A Golden Chain

Or,

The Description of *Theology*,

Containing the Order of the Causes of Salvation and Damnation, according to God's Word.

Written in Latin by that man of God, WILLIAM PERKINS, translated into English by ROBERT HILL, and edited by MARK SMITH and MATTHEW PAYNE.

Published at Lansvale by TULIP PUBLISHING, 2021.

A Golden Chain

By William Perkins

Edited by Mark Smith and Matthew Payne

Tulip Publishing Edition, 2021.

This text is of the 1597 edition and was transcribed from scanned TIF files downloaded from Early English Books Online (EEBO - http://eebo.chadwyck.com) and accessed through the University of Sydney Library. The original book is held in the Henry E. Huntington Library at the Henry E. Huntington Library and Art Gallery. Reel position: STC / 260:03.

Transcription by Mr Mark Smith, A Reformed Baptist's Disk (http://www.vor.org/rbdisk/). © 2014, 2020. Mark Smith substituted the original Bible quotations for the text of the English Standard Version of the Bible (ESV, 2001). All biblical quotations are from the ESV except where otherwise indicated.

Introduction, footnoted material, and editing by Matthew Payne, Stretch Theology (http://stretchtheology.com). © 2019–2021.

For information contact:

Tulip Publishing, PO Box 3150, Lansvale, NSW, Australia 2166

www.tulippublishing.com.au

Book and Cover design by Tulip Publishing

PAPERBACK ISBN: 978-0-6487250-5-3

DIGITAL ISBN: 978-1-922584-00-7

NATIONAL LIBRARY OF AUSTRALIA

A catalogue record for this work is available from the National Library of Australia

PREFACE

William Perkins' *A Golden Chain* is a classic work of Reformed theology. It offers a practical account of the Christian life built on the foundation of God's sovereign predestination. According to Romans 8:29-30, God lovingly *calls*, *justifies*, and *sanctifies* his elect, that he might lead them to *glorification* in his eternal kingdom. For Perkins, this sequence—or 'golden chain'—of God's action for his elect provides the proper framework to understand the Christian life. Perkins regarded this 'chain' as the centrepiece of all theology, Christian living, and pastoral practice.

Until recently Perkins' writings have suffered from widespread neglect. We appreciate the recent republication of Perkins' Works (10 volumes, Reformed Heritage Books, 2014-2020), but many readers will want a more concise entry point into Perkins' thought. We believe that *A Golden Chain* fills that need admirably.

This edition of *A Golden Chain* began its life in 2014, when Mark transcribed the 1597 edition of the work. He was motivated to do so after attending Dr James M. Renihan's course "Puritanism in Context" at a School of Theology in New Zealand in 2011. In early 2019, Brett Lee-Price of Tulip Publishing approached us to produce a modernised version of that text. At this time Matthew was in the middle of his PhD studies on William Perkins' life and thought, and eager to partner in an opportunity to bring Perkins' work before a wider audience.

This edition of *A Golden Chain* is intended to help modern readers benefit from Perkins' work. The language has been modernised, and occasionally paraphrased or lightly abridged. *The English Standard Version* (ESV, 2001) has been used for the Scripture quotations (which are extensive), except where otherwise stated. In some places we have kept the sixteenth century wording when we thought it was necessary to preserve Perkins' point.

One of the main distinctives of this edition of Perkins' *A Golden Chain* is the way Matthew has laid out the structure and flow of the book and provided structural diagrams to make Perkins' writing easy to follow. The main golden chain chart has been reduced and simplified for the sake of space (p. 18). A modernised version of the full chart is available on the publishers website. We believe we have preserved the overall sense and emphases of the original whilst making it more accessible. Indeed, this was Perkins' own goal for the work in his day: to make theology available to ordinary Christians. We share his passion for that goal.

While neither of us agree with everything in Perkins' book, we have a deep affinity with its overall theology. Like Perkins, we believe that God's sovereign, predestinating grace is enormously important for Christians to understand, and is of direct practical importance for living as Christians today.

Mark wishes to thank: Dr James M. Renihan for introducing him to William Perkins; Matthew for his fellowship and for the skill and diligence he brought to the project to make it a reality; and his wonderful wife Carmel, for her love and support through the many hours invested in this project.

Matthew wishes to thank: Mark for his careful attention to detail in this project and warm fellowship in Christ; and the faculty of Moore Theological College through whom he has grown both in passion and ability to serve the Lord Jesus.

We both want to thank Brett Lee-Price for inviting us to work on this project and for undertaking its production and publication.

Above all, we thank our great God who has graciously saved us and provided for us in every way in Christ Jesus. His generosity to us was established in his eternal purposes in Christ before creation and extends to our ultimate glorification in his presence. Until then, God longs to lead his children into a deeper love, knowledge, and experience of his grace each day. It is our prayer that this book might be used to that end for his glory.

Mark Smith & Matthew Payne
Sydney, Australia
July 2020

CONTENTS

LIST OF DIAGRAMS

INTRODUCTION

William Perkins (1558–1602) is not as well known today as might be expected. In the 1590s Perkins was widely known as an exceptionally gifted preacher and theological author. His book sales in England even rivalled those of Reformed greats such as John Calvin and Theodore Beza. Perkins was not only eagerly read in England but also became the first English Protestant theologian to gain a significant readership in Europe. The book you are holding, *A Golden Chain*, was quickly translated into Dutch, German, and French, in addition to its English and Latin versions. Perkins' collected *Works* were translated into many more languages besides, including Spanish, Welsh, Irish, Italian, Hungarian, and Czech. Perkins' influence extended into the Americas too. The Puritan pilgrims of the early seventeenth century brought Perkins' *Works* with them to New England where they became a standard pastoral resource. Not only was Perkins an internationally acclaimed theologian, but he is now regarded by many as 'the father of Puritanism', despite working his entire career within the established Church of England.

But who was William Perkins? We don't know many details of his story, though perhaps there isn't all that much to know. Perkins was born and raised in a rural parish in Warwickshire before spending his entire adult life in Cambridge. He enrolled as a student at Christ's College in 1577, attained his *Bachelor of Arts* (1581) and then his *Master of Arts* (1584) at which time he also became a fellow at the college. From this position in the college he was to have a formative influence on many notable students, including William Ames (1576–1633), Richard Sibbes (1577–1635), and Samuel Ward (1577–1640). In 1595 Perkins resigned his fellowship in order to get married (college fellows were not permitted to marry). But he continued his work in Cambridge just across the road from Christ's College, serving as the 'lecturer' (i.e. preacher) at St Andrews the Great church. He continued there until he died of illness in 1602, aged 44.

Although Perkins' life was short, it was not unproductive. In his brief career Perkins authored no fewer than 31 works. In addition, many of his sermons were collected and published after his death.[1]

Perkins' brief career took place during the final years of the Tudor dynasty. Elizabeth I (1533–1603) ruled England for all of Perkins' life, dying the year after he did. The English Reformation had been a tumultuous process up to Elizabeth's reign. Her father Henry VIII (1491–1547) had severed England from the authority of the Pope in 1534, opening the way for evangelical reformers to cautiously pursue change along biblical lines. When Henry's son Edward VI (1537–1553) became king, this process of reforming English religion took off in earnest. However, Edward's reign would prove brief when he suddenly died of illness, and his Roman Catholic sister Mary I (1516–1558) seized the throne. Mary's religious policy was the opposite of her brother's: she set out to recommit England to the Pope's authority and to make England a thoroughly Roman Catholic nation once more. Key reforming leaders of Edward's reign—Thomas Cranmer, Nicolas Ridley, Hugh Latimer, John Hooper, John Bradford—became martyrs under Mary, executed for heresy. However, restoring England to Roman Catholic devotion proved more difficult than expected. When Mary's brief reign ended with her death in 1558, this ambition died with her.

When Elizabeth ascended the throne that year, she quickly made it clear that England would be a Protestant nation. She repealed all of Mary's Roman Catholic legislation, and restored England's official standards of doctrine and church practice to something very close to what it was at the end of Edward's reign in 1553. English clergy were to conduct church services according to the liturgy of *The Book of Common Prayer* (1552, 1559). The sermons of the *Books of Homilies* (1547, 1562, 1571) were to be read in churches whenever a licensed preacher was not present, and all clergy were to subscribe to the doctrine laid out in *The Thirty-Nine Articles of Religion* (1563, 1571).

What all this amounted to was that the Church of England was a decidedly Reformed, Protestant, and evangelical church. However, it differed in character from the Edwardian church in one major way, and this would be a fundamental source of contention throughout Elizabeth's long reign. The Edwardian reformers regarded their program of reform

1. Perkins' complete works have recently been republished: Joel R. Beeke & Derek W.H. Thomas (gen. eds.), *The Works of William Perkins* (10 vols; Grand Rapids: Reformed Heritage Books, 2014–2020).

as a work in progress, yet to be completed. For example, Cranmer's first edition of *The Book of Common Prayer* (1549) was soon revised (1552), and it appears likely that he would have revised it again, given the opportunity. Elizabeth's attitude to reform was the opposite. She regarded her religious settlement as just that—*settled*—and she was extremely resistant to calls for further changes or development. Elizabeth's personal motto—"always the same" (*semper eadem*)—encapsulated her attitude toward religious matters.

This was a source of enormous frustration to reform-minded Christians. Many had spent Mary's reign in exile, living in various Reformed cities in Europe where they observed how far truly 'biblical' church reform could progress. They eagerly imagined what the English church might look like if they were ever given the opportunity to continue the process of reform from where they left off in 1553. However, after Elizabeth became queen and they returned home, they found that their church was essentially 1553 set in stone. No further reforms would proceed whilst Elizabeth lived, leaving many to lament that their church was 'only half reformed.' Eventually the term 'Puritan' was coined to describe those who sought further reform of Elizabeth's church settlement, whether in terms of clerical vestments, liturgy, church governance, or issues of doctrine and piety. The Church of England remained a Reformed church which identified with the other national Reformed churches of Europe, but it also bore its own distinct characteristics and struggled with its own inner tensions. It was a church in which enthusiastic Reformed believers like William Perkins could find much to be thankful for, though points of frustration remained.

Puritan or Anglican?

Putting a label to Perkins' theological identity is not a straightforward task. Was he a 'Puritan'? Was he an 'Anglican'? Was he both? Or are both terms misleading? Scholars struggle to find consensus on these basic questions, in part because the meaning and connotations of these terms has changed over time. It is probably most accurate to say that Perkins was *both* an Anglican and a Puritan, provided we clarify what those terms mean.

Whilst the word 'Anglican' didn't come into general usage until the nineteenth century, it is difficult to avoid using it to refer to the Church of England of Perkins' day. If 'Anglican' merely refers to the legally established Church of England along with its official theology and practices, William Perkins was certainly an Anglican. He belonged to the first generation of English Christians raised under the terms of Elizabeth's religious settlement, and the *Book of Common Prayer* and *Thirty-Nine Articles* had a formative influence on him. In his sermons of the 1590s, Perkins would often confront his listeners with the fact that sound doctrine had been preached and taught under Elizabeth for decades, and yet this had produced very limited fruit among them. Perkins never expressed dissatisfaction with the doctrine of the English church, but strongly opposed separatism (i.e. creating a church of genuine believers outside the national church) and became one of the established Church of England's most capable advocates and defenders.[2]

Thus, *A Golden Chain* is a work of Anglican confessional theology. As Perkins states in his preface, it was intended as a contribution to 'the treasury of the Church of England' (p. 20). His book teaches doctrine which is entirely in accordance with the Anglican confessional standard, *The Thirty-Nine Articles*, and Perkins intended that it would enrich the understanding and piety of the English people within that church. One primary application of *A Golden Chain* was that all readers should seek God through the means of grace provided in their local parish church, namely the (preached) Bible and the sacraments (ch. 58). At a theological level, *A Golden Chain* bears striking similarities to Article 17 of the *Thirty-Nine Articles*. Both emphasise that election is 'in Christ,' are structured around Romans 8:29–30, and expect the doctrine to provide 'sweet, pleasant, and unspeakable comfort to godly persons [who] feel in themselves the working of the Spirit of Christ...' (Article 17). Of course, Perkins developed the theme of predestination beyond what this Article explicitly stated, most notably by teaching double-predestination, supralapsarianism, and a more developed doctrine of assurance (see below). However, this makes his work no less confessional. The role of a confession of faith is to set the foundations and boundaries of theological opinion, not to outlaw theological developments and fresh articulations of biblical truth that are compatible with it.

'Perkins the Anglican' will no doubt come as a surprise to many

2. Perkins' place in the mainstream of the Church of England is emphasised by: W.B. Patterson, *William Perkins and the Making of a Protestant England* (Oxford: Oxford University Press, 2014).

readers. It is generally thought that Perkins' contemporary Richard Hooker (1554–1600) was the quintessential Anglican of the Elizabethan era, whereas Perkins was a Puritan. Yet, both were confessional theologians of their day, and Perkins was far more influential. It is a pure accident of later history that Hooker has been remembered as the 'Anglican' and Perkins as the 'Puritan.' Party-lines shift over time, and the champions of the past are recruited to serve fresh concerns and positions that didn't exist in their day. If we describe any theologian of the Elizabethan period 'Anglican,' then Perkins certainly warrants the label.

Yet, neither should we hesitate to regard Perkins as a Puritan. Most Puritans of Perkins' day were insiders to the Church of England who sought further reform from within. Some of the more outspoken and controversial Puritans were forced out of the national church, such as Thomas Cartwright (1535–1603) who promoted the adoption of presbyterian church governance in England and suffered the shipwreck of his career as a result. Others, such as Perkins and many of his Cambridge colleagues, were content to bear the flaws of the Elizabethan settlement as relatively minor imperfections on a fundamentally sound national church establishment.[3] Rather than quibble on lesser issues, they sought to promote and enrich its official theology and piety. Too many English people were ignorant or hardhearted. Too many had yet to embrace the gospel that their nation formally endorsed, much less wholehearted devoted themselves to Jesus' way of godliness. There was important work to do.

This concern for the thorough conversion of England was where official church policy and Puritan enthusiasm intersected.[4] William Perkins was both an Anglican and a Puritan precisely because he was enthusiastically devoted to the Reformed theology of the English church, and desired that all of England should embrace it.

---

3. For Perkins' views on the Church of England, see: Donald John MacLean, *'Ours is a True Church of God': William Perkins and the Reformed doctrine of the church* (London: The Latimer Trust, 2019).
4. On this point, the work of Peter Lake is especially useful. See his essay "Puritans' and 'Anglicans' in the History of the Post-Reformation English Church' in *The Oxford History of Anglicanism. Volume 1: Reformation and Identity, c.1520-1662* Edited by Anthony Milton. Oxford: Oxford University Press, 2017), 352–379, and *Moderate Puritans and the Elizabethan Church* (Cambridge: Cambridge University Press, 1982).

Corrupter of Calvinism?

In recent times it has become fashionable to regard Perkins as a kind of theological villain. His main crime is allegedly distorting the legacy of John Calvin (1509-1564). According to the influential account of R.T. Kendall, English theology gradually moved away from the theology of Calvin by means of an overly scholastic interest in predestination and related issues. Gradually Calvin's theology became so distorted in England that it became a case of 'Calvin versus the Calvinists.' Calvin (it is claimed) would have opposed the theology of William Perkins and that of the later *Westminster Confession of Faith* (1647), upon which Perkins had significant influence.[5]

This historical narrative has been repeatedly and exhaustively debunked, however its influence remains.[6] Much of the problem stems from the term 'Calvinism,' which implies that the measure of Reformed orthodoxy is one's faithful adherence to the views of John Calvin. 'Reformed' is a far more accurate term, and immediately highlights that Calvin was but one (very influential) Reformed theologian alongside others. In this broader context it becomes clear that Perkins' theology sits comfortably alongside that of other Reformed theologians including Heinrich Bullinger, Peter Martyr Vermigli, Martin Bucer, Theodore Beza, Thomas Cranmer, John Knox, and others, including John Calvin.[7]

However, this kind of historical critique of Perkins is often more fundamentally concerned with theology. For example, many of those influenced by the theology of Karl Barth (1886-1968) and of T.F. Torrance (1913-2007), such as 'Evangelical Calvinists,' charge Perkins with distorting the Reformation understanding of God's love, election, covenant, assurance, and more.[8] At a theological level such critical

5. R.T. Kendall, *Calvin and English Calvinism to 1649* (Oxford: Oxford University Press, 1979).
6. For an accessible critique, see: Paul Helm, *Calvin and the Calvinists* (Edinburgh: Banner of Truth, 1982).
7. On the diversity of the Reformed tradition see: Richard A. Muller, *Calvin & the Reformed Tradition: On the Work of Christ and the Order of Salvation* (Grand Rapids: Baker, 2012) and Kenneth Stewart, *Ten Myths about Calvinism: Recovering the Breadth of the Reformed Tradition* (Grand Rapids: IVP, 2011).
8. For an extensive (and misleading) engagement with Perkins from this perspective, see: Ronald Norman Frost, *Richard Sibbes: God's Spreading Goodness* (Vancouver: Cor Deo Press, 2012). More broadly, this perspective is capably expounded in two volumes edited by Myk Habets and Bobby Grow:

engagement is welcome and important when made on biblical grounds. Perkins himself appealed to the authority of the Bible in all theological matters, as witnessed by the enormous number of biblical quotations throughout *A Golden Chain*. Yet, many critics of Perkins' theology have failed to read him fairly, resulting in misrepresentation of his theological and pastoral concerns.

For example, some critiques of Perkins extend no deeper than the impressions given by his famous predestinarian chart, or 'ocular catechism,' which visually lays out the structure of *A Golden Chain*. As a seventeenth-century English bishop would muse:

> I observed in Perkins Tables
> Those black Lines of Damnation:
> Those crooked veins
> So struck in my brains,
> That I feared my Reprobation.[9]

The doctrine of predestination has long been a cause of anxiety to many. Perkins' chart appears to reinforce the worst fears of some by explicitly laying out the path of reprobation. It is easy to conceive how an anxious reader might relate to the experiences of the reprobate described there ('zeal,' 'deceit of sin,' and so on), and conclude that they are reprobate. The potential for such disastrous responses to Perkins' chart might seem to prove how theologically misguided his approach is. Yet this is not a fair criticism. We ought to expect that superficial engagement with any doctrine will result in misunderstanding. More to the point, those who read the work itself will find that Perkins' account of predestination, and even of reprobation, is balanced, practical, and warmly pastoral.

The Structure of *A Golden Chain*

Readers will quickly discover that Perkins' writing style is highly structured. At times the work reads a bit like a dictionary, setting out precise definitions of theological terms and subdividing them into their

---

Evangelical Calvinism: Essays Resourcing the Continuing Reformation of the Church (Oregon: Wipf & Stock, 2012), and *Evangelical Calvinism: Volume 2: Dogmatics and Devotion* (Oregon: Wipf & Stock, 2017).

9. Richard Corbett, 'The Distracted Puritane' in *Poëtica Stromata: or A Collection of Sundry Pieces in Poetry: Drawne by the known and approved Hand of R. C.* (Holland, 1648), 74.

component parts. This form of structuring human knowledge comes from a sixteenth-century educational philosophy called *Ramism* which Perkins learned as a student at Christ's College. In brief, Ramism sought to lay out the inherent structure of a topic by rightly subdividing and ordering its component parts. Ramists believed that this was the best way to produce true and unconfused knowledge of any subject, and that it greatly aided memory recall.[10]

This Ramist structuring of knowledge was highly conducive to visual representation. For example, at the beginning of *A Golden Chain* Perkins includes a diagram laying out the 'sacred sciences', of which theology is preeminent. However, most of the time the Ramist structure of Perkins' writing is merely expressed verbally, and readers are expected to keep up with his place in the structure. Occasionally he says 'thus much [topic]' to indicate to the reader that he has concluded the topic mentioned and is moving on to the next one. Virtually the entire work could be represented as a massive tree diagram.

This approach is foreign to modern readers, and it is easy to get lost when subdivisions extend to multiple layers or over several chapters. For that reason, this edition of *A Golden Chain* includes new diagrams that make the structure of the work explicit wherever it seemed beneficial. For example, the main topic of the book (predestination) is divided into its component parts which are treated over the course of chapters 15 to 53, as follows:

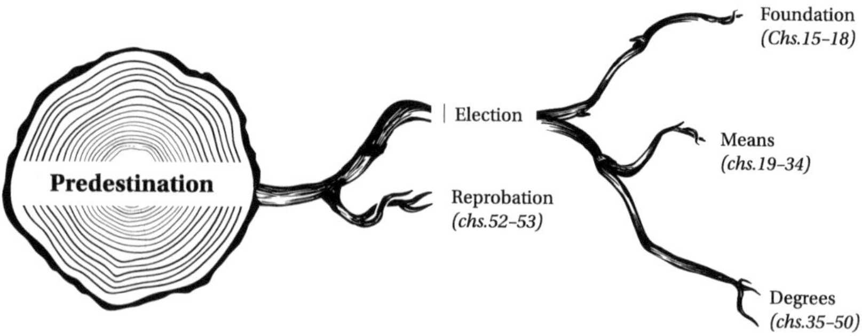

Each of those sections subdivides into further points as laid out at the start of relevant chapters.

10. See further: Donald K. McKim, *Ramism in William Perkins' Theology* (New York: Peter Lang, 1987).

Some of the longest chapters of *A Golden Chain* are those which expound each of the Ten Commandments (chs. 20-29) and the polemical chapters which criticise the Roman Catholic (ch. 51) and Lutheran (ch. 54) views of predestinarian. Together this material amounts to nearly half the length of the book. Whilst these chapters are of great practical and polemical importance, they are of little significance to the main argument. First-time readers should feel free to skim past these chapters whilst familiarising themselves with the book's overall argument. Those chapters can then be read in their larger theological context.

The Theology of *A Golden Chain*

Perkins' *A Golden Chain* is a classic of Reformed predestinarian theology and pastoral care. Those two topics might not sound like they belong together, yet at the heart of Perkins' ministry was his conviction that good pastoral practice flowed from a right understanding of predestination. That connection is especially clear in *A Golden Chain*.

The Causes of Predestination

As with many works of the sixteenth century, the full title of Perkins' book was lengthy and offers a detailed description of its contents: *A Golden Chain, or The Description of Theology, containing the Order of the Causes of Salvation and Damnation, according to God's Word.* In this book Perkins is concerned to lay out the 'causes' of salvation. This not only refers to God's sovereign work of saving sinners, but to the interconnections between God's eternal decree, the work of Christ in history, and the application of Christ's work to the elect. These causal connections are represented in the ocular catechism accompanying the book. However, the central causal 'chain' referred to in the book's title consists of five steps, as laid out in Romans 8:29–30:

> For those whom he foreknew he also predestined (**elected**) to be conformed to the image of his Son (**sanctified**), in order that he might be the firstborn among many brothers. And those whom he predestined he also **called**, and those whom he called he also **justified**, and those whom he justified he also **glorified**.

This chain extends from eternity past to eternity future in continuous and unbreakable sequence: election, call, justification, sanctification, and glorification. The unbreakability of this chain is implied by the passage's repeated specification that 'those' who experience one step are the same 'those' who experience the next, right up to glorification. An immediate implication of this 'chain' is the doctrine of *perseverance of the saints*, meaning that all who are subject of any stage in the chain are subject of all the others, and thus will necessarily reach glory. The sequence always flows on to its invincible conclusion.

The foundational cause of this chain is the will of God. Perkins places particular emphasis on the will of God as the cause of things, both in creation and redemption. God exists outside of time and space, eternal and unchangeable (ch. 2). This means that God's will is not a series of decisions but is one eternal act (p. 41) or 'decree', by which all things are transcendently determined. This eternal decree comes into effect in history and human experience in unfolding 'degrees' of the application of God's decree, each caused by the previous in sequence, and compelling the elect onward to glory (ch. 35).

One of the most important aspects of Perkins' ocular catechism is at its centre: the series of acts comprising Jesus' mission to save sinners, from his incarnation through to his present heavenly intercession. In Perkins' chart, each aspect of the believer's experience of the gospel (faith, mortification of sin, etc) is directly linked to a step of the golden chain (on its left), and to one or more parts of the work of Christ (on its right). This is extremely theologically significant. It links the invisible regenerative unfolding of God's saving activity in his elect by the Holy Spirit with its redemptive basis in the work of Christ the mediator. Thus, for Perkins salvation is not only decretal, but Trinitarian and Christocentric. The Christocentric character of Perkins' chart is particularly noteworthy; it is the fundamental difference between it and the otherwise similar charts by Theodore Beza (1519–1605) and later by John Bunyan (1628–1688). It rightly emphasises that the centrepiece of God's predestinating work is the mission of Jesus Christ, who came into the world to save sinners. In other words, Perkins' predestinarian scheme is profoundly gospel-centred.

As noted above, Perkins not only lays out the path of the elect to glory, but also that of the reprobate to condemnation. Perkins teaches the doctrine of *double-predestination*, meaning that God not only actively predestined the elect to glory, but also actively predestined the reprobate to destruction. In double-predestination, God's active decision making is involved on both sides, in contrast to single-predestination where God actively chooses the salvation of the elect only and passively passes by the rest, leaving them to just condemnation by implication. For Perkins, God must actively will both parts of his predestinating decree, since by it he intends to demonstrate both his grace in saving the elect (ch. 15), and his justice in condemning the reprobate (ch. 52).

Given that Perkins was a Reformed theologian (or 'Calvinist'), one might expect his main opponents to be Arminians. However, at the time *A Golden Chain* was written, Jacob Arminius (1560-1609) was quietly serving as a pastor in Amsterdam and had not yet risen to prominence in the theological world. There would be no English 'Arminians' until the early seventeenth century. Instead, Perkins mainly describes views in terms of how they formulate the causality of salvation. These issues were becoming controversial in Cambridge at the time. Indeed, the popularity of *A Golden Chain* was a significant part of what led to tensions boiling over into a serious theological controversy at Cambridge in 1595. This controversy would produce the *Lambeth Articles* (1595), an attempt to further specify the boundaries of orthodox predestinarian doctrine. However, this document was immediately censored by Elizabeth, who detected an effort to further reform her religious settlement.[11]

Though the terminology had not yet been developed, we might accurately describe Perkins' position on predestination as *supralapsarian* (a natural complement to the double-predestinarian position). The issue with which supralapsarianism (and its alternative, infralapsarianism) are concerned is whether God sovereignly chose his elect out of humanity envisioned as sinners (infralapsarian), or as created and not yet fallen (supralapsarian). This might seem a small and perhaps speculative issue, but it has implications for how we understand God and his plans.

Perkins' advocacy of supralapsarianism was motivated by his conviction that God alone must be the determining cause of all things,

11. Perkins would write two further works on predestination in the aftermath of this controversy: *A Christian and Plain Treatise of the Manner and Order of Predestination, and the largeness of God's grace* (1598) and *A Treatise on God's Free Grace and Man's Free Will* (1601). These may be found in *The Works of William Perkins: Volume 6*. (ed. Joel R. Beeke & Greg A. Salazar; Grand Rapids: Reformation Heritage Books, 2018).

particularly of things relating to salvation. He believed that human beings have 'free will' in earthy matters (p. 65), but that sinners could only reach out to God by God's enabling grace. He therefore opposed those who hold that God's predestinating decree was based on foresight of who would come to faith by their free will ('Pelagians'), as well as Roman Catholics who argue that conversion is partly by grace and partly by the exercise of human free-will ('Semi-Pelagians'). It is worth noting that both positions were contrary to Article 10 of the *Thirty-Nine Articles*, which states that human beings 'cannot turn and prepare' themselves for repentance and faith without God's prior gracious enabling. This point is essential to Reformed thought.

The more subtle alternative that Perkins engaged with was that offered by contemporary Lutheranism. Basically, it argued that God foresaw both the fall and that all sinners would reject his grace, and on that basis elected some sinners to salvation, passing by the rest. (This view involved a form of infralapsarianism, a universal atonement, and a universal call; see chapter 54). Perkins rejected this option because it still made God's saving decisions reactive to human causes, even if in a lesser way. Perkins' objection to each of these three views was the same: God alone can be sovereign in salvation.

Perkins was not insensitive to the accusation that this appeared to make God the cause of sin, and that it made salvation and condemnation appear to be two arbitrary sides of the same fatalistic coin. Is God really the predestinating cause of salvation and of condemnation *in the same way*? (This idea is often referred to as 'equal ultimacy'). Perkins is clear that this is not the case. The difference between election and reprobation is that only election is according to God's decree without reference to anything in those he chooses to save. That is, no point in the 'golden chain'—election, call, justification, sanctification, glorification—has reference to something inherent in the elect. God's entire saving work, from eternity past to eternity future, is entirely of his sovereign grace. In contrast, God's condemnation of the reprobate is not according to 'any *absolute* decree of damnation' (p. 361, emphasis added), but has reference to something inherent in those condemned, namely their sin. Condemnation is always an act of justice on God's part.

The foundation of this point is the common theological distinction between primary and secondary causality (ch. 6). God is the transcendent cause of all things, but what he has created also has its own (secondary) causality. Primary and secondary causality operate at entirely different levels and must not be conceived as competing forces. The relationship of God's will (primary cause) to created things (secondary causes) is that he 'brings them into a certain order' and 'directs them to a determined end', yet without compromising 'the nature and property of secondary causes' in any way (p. 42). Creation is not a lifeless puppet of which God is the controlling puppet-master. Describing the relationship between divine and creaturely realities is far more complicated than can be represented by such simplistic illustrations. Thus, to return to the point, Perkins argues that whilst God's will is the primary cause of reprobation, condemnation never occurs apart from the presence of sin in those reprobated (i.e. an attending secondary cause).

In this way, secondary causes are never the underlying reason for God's decision making. God is not the author of sin (chs. 10–11), nor is he unjust to predestine the reprobate to condemnation. However, these clarifications notwithstanding, the root cause of all things is God's will and decree without the influence of secondary causes. God's will is the deepest explanation of reality that there is.[12]

Even with these clarifications, many modern readers will baulk at Perkins' doctrine of supralapsarian double-predestination. These remain deep and complex issues, and many great minds have wrestled with them.[13] However, regardless of one's personal conclusions on these theological questions, readers should observe that, for Perkins, this predestinarian position finds its proper expression in his concern that all people would hear God's offer of salvation in Christ, and be urged to repentance and faith.

12. For an extensive discussion of Perkins' views of primary and secondary causality, see: Richard A. Muller, *Grace and Freedom: William Perkins and the Early Modern Reformed Understanding of Free Choice and Divine Grace* (Oxford: Oxford University Press, 2020), esp. 155–181.
13. Readers interested in delving into the way Reformed theologians have navigated these issues should consult: Joel R. Beeke, *Debated Issues in Sovereign Predestination: Early Lutheran Predestination, Calvinian Reprobation, and Variations in Genevan Lapsarianism* (Reformed Historical Theology 42. Göttingen: Vandenhoeck & Ruprecht, 2017).

The Practical Importance of Predestination

Perkins has fittingly been described as an *experimental* or *practical* predestinarian.[14] He believed that the doctrine of predestination directly expressed itself in Christian spiritual experience. In fact, Perkins held that all theology is practical: *A Golden Chain* begins by defining theology as 'the science of living blessedly forever' (p. 23). Echoing Calvin, he held that our knowledge of God is tightly bound-together with knowledge of ourselves.[15] Perkins placed particular emphasis on this latter point, even claiming that: '...we know God by looking into ourselves' (p. 23).

Why this emphasis on inwardness? Stereotypes of the 'naval-gazing Puritan' abound and there are certainly dangers in overemphasising introspection. However, we must not dismiss it altogether. Perkins' point is that the process of coming to know God involves self-knowledge. Knowing God is not simply a matter of true doctrine and right outward confession, but of inner transformation. For a start, sinners only turn to Christ once they come to personal knowledge of the depths of their own sinfulness and of how utterly deserving they are of condemnation. Furthermore, coming to the fullness of assurance involves personal knowledge of how God's Spirit is actively renewing one's own heart, changing our spiritual desires (ch. 36). The Christian life involves being attuned to one's own conscience and ensuring that it is well instructed by the word of God (pp. 63–4, 282). Christians must also understand how temptation arises within them to be able fight against it (chs. 13, 40-43). Each step of the golden chain is directly connected to inward Christian experience, and thus to the life of obedience it produces.

It is noteworthy that in Perkins' day virtually everyone was considered "Christian" and went to church on Sunday whether they were converted or not. The pressing pastoral need of the day was therefore helping unconverted "Christians" to identify their spiritual poverty and to genuinely, inwardly encounter the gospel for the first time. People must *experience* salvation to know that they have it.

Perkins' influential teaching on assurance was developed in this context. Many English people were spiritually presumptuous and

14. These terms were respectively coined by R.T. Kendall (*Calvin and English Calvinism*, 8) and Leif Dixon (*Practical Predestinarians in England, c. 1590-1640*. (Surrey: Ashgate, 2014), 11–2).
15. Cf. John Calvin, *Institutes of the Christian Religion* (1559), 1.1.1.

apathetic. Others had the extreme opposite problem, experiencing anxiety and even despair about whether they were elect. Perkins' teaching addressed both problems. Using the illustration of a mustard seed, Perkins distinguishes between faith and the fullness of assurance that faith grows into (ch. 36). He doesn't *separate* faith and assurance (as he is sometimes accused of doing) but distinguishes between the regenerate beginnings of faith and what it becomes at full maturity, like a seed growing into a tree.[16] The spiritually mature person is assured of their election whereas the infant in Christ has not yet reached that degree of assurance.

Yet Perkins offers a word of comfort to seekers too. The most microscopic starting point of saving faith is regenerate desire. Even before the mind understands the gospel clearly enough to express faith, the Holy Spirit produces a genuine desire for spiritual things in the heart. Therefore, anyone with this 'mustard seed' of spiritual desire should be encouraged that God is evidently at work in them. They, in turn, must work at cultivating the growth of that spirituality desire toward full maturity in Christ. Such growth generally takes time, effort, and long spiritual experience on the part of the believer.[17]

This point is not only of comfort to the spiritually weak and struggling, but it also rebukes to the spiritually complacent. Apathy in spiritual matters is the opposite of regenerate desire. Without it all outward religiosity is mere show. Regenerate desire is the very first transformation that invades the sinful human heart, and all genuine Christian experience flows out of it.

But what of 'temporary faith'? Perkins argues that many reprobate people experience an 'ineffectual calling' and a lesser spiritual experience that can easily be confused with genuine conversion (ch. 53). Doesn't this undermine any notion of assurance?

This point requires care and precision. Perkins' teaching on temporary faith is largely based on Hebrews 6:4—which famously describes the possible falling away of those who have had some measure of genuine spiritual experience—as well as Jesus' parable of the soils (Mark 4). The

16. Perkins' position is essentially the same as that expressed in the *Westminster Confession of Faith* (1647), 18.1–4.
17. See further: Matthew N. Payne, 'William Perkins's Doctrines of Faith and Assurance through the Lens of Early-Modern Faculty Psychology'. *Westminster Theological Journal* (2021): forthcoming.

main difference between temporary faith and genuine faith (including the 'least faith' of the mustard seed) is whether it produces superficial or genuine desire for spiritual things. At best, the reprobate fears God rather than loves him, and the word of God only superficially touches their desires rather than transforming them. Such an experience lacks the spiritual vitality to persevere. In contrast, regenerate hearts sincerely desire Christ and, in God's grace, *always* find him.

Some might expect Perkins' supralapsarian predestinarian views to contradict the idea of a national church or even the free offer of the gospel to all. On the contrary, Perkins rejoiced that the gospel was to be offered to all of England by means of a national Reformed church: '...the evangelical promises are indefinite and exclude no man, unless any man excludes himself' (p. 298). Similarly, Perkins' explicit teaching on the signs of reprobation might seem to imply a reprobate caste in England, the ungodly who had rejected the gospel in the ways which Perkins describes. Yet Perkins forbids anyone from concluding that they or anyone else is reprobate. Instead, all should 'use the word of God and the sacraments that he may have an inward sense of the power of Christ drawing him to Christ, and an assurance of his redemption by Christ's death and passion' (p. 393). All must heed the call to turn to Christ. So long as a person lives, there remains a possibility that they might find salvation. So, whatever one's present relation to Christ, the application is the same: *seek Christ through the means of grace that you might find him* (ch. 58).

Despite his reputation in some quarters, readers will find Perkins' theology decidedly anti-fatalistic. Fatalism is a sombre classical philosophy, teaching that everyone will end up at their predetermined destiny regardless of what they do. If you try to fight your destiny then you will only end up making it happen. It is a philosophy of hopelessness, which can only breed complacency, passivity, and despair. In contrast, Perkins taught that not only do people play an active role in reaching their predestined end, but that the offer of salvation is sincerely made by God to all people. Fatalistic complacency is a dire error. Predestination calls all people to faith, repentance, obedience, perseverance, and active dependence upon God in all things. It doesn't undermine the role of the means of grace and human obedience but establishes their place in God's plans. Here Perkins' teaching has great affinity with the words of the Apostle Paul:

> Therefore, my beloved, as you have always obeyed, so now, not only as in my presence but much more in my absence, work out your own salvation with fear and trembling, for it is God who works in you, both to will and to work for his good pleasure. (Philippians 2:12–13)

As indicated in the preface, a simplified version of the main golden chain chart is on the next page. However, the updated version of the full chart is available by heading to http://tulippublishing.com.au/a-golden-chain/ or by using this QR Code.

A table surveying the **Order of the Causes of Salvation and Damnation** according to God's word. It may be used as an *Ocular Catechism* to instruct those who cannot read, so that they might understand the chief points of religion and their proper order.

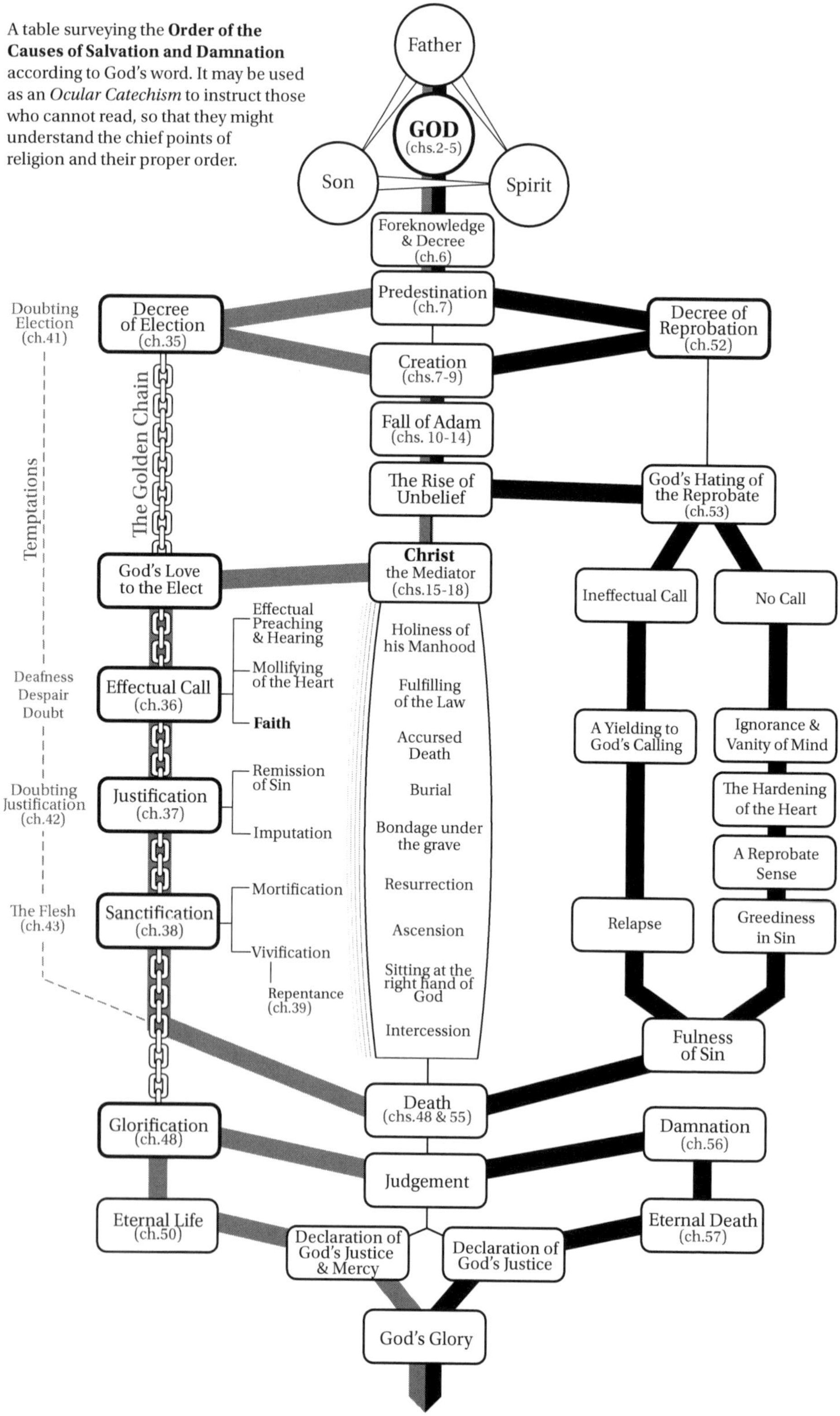

TO THE CHRISTIAN READER

Christian Reader, there are today four opinions regarding the order of God's predestination.

1. The old and new **Pelagians** place the cause of God's Predestination in man.[1] They hold that God ordained men either to life or death according to his foresight of whether they would, by their natural free-will, either reject or receive grace offered.
2. Those called **Lutherans** teach that God foresaw how all mankind would be bound in unbelief and would therefore reject grace offered. He therefore chose some to salvation out of his mere mercy, without any reference to their faith, or good works. The rest he rejected, being moved to do this because he eternally foresaw that they would reject his grace offered to them in the gospel. (See ***chapter 54***).
3. The **Semipelagian Papists**[2] ascribe God's Predestination partly to mercy and partly to men's foreseen preparations and meritorious works. (See ***chapter 51***).
4. Others teach that the cause of the execution of God's Predestination is his mercy in Christ in those who are saved, and the fall and corruption of man in those who perish. Yet this is such that the decree and eternal counsel of God concerning both has no cause except his will and pleasure.

---

1. Perkins refers to this group as 'Pelagians' to identify their free-will theology with that of the heretic Pelagius (360-420), who was opposed by Augustine of Hippo (354–430).
2. In the sixteenth century, 'Papist' was a common Protestant term for Roman Catholics, as was 'Popery' for their religious practices. These terms captured the idea that instead of being devoted to the teaching of Scripture, Roman Catholics were committed to Papal traditions regardless of whether they contradicted the Bible.

Of these four opinions, I have laboured to expose the first three as errors. I maintain that the last is true.

I offer this discourse for your godly consideration, asking the reader to regard my intent and affection more than the slender size of the work itself. Along with others, I desire to make my humble contribution to the treasury of the Church of England (Mark 12:41–44), and (lacking gold, pearl, and precious stone) to bring a ram's skin or two, and a little goats hair to the building of the Lord's tabernacle (Exod. 35:23).

May the Father of our Lord Jesus Christ grant that according to the riches of his glory, you may be strengthened by his Spirit in the inner man, that Christ may dwell in your hearts by faith; to the end that you, being rooted and grounded in love, may be able to comprehend with all Saints, what is the breadth and length, and height thereof; and to know the love of Christ which pass knowledge, that you may be filled with all fullness of God (Eph 3:16–19). Amen. Farewell.

Yours in Christ Jesus,

William Perkins.

23 July 1592.

The body of Holy Scripture is distinguished into sacred sciences, of which

One is principle. **Theology** is a science of living well and blessedly forever.

Others are **attendants** or handmaids.

1. **Ethics**, a doctrine of living honestly and civilly.
2. **Economics**, a doctrine of governing a family well.
3. **Politics**, a doctrine of the right administration of a commonwealth.
4. **Ecclesiastic discipline**, a doctrine of well ordering the Church.
5. **The Jews commonwealth**, inasmuch as it differs from Church government.
6. **Prophecy**, the doctrine of preaching well.
7. **Academic,** the doctrine of governing Schools well: especially those of the Prophets.

Chapter One

THE BODY OF SCRIPTURE AND THEOLOGY

The **Body of Scripture** sets forth doctrine sufficient to live well. It includes many holy sciences, of which one is principal, and the others are attendants or servants.

The principal science is Theology.

Theology is the science of living blessedly forever. Blessed life consists in the knowledge of God. *"And this is eternal life, that they know you the only true God, and Jesus Christ whom you have sent"* (Joh 17:3). *"By his knowledge shall the righteous one (i.e. Christ), my servant, make many to be accounted righteous, and he shall bear their iniquities"* (Isa. 53:11). Therefore, theology also involves knowledge of ourselves since we know God by looking into ourselves.

Theology has two parts: the first of God (***chapters 2–5***), the second of his works (***chapters 6–7***).

CHAPTER 2:

God's Nature & Life

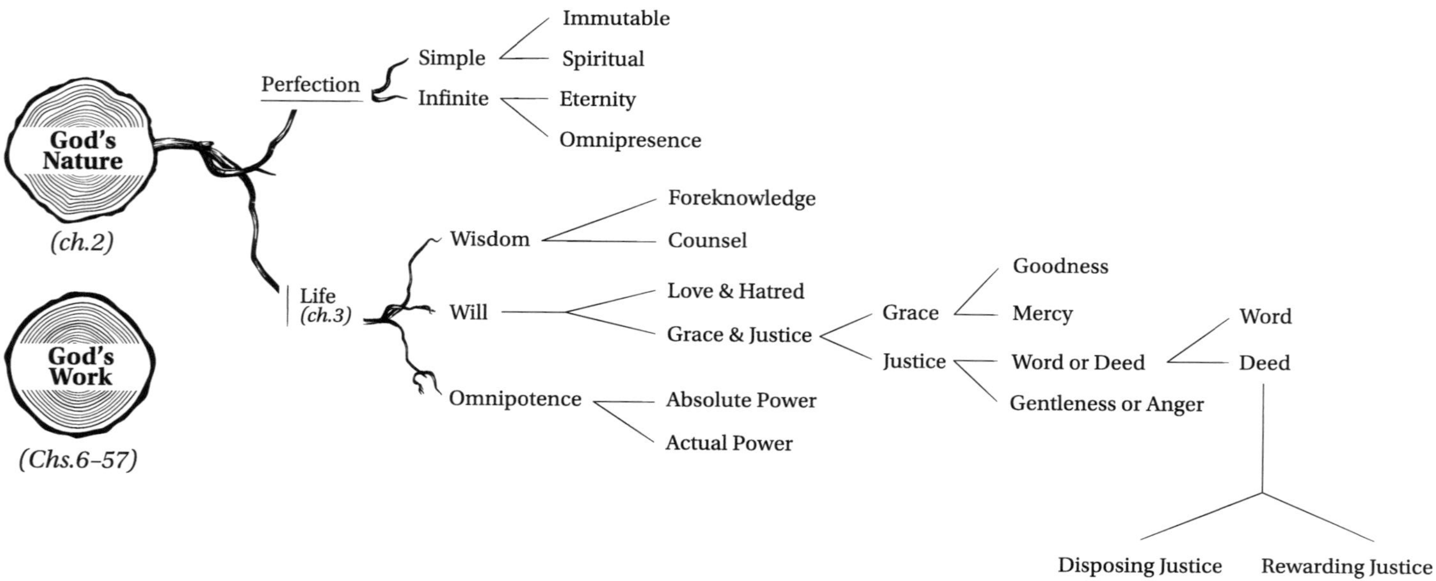

Chapter Two

GOD AND HIS NATURE

That there is a God is evident by:

1. the course of nature
2. the nature of the soul of man
3. the distinction of things honest and dishonest
4. the terror of conscience
5. the governance of civil societies
6. the order of all causes always having recourse to some former beginning
7. the determination of all things to their various ends
8. the consent of all sane people

God is Jehovah Elohim. *"God spoke to Moses and said to him, "I am the LORD. I appeared to Abraham, to Isaac, and to Jacob, as God Almighty, but by my name the LORD I did not make myself known to them"* (Exod. 6:2–3). *""and they ask me, 'What is his name?' what shall I say to them?" God said to Moses, "I AM WHO I AM." And he said, "Say this to the people of Israel, 'I AM has sent me to you.'""* (Exod. 3:13–14). In these words, the first title of God declares his Nature, the second his Persons.

The **Nature of God** is his most lively and most perfect essence.

The **Perfection of the Nature of God** is the absoluteness of his constitution by which he is entirely complete within himself. *"I AM WHO I AM."* (Exod. 3:13). *"The God who made the world and everything in it, being Lord of heaven and earth, does not live in temples made by man, nor is he served by human hands, as though he needed anything, since he himself gives to all mankind life and breath and everything"* (Acts 17:24–25).

The **Perfection of God's Nature** consists of its Simplicity and Infinity.

The **Simplicity** of his nature is that by which he is completely without logical relation in arguments (in him there is neither subject nor adjoining parts).[1] *"For as the Father has life in himself, so he has granted the Son also to have life in himself"* (John 5:26). Conferred with John 14:6, *"I am the way, and the truth, and the life". "But if we walk in the light, as he is in the light"* (1 John 1:7). Conferred with v.5 *"God is light, and in him is no darkness at all"*. Hence it is evident that in God these are all one: to have Life and to be Life, or to be in Light and to be Light. Neither is God subject to generality or speciality, whole or parts, matter or that which is made of matter. Otherwise there would be diverse things in God, and one more perfect than another. Therefore, whatever is in God *is* his essence; and all that he is, he is by his essence. The saying of Augustine is fit to prove this: "In God, to exist, and to be just or mighty, are all one. But in the mind of man, it is not all one to exist, and to be mighty or just: for the mind may be destitute of virtues and yet be a mind".[2]

Hence it is clear that **the Nature of God** is Immutable and Spiritual.

God's **Immutability of Nature** is that by which he is void of all composition, division, and change.[3] *"(God) the Father of lights with whom there is no variation or shadow due to change"* (James 1:17). *"For I the LORD do not change"* (Mal. 3:6). Where it is said, that *"God repents etc."* (Gen. 6:6). The meaning is that God changes his action like people do when they repent. Therefore, repentance does not signify any change *in* God, but only in his actions, and in such things as are made and changed by him.

God's Nature is **Spiritual** in that it is incorporeal and therefore invisible. *"God is spirit"* (John 4:24.). *"The Lord is the spirit"* (2 Cor. 3:17.). *"To the King of ages, immortal, invisible, the only God, be honour and*

1. That is, the *Simplicity* of God's Being means that he is not composed of parts. If he were so composed (for example, if God could be divided up into his attributes) then 'God' would be the sum of things more fundamental than his own existence. As Perkins asserts here, the doctrine of Divine Simplicity states that God simply *is* his attributes. This is a fundamental difference between God's Being (or *essence*) and all beings created by him.
2. Augustine, *On the Trinity*, 6.4.
3. *Immutable* means unchangeable. Perkins defines immutability in terms of God's simplicity, as previously discussed. In God there is no unfulfilled potential to fulfill or make use of. God is perfect and therefore unchangeable.

glory forever and ever. Amen" (1 Tim. 1:17). *"He is the image of the invisible God"* (Col. 1:15).

The **Infinity of God** is twofold: his Eternity and Omnipresence.

God's **Eternity** is that by which he is without beginning and ending, *"Before the mountains were brought forth, or ever you had formed the earth and the world, from everlasting to everlasting you are God"* (Psalm 90:2). *"'I am the Alpha and the Omega,' says the Lord God, 'who is and who was and who is to come, the Almighty'"* (Rev. 1:8).

God's **Omnipresence** is that by which his incomprehensible nature is everywhere present, both within and without the world. *"Great is the LORD, and greatly to be praised, and his greatness is unsearchable"* (Psalm 145:3). *"But will God indeed dwell on the earth? Behold, heaven and the highest heaven cannot contain you; how much less this house that I have built!"* (1 Kings 8:27). *"Do I not fill heaven and earth? declares the LORD"* (Jer. 23:24). Hence it is clear that:

First, that he is only one and indivisible, not many. *"One Lord, one faith, one baptism, one God and Father of all, who is over all and through all and in all"* (Eph. 4:5-6). *"To you it was shown, that you might know that the LORD is God; there is no other besides him"* (Deut. 4:35). *"We know that 'an idol has no real existence,' and that 'there is no God but one'"* (1 Cor. 8:4). And there can be but one thing infinite in nature.

Secondly, God knows our hearts. Nothing is hidden from that nature, which is within all things and without all things, which is included in nothing nor excluded from anything. Because *"(the Lord) only, know(s) the hearts of all the children of mankind"* (1 Kings 8:39). *"O LORD, you have searched me and known me! You know when I sit down and when I rise up; you discern my thoughts from afar"* (Psalm 139:1-2).

Chapter Three

THE LIFE OF GOD

So far we have spoken of the perfection of God's Nature. Now follows the life of God, by which the Divine Nature is in perpetual action, living, and moving in itself.[1] *"My soul thirsts for God, for the living God. When shall I come and appear before God?"* (Psalm 42:2). *"Take care, brothers, lest there be in any of you an evil, unbelieving heart, leading you to fall away from the living God"* (Heb. 3:12).

The **Divine Nature** is especially in perpetual operation by three attributes by which God acts towards his creatures. These are his Wisdom, Will, and Omnipotence.

The **Wisdom** or **Knowledge** of God is that by which God distinctly and perfectly knows himself and all other things, whether they have been or not. (God's knowledge is not by notions abstracted from the things themselves, but by his own essence. Nor is it successive and by course of reason, but by one eternal and unchanging act of understanding). *"No one knows the Son except the Father, and no one knows the Father except the Son and anyone to whom the Son chooses to reveal him"* (Matt. 11:27). *"And no creature is hidden from his sight, but all are naked and exposed to the eyes of him to whom we must give account"* (Heb. 4:13). *"His understanding is beyond measure"* (Psalm 147:5).

God's **Wisdom** has two parts: His Foreknowledge and his Counsel.

The **Foreknowledge** of God is that by which he most assuredly foresees all things that are to come. *"This Jesus, delivered up according to the definite plan and foreknowledge of God, you crucified and killed by the hands of lawless men"* (Acts 2:23). *"For those whom he foreknew he also predestined to be conformed to the image of his Son"* (Rom. 8:29).

1. This is the classic philosophical way of describing God's perfect Being in action. Whilst God is unchangeable and has no potential to fulfil, this must not be confused with being static or lifeless. God is completely full of energy, life, and joy.

Foresight is not properly spoken of God (who is eternal), except for the sake of human understanding, to whom things are either past or to come.

The **Counsel** of God is that by which he immediately perceives the best reason for all things that exist. *"I have counsel and sound wisdom; I have insight; I have strength"* (Prov. 8:14).

The **Will** of God is that by which he both most freely and justly, with one act, wills all things. *"So then he has mercy on whomever he wills, and he hardens whomever he wills"* (Rom. 9:18). *"He predestined us for adoption as sons through Jesus Christ, according to the purpose of his will"* (Eph. 1:5). *"Instead you ought to say, 'If the Lord wills, we will live and do this or that'"* (James 4:15).

God wills that which is good by approving it, but that which is evil (inasmuch as it is evil) by disallowing and forsaking it.[2] And yet he voluntarily does permit evil because it is good that there should be evil. *"In past generations he allowed all the nations to walk in their own ways"* (Acts 14:16). *"So I gave them over to their stubborn hearts, to follow their own counsels"* (Psalm 81:12).

The **Will** of God has diverse names depending on the object of its action. It is therefore called Love and Hatred, or Grace and Justice.

The **Love** of God is that by which God approves first himself, and then all his creatures (without their deserving). In them he takes delight. *"God is love, and whoever abides in love abides in God, and God abides in him"* (1 John 4:16). *"For God so loved the world, that he gave his only Son, etc."* (John 3:16). *"God shows his love for us in that while we were still sinners, Christ died for us"* (Rom. 5:8).

The **Hatred** of God is that by which he dislikes and detests his offending creature for its faults. *"Nevertheless, with most of them God was not pleased, for they were overthrown in the wilderness"* (1 Cor. 10:5.) *"You hate all evildoers"* (Psalm 5:5). *"You have loved righteousness and hated wickedness"* (Psalm 45:7).

The **Grace** of God is that by which he freely declares his favour to his creatures. *"But if it is by grace, it is no longer on the basis of works; otherwise grace would no longer be grace"* (Rom. 11:6). *"For the grace*

2. That is, evil is parasitic on good things. Created things are 'good' by nature (Genesis 1) but evil manipulates good things to bad ends. See ***chapters 10–12***.

of God has appeared, bringing salvation for all people, training us to renounce ungodliness and worldly passions, etc." (Titus 2:11–12).

The **Grace** of God is either his Goodness or his Mercy.

The **Goodness** of God is that by which he, being in himself absolutely good, freely exercises his generosity upon his creatures. *"Why do you ask me about what is good? There is only one who is good"* (Matt. 19:17). *"For he makes his sun rise on the evil and on the good, and sends rain on the just and on the unjust"* (Matt. 5:45).

God's **Mercy** is that by which he freely assists all his creatures in the miserable consequences of their sinful state. *"Therefore the LORD waits to be gracious to you"* (Isa. 30:18). *"His mercies never come to an end"* (Lam. 3:22). *"I will be gracious to whom I will be gracious, and will show mercy on whom I will show mercy"* (Exod. 33:19).

God's **Justice** is that by which he, in all things, wills that which is just. *"For the LORD is righteous; he loves righteous deeds;* (Psalm 11:7) *"For you are not a God who delights in wickedness"* (Psalm 5:4).

God's **Justice** is in Word or Deed.

Justice in Word is that truth by which God constantly wills that which he has said. *"Let God be true though everyone were a liar"* (Rom. 3:4). *"Heaven and earth shall pass away, but my words will not pass away"* (Matt. 24:35). Hence it is that God is just in keeping his promise. *"If we confess our sins, he is faithful and just to forgive us our sins"* (1 John 1:9). *"Henceforth there is laid up for me the crown of righteousness, which the Lord, the righteous judge, will award to me on that Day"* (2 Tim. 4: 8).

Justice in Deed is that by which he either disposes or rewards.

God's **Disposing Justice** is that by which he, as a most free Lord, rightly orders all things in his actions. *"The Lord is righteous in all his ways"* (Psalm 145:17).

God's **Rewarding Justice** is that by which he renders to his creature according to his work. *"God considers it just to repay with affliction those who afflict you, and to grant relief to you who are afflicted as well as to us"* (2 Thess. 1:6). *"And if you call on him as Father who judges impartially according to each one's deeds, conduct yourselves with fear throughout the time of your exile"* (1 Pet. 1:17). *"The LORD is a God of recompense; he will surely repay"* (Jer. 51:56).

The **Justice of God** is either his Gentleness or Anger.

God's **Gentleness** is that by which he freely bestows upon his creature a reward. *"This is evidence of the righteous judgement of God, that you may be considered worthy of the kingdom of God, for which you are also suffering"* (2 Thess. 1:5). *"The one who receives a prophet because he is a prophet will receive a prophet's reward, and the one who receives a righteous person because he is a righteous person will receive a righteous person's reward. And whoever gives one of these little ones even a cup of cold water because he is a disciple, truly, I say to you, he will by no means lose his reward"* (Matt. 10:41, 42).

God's **Anger** is that by which he punishes the transgressions of his creatures. *"For the wrath of God is revealed from heaven against all ungodliness and unrighteousness of men, who by their unrighteousness suppress the truth"* (Rom. 1:18). *"Whoever believes in the Son has eternal life; whoever does not obey the Son shall not see life, but the wrath of God remains on him"* (John 3:36).

Thus much concerning the will of God. Now follows his omnipotence.

God's **Omnipotence** is that by which he is most able to perform every work. *"With man this is impossible, but with God all things are possible"* (Matt. 19:26).

God's omnipotence excludes certain things:

1. First, whatever involves an impotence or lack, such as to lie or to deny his word. *"Which God, who never lies, promised before the ages began"* (Titus 1:2). *"He cannot deny himself"* (2 Tim. 2:13).
2. Such things as are contrary to the Nature of God, such as to destroy himself, and not to beget his Son from eternity.
3. Such things as imply contradiction. For God cannot make a truth false or make something simultaneously both exist and not exist.

God's **Power** may be distinguished into an absolute and actual power.

God's **Absolute Power** is that by which he can do more than he either does or will do. *"I tell you, God is able from these stones to raise up children for Abraham"* (Matt. 3:9). *"By the power that enables him even to* *subject all things to himself"* (Phil. 3:21).

God's **Actual Power** is that by which he causes all things to occur which he freely wills. *"Whatever the LORD pleases, he does, in heaven and on earth, in the seas and all deeps"* (Psalm 135:6).

Chapter Four

GOD'S GLORY AND BLESSEDNESS

Out of the former attributes, by which the true Jehovah is distinguished from a false god and from idols, arise the glory of God and his blessedness.

God's **Glory** or **Majesty** is the infinite excellence of his most simple and most holy divine Nature. *"He is the radiance of the glory of God and the exact imprint of his nature, etc."* (Heb. 1:3).

By this we see that God alone can know himself perfectly. *"Not that anyone has seen the Father except he who is from God; he has seen the Father"* (John 6:46), *"who alone has immortality, who dwells in unapproachable light, whom no one has ever seen or can see"* (1 Tim. 6:16), *"you cannot see my face"* (Exod. 33:20).

This notwithstanding, there is a certain **Manifestation of God's Glory**: partly more obscure, partly more apparent.

The **more obscure manifestation** is the vision of God's majesty in this life by the eyes of the mind, through the help of the things perceived by the outward senses. *"I saw the Lord sitting upon a throne, high and lifted up; and the train of his robe filled the temple"* (Isa. 6:1). *"And while my glory passes by I will put you in a cleft of the rock, and I will cover you with my hand until I have passed by. Then I will take away my hand, and you shall see my back, but my face shall not be seen"* (Exod. 33:22–23). *"For now we see in a mirror dimly"* (1 Cor. 13:12).

The clearer and **more apparent manifestation** of God is the contemplation of him in heaven face to face. *"But then face to face"* (1 Cor. 13:12). *"As I looked, thrones were placed, and the Ancient of Days took his seat; his clothing was white as snow, etc."* (Dan. 7:9, 10; Matt. 19:16).

God's **Blessedness** is that by which God is, in and of himself, all sufficient. *"I am God Almighty; walk before me, and be blameless"* (Gen.

17:1). *"For in him the whole fullness of deity dwells bodily"* (Col. 2:9). *"Which he will display at the proper time—he who is the blessed and only Sovereign, etc."* (1 Tim. 6:15).

Chapter Five

THE PERSONS OF THE GODHEAD

The **Persons** are they which, subsisting in one Godhead,[1] are distinguished by incommunicable properties.[2] *"For there are three that testify: the Spirit and the water and the blood; and these three agree"* (1 John 5:7–8). *"Then the LORD rained on Sodom and Gomorrah sulphur and fire from the LORD out of heaven"* (Gen. 19:24). *"In the beginning was the Word, and the Word was with God, and the Word was God"* (John 1:1).

They therefore are co-equal, and are distinguished not by degree, but by order.[3]

The **Constitution** of a person is the joining of a personal property to the one divine Nature.

Distinction of Persons is that by which every divine person is one and the same perfect God, yet the Father is not the Son or the Holy Spirit, but the Father alone; and the Holy Spirit is not the Father or the Son, but the Holy Spirit alone. Neither can they be divided by reason of the infinity of their most simple essence. The divine essence is all one in number, and the same in the Father, the same in the Son, the same in the Holy Spirit, so that in these there is diversity of persons but unity in essence.

The **Communion of the Persons** is that by which each one is in and with the rest by reason of the unity of the Godhead. Therefore, each one possesses, loves, and glorifies the others, and all work the same thing.

---

1. *Subsisting* is a way of distinguishing the particularity of the persons of the Trinity without compromising the oneness of God (his *Simplicity*, see above). This rules out any possibility that the divine persons might be mere parts or expressions of God (i.e. *Modalism*), or that there are three gods (i.e. *Tritheism*).
2. *Incommunicable Properties* are those attributes which God alone possesses, and which created beings do not.
3. That is, the necessary order (or *taxis*) of the divine persons is: Father → Son → Spirit. This order and priority of relation is expressed in all of God's acts, both in creation and redemption.

"Do you not believe that I am in the Father and the Father is in me? The words that I say to you I do not speak on my own authority, but the Father who dwells in me does his works" (John 14:10). *"The LORD possessed me at the beginning of his work, the first of his acts of old"* (Prov. 8:22), and verse 30, *"then I was beside him, like a master workman, and I was daily his delight, rejoicing before him always". "In the beginning was the Word, and the Word was with God, and the Word was God"* (John 1:1), and John 15:19 *"the Son can do nothing of his own accord, but only what he sees the Father doing. For whatever the Father does, that the Son does likewise".*

There are **three Persons**: the Father, the Son, and the Holy Spirit, *"And when Jesus was baptized, immediately he went up from the water, and behold, the heavens were opened to him, and he saw the Spirit of God descending like a dove and coming to rest on him; and behold, a voice from heaven said, 'This is my beloved Son, with whom I am well pleased'"* (Matt. 3:16–17).

The **Father** is a person without beginning, who from all eternity begat the Son. *"He is the radiance of the glory of God and the exact imprint of his nature"* (Heb. 1:3). *"You are my Son; today I have begotten you"* (Psalm 2:7).

In the generation of the Son, these properties must be noted:

1. He that begets and he that is begotten are together, and not one before another in time.
2. He that begets communicates his whole essence with him that is begotten, not just one part.
3. The Father begot the Son not out of himself, but within in himself.

The incommunicable property of the Father is to be unbegotten, to be a Father, and to beget. He is the beginning of actions, because he begins every action of himself, effecting it by the Son and the Holy Spirit. *"Yet for us there is one God, the Father, from whom are all things and for whom we exist, and one Lord, Jesus Christ, through whom are all things and through whom we exist"* (1 Cor. 8:6). *"For from him and through him and to him are all things"* (Rom. 11:36).

The Son and the Holy Spirit have the Godhead (the whole divine essence) of the Father by communication.

The **Son** is the second person, begotten of the Father from all Eternity. *"For to which of the angels did God ever say, 'You are my Son, today I have begotten you'?"* (Heb. 1:5). *"He is the image of the invisible God, the firstborn of all creation"* (Col. 1:15). *"And we have seen his glory, glory as of the only Son from the Father, full of grace and truth"* (John 1:14). *"He who did not spare his own Son ...."* (Rom. 8:32).

For this reason he is said to be sent from the Father. *"For I came from God and I am here. I came not of my own accord, but he sent me"* (John 8:42). This sending does not take away equality of essence and power but declares the order of the persons. *"This was why the Jews were seeking all the more to kill him, because not only was he breaking the Sabbath, but he was even calling God his own Father, making himself equal with God"* (John 5:18). *"Who, though he was in the form of God, did not count equality with God a thing to be grasped"* (Phil 2:6).

Although the Son is begotten of his Father, yet nevertheless he is of and by himself very God: for he must be considered either according to his essence, or according to his filiation or sonship. In regard of his essence, he is '*autotheos*': of and by himself very God. (For the Deity which is common to all the three persons is not begotten). But as he is a person, and the Son of the Father, he is not of himself but from another: for he is the eternal Son of his father. And thus he is truly said to be "very God of very God".[4]

For this reason he is also "the Word of the Father", not a vanishing word (like our spoken words which last for an instant), but an essential word. As a word is, as it were, 'begotten of the mind', so is the Son begotten of the Father; and also, because he brings glad tidings from the bosom of the Father.[5]

The property of the Son is to be begotten.

His proper manner of working is to execute actions from the Father,

4. *Nicene Creed* (325AD).

5. Here Perkins directs readers to two early works on the Trinity: *Oration of the Son* by Gregory of Nazianzus (329–390AD), and a preface on John's Gospel by Basil of Caesarea (330-379AD). These can be found online. Alternatively, the following are particularly good modern translations: St Gregory of Nazianzus, *On God and Christ: The Five Theological Orations and Two Letters to Cledonius* (Popular Patristics 23; New York: St Vladimirs Seminary Press, 2002) and St Basil the Great, *On Christian Doctrine and Practice* (Popular Patristics 47; New York: St Vladimirs Seminary Press, 2013).

by the Holy Spirit. *"One Lord, Jesus Christ, through whom are all things and through whom we exist"* (1 Cor. 8:6). *"For whatever the Father does, that the Son does likewise"* (John 5:19).

The **Holy Spirit** is the third person, proceeding from the Father and the Son. *"But when the Helper comes, whom I will send to you from the Father, the Spirit of truth, who proceeds from the Father, he will bear witness about me"* (John 15:26). *"You, however, are not in the flesh but in the Spirit, if in fact the Spirit of God dwells in you. Anyone who does not have the Spirit of Christ does not belong to him"* (Rom. 8:9). *"When the Spirit of truth comes, he will guide you into all the truth, for he will not speak on his own authority, but whatever he hears he will speak, and he will declare to you the things that are to come. He will glorify me, for he will take what is mine and declare it to you"* (John 16:13–14).

What may be the essential difference between proceeding and begetting, neither the Scriptures determine, nor the Church knows.

The incommunicable property of the Holy Spirit is to proceed.

His proper manner of working is to finish an action, effecting it, as from the Father and the Son.

The Father and the Son are two distinct persons yet are they both but one beginning of the Holy Spirit.[6]

6. Here Perkins endorses the western addition of the word 'filioque' ("and the Son") to the *Nicene Creed*, which occurred during the medieval period. The idea is that the Spirit proceeds from the Father *and* the Son, not from the Father alone. This is reflected on the *ocular catechism* accompanying this book). The *filioque* position is endorsed by both Protestant and Roman Catholic churches, in contrast to East Orthodoxy who reject it. See John 14:26, 15:26, 16:7, 20:22.

Chapter Six

GOD'S WORKS AND HIS DECREE

Thus far concerning the first part of Theology. The second follows, concerning the works of God.

The **Works of God** are all those which he does out of himself, that is, out of his divine essence. These are common to the Trinity, always referring the particular manner of working to each person.

The end goal of all these is the manifestation of the glory of God. *"For from him and through him and to him are all things"* (Rom. 11:36).

The work, or action of God, is either his Decree or the Execution of his Decree.

The **Decree of God** is that by which God in himself has necessarily and yet freely, from all Eternity, determined all things. *"In him we have obtained an inheritance, having been predestined according to the purpose of him who works all things according to the counsel of his will"* (Eph. 1:11) and verse 4: *"even as he chose us in him before the foundation of the world." "Are not two sparrows sold for a penny? And not one of them will fall to the ground apart from your Father"* (Matt. 10:29). *"Has the potter no right over the clay, to make out of the same lump one vessel for honourable use and another for dishonourable use?"* (Rom. 9:21).

Therefore, the Lord, according to his good pleasure, has most certainly decreed every action and thing, whether past, present, or to come, together with their circumstances of place, time, means, and end.

Indeed, he has most justly decreed the wicked works of the wicked. For if it had not so pleased him, they would never have happened at all. And though they, of their own nature, are and remain wicked, yet in respect of God's decree they are to be accounted good. For there is nothing absolutely evil,[1] *"For it is better to suffer for doing good, if that should be God's will, than for doing evil"* (1 Pet. 3:17).

The thing which in its own nature is evil, in God's eternal counsel comes as in the place of a good thing. Here it is an occasion and way to manifest the glory of God in his justice and mercy.

God's Foreknowledge is joined to his decree, and indeed is in nature before it (not in relation to God but to us) since knowledge goes before willing and effecting a work. For we only do those things that we have already willed and know.

God's foreknowledge (in itself) is not a cause of why things are, except as it is joined with his decree. For things do not come to pass because God foreknew them, but because he decreed and willed them.

The **Execution of God's Decree** is that by which all things (which were foreknown or decreed) are accomplished in their time, just as they were foreknown and decreed.

This same decree of God is the first cause of all things, and their primary working cause. It is before all other causes in order and in time. For God's decree always has his will joined to it, by which he can willingly effect that which he has decreed. It would be a sign of powerlessness for God to decree anything which he could not willingly accomplish. And with God's will is joined an effectual power, by which the Lord can bring to pass whatever he has freely decreed.

This first and principle cause, though in itself necessary, does not take away freedom of will in election, or the nature and property of secondary causes, but only brings them into a certain order.[2] That is, it directs them to a determined end. Consequently, the effects and events of things are either contingent or necessary according to their own nature as a secondary cause.[3] So Christ, according to his Father's decree, died necessarily (Acts 17:3), yet willingly (Matt. 25:39). Yet if we consider the physical nature of Christ's body, he might have prolonged his life, and

1. On the nature of evil, see ***chapter 10***.
2. *Primary Causality* refers to God's actions, whereas *Secondary Causality* refers to the actions of created things (including human decisions). God's acts are sovereign and transcendent, whereas creaturely existence and actions only occur by God's upholding of creation and under his sovereign will.
3. *Contingency* means that something might potentially have been otherwise. *Necessity* refers to things that could not have been otherwise.

therefore in this respect may be said to have died contingently.

The Execution of God's decree has two branches, his Operation and his Operative Permission.

God's **Operation** is his effectual producing of all good things, which either have being or moving, or which are done.

God's **Operative Permission** is that by which he only *permits* a work to be done inasmuch as it is evil, but *effectually works* it inasmuch as it is good. *"As for you, you meant evil against me, but God meant it for good, to bring it about that many people should be kept alive, as they are today"* (Gen. 50:20), and *"God sent me before you to preserve for you a remnant on earth"* (Gen. 45:7). *"Ah, Assyria, the rod of my anger; the staff in their hands is my fury! Against a godless nation I send him, and against the people of my wrath I command him, to take spoil and seize plunder, and to tread them down like the mire of the streets. But he does not so intend, and his heart does not so think; but it is in his heart to destroy, and to cut off nations not a few"* (Isa. 10:5–7).

God permits evil by a certain voluntary permission in that he forsakes the secondary cause in its working of evil. He forsakes his creature either by detracting the grace it had, or by not bestowing that which it lacks. *"For this reason God gave them up to dishonourable passions"* (Rom. 1:26). *"Correcting his opponents with gentleness. God may perhaps grant them repentance leading to a knowledge of the truth, and they may come to their senses and escape from the snare of the Devil, after being captured by him to do his will"*(2 Tim. 2:25–26).

We must not think that God is unjust, since he is indebted to none. *"I will have mercy on whom I have mercy, and I will have compassion on whom I have compassion"* (Rom. 9:15). It is in God's pleasure to bestow however much grace he chooses, and upon whomever he will. *"Am I not allowed to do what I choose with what belongs to me?"* (Matt. 20:15).

That which is evil has some respect of goodness with God. First, in that it is the punishment of sin, and punishment is accounted a moral good in that it is the part of a just judge to punish sin. Secondly, as it is a mere action or act. Thirdly, as it is a chastisement, a trial of one's faith, martyrdom, or propitiation for sin, as was the death and passion of Christ (Acts 2:23; 4:24). And if we observe these caveats, God is not a mere permissive agent in an evil work, but a powerful effector of it, yet in such a way that he neither instils an aberration into the action, nor supports or intends the same, but that he most freely permits evil and best directs it toward his own glory. Consider the following analogy: a man spurs forward a lame horse. The rider is the cause of the horse moving forward, but the horse itself is the cause of it stumbling due to its injury. Similarly, we see that when sun beams converge through glass they burn whatever they focus upon. Now, the cause of their burning is not in the sun, but in the glass. The same may be said of God's action in an evil subject.

Chapter Seven

PREDESTINATION AND CREATION

God's **Decree**, inasmuch as it applies to man, is called **Predestination**, which is the decree of God by the which he has ordained all men to a certain and everlasting estate: that is, either to salvation or condemnation, for his own glory. *"For God has not destined us for wrath, but to obtain salvation through our Lord Jesus Christ"* (1 Thess. 5:9). *"As it is written, "Jacob I loved, but Esau I hated .... What if God, desiring to show his wrath and to make known his power, has endured with much patience vessels of wrath prepared for destruction, in order to make known the riches of his glory for vessels of mercy, which he has prepared beforehand for glory"* (Rom. 9:13, 22–23).

The means of accomplishing God's Predestination are twofold: The Creation (***as follows***), and the Fall (***chapter 11***).

The **Creation** is that by which God made all things very good, out of nothing, that is, of no matter which was before the creation. *"In the beginning, God created the heavens and the earth, etc."* (Gen. 1:1ff).

God's manner of creating, as also of governing, is by his word alone, such that he produced everything without any instruments, means, assistance, or motion. For with God, to will anything is to be able to perform it. *"By faith we understand that the universe was created by the word of God, so that what is seen was not made out of things that are visible"* (Heb. 11:3). *"Let them praise the name of the LORD! For he commanded and they were created"* (Psalm 148:5).

The **Goodness** of the creature is a kind of excellence by which it was void of all sin, that is, free from punishment and transgression.

The **Creation** is of the world, or inhabitants in the world.

The World is a most beautiful palace, framed out of a deformed substance, and fit to be inhabited.

The **parts of the world** are the heavens and earth.

The **heavens** are threefold: the first is the air, the second the sky, the third an invisible and incorporeal essence, created to be the seat of all the blessed, both men, and Angels. This third heaven is called Paradise (2 Cor. 13:4).

The inhabitants of the world are reasonable creatures, made according to God's own image. These are either Angels or men. *"Then God said, "Let us make man in our image, after our likeness"* (Gen. 1:26). *"When the sons of God came to present themselves before the LORD, and Satan also came among them"* (Job 1:6).

The image of God is the integrity of the reasonable creature, resembling God in holiness, *"and to put on the new self, created after the likeness of God in true righteousness and holiness"* (Eph. 4:24).

Chapter Eight

ANGELS

The Angels were each created in the beginning and established in an upright estate. In them these things are to be noted.

1. Their **Nature**. Angels are spiritual and incorporeal essences. *"For surely it is not angels that he helps, but he helps the offspring of Abraham"* (Heb. 2:16). *"Of the angels he says, 'He makes his angels winds, and his ministers a flame of fire'"* (Heb. 1:7).

2. Their **Qualities**.

   i. They are wise, *"But my lord has wisdom like the wisdom of the angel of God to know all things that are on the earth"* (2 Sam. 14:20).

   ii. They are of great might, *"when the Lord Jesus is revealed from heaven with his mighty angels"* (2 Thess. 1:7). *"David spoke to the LORD when he saw the angel who was striking the people"* (2 Sam. 24:17). *"And that night the angel of the LORD went out and struck down 185,000 in the camp of the Assyrians"* (2 Kings 19:35).

   iii. They are swift and agile, *"Then one of the seraphim flew to me, having in his hand a burning coal that he had taken with tongs from the altar"* (Isa. 6:6). *"While I was speaking in prayer, the man Gabriel, whom I had seen in the vision at the first, came to me in swift flight at the time of the evening sacrifice"* (Dan. 9:21). This is why the Cherubim in the Tabernacle were painted with wings.

3. They are **Innumerable**, *"Jacob went on his way, and the angels of God met him"* (Gen. 32:1). *"A thousand thousands served him, and ten thousand times ten thousand stood before him"* (Dan. 7:10). *"Do you think that I cannot appeal to my Father, and he will at once send me more than twelve legions of angels?"* (Matt. 26:53). *"To innumerable angels in festal gathering"* (Heb. 12:22).

4. They are in the **Highest Heaven**, where they ever attend upon God and have fellowship with him. *"I tell you that in heaven their angels always see the face of my Father who is in heaven"* (Matt. 18:10). *"The chariots of God are twice ten thousand, thousands upon thousands; the Lord is among them; Sinai is now in the sanctuary"* (Psalm 68:17). *"But are like angels in heaven"* (Mark 12:25).
5. Their **Degree**. It is clear that there are degrees of Angels. *"For by him all things were created, in heaven and on earth, visible and invisible, whether thrones or dominions or rulers or authorities"* (Col. 1:16). *"Neither death nor life, nor angels nor rulers, etc."* (Rom. 8:38) *"For the Lord himself will descend from heaven with a cry of command, with the voice of an archangel, and with the sound of the trumpet of God"* (1 Thess. 4:16). But it is not for us to search who or how many are of each order. Neither ought we curiously to enquire how they are distinguished, whether in essence or qualities. *"Let no one disqualify you, insisting on asceticism and worship of angels, going on in detail about visions, puffed up without reason by his sensuous mind"* (Col. 2:18).
6. Their **Office**. Their office is partly to magnify God and partly to perform his commandments. *"Bless the LORD, O you his angels, you mighty ones who do his word, obeying the voice of his word! Bless the LORD, all his hosts, his ministers, who do his will!"* (Psalm 103:20-21).

The **Establishing** of some Angels in that integrity in which they were created.

Chapter Nine

MAN IN HIS STATE OF INNOCENCE

After he was created by God, man was established in an excellent estate of innocence. Of this estate seven things are mainly to be regarded.

1. The **Place**. The garden of Eden, that most pleasant garden. *"The LORD God took the man and put him in the garden of Eden to work it and keep it"* (Gen. 2:15).
2. The **Integrity** of man's nature. Which was *"created after the likeness of God in true righteousness and holiness"* (Eph. 4:24). This integrity has two parts:

    a. Wisdom, which is true and perfect knowledge of God, and of his will (inasmuch as it is to be performed by man), and indeed of the counsel of God in all his creatures. *"And have put on the new self, which is being renewed in knowledge after the image of its creator"* (Col. 3:10). *"Now out of the ground the LORD God had formed every beast of the field and every bird of the heavens and brought them to the man to see what he would call them. And whatever the man called every living creature, that was its name"* (Gen. 2:19).

    b. Justice, which is a conformity of the will, affections, and powers of the body to the will of God.

3. Man's **Dignity** consists of four parts.

    a. His communion with God, by which God rejoiced in his own image and likewise man loved God. This is apparent by God's familiar conference with Adam, *"and God said, "Behold, I have given you every plant yielding seed that is on the face of all the earth, etc."* (Gen. 1:29).

    b. His dominion over all the creatures of the earth (Gen. 2:19). *"You have given him dominion over the works of your hands;*

you have put all things under his feet, etc" (Psalm 8:6).

c. The decency and dignity of the body in which there was imprinted a princely majesty. *"Yet you have made him a little lower than the heavenly beings and crowned him with glory and honour"* (Psalm 8:5). *"And the man and his wife were both naked and were not ashamed"* (Gen. 2:25). *"And on those parts of the body that we think less honourable we bestow the greater honour, and our unpresentable parts are treated with greater modesty"* (1 Cor. 12:23).

d. Labour of the body without pain or grief. *"Because you have listened to the voice of your wife... cursed is the ground because of you... By the sweat of your face you shall eat bread, etc."* (Gen. 3:17, 19).

4. **Subjection to God**, whereby man was bound to perform obedience to the commandments of God, of which there were two: one concerning the two trees, and the other the observation of the Sabbath.

God's commandment concerning the trees was ordained to make examination and trial of man's obedience. It consists of two parts:

a. The giving of the tree of life as a sign, that it might confirm to man his perpetual abode in the garden of Eden, if he persists in his obedience. *"To the one who conquers I will grant to eat of the tree of life, which is in the paradise of God"* (Rev. 2:7). *"She is a tree of life to those who lay hold of her; those who hold her fast are called blessed"* (Prov. 3:18).

b. The prohibition to eat of the tree of the knowledge of good and evil, together with a communication of temporal and eternal death, after the transgression of this commandment. *"But of the tree of the knowledge of good and evil you shall not eat, for in the day that you eat of it you shall surely die"* (Gen. 2:17). The observation of God's command would have brought perpetual happiness, but the violation gave experience of evil and misery, namely of punishment and of guiltiness of sin.

God's commandment concerning the observation of the Sabbath is that, by which God ordained the sanctification of the Sabbath. *"So God blessed the seventh day and made it holy"* (Gen. 2:3).

5. His **Calling**, which is his service of God in the observation of his commandments and the tending of the garden of Eden. *"God made all things for himself"* (Prov. 16:4). *"The LORD God took the man and put him in the garden of Eden to work it and keep it"* (Gen. 2:15).
6. His **Diet** was the herbs of the earth and fruit of every tree, except for the tree of the knowledge of good and evil. *"Behold, I have given you every plant yielding seed that is on the face of all the earth, and every tree with seed in its fruit. You shall have them for food"* (Gen. 1:29) and *"but of the tree of the knowledge of good and evil you shall not eat"* (Gen. 2:17).
7. His **Free Choice**, both to will and perform the commandment concerning the two trees, and also to neglect and violate the same. By this we see that our first parents were created perfect, but changeable. For it pleased God to prepare a way for the execution of his decree in this way.

Chapter Ten

THE NATURE OF SIN AND THE FALL OF ANGELS

The **Fall** is a revolt of the reasonable creature, a movement from obedience to sin.[1]

Sin is the corruption, or rather deprivation, of the first integrity. More plainly, it is falling or turning from God, binding the offender by the course of God's justice to undergo due punishment.

Here a doubt may be resolved, namely whether sin is a 'thing' that exists or not. The answer is this: some things which exist are positive, others privative.[2]

Positive things are substances together with their properties, effects, inclinations, and affections which the Lord has created and imprinted in their natures. 'Privative' refers to the absence of something that ought to be in it. Such is sin, which (properly and of itself) is not created and existing, but rather the absence of that good which ought to be in the creature.

Sin has two parts: a Defect or Impotence, and Disorder:

1. **Impotence** is the lack or loss of that good which God grafted into the nature of his creature.
2. **Disorder** is a confusion or disturbance of all the powers and actions of the creature.

---

1. Sin is only possible for 'reasonable' beings. Since humans and angels have intellectual natures, they have the innate capacity to choose to obey or reject God's commands. Animals don't have this capacity, and therefore their actions can never be regarded as sinful.
2. *Privation* is a classic way of describing sin as a lack of goodness or wholeness. Technically, sin doesn't 'exist' since by nature created existence is good (Genesis 1). 'Sin' therefore describes a distortion of the goodness of creation.

The Fall came about in this manner:

1. God created his reasonable creatures good indeed, but changeable, as we showed earlier. For to be unchangeably good belongs to God alone.
2. God tested their obedience in those things about which they knew: *"you shall not listen to the words of that prophet or that dreamer of dreams. For the LORD your God is testing you, to know whether you love the LORD your God with all your heart and with all your soul"* (Deut. 13:3).
3. In this trial God didn't assist them with new grace to stand, but for just causes forsook them. Lastly, after God had forsaken them and left them to themselves, they fell from God. This can be compared to a man balancing a staff on the ground: if he withdraws his hand, the staff falls over on account of its own weight.

The **Fall** is of Men and Angels.

The **Fall of Angels** is that by which they were the sole instruments of their fall from God, since by their understanding and will, they could have chosen contrary. *"For if God did not spare angels when they sinned, but cast them into hell and committed them to chains of gloomy darkness to be kept until the judgement, etc."* (2 Pet. 2:4). *"And the angels who did not stay within their own position of authority, but left their proper dwelling, he has kept in eternal chains under gloomy darkness until the judgement of the great day"* (Jude 6). *"He was a murderer from the beginning, and has nothing to do with the truth, because there is no truth in him"* (John 8:44).

In the fall of Angels consider:

1. Their **Corruption**, which is the depravation of their nature arising from their fall. This is either that fearful malice and hatred by which they set themselves against God, or their insatiable desire to destroy mankind whether by force or fraud. *"Whoever makes a practice of sinning is of the Devil, for the Devil has been sinning from the beginning. The reason the Son of God appeared was to destroy the works of the Devil"* (1 John 3:8). *"Your adversary the Devil prowls around like a roaring lion, seeking someone to devour"* (1 Pet. 5:8). *"For we do not wrestle against flesh and blood, but against the rulers, against the authorities,*

against the cosmic powers over this present darkness, against the spiritual forces of evil in the heavenly places" (Eph. 6:12).

2. Their **Degree** and **Diversity**. Of these Angels one is chief and the rest are attendants. The chief is Beelzebub, prince of the rest of the Devils and the world, exceeding them all in malice. *"Depart from me, you cursed, into the eternal fire prepared for the Devil and his angels"* (Matt. 25:41). *"In their case the god of this world has blinded the minds of the unbelievers"* (2 Cor. 4:4). *"Now war arose in heaven, Michael and his angels fighting against the dragon. And the dragon and his angels fought back"* (Rev. 12:7). Ministering Angels are those who wait upon the Devil to accomplish his wicked schemes.
3. **Their Punishment**. God, after their fall, gave them over to perpetual torments without any hope of pardon. Jude verse 6. *"God did not spare angels when they sinned, but cast them into hell and committed them to chains of gloomy darkness to be kept until the judgement"* (2 Pet. 2:4). He did this, first, to admonish men regarding what great punishment they deserved. Secondly, to show that grievous sins must be punished more grievously.

The fall of Angels was the more grievous, because both their nature was more able to resist, and the Devil was the first founder of sin.

Their punishment may be divided into the easier and more grievous parts.

Their easier punishment is twofold. First is their ejection from heaven. *"God did not spare angels when they sinned, but cast them into hell"* (2 Pet. 2:4). Second is the limitation of their powers, *"And the LORD said to Satan, 'Behold, all that he has is in your hand. Only against him do not stretch out your hand'"* (Job 1:12).

The more grievous pain is that torment in the deep, which is endless and infinite in time and measure. *"And they begged him not to command them to depart into the abyss"* (Luke 8:31).

Chapter Eleven

MAN'S FALL AND DISOBEDIENCE

Adams Fall was his willing revolt to disobedience by eating the forbidden fruit. In Adams fall we may note its manner, greatness, and fruit.

1. **The Manner of Adams fall** was as follows:

    a. The Devil, having immediately before fallen himself, insinuated to our first parents that both the punishment for eating the forbidden fruit was uncertain and that God was not true in his word to them.

    b. By this his deception he blinded the eyes of their understanding.

    c. Being thus blinded, they begin to distrust God and to doubt God's favour toward them.

    d. Thus doubting they were moved to behold the forbidden fruit.

    e. They no sooner saw its beauty but they desired it.

    f. That they might satisfy their desire they ate the fruit, which the woman took from the tree. By this act they become utterly disloyal to God (Gen. 3:1–8).

    Thus, without constraint they willingly fell from their integrity. God, with just cause, left them to themselves and freely suffered them to fall. For we must not think that man's fall was either by chance, or by God not knowing it or barely winking at it, or by his bare permission, or against his will. Rather, it was not without the will of God yet was without the full approval of it.

2. **The Greatness of this Transgression** is not to be understood by the external object (the apparent triviality of an apple), but by the offence it contained against God's majesty. This offence appears by the many trespasses committed in that action. These are:

a. Doubting God's word.

b. Lack of faith. For they didn't believe God's threatening, *"For in the day that you eat of it you shall surely die"* (Gen. 2:17). But being bewitched with the Devil's promise, *"you will be like God"* (Gen. 3:5) they ceased to fear God's punishment and were inflamed with desire for greater dignity.

c. Their curiosity, in forsaking God's word and seeking other wisdom.

d. Their pride, in seeking to magnify themselves and to become like God.

e. Contempt of God, in transgressing his commandments against their own conscience.

f. In that they prefer the Devil before God.

g. Ingratitude, by which they expel God's spirit dwelling in them and despise that blessed union.

h. They murder both themselves and their descendants.

3. **The Fruit or Effects**. Out of this corrupt state of our first parents arose the state of unfaithfulness or unbelief. In this God has included all men under sin, that he might manifest his mercy in the salvation of some and his justice in condemnation of others. *"For God has consigned all to disobedience, that he may have mercy on all"* (Rom. 11:32). *"But the Scripture imprisoned everything under sin, so that the promise by faith in Jesus Christ might be given to those who believe"* (Gal. 3:22).

   Of this state we must consider Sin and the Punishment of Sin.

   Sin is threefold:

   1. Participation in Adam's Guilt (***as follows***).
   2. Original Corruption (***chapter 12***)
   3. Actual Sin (***chapter 13***).

The first part of Sin is **Participation** in both **Adam's Transgression and Guilt**, whereby in his sin all his descendants sinned. *"Therefore, just as sin came into the world through one man, and death through sin, and so death spread to all men because all sinned"* (Rom. 5:12). The reason for this is as follows. Adam was not a private man but represented all mankind. Therefore, whatever good or evil he received from God were common to others with him. *"For as in Adam all die, so also in Christ shall all be made alive"* (1 Cor. 15:22).

Again, when Adam offended his descendants were in his loins, from whom they would (by the course of nature) issue. They therefore take part in the guilt with him. *"One might even say that Levi himself, who receives tithes, paid tithes through Abraham, for he was still in the loins of his ancestor when Melchizedek met him"* (Heb. 7:9–10).

Chapter Twelve

ORIGINAL SIN AND THE CORRUPTION OF MAN'S NATURE

Out of the former transgression arises another, namely **Original Sin**, which is corruption ingrained within us from our first conception whereby every faculty of soul and body is prone and disposed to evil. *"Behold, I was brought forth in iniquity, and in sin did my mother conceive me"* (Psalm 51:5, Gen. 6:5). *"For we ourselves were once foolish, disobedient, led astray, slaves to various passions and pleasures, passing our days in malice and envy, hated by others and hating one another"* (Titus 3:3). *"Let us also lay aside every weight, and sin which clings so closely"* (Heb. 12:1).

By this we see that sin is not a corruption of man's substance, but only of his faculties. Otherwise men's souls could never be immortal, nor could Christ take man's nature upon himself.

All Adam's descendants equally share in this corruption. The reason that it doesn't show itself equally in all is because some have the Spirit of sanctification, some the Spirit only to bridle corruption, some neither.

The propagation of sin from the parents to the children is either because the soul is infected by the contagion of the body (as a good ointment by a filthy vessel), or because God, in the very moment of creation and infusion of souls into infants, does utterly forsake them. For as Adam received the image of God both for himself and others, so he lost it for himself and others.

The propagation of sin is like a common fire in a town: men ought not to be as concerned to understand how it came about as to know how to extinguish it.

In order that we may better understand the effects of original sin on the faculties of man's nature, three circumstances must be considered:

(a) How much of God's image sinful man retains.

(b) How much sin man received from Adam.

(c) How sin increases afterwards

We here examine each of these three circumstances with respect to each in order, namely: Mind, Conscience, Will, and Affections, and finally the Body.

The Mind

(a) In the mind the remnant of God's image consists of certain notions of good and evil, such as that there is a God, that this same God punishes transgressions, that there is everlasting life, that we must respect our superiors and not harm our neighbours. But even these notions are general and corrupt, and they have no other use but to deprive man of all excuse before God's judgement seat. *"For what can be known about God is plain to them, because God has shown it to them. For his invisible attributes, namely, his eternal power and divine nature, have been clearly perceived, ever since the creation of the world, in the things that have been made. So they are without excuse"* (Rom. 1:19–20).

(b) Men's minds received from Adam:

1. Ignorance, namely a lack or deprivation of knowledge in the things of God, whether concerning sincere worship or eternal happiness. *"The natural person does not accept the things of the Spirit of God, for they are folly to him, and he is not able to understand them because they are spiritually discerned"* (1 Cor. 2:14). *"For the mind that is set on the flesh is hostile to God, for it does not submit to God's law; indeed, it cannot"* (Rom. 8:7).

2. Impotence, whereby the mind of itself is unable to understand spiritual things, though they be taught. *"Then he opened their minds to understand the Scriptures"* (Luke 24:45). *"Not that we are sufficient in ourselves to claim anything as coming from us, but our sufficiency is from God"* (2 Cor. 3:5).

3. Vanity, in that the mind thinks falsehood truth and truth falsehood. *"You must no longer walk as the Gentiles do, in the futility of their minds"* (Eph. 4:17). *"It pleased God through the*

folly of what we preach to save those who believe, ... but we preach Christ crucified, a stumbling block to Jews and folly to Gentiles" (1 Cor. 1:21–23). *"There is a way that seems right to a man, but its end is the way to death"* (Prov. 14:12).

4. A natural inclination only to conceive and devise things which are evil. *"The LORD saw that the wickedness of man was great in the earth, and that every intention of the thoughts of his heart was only evil continually"* (Gen. 6:5). *"They are 'wise'—in doing evil! But how to do good they know not"* (Jer. 4:22).

   Hence it is apparent that the substance of all heresies is naturally grafted in man's nature. This is an important observation for students of theology.

(c) The increase of sin in the understanding is:

1. A sense of reprobation when God withdraws the light of nature. *"He has blinded their eyes and hardened their heart, lest they see with their eyes, and understand with their heart, and turn, and I would heal them"* (John 12:40). *"And since they did not see fit to acknowledge God, God gave them up to a debased mind to do what ought not to be done"* (Rom. 1:28).
2. The spirit of slumber, *"God gave them a spirit of stupor, eyes that would not see and ears that would not hear, etc."* (Rom. 11:8).
3. A spiritual drunkenness, *"Be drunk, but not with wine; stagger, but not with strong drink!"* (Isa. 29:9).
4. Strong delusions, *"Therefore God sends them a strong delusion, so that they may believe what is false"* (2 Thess. 2:11)

The Conscience[1]

(a) The remnant of God's image in the conscience is an observing and watchful power. It is like the eye of a keeper, reserved in man both to reprove and repress the unbridled course of his affections. *"They show that the work of the law is written on their hearts, while their conscience also bears witness, and their conflicting thoughts accuse or*

1. For Perkins's fuller discussion of the nature of the conscience, see his *Discourse on Conscience* (1596) in *The Works of William Perkins: Volume 8* (ed. J. Stephen Yuille; Grand Rapids: Reformation Heritage Books, 2019).

even excuse them" (Rom. 2:15).

(b) From Adam the conscience has received Impurity. *"But to the defiled and unbelieving, nothing is pure; but both their minds and their consciences are defiled"* (Titus 1:15). This impurity has three effects:

1. To excuse sin. For example, if a man outwardly serves God he will excuse and cloak his inward impiety. *"You know the commandments: 'Do not murder, etc, ... And he said to him, "Teacher, all these I have kept from my youth"* (Mark 10:19–20). Again, it excuses intentions not warranted in God's word, *"And when they came to the threshing floor of Chidon, Uzzah put out his hand to take hold of the ark, for the oxen stumbled"* (1 Chron. 13:9).

2. To accuse and terrify for doing good. This we may see in superstitious idolaters, who are grieved when they omit to perform counterfeit and idolatrous worship to their gods. *""Do not handle, Do not taste, Do not touch" (referring to things that all perish as they are used)—according to human precepts and teachings?"* (Col. 2:21–22). *"And their fear of me is a commandment taught by men"* (Isa. 29:13).

3. To accuse and terrify for sin. *"When Joseph's brothers saw that their father was dead, they said, 'It may be that Joseph will hate us and pay us back for all the evil that we did to him.'"* (Gen. 50:15). *"But when they heard it, they went away one by one, beginning with the older ones"* (John 8:9). *"For whenever our heart condemns us, God is greater than our heart, and he knows everything"* (1 John 3:20). Though the conscience shall accuse a man truly, yet that does not prove that there is any holiness in it. This is seen in Adam in whose innocence had a God, yet no accusing conscience.

(c) Impurity increased in the conscience is:

1. Such a senseless numbness as that it can hardly accuse a man of sin. *"They have become* callous *and have given themselves up to sensuality, greedy to practice every kind of impurity"* (Eph. 4:19). *"The insincerity of liars whose consciences are seared"* (1 Tim. 4:2). This senselessness springs from a habit of sinning. *"In the morning, when the wine had gone out of Nabal, his wife told him these things, and his heart died within him, and he became*

as a stone" (1 Sam. 25:37).

2. Some grievous horror and terror of the conscience, *"Behold, you have driven me today away from the ground, and from your face I shall be hidden"* (Gen. 4:14), and verse 13 *"My punishment is greater than I can bear".* The symptoms of this disease, are blasphemies, trembling of body, and fearful dreams, *"And as he reasoned about righteousness and self-control and the coming judgement, Felix was alarmed, etc.'"* (Acts 24:25). *"Then King Belshazzar was greatly alarmed, and his colour changed, and his lords were perplexed"* (Dan. 5:9).

The Will

(a) In the will, the remnant of God's image is free choice:

1. In every natural action, belonging to each living creature, as to nourish, to engender, to move, to perceive.
2. In every human action, that is, such as belong to all men. Thus man has free will in outward actions, whether they concern manners, a family, or the commonwealth, though both in the choice and refusal of these things it is very weak. *"For when Gentiles, who do not have the law, by nature do what the law requires"* (Rom. 2:14).

(b) The will received from Adam has:

1. An Impotence, whereby it cannot will (or even desire after) what is good, that is, what may please and be acceptable to God. *"The natural person does not accept the things of the Spirit of God, for they are folly to him, and he is not able to understand them because they are spiritually discerned"* (1 Cor. 2:14). *"For while we were still weak, at the right time Christ died for the ungodly"* (Rom. 5:6; 2 Tim 2:26). *"For it is God who works in you, both to will and to work for his good pleasure"* (Phil. 2:13).
2. An inward rebellion, whereby it utterly hates that which is good, desiring and willing that which is evil alone.

   By this it appears that in the first act of conversion to God the will is no agent, but a mere patient. By itself it can neither begin that conversion, or any other inward and sound obedience due to God's law.

The Affections[2]

(b) That which the affections receive is a disorder, by which they hate that which is good and pursue that which is evil. *"And those who belong to Christ Jesus have crucified the flesh with its passions and desires"* (Gal. 5:24). *"For this reason God gave them up to dishonourable passions"* (Rom. 1:26). *"And the king of Israel said to Jehoshaphat, 'There is yet one man by whom we may inquire of the LORD, Micaiah the son of Imlah, but I hate him, for he never prophesies good concerning me, but evil etc.'"* (1 Kings 22:8) and 1 Kings 21:4, *"And Ahab went into his house vexed and sullen because of what Naboth the Jezreelite had said to him, for he had said, 'I will not give you the inheritance of my fathers.' And he lay down on his bed and turned away his face and would eat no food".*

The Body[3]

(b) That which the body has received is:

1. A role in the beginning of sinful acts. The body does this in transporting all objects and occasions of sin to the soul. *"So when the woman saw that the tree was good for food, and that it was a delight to the eyes, and that the tree was to be desired to make one wise, she took of its fruit and ate."* (Gen. 3:6).
2. A readiness to execute sin as soon as the heart has begun it. *"Do not present your members to sin as instruments for unrighteousness... For just as you once presented your members as slaves to impurity and to lawlessness"* (Rom. 6:13, 19).

---

2. *Affections* are emotional-attitudes. They are not equivalent to what modern people mean by 'emotions'. We tend to think of emotions as feelings that happen to us. Emotions don't necessarily have an object or even involve thinking (e.g. you can feel happy about something, or just feel happy without any identifiable reason). In contrast, Affections combine thinking and feeling. They are emotional-attitudes that reflect the strength of our opinion about something. (E.g. to love God is an affection: it involves knowledge of God which leads to love and desire for him). Much of what we call emotions (intense, irrational feelings), the Bible calls 'passions' arising from the 'flesh'. Perkins later discusses such inclinations as arising from 'concupiscence' (see ***chapters 26 & 29***).
3. Perkins doesn't consider points (a) or (c) for the Affections or the Body.

CHAPTER 13:

Actual Sin

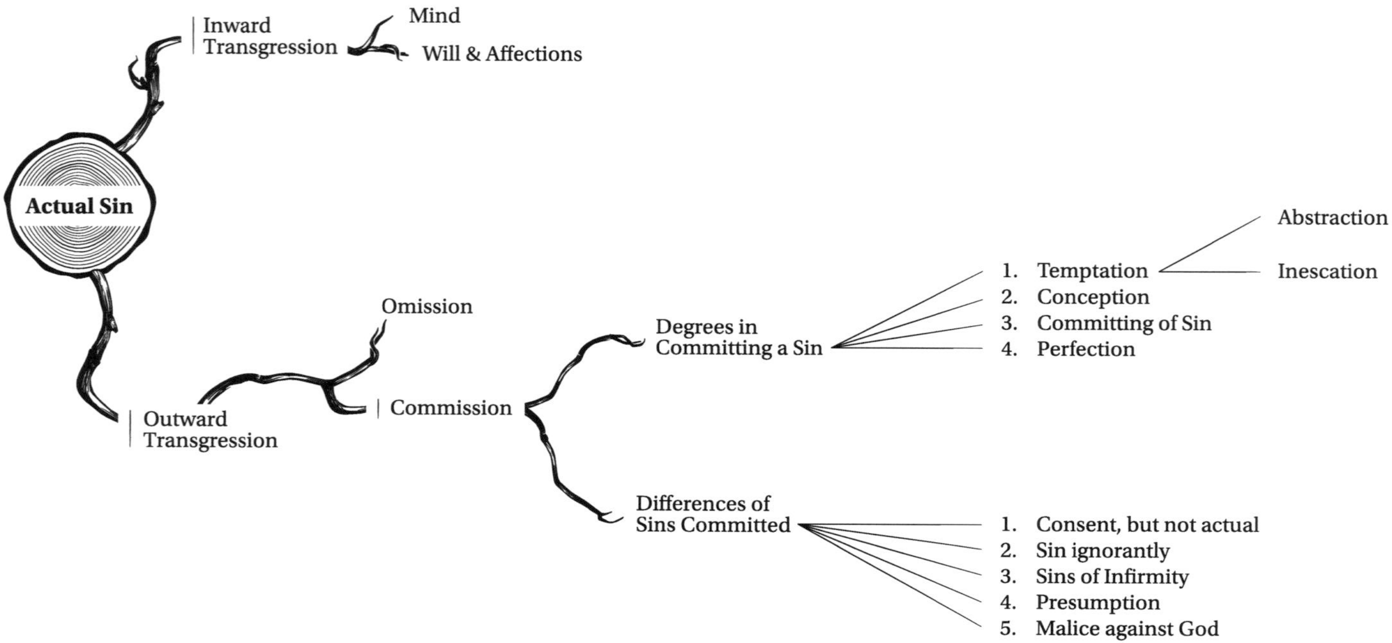

Chapter Thirteen

ACTUAL SIN

After original sin in Adams descendants, **Actual Transgression** takes place. It is either Inward or Outward.

Inward Transgression is of the mind, will, and affections.

The actual sins of the **Mind** are evil thoughts or intentions, contrary to God's law. God (who alone knows our hearts) has given many examples of evil thoughts in his word:

1. That there is no God. *"In the pride of his face the wicked does not seek him; all his thoughts are, 'There is no God'"* (Psalm 10:4). *"The fool says in his heart, 'There is no God'"* (Psalm 14:1).
2. That there is neither providence nor presence of God in the world. *"He says in his heart, 'God has forgotten, he has hidden his face, he will never see it'"* (Psalm 10:11). Therefore *"Why does the wicked renounce God and say in his heart, 'You will not call to account'?"*
3. It imagines safety for itself to itself from all perils. *"He says in his heart, 'I shall not be moved; throughout all generations I shall not meet adversity'"* (Psalm 10:6). *"She says, 'I sit as a queen, I am no widow, and mourning I shall never see'"* (Rev. 18:7).
4. It esteems itself more excellent than others. *"I sit as a Queen"* (Rev. 18:7). *"The Pharisee, standing by himself, prayed thus: 'God, I thank you that I am not like other men, extortioners, unjust, adulterers, or even like this tax collector. I fast twice a week; I give tithes of all that I get"* (Luke 18:11–12).
5. That the gospel of God's kingdom is mere foolishness. *"The natural person does not accept the things of the Spirit of God, for they are folly to him"* (1 Cor. 2:14).
6. To think uncharitably and maliciously of others who serve God sincerely. *"But when the Pharisees heard it, they said, 'It is only by Beelzebul, the prince of demons, that this man casts out demons'"*

(Matt. 12:24) *"They said to themselves, 'We will utterly subdue them'; they burned all the meeting places of God in the land"* (Psalm 74:8).

7. To think the day of death far off. *"You have said, 'We have made a covenant with death, and with Sheol we have an agreement, when the overwhelming whip passes through it will not come to us'"* (Isa. 28:15).
8. That the pains of hell may be ignored. As in the passage before mentioned, they say, *"We have made a covenant with death, and with Sheol"* (Isa. 28:15).
9. That God will defer both our death and his final coming to judgement. *"And I will say to my soul, Soul, you have ample goods laid up for many years'; .... But if that servant says to himself, 'My master is delayed in coming'"* (Luke 12:19, 45).

Many carnal men pretend their good meaning but when God opens their eyes they shall see these rebellious thoughts rising in their minds, as sparks out of a chimney.

The actual sin of both **Will and Affections** is every wicked motion, inclination, and desire. *"For the desires of the flesh are against the Spirit"* (Gal. 5:17).

An **Actual Outward Sin** occurs where the members of the body concur with the faculties of the soul. Such sins as these are infinite. *"For evils have encompassed me beyond number; my iniquities have overtaken me, and I cannot see; they are more than the hairs of my head; my heart fails me."* (Psalm 40:12).

Actual Sin is of Omission or Commission: Again, both these are in words or deeds.

In the **Sin of Commission**, observe these two points: the degrees in committing a sin and the differences of sins committed.

There are four degrees in committing a sin. *"But each person is tempted when he is lured and enticed by his own desire. Then desire when it has conceived gives birth to sin, and sin when it is fully grown brings forth death"* (James 1:14–15).

The first degree is **Temptation**, whereby man is allured to sin. Satan does this by offering evil to the mind. *"The Devil had already put it into the heart of Judas Iscariot, Simon's son, to betray him"* (John 13:2). *"Peter said, 'Ananias, why has Satan filled your heart to lie to the Holy Spirit?'"* (Acts 5:3). *"Then Satan stood against Israel and incited David to number Israel"* (1 Chron. 21:1). This also is effected upon occasion of some external object, which the senses perceive *"I have made a covenant with my eyes; how then could I gaze at a virgin?"* (Job 31:1).

Temptation has two parts: Abstraction and Allurement.

> **Abstraction** is the first thought of committing sin, when the mind is withdrawn from God's service (to which it should always be ready). *"You shall love the Lord your God with all your heart and with all your soul and with all your strength and with all your mind"* (Luke 10:27).
>
> **Allurement** is where an evil thought is retained in the mind for a time, so as to delight the will and affections. Thus, it lays a bait for them to draw out their consent.

The second degree is **Conception**, which is a consent and resolution to commit sin. *"Behold, the wicked man conceives evil and is pregnant with mischief and gives birth to lies"* (Psalm 7:14).

The third degree is the birth of sin, namely the **Committing of Sin** by the assistance of the faculties of the soul and the powers of the body.

The fourth degree is **Perfection**, where a sin becomes a habit or custom. Thus 'ripe', the sin reaps death, that is damnation. This appears in the example of Pharaoh (Exodus Ch. 7-10). Therefore a habit in any sin is fearful.

Sins Actually Committed are of kinds:

First, to **Consent with an Offender** but not actually to commit sin. *"Take no part in the unfruitful works of darkness, but instead expose them"* (Eph. 5:11). This might be done in three ways:

1. When a man's judgement somewhat allows the sin of another. *"Then Moses and Aaron gathered the assembly together before the rock, and he said to them, 'Hear now, you rebels: shall we*

bring water for you out of this rock?' .... And the LORD said to Moses and Aaron, 'Because you did not believe in me, to uphold me as holy in the eyes of the people of Israel, therefore you shall not bring this assembly into the land that I have given them'" (Num. 20:10, 12).

2. When the heart approves with affection and consent. For example, where ministers and magistrates conceal and wink at offences. *"And he (Eli) said to them, 'Why do you do such things? For I hear of your evil dealings from all the people'". Now that Eli will agree with his sons sins, it is manifest, "Why then do you scorn my sacrifices and my offerings that I commanded, and honour your sons above me"* (1 Sam. 2:23, 29).
3. By counsel, presence, or enticement. *"They not only do them but give approval to those who practice them"* (Rom. 1:32). *"And she went out and said to her mother, "For what should I ask?" And she said, 'The head of John the Baptist'"* (Mark 6:24). *"And when the blood of Stephen your witness was being shed, I myself was standing by and approving and watching over the garments of those who killed him"* (Acts 22:20).

The second is to **Sin Ignorantly**, as when a man does not distinctly know whether what he does is a sin or not (or if he knew it, he didn't acknowledge and make note of it). *"Though formerly I was a blasphemer, persecutor, and insolent opponent. But I received mercy because I had acted ignorantly in unbelief"* (1 Tim. 1:23). *"But if he pushed him suddenly without enmity, or hurled anything on him without lying in wait or used a stone that could cause death, and without seeing him dropped it on him, so that he died, though he was not his enemy and did not seek his harm, then the congregation shall judge between the manslayer and the avenger of blood, in accordance with these rules"* (Num. 35:22–24). *"For I am not aware of anything against myself, but I am not thereby acquitted"* (1 Cor. 4:4). *"Keep back your servant also from presumptuous sins"* (Psalm 19:13).

The third is to sin upon knowledge but of **Infirmity**, as when a man fears some imminent danger and denies a truth which he knows, and which he would otherwise acknowledge and embrace. Such was Peter's fall, arising from rashness of mind, mingled with some fear.

Thus, all men offend when the flesh and inordinate desires so overrule the will and every good endeavour that they may provoke man to do that which he from his heart detests. *"For I do not do the good I want, but the evil I do not want is what I keep on doing"* (Rom. 7:19).

The fourth is **Presumption**, which is of two kinds:

1. Presumptuous sinning upon knowledge. *"Keep back your servant also from presumptuous sins"* (Psalm 19:13). To this belongs every sin committed with a high hand, that is, in contempt of God. *"But the person who does anything with a high hand, whether he is native or a sojourner, reviles the LORD, and that person shall be cut off from among his people"* (Num. 15:30).
2. Presumption of God's mercy in doing evil. *"Because the sentence against an evil deed is not executed speedily, the heart of the children of man is fully set to do evil"* (Eccl. 8:11). *"Or do you presume on the riches of his kindness and forbearance and patience, not knowing that God's kindness is meant to lead you to repentance?"* (Rom. 2:4).

The fifth is to sin upon knowledge and settled **Malice against God**, which is the sin against the Holy Spirit (Mark 3:28–29).

Chapter Fourteen

THE PUNISHMENT OF SIN

So far we have discussed sin, with which all mankind is infected. In the next place follows the punishment of sin, which is threefold.

The first is **In this Life**, in several ways:

1. Concerns of the body, either in trouble providing for the things of this life (Gen. 3:17), or a proneness to disease: *"Take heart, my son; your sins are forgiven"* (Matt. 9:2). *"See, you are well! Sin no more, that nothing worse may happen to you"* (John 5:14). *"The LORD will make the pestilence stick to you until he has consumed you off the land that you are entering to take possession of it, etc."* (Deut. 28:21–22). Or shame of nakedness (Gen. 3:7). Or in women's pains in childbirth: *"To the woman he said, "I will surely multiply your pain in childbearing; in pain you shall bring forth children"* (Gen. 3:16).
2. The soul is punished with trembling of conscience, care, trouble, hardness of heart, and madness. *"The LORD will strike you with madness and blindness and confusion of mind"* (Deut. 28:28).
3. The whole man is punished:
    a. With fearful subjection to the government of Satan. *"He has delivered us from the domain of darkness and transferred us to the kingdom of his beloved Son"* (Col. 1:13). *"He himself likewise partook of the same things, that through death he might destroy the one who has the power of death, that is, the Devil"* (Heb. 2:14).
    b. A separation from the fellowship of God and trembling at his presence. *"They are darkened in their understanding, alienated from the life of God"* (Eph. 4:18). *"I heard the sound of you in the garden, and I was afraid, because I was naked, and I hid myself"* (Gen. 3:10).

c. By various calamities and damages upon a man's goods: *"And you shall be only oppressed and robbed continually, and there shall be no one to help you, etc."* (Deut. 28:29-68). This also relates to worldly rulers, their desire to enlarge their domains, and bargaining with all manner of civil servitudes.

d. The loss of that lordly authority which man had over all creatures. Also their vanity, which is not only a weakening, but also a corrupting of the virtues and powers which God first put into them. *"For the creation was subjected to futility* [vanity], *not willingly, but because of him who subjected it, in hope."* (Rom. 8:20).

e. Sometimes by a bad reputation after his death (Jer. 24:9).

The second is living under the state of **Death**. *"For the wages of sin is death"* (Rom. 6:23).

The third is **After this Life**, namely eternal destruction away from God's presence and his exceeding glory. *"They will suffer the punishment of eternal destruction, away from the presence of the Lord and from the glory of his might"* (2 Thess. 1:9).

CHAPTER 15:
Election

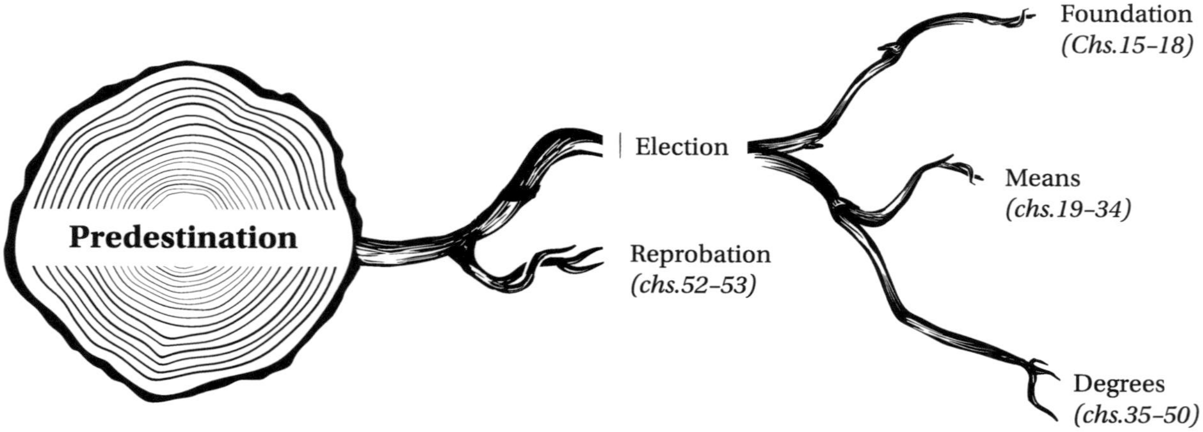

Chapter Fifteen

ELECTION AND JESUS CHRIST, ITS FOUNDATION

Predestination has two parts: Election and Reprobation. *"For God has not destined us for wrath, but to obtain salvation through our Lord Jesus Christ"* (1 Thess. 5:9).

Election is God's decree, whereby of his own free will he has ordained certain men to salvation, to the praise of the glory of his grace. *"Even as he chose us in him before the foundation of the world, ... according to the purpose of his will, to the praise of his glorious grace"* (Eph. 1:4–6).

This **Decree** is the book of life, in which are written the names of the Elect. *"Then another book was opened, which is the book of life. And the dead were judged by what was written in the books, according to what they had done"* (Rev. 20:12). *"But God's firm foundation stands, bearing this seal: 'The Lord knows those who are his'"* (2 Tim. 2:19).

The **Execution of this Decree** is God's action by which he works all those things which he decreed for the salvation of the elect, just as he purposed with himself. For they whom God elected to inherit eternal life were also elected to those subordinate means whereby, as though step by step, they might attain this end, and without which it were impossible to obtain it. *"For those whom he foreknew he also predestined to be conformed to the image of his Son, in order that he might be the firstborn among many brothers. And those whom he predestined he also called, and those whom he called he also justified, and those whom he justified he also glorified"* (Rom. 8:29–30).

There are three things to consider regarding the execution of this decree:

1. The **Foundation** ***(as follows, chapters 15–18)***
2. The **Means** ***(chapters 19–34)***
3. The **Degrees** ***(chapters 35–50)***

The **Foundation** is Christ Jesus, called by his Father from all eternity to perform the office of the Mediator, that in him all those who should be saved might be chosen. *"So also Christ did not exalt himself to be made a high priest, but was appointed by him who said to him, 'You are my Son, today I have begotten you'"* (Heb. 5:5). *"Behold my servant, whom I uphold, my chosen, in whom my soul delights; I have put my Spirit upon him; he will bring forth justice to the nations"* (Isa. 42:1). *"Even as he chose us in him"* (Eph. 1:4), meaning Christ.

Question. How can Christ be subordinate to God's election, since he together with the Father decreed all things?

> *Answer.* Christ as he is Mediator is not subordinate to the decree of election itself, but only to its execution. *"He (Christ) was foreknown before the foundation of the world"* (1 Pet. 1:20). As Augustine says: *"Christ was predestined that he might be our head"*.[1]

In Christ we must especially observe two things: his Incarnation, & his Office.

Three things concur in Christ's **Incarnation**. First, both his Natures (***as follows***). Secondly, their Union (***chapter 16***). Thirdly, their Distinction (***chapter 17***).

Christ's first **Nature** is the **Godhead**, inasmuch as it belongs to the Son, whereby he is God. *"Who, though he was in the form of God, did not count equality with God a thing to be grasped"* (Phil. 2:6). *"In the beginning was the Word, and the Word was with God, and the Word was God"* (John 1:1).

It was necessary for the Mediator to be God:

1. That he might better sustain the great misery with which mankind has been overwhelmed. This great misery declares four things:
    a. The grievousness of sin, by which God's majesty was infinitely offended.
    b. God's infinite anger against this sin.
    c. The fearful power of death.

1. Augustine, *On the Predestination of the Saints*, ch. 31.

   d. The tyranny of the Devil, who is prince of this world.

2. That he might make his human nature to be both of plentiful merit and of sufficient efficacy for the work of man's redemption.
3. That he might instil eternal life and holiness into all the elect. *"'I declared and saved and proclaimed, when there was no strange god among you; and you are my witnesses,' declares the LORD, 'and I am God'"* (Isa. 43:12).

The Godhead of the Son is Christ's divine nature, not the Godhead of the Father or the Holy Spirit. For it is the office of the Son to have the administration of every outward action of the Trinity, from the Father to the Holy Spirit (1 Cor. 6:8). And he, being by nature the Son of the Father, bestows this privilege on those that believe that they might be the sons of God by adoption. *"But to all who did receive him, who believed in his name, he gave the right to become children of God"* (John 1:12).

If either the Father or the Holy Spirit had been incarnate, the title of Son would have been given to one of them. In that case it would be given to one who was not the Son by eternal generation, and so there would be more than one son.

Christ's other nature is his **Humanity**, whereby he, the Mediator, is truly man. *"For there is one God, and there is one mediator between God and men, the man Christ Jesus"* (1 Tim. 2:5).

It was necessary that Christ become man. First, in order that God's wrath might be pacified in the same nature by which he was offended. Secondly, that he might undergo the punishment due to sin, which the Godhead could not since it is free from all passion.[2]

Furthermore, Christ as he is man is like us in all things, except sin alone. *"Therefore he had to be made like his brothers in every respect"* (Heb. 2:17; cf. 1 Cor. 13:4).

Christ therefore is a perfect man, consisting of an eternal and true soul and body, which includes all the faculties and properties that are essential to both. In his soul is understanding, memory, will, and so on.

2. That is, God is *Impassible*. Since God is the unchangeable source of all things, created things cannot cause him change or suffering. The incarnation was necessary for God to experience suffering.

In his body is length, breadth, and thickness. It is located in one place at a time, visible, subject to feeling. There is nothing of man's being or nature lacking in him.

Again, Christ in his humanity was subject to the infirmities of man's nature, which are these:

1. To be tempted. *"Then Jesus was led up by the Spirit into the wilderness to be tempted by the Devil"* (Matt. 4:1).
2. To fear. *"In the days of his flesh, Jesus offered up prayers and supplications, with loud cries and tears, to him who was able to save him from death, and he was heard because of his reverence"* (Heb. 5:7).
3. To be angry. *"And he looked around at them with anger, grieved at their hardness of heart, and said to the man, 'Stretch out your hand.' He stretched it out, and his hand was restored"* (Mark 3:5).
4. Forgetfulness of his office by reason of agony astonishing his senses, *"And going a little farther he fell on his face and prayed, saying, 'My Father, if it be possible, let this cup pass from me; nevertheless, not as I will, but as you will'"* (Matt. 26:39).

We must believe the following concerning Christ's infirmities:

1. They were such qualities as only affect his human nature, but do not constitute it. They were therefore temporary.
2. They were such as were common to all men, such as to thirst, to be weary, and to die. They were not personal, as are illness, consumption, leprosy, blindness, and so on.
3. He was subject to these infirmities not by necessity of his human nature, but by his freewill and pleasure, motivated by his pity of mankind. Therefore in him such infirmities were not the punishment of his own sin, as they are in us, but rather part of his humiliation which he willingly underwent for our sake.

Chapter Sixteen

THE UNION OF THE TWO NATURES IN CHRIST

Now follows the Union of the two Natures in Christ, which especially concerns his Office as Mediator. For by his humanity he suffered death upon the cross in such a way that he could neither be overcome, nor perpetually overwhelmed by it.

Three things belong to this **Uniting of Natures**:

1. **Conception**, by which his human nature was, by the wonderful power and operation of God, both immediately and miraculously framed of the substance of the Virgin Mary without man's help. *"The Holy Spirit will come upon you, and the power of the Most High will overshadow you"* (Luke 1:35). The Holy Spirit cannot be said to be the father of Christ since he didn't contribute matter to the making of the humanity, but only fashioned and framed it from the substance of the Virgin Mary.
2. **Sanctification**, whereby the same human nature was purified, that is, altogether severed by the power of the Holy Spirit from the least stain of sin, in order that it might be holy and be made fit to die for others. *"Therefore the child to be born will be called holy—the Son of God"* (Luke 1:35). *"For Christ also suffered once for sins, the righteous for the unrighteous"* (1 Pet. 3:18). *"He committed no sin, neither was deceit found in his mouth"* (1 Pet. 2:22).
3. **Assumption**, whereby the Word and second person in Trinity took upon himself flesh, the seed of Abraham. In this way his human nature, being without its own personal subsistence, might obtain this in the person of the Word: subsisting and, as it were, being supported by the Word for ever.[1] *"And the Word became flesh"* (John 1:14). *"He*

1. Perkins is summarising two precise theological points about the nature of Christ's incarnation which were formulated in the sixth century. Jesus' humanity was not a person of itself, as though God the Son took over a complete human person.

took not upon him the nature of Angels, but the seed of Abraham" (Heb. 2:16 KJV).

In the Assumption we have three things to consider:

a. the *difference* of the two natures in Christ. For the divine nature, as it is limited to the person of the Son, is perfect and subsisting in itself; the other not.

b. The *manner* of union. By assuming human nature, the person of the Son created it, and by creating assumed it.

c. The *product* of the Union. The whole Christ—God and man —was not made a new person of the two natures, as if by combining parts to make a new thing. Rather, he remained the same person. Now whereas the ancient Fathers termed Christ a compound person, we must understand them as here referring to proportion.[2] For as the parts are united in the whole, so these two natures concur together in one person, which is the Son of God.

By this we may see that Christ is one Son of God, not two. Yet he is the Son of God in two respects. As he is the eternal Word, he is by nature the Son of the Father. As he is man, he is also Son, yet not by nature or by adoption but only by personal union (Luke 1:35). *"This is my beloved Son, with whom I am well pleased"* (Matt. 3:17).

Relating to this union is the **Communion of Properties**, concerning which, observe two rules:

1. Of those things which are spoken or attributed to Christ, some only relate to his divine nature. As in John 8:58, *"before Abraham was, I am"*. And in Colossians 1:15, *"He is the image of the invisible God, the firstborn of all creation"*. Some again refer only to his humanity, as "born, suffered, dead, buried", and so on. *"And Jesus increased in wisdom and in stature and in favour with God and man"* (Luke 2:52). Lastly, other things are understood of both natures united together. As *"This is my beloved Son, with whom I am well pleased; listen to him"* (Matt. 17:5). *"And he put all things under his feet and*

Rather Jesus' humanity is impersonal (*anhypostasis*). The personhood of Jesus' humanity is God the Son (*enhypostasis*), who was the same person both before and after the incarnation.

2. That is, the entirety of both natures are present in the one person.

gave him as head over all things to the church" (Eph. 1:22).

2. Some things are spoken of Christ as he is God, which properly relate to his human nature. *"Care for the church of God, which he* (Christ, according to his manhood) *obtained with his own blood"* (Acts 20:28). *"None of the rulers of this age understood this, for if they had, they would not have crucified the Lord of glory"* (1 Cor. 2:8). On the contrary, some things are mentioned of Christ as he is man which properly relate to his divine nature. *"No one has ascended into heaven except he who descended from heaven, the Son of Man"* (John 3:13). This is spoken of his manhood, whereas we must understand that only his deity came down from heaven. *"Then what if you were to see the Son of Man* (i.e. Christ's human nature) *ascending to where he* (i.e. his Deity) *was before?"* (John 6:62).

Lastly, by this union, Christ as he is a man is exalted above every name. Indeed, he is adored and has such a great (though not infinite) measure of gifts as far surpass the gifts of all saints and angels. *"And seated him at his right hand in the heavenly places, far above all rule and authority and power and dominion, and above every name that is named, not only in this age but also in the one to come"* (Eph. 1:20-21). *"And again, when he brings the firstborn into the world, he says, 'Let all God's angels worship him'"* (Heb. 1:6). *"In whom are hidden all the treasures of wisdom and knowledge"* (Col. 2:3). *"Therefore God has highly exalted him and bestowed on him the name that is above every name, so that at the name of Jesus every knee should bow (namely worship and be subject to him), in heaven and on earth and under the earth"* (Phil. 2:9–10).

Chapter Seventeen

THE DISTINCTION OF BOTH NATURES

The **Distinction of both Natures** is that whereby they remain distinct with their properties and effects remaining, without composition, mingling, or conversion. *"For this reason the Father loves me, because I lay down my life that I may take it up again. No one takes it from me, but I lay it down of my own accord. I have authority to lay it down, and I have authority to take it up again. This charge I have received from my Father"* (John 10:17–18). *"Now is the Son of Man glorified, and God is glorified in him. If God is glorified in him, God will also glorify him in himself, and glorify him at once"* (John 13:31–32). Here we may observe that there is one will in Christ as God, and another as man.[1] *"Not as I will, but as you will"* (Matt. 26:39). This also approves that sentence of the Chalcedon Creed: *"We confess, that one and the same Christ Jesus, both Son, Lord, and only begotten, is known and preached to be in two natures without confusion, change, distinction, or separation".*

By this it is clear that Christ, when he became that which he was not (namely man), continued being that which he was (very God).

1. Perkins' endorses the mainstream view that Christ had 'two wills' (*Dyothelitism*) rather than one (*Monothelitism*). In the seventh century the church agreed that since Christ had two entire natures, he must have two wills, one belonging to each nature.

CHAPTER 18:

Christ's Nativity & Office

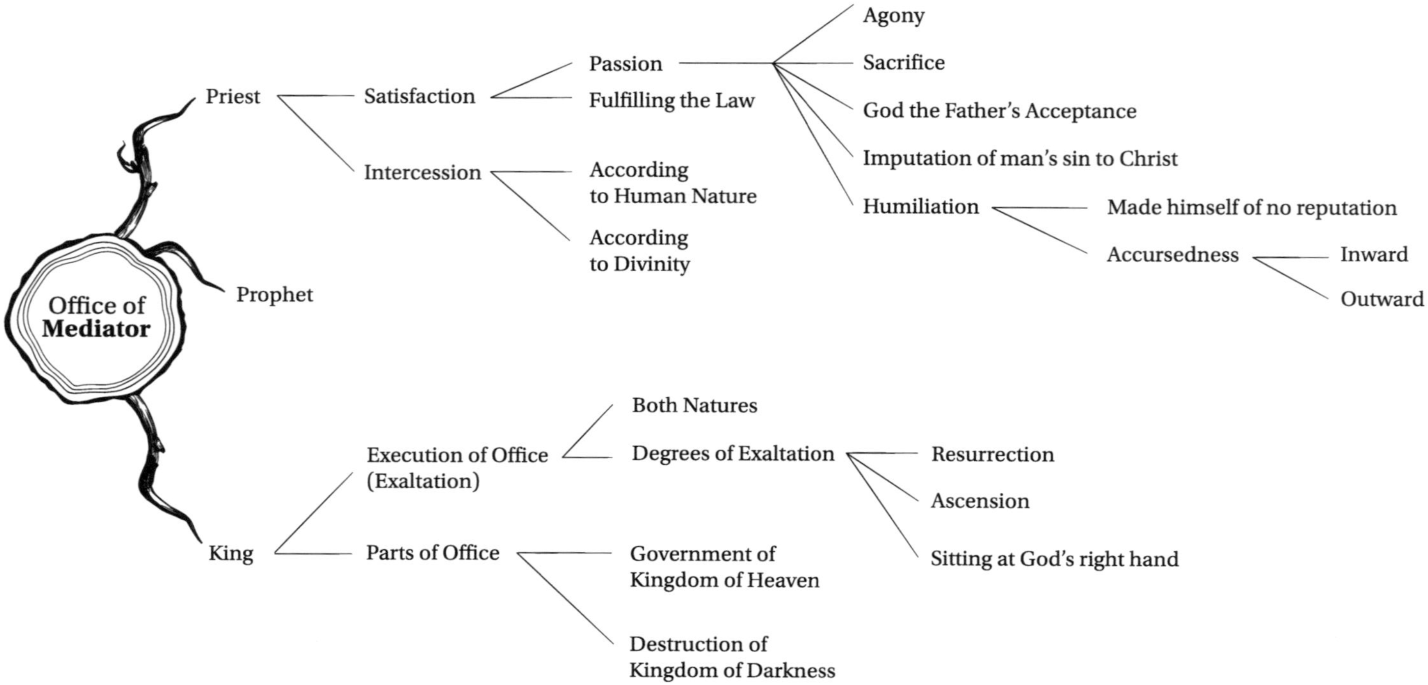

Chapter Eighteen

CHRIST'S NATIVITY AND MEDIATORIAL OFFICE

Thus much concerning the nature of Christ's incarnation, which was clearly declared in his Nativity.

The **Nativity of Christ** is that whereby Mary, a virgin, naturally gave birth to Christ, who is both the Word of the Father and the Son of David. Therefore, those who are of the opinion that Christ came into the world in a miraculous manner rather than being naturally born are greatly deceived. *"Every male who first opens the womb shall be called holy to the Lord"* (Luke 2:23). This passage of scripture is applied to Mary and our Saviour Christ. Hence is it that the Virgin Mary is called *theotokos*, meaning "God bearer", though she is not in any way the mother of the Godhead.[1] For Christ as he is God is without mother, and as man without father.

It is fitting to assume that Mary continued a virgin until her dying day, though we do not make this opinion an article of our belief. In support of this opinion we observe that:

1. Christ, being ready to depart the world, committed his mother to the tuition and custody of his disciple John. It is unlikely that he would have done this if she had any other children by whom she might have been provided for (John 19:26).
2. It is likely that she who was with child by the Holy Spirit would not afterwards know any man.
3. It is agreed by the Church in all ages.

Christ, now being born, was circumcised on the eight day so that he

1. Here Perkins endorses the orthodox position that emerged from a fifth century debate regarding whether Mary could truly be described as 'God-bearer' (*theotokos*). The issue has less to do with Mary herself as it does with recognising that from conception, Mary was pregnant with God the Son.

might fulfil all the righteousness of the law. And being thirty years of age he was baptised, that he (being publicly and solemnly invested into the office of his Mediatorship) might take upon himself the guilt of our sins. He was both circumcised and baptised that we might learn:

1. That the whole efficacy of the sacraments depends alone and wholly upon him.
2. That he was the Mediator of mankind both before and after the Law, as also under grace.
3. That he is the knot and bond of both covenants.

His **Office** follows. For the perfect accomplishing of his office, he was anointed by his Father, that is, he was sufficiently furnished both with gifts and authority: *"therefore God, your God, has anointed you with the oil of gladness beyond your companions"* (Heb. 1:9). *"The Spirit of the Lord God is upon me, because the LORD has anointed me"* (Isa. 61:1). *"For he whom God has sent utters the words of God, for he gives the Spirit without measure"* (John 3:34).

If any man reasons that Christ could not perform the Office of a Mediator since he is not an intermediate figure between God and man, but the party offended, we must see that Christ is said to be an intermediate figure in two ways.

1. Between God and all men. For being both God and man he participates with both extremes.
2. Between God and the faithful only. Firstly, according to his humanity, whereby he received the Spirit without measure. Secondly, according to his divine nature, namely as he is the Word. Now the Word is *middle*, between the Father and the faithful:
    a. In regard of *order*, because the Word was begotten of the Father and by him we have access to the Father. This subordination of the Son to the Father is not in the divine essence, but in the relation or manner of having the essence. And in this manner those things which are subordinate cannot be unequal if they have one and the same singular essence.
    b. In regard of his *office*, which being imposed on him by his Father he willingly underwent of his own accord.

Christ exercises this office according to both natures united in one person, and according to each nature distinct one from the other. For in reconciling God and man together the flesh performs some things distinctly, and the word other things distinctly. Again, some other things are done not by the word or flesh alone, but by both together.

This office is so appropriate to Christ, that it cannot be transferred to any other, either in whole or in part. *"He holds his priesthood permanently, because he continues forever"* (Heb. 7:24).

Therefore Christ, as he is God, has under him emperors, kings, and princes to be his vicegerents.[2] They are therefore called gods (Psalm 82:1). But as he is mediator—that is, as a priest, a prophet, and king of the Church—he has no vicegerent, vicar, or lieutenant who can occupy his kingly or priestly office in his stead, whether in one or both.

Christ's **Mediatorial Office** is threefold: Priest, Prophet, and King (Psalm 110:1-4; Isa. 42:1).

Christ's Priesthood is the office by which he performed all those things to God, by which eternal life was attained. *"And being made perfect, he became the source of eternal salvation to all who obey him, being designated by God a high priest after the order of Melchizedek"* (Heb 5:9). *"But he holds his priesthood permanently, because he continues forever. Consequently, he is able to save to the uttermost those who draw near to God through him, since he always lives to make intercession for them."* (Heb 7:24–25).

His **Priesthood** consists of two parts: Satisfaction and Intercession.

Satisfaction is that by which Christ was a full propitiation to his Father for the elect. *"If there be for him an angel, a mediator, one of the thousand, to declare to man what is right for him, and he is merciful to him, and says, 'Deliver him from going down into the pit; I have found a ransom"* (Job 33:23–24). *"And are justified by his grace as a gift, through the redemption that is in Christ Jesus, whom God put forward as a propitiation by his blood, to be received by faith"* (Rom. 3:24). *"He is the propitiation for our sins"* (1 John 2:2).

2. A *vicegerent* exercises the delegated power of a monarch on their behalf.

Christ satisfied God's anger for man's offence in two ways:

1. According to his humanity, by performing perfect obedience to the will of God.
2. According to his Deity, by supplying such special dignity to his perfect obedience as was both full of merit and efficacy before God, for the salvation of the elect. *"And for their sake I consecrate myself, that they also may be sanctified in truth"* (John 17:19). *"To care for the church of God, which he obtained with his own blood"* (Acts 20:28). *"In Christ God was reconciling the world to himself, not counting their trespasses against them"* (2 Cor. 5:19).

Satisfaction includes his Passion and Fulfilling the Law.

His **Passion** is the first part of satisfaction. In this, having undergone the punishment of sin, he satisfied God's justice and appeased his anger for the sins of the faithful. His passion was in this manner.

Before his death, fear arose in him from the sense of God's wrath imminent upon him, and grief possessing each part of him. This so disturbed his sacred mind (Mark 4:34; Matt. 26:38), that inwardly for a while it struck into him a strange kind of astonishment (John 12:27; Mark 14:35) and oblivion of his duty imposed upon him. This made him outwardly pray to his Father to remove (if he would) the cup from him (Matt. 26:37, 42; John 12:27; Heb. 5:7). He expressed this with no small cry, many tears, and a bloody sweat, trickling from his body to the ground (Luke 22:44). But when he came to himself again, he freely yielded himself to his Father to satisfy upon the cross for the transgression of man (Heb. 9:5; 1 Cor. 5:5, 7; Isa. 53:10–11). After this, his agony was overtaken by Judas' treachery, and Christ was apprehended (Matt. 26:47). He was first brought to Annas, then to Caiaphas, where Peter denied him (John 18:13–14). From Caiaphas he was led bound to Pilate (Joh 18:28), and Pilate passed him over to Herod (Luke 23:7–8), who sent him back again to Pilate (Luke 23:15). Pilate acknowledged his innocence, and yet condemned him as an offender (Matt. 27:24, 26). Thus condemned, this innocent man was pitifully scourged, crowned with thorns, scoffed, spat at, and spitefully condemned to death on the cross, onto which his hands and feet are fastened with nails (John 19:18). He didn't end his suffering there, but after all this he became accursed to God the Father (Gal. 3:13).

That is, God poured upon him—who was innocent—such a sea of his wrath as was equivalent to the sins of the whole world. Being under this curse he complained to his Father, through the sense and feeling of this strange terror, that he was forsaken (Matt. 27:35, 46). Nonetheless, Christ then encountered Satan and his angels and utterly vanquished and overcame them (Col. 1:14–15). When this was over, his heart was pierced with a spear until the blood gushed out from his side (John 19:34), and he gave up the ghost (John 19:30; Heb 9:15–16). He commended his spirit to his Fathers protection (Luke 23:43, 46), which immediately went into Paradise (John 19:33, 42). His body, of which not one bone was broken, was buried and for three days was ignominiously the captive of death.

In this description of Christ's passion we may especially note five circumstances:

1. His Agony, namely a vehement anguish arising upon the conflict of two contrary desires in him. The first was to be obedient to his Father; the second to avoid the horror of death. *"And being in an agony he prayed more earnestly; and his sweat became like great drops of blood falling down to the ground"* (Luke 22:44). *"In the days of his flesh, Jesus offered up prayers and supplications, with loud cries and tears, to him who was able to save him from death, and he was heard because of his reverence"* (Heb. 5:7).
2. His Sacrifice, which is Christ's offering himself to God the Father as a ransom for the sins of the elect. *"He has appeared once for all at the end of the ages to put away sin by the sacrifice of himself"* (Heb. 9:26). In this sacrifice the oblation was Christ, as he was man. *"And by that will we have been sanctified through the offering of the body of Jesus Christ once for all"* (Heb. 10:10). The Altar too was Christ, as he was God. *"We have an altar from which those who serve the tent have no right to eat"* (Heb. 13:10). *"How much more will the blood of Christ, who through the eternal Spirit offered himself without blemish to God, purify our conscience from dead works to serve the living God"* (Heb. 9:14). Hence is it that Christ is said to sanctify himself, as he is man: *"And for their sake I consecrate myself"* (John 17:19). As the altar, so the gift; and as the temple, so the gold (Matt. 23:17).
   Christ is the Priest, as he is God and man, *"You are a priest forever, after the order of Melchizedek"* (Heb. 5:6). *"For there is one*

God, and there is one mediator between God and men, the man Christ Jesus, who gave himself as a ransom for all, which is the testimony given at the proper time" (1 Tim. 2:5–6).

3. God the Father's acceptance of his sacrifice, by which he was well pleased. For, had God had not allowed it, Christ's suffering had been in vain. *"This is my beloved Son, with whom I am well pleased"* (Matt. 3:17). *"As Christ loved us and gave himself up for us, a fragrant offering and sacrifice to God"* (Eph. 5:2).
4. Imputation of man's sin to Christ, whereby his Father accounted him as a transgressor, having translated the burden of man's sins onto his shoulders. *"Surely he has borne our griefs and carried our sorrows; yet we esteemed him stricken, smitten by God, and afflicted. But he was wounded for our transgressions; he was crushed for our iniquities, etc. .... yet he bore the sin of many, and makes intercession for the transgressors"* (Isa. 53:4, 12). *"For our sake he made him to be sin who knew no sin, so that in him we might become the righteousness of God"* (2 Cor. 5:21).
5. His wonderful **Humiliation**, consisting of two parts.
    a. In that he made himself of small or no reputation in respect of his Deity. *"but made himself nothing, ... he humbled himself by becoming obedient to the point of death, even death on a cross"* (Phil. 2:7–8). We may not think that this debasing of Christ came because his divine nature was either wasted or weakened. Rather, his deity laid aside and concealed his power and majesty for a season. As Irenaeus says: *"The Word rested, that the human nature might be crucified, and dead"*.
    b. In that he became accursed by the law for us. *"Cursed be everyone who does not abide by all things written in the Book of the Law, and do them"* (Gal. 3:10).

    This **Accursedness** is both inward and outward.

    i. Christ's **Inward Accursedness** was the sense of God's fearful anger upon the cross. *"He will tread the winepress of the fury of the wrath of God the Almighty"* (Rev. 19:15). *"But he was wounded for our transgressions; he was crushed for our iniquities; upon him was the chastisement that brought us peace, and with* *his stripes we are healed"* (Isa. 53:5). This appeared by those drops of blood which issued from him, by his cryings to his Father upon the cross, and by the Angels sent to comfort him. Hence was it that he so much feared death which many Martyrs entertained most willingly.

ii. His **Outward Accursedness** was of three degrees.

1. **Death upon the Cross**, which was not imaginary but true, for blood and water issued from his heart. Since the water and blood gushed forth together (John 19:34), it is very likely that the pericardium was pierced (the casket or coat which surrounds the heart).[3] His death was necessary that be might confirm to us the testament (or *covenant of grace*) promised for our sake. *"Therefore he is the mediator of a new covenant, so that those who are called may receive the promised eternal inheritance, since a death has occurred that redeems them from the transgressions committed under the first covenant. For where a will is involved, the death of the one who made it must be established. For a will takes effect only at death, since it is not in force as long as the one who made it is alive"* (Heb. 9:15–16).

2. **Burial**, to ratify the certainty of his death.

3. **Descent into Hell**, by which we must understand not that he went locally into the place of the damned, but that for the time of his abode in the grave he was under the ignominious dominion of death. *"God raised him up, loosing the pangs of death, because it was not possible for him to be held by it"* (Acts 2:24). *"In saying, "He ascended," what does it mean but that he had also descended into the lower regions, the earth?"* (Eph. 4:9). It was necessary that Christ should be captured by death so that he might abolish the sting, that is,

3. Columbus, *Anatomie*, book 7.

the power thereof. *"O death, where is your victory? O death, where is your sting?"* (1 Cor. 15:55).

Thus we have heard of Christ's marvellous passion, by which he abolished both the first and second death due to us for our sins. We may further observe that his passion was a perfect ransom for the sins of all and every one of the elect. *"Who gave himself as a ransom for all"* (1 Tim. 2:6). Moreover, Christ—the only begotten Son of God and indeed God himself—bore the curse of the Law for a short while rather than the whole world suffering eternal punishment.

This also is worthy of our meditation. A man is well grounded in the doctrine of Christ's passion when his heart ceases to desire sin and is pricked with the grief of those sins whereby, as with spears, he pierced the side of the immaculate lamb of God. *"No one who keeps on sinning has either seen him or known him"* (1 John 3:6). *"When they look on me, on him whom they have pierced, they shall mourn for him, as one mourns for an only child, and weep bitterly over him, as one weeps over a firstborn"* (Zech. 12:10).

After Christ's passion follows his **Fulfilling of the Law**, by which he satisfied God's justice. *"By sending his own Son in the likeness of sinful flesh and for sin, he condemned sin in the flesh, in order that the righteous requirement of the law might be fulfilled in us"* (Rom. 8:3–4).

He fulfilled the Law, partly by the holiness of his human nature and partly by obedience in the works of the Law. *"For the law of the Spirit of life has set you free in Christ Jesus from the law of sin and death"* (Rom. 8:2). *"For thus it is fitting for us to fulfil all righteousness"* (Matt. 3:15; John 17:19).

Now follows the second part of Christ's priesthood, namely **Intercession**, whereby Christ is an advocate who pleads with God the Father for the faithful. *"Christ Jesus is the one who died—more than that, who was raised—who is at the right hand of God, who indeed is interceding for us"* (Rom. 8:34). Christ's intercession is directed immediately to God the Father. *"But if anyone does sin, we have an advocate with the Father, Jesus Christ the righteous"* (1 John 2:1). Since the Father is first of the Trinity in order, if he is appeased then the Son and the Holy Spirit are appeased also. For there is one and the same agreement and will of all the persons of the Trinity.

Christ makes intercession according to both natures.

First, Christ **Intercedes according to his Humanity** partly by appearing before his Father in heaven and partly by desiring the salvation of the elect. *"For Christ has entered, not into holy places made with hands, which are copies of the true things, but into heaven itself, now to appear in the presence of God on our behalf"* (Heb. 9:24) and *"Consequently, he is able to save to the uttermost those who draw near to God through him, since he always lives to make intercession for them"* (Heb. 7:25).

Secondly, Christ **Intercedes according to his Deity** party by applying the merit of his death and partly by making request by his Holy Spirit in the hearts of the elect with sighs unspeakable. *"Elect exiles .... according to the foreknowledge of God the Father, in the sanctification of the Spirit"* (1 Pet. 1:1–2). *"Likewise the Spirit helps us in our weakness. For we do not know what to pray for as we ought, but the Spirit himself intercedes for us with groanings too deep for words"* (Rom. 8:26).

We are not therefore to imagine or surmise that Christ prostrated himself upon his knees before his Father's throne for us. Neither is it necessary since his very presence before his Father has in it the force of a humble petition.

The goal of Christ's intercession is that all those justified by his merits should, by this means, continue in the state of grace. Now Christ's intercession preserves the elect in covering their continual slips, infirmities, and imperfect actions by a special and continual application of his merits. By this means a man's person may remain just and his works acceptable to God. *"He is the propitiation for our sins, and not for ours only but also for the sins of the whole world"* (1 John 2:2). *"You yourselves like living stones are being built up as a spiritual house, to be a holy priesthood, to offer spiritual sacrifices acceptable to God through Jesus Christ"* (1 Pet. 2:5). *"And another angel came and stood at the altar with a golden censer, and he was given much incense to offer with the prayers of all the saints on the golden altar before the throne, and the smoke of the incense, with the prayers of the saints, rose before God from the hand of the angel"* (Rev. 8:3–4).

Thus far concerning Christ's Priesthood; now follow his Prophetic and Royal offices.

Christ's **Prophetic Office** is that by which he reveals his word and all the means of salvation directly from his Father. *"The only God, who is at the Father's side, he has made him known"* (John 1:18). *"I declare to the world what I have heard from him"* (John 8:26). *"I will raise up for them a prophet like you from among their brothers, etc."* (Deut. 18:18).

The word was first revealed partly by visions, dreams, and speech, and partly by the motion of the Holy Spirit. *"Long ago, at many times and in many ways, God spoke to our fathers by the prophets, but in these last days he has spoken to us by his Son"* (Heb. 1:1-2). As for prophecy: *"no prophecy was ever produced by the will of man, but men spoke from God as they were carried along by the Holy Spirit"* (2 Pet. 1:21).

This revealing is ordinarily done only by the preaching of the word, whereby the Holy Spirit inwardly illuminates the understanding. *"Then he opened their minds to understand the Scriptures"* (Luke 24:45). *"I will give you a mouth and wisdom, which none of your adversaries will be able to withstand or contradict"* (Luke 21:15). *"The Lord opened her heart to pay attention to what was said by Paul"* (Acts 16:14). For this reason Christ is called the Doctor[4], Lawgiver, and Counsellor of his Church. *"Neither be called instructors, for you have one instructor, the Christ"* (Matt. 23:10). *"There is only one lawgiver and judge, he who is able to save and to destroy"* (James 4:12). *"His name shall be called Wonderful Counsellor, etc."* (Isa. 9:6). Yes, he is the Apostle of our profession (Heb. 3:1). The Angel of the covenant (Mal. 3:1). And the Mediator of the new covenant (Heb. 9:15). Therefore, the sovereign authority of expounding the Scripture belongs to Christ alone. The Church only has the ministry of judgement and interpretation committed to her.

Christ's **Royal Office** is that by which he distributes his gifts and orders all things for the benefit of the Elect (Psalm 2). *"The LORD says to my Lord: 'Sit at my right hand, until I make your enemies your footstool'"* (Psalm 110:1-2).

The execution of Christ's royal office includes his Exaltation.

Christ's **Exaltation** is that by which after his humiliation he was exalted to glory little by little, and in various respects according to both

4. In the early-modern context, doctor was the title for someone who served in a capacity where they gave instruction in a branch of knowledge.

of his natures.

The exaltation of his Divine Nature was a clear declaration of his divine properties in his human nature, without its least alteration. *"And was declared to be the Son of God in power according to the Spirit of holiness by his resurrection from the dead, Jesus Christ our Lord"* (Rom. 1:4). *"God has made him both Lord and Christ, this Jesus whom you crucified"* (Acts 2:36).

The exaltation of his Humanity was a putting off of his servile condition and all infirmities, and putting on of such habitual gifts which (though they are created and finite) have so great and marvellous a perfection as possibly can be ascribed to any creature. The gifts of his mind are wisdom, knowledge, joy, and he has other unspeakable virtues of body as immortality, strength, agility, brightness. *"Who will transform our lowly body to be like his glorious body"* (Phil. 3:21). *"And he was transfigured before them, and his face shone like the sun, and his clothes became white as light"* (Matt. 17:2). *"Therefore God, your God, has anointed you with the oil of gladness beyond your companions"* (Heb. 1:9). See also Eph. 1:20-22.

Christ's body, though glorified, is still of a solid substance, compassed about, visible, palpable, and shall perpetually remain in some certain place. *"See my hands and my feet, that it is I myself. Touch me, and see. For a spirit does not have flesh and bones as you see that I have"* (Luke 24:39).

There are three degrees of Christ's exaltation.

1. His **Resurrection**, wherein by his divine power he subdued death and raised himself up to eternal life. *"For he was crucified in weakness, but lives by the power of God. For we also are weak in him, but in dealing with you we will live with him by the power of God"* (2 Cor. 13:4). *"He is not here, for he has risen, as he said. Come, see the place where he lay"* (Matt. 28:6).

   Christ's resurrection was to show that his satisfaction, by his passion and death, was complete and absolute. For only one sin would have enslaved the Mediator under the dominion of death, even if he had fully satisfied for all the rest. *"And if Christ has not been raised, your faith is futile and you are still in your sins"* (1 Cor. 15:17). *"Who was delivered up for our trespasses and raised for our justification"* (Rom. 4:25).

2. His **Ascension** into heaven was a true, local, and visible translation of Christ's human nature from earth into the highest heaven, by the virtue and power of his Deity. *"And when he had said these things, as they were looking on, he was lifted up, and a cloud took him out of their sight. And while they were gazing into heaven as he went, behold, two men stood by them in white robes, and said, 'Men of Galilee, why do you stand looking into heaven? This Jesus, who was taken up from you into heaven, will come in the same way as you saw him go into heaven'"* (Acts 1:9–11). *"He .... also ascended far above all the heavens"* (Eph. 4:10).

   The goal of Christ's ascension was that he might prepare a place for the faithful, give them the Holy Spirit, and prepare their eternal glory. *"In my Father's house are many rooms. If it were not so, would I have told you that I go to prepare a place for you?"* (John 14:2). *"If I do not go away, the Helper will not come to you. But if I go, I will send him to you"* (John 16:7).

3. His **Sitting at the Right Hand of God the Father** demonstrates that Christ has all glory, power, and dominion in the highest heavens. *"After making purification for sins, he sat down at the right hand of the Majesty on high"* (Heb. 1:3). *"The LORD says to my Lord: 'Sit at my right hand, until I make your enemies your footstool'"* (Psalm 110:1). *"For he must reign until he has put all his enemies under his feet"* (1 Cor. 15:25). *"But he, full of the Holy Spirit, gazed into heaven and saw the glory of God, and Jesus standing at the right hand of God"* (Acts 7:55). See also: Mark 20:22.

His Royal Office has two parts:

1. His **Governance of the Kingdom of Heaven**, that is, the congregation of the faithful, part of which is in heaven and part upon the earth. In the government of his Church Christ exercises two royal prerogatives:
   a. To make laws. *"There is only one lawgiver and judge, he who is able to save and to destroy"* (James 4:12).
   b. To ordain his ministers. *"And he gave the apostles, the prophets, the evangelists, the shepherds and teachers, etc."*

(Eph. 4:11). *"And God has appointed in the church first apostles, second prophets, third teachers, then miracles, then gifts of healing, helping, administrating, and various kinds of tongues"* (1 Cor. 12:28).

Christ's government of the Church involves his gathering it out of the world, and his conserving it once collected (Eph. 4:12; Psalm 10).

2. The **Destruction of the Kingdom of Darkness**. *"He has delivered us from the domain of darkness"* (Col. 1:13). *"You shall break them with a rod of iron and dash them in pieces like a potter's vessel"* (Psalm 2:9). *"But as for these enemies of mine, who did not want me to reign over them, bring them here and slaughter them before me"* (Luke 19:27).

   The Kingdom of Darkness is the whole company of Christ's enemies. The Prince of this kingdom and of all its members is the Devil. *"In which you once walked, following the course of this world, following the prince of the power of the air, the spirit that is now at work in the sons of disobedience"* (Eph. 2:2). *"In their case the god of this world has blinded the minds of the unbelievers"* (2 Cor. 4:4). *"What accord has Christ with Belial? Or what portion does a believer share with an unbeliever?"* (2 Cor. 6:15).

   The members of this kingdom (and subjects of Satan) are his angels and unbelievers. Among these the principle members are:

   1. Atheists, who say in their heart that there is no God (Psalm 14:1).
   2. Magicians, who bargain with the Devil to accomplish their desires (1 Sam. 28:7, Psalm 58:5).
   3. Idolaters, who either adore false gods, or the true God by means of an idol (1 Cor. 10:17, 20). Muslims and Jews are of this group, as are Heretics, meaning those who persist in error in the very foundations of religion (2 Tim. 2:18).
   4. Apostates from faith in Christ Jesus (Heb. 6:6).
   5. False Christs, who present themselves as true Christs (Matt. 24:26). There were many such persons about during the time of our Saviour Christ's first coming, as Josephus

witnesses.[5]

6. The Antichrist who (as it is now apparent) can be none other but the Pope of Rome.[6] *"Let no one deceive you in any way. For that day will not come, unless the rebellion comes first, and the man of lawlessness is revealed, the son of destruction, who opposes and exalts himself against every so-called god or object of worship, so that he takes his seat in the temple of God, proclaiming himself to be God"* (2 Thess. 2:3–4). *"Then I saw another beast rising out of the earth. It had two horns like a lamb and it spoke like a dragon. It exercises all the authority of the first beast in its presence, and makes the earth and its inhabitants worship the first beast, whose mortal wound was healed"* (Rev. 13:11).

   Thus, the first Antichrists were at Rome, when the Bishops there would be decreed "Universal",[7] or supreme governors of the whole world. This scheme was completed through use of civil authority and censure.

After Christ has subdued all his enemies, two things shall ensue:

1. The surrendering over of his kingdom to God the Father, as regards its civil and spiritual governance.
2. The subjection of Christ (in regard to his humanity only) when the Son of God shall most fully demonstrate his majesty, which before was obscured by the flesh as a

---

5. Josephus, *Jewish Antiquities*, 20.11–12, 14.
6. Early Protestants generally believed that the Pope was the Antichrist. Not only did Roman Catholicism promote idolatry and false doctrine, but Roman Catholics sought to subdue Protestant nations like England, and to secure their return to Roman Catholic devotion. For example, at the time of writing, the Spanish Armada (1588) was fresh in memory and this threat of invasion was not over.
7. 'Universal', or *Catholic*, refers to all orthodox Christian believers. Reformed Protestants (such as Perkins) argued that true catholicity was a matter of holding to the doctrine of the Apostles, as found in the Bible. In contrast, *Roman* Catholics claimed that catholicity centred on fellowship with the Bishop of Rome, the Pope. This involved holding to the doctrines developed by Roman Catholicism through the centuries (e.g. purgatory, transubstantiation, and so on). See further ***chapter 51***.

veil, so that the same flesh (remaining both glorious and united to the Son of God) may by infinite degrees appear inferior.

Therefore, we may not imagine that the subjection of Christ consists in diminishing the glory of the humanity, but rather consists in demonstrating the majesty of the Word most fully.

CHAPTER 19–31:

Outward Means

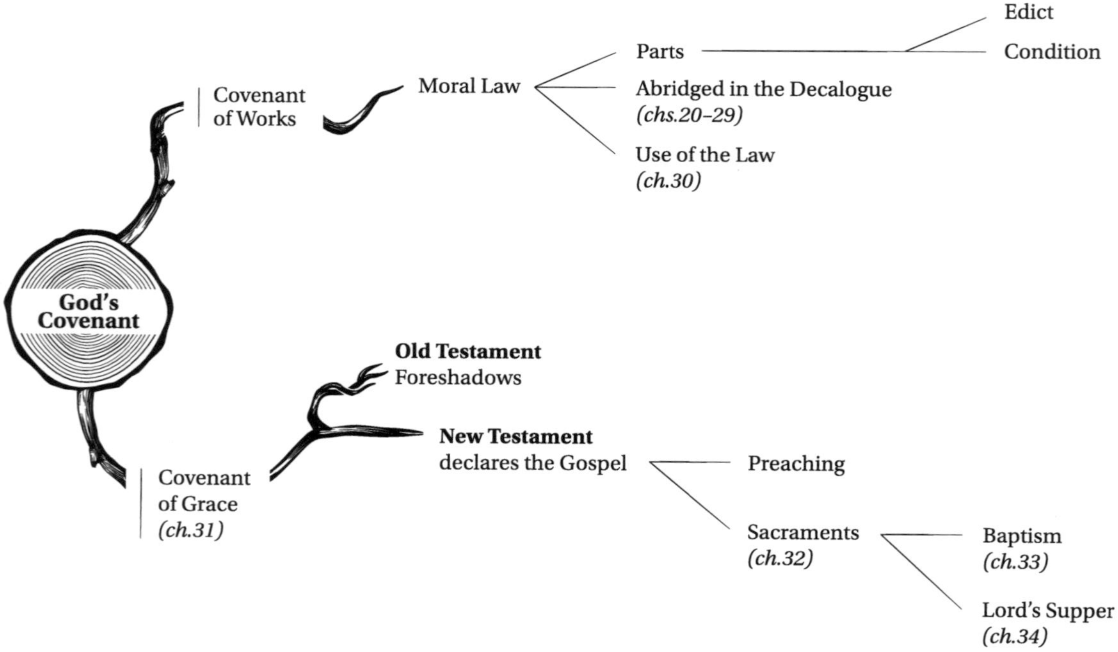

Chapter Nineteen

THE OUTWARD MEANS OF EXECUTING THE DECREE OF ELECTION, AND THE DECALOGUE

After the Foundation of Election (***chapters 15–18***, above) it follows that we should treat its **Outward Means (*chapters 19–34*)**.

The means are God's Covenant and its Seal.

God's Covenant is his contract with man concerning life eternal, upon the fulfilment of certain conditions. This covenant consists of two parts: God's promise to man, and man's promise to God. God's promise to man is that whereby he binds himself to man to be his God, if he doesn't break the condition. Man's promise to God is that whereby he vows his allegiance to his Lord, and to perform the condition between them.

There are **two kinds of this Covenant**: the Covenant of Works (***as follows***), and the Covenant of Grace (***chapter 31***). *"Behold, the days are coming, declares the LORD, when I will make a new covenant with the house of Israel and the house of Judah, not like the covenant that I made with their fathers on the day when I took them by the hand to bring them out of the land of Egypt, my covenant that they broke, though I was their husband, declares the LORD. But this is the covenant that I will make with the house of Israel after those days, declares the LORD: I will put my law within them, and I will write it on their hearts. And I will be their God, and they shall be my people"* (Jer. 31:31–33).

The **Covenant of Works** is God's covenant made with the condition of perfect obedience. It is expressed in the Moral Law.

The **Moral Law** is that part of God's word which commands perfect obedience (in both man's nature and actions) and forbids the contrary. *"For Moses writes about the righteousness that is based on the law, that the person who does the commandments shall live by them"* (Rom. 10:5). *"The aim of our charge is love that issues from a pure heart and a good conscience and a sincere faith"* (1 Tim. 1:5). *"And he said, 'Then I beg you, father, to send him to my father's house"* (Luke 16:27). *"For we know that the law is spiritual"* (Rom. 7:14).

The Law has two parts: the **Edict** commanding obedience, and the **Condition** binding man to obedience. The condition is that eternal life will be given to those who fulfil the law, but everlasting death to transgressors.

The **Decalogue** or Ten Commandments is an abridgement of the whole Law, and of the Covenant of Works. *"And the LORD said to Moses, 'Write these words, for in accordance with these words I have made a covenant with you and with Israel.' So he was there with the LORD forty days and forty nights. He neither ate bread nor drank water. And he wrote on the tablets the words of the covenant, the Ten Commandments"* (Exod. 34:27–28). *"There was nothing in the ark except the two tablets of stone that Moses put there at Horeb, where the LORD made a covenant with the people of Israel, when they came out of the land of Egypt"* (1 Kings 8:9). *"On these two commandments depend all the Law and the Prophets"* (Matt. 22:40).

The true interpretation of the Decalogue must be according to these rules:

1. In negative commands, the affirmative must be understood as also commanded. Likewise, the negative is commanded in the affirmative.
2. The negative binds at all times and to all times. The affirmative binds at all times but not to all times. Therefore, negative commands are of more force.
3. Under one expressly forbidden vice are included all vices of that kind.[1] The least cause, occasion, or enticement thereto a vice is likewise forbidden. *"Everyone who hates his brother is a murderer"* (1 John 3:15). Evil thoughts are condemned,

1. Vices (wicked actions or habits) are the opposite of virtues.

as well as evil actions (Matt. 5:21 ff.).

4. The smallest sins are entitled with the same names as the expressly forbidden sin to which they appertain. Thus, hatred is called 'murder' and to look after a woman with a lusting eye is adultery.
5. Every commandment of the law stands except where God commands otherwise. For God, being an absolute Lord and so above the law, may command that which his law forbids. So he commanded Isaac to be offered (Gen. 22:2), the Egyptians to be plundered (Exod. 3:21–22), the bronze Serpent to be erected which was a figure of Christ (Num. 21:8), and so on.

The Decalogue is described in two Tables.

The sum of the first Table is that we love God with our mind, memory, affections, and all our strength. *"And he said to him, "This is the greatest* (in excellence, and dignity) *and first* (in nature and order) *commandment"* (Matt. 22:37).

Chapter Twenty

THE FIRST COMMANDMENT

The first Table has four commandments.

The First Commandment teaches us to have and to choose the true God for our God. The words are these:

> *"I am the LORD your God, who brought you out of the land of Egypt, out of the house of slavery. "You shall have no other gods before me."* (Exod. 20:2–3).

The Resolution

"I am". If anyone judges that these words are a preface to all the commandments rather than a part of the first, then I won't hinder him. Nevertheless, it is likely that they are intended as a persuasion to keep the first commandment, since it is harder to receive than the rest. Moreover, the three following commandments have their own reasons.

"The LORD".[1] This word signifies three things:

1. That God who from all eternity is of himself and in himself. *"Who is and who was and who is to come"* (Rev. 1:8).
2. That He gave existence to all things, partly by creating and partly by preserving them.
3. That He mightily causes his promises be fulfilled (Exod. 6:1; Rom. 4:17).

Here begins the first reason of the first commandment taken from the

1. Original: 'Jehovah'. This Old Testament name for God is better translated 'Yahweh' (Exod. 3:15).

name of God. It is thus framed:

> He that is Jehovah, must alone be your God.
> I am Jehovah.
> Therefore I alone must be God.[2]

Your God. These are the words of the covenant of grace (Jer. 32:33) by which the Lord promises to his people remission of sins and eternal life. Indeed, these words are the second reason for the commandments drawn from the mutual relationship between God and his people:

> If I am your God, you must be my people and take me alone as your God.
> I am your God.
> Therefore you must be my people and take me alone as your God.

The second part of this reason ('I am your God') is confirmed by the time when God delivered his people out of Egypt, from the servitude of a most tyrannous master. This delivery applies not only to the Israelites, but in some respect to the Church in all ages, since it was a foreshadowing of a greater delivery from that fearful kingdom of darkness. *"For I want you to know, brothers, that our fathers were all under the cloud, and all passed through the sea, and all were baptized into Moses in the cloud and in the sea"* (1 Cor. 10:1–2). *"He has delivered us from the domain of darkness and transferred us to the kingdom of his beloved Son"* (Col. 1:13).

Other gods or strange gods. They not so called because they are gods by nature, but because the corrupt and devilish hearts of carnal man esteem them to be. *"Their god is their belly"* (Phil. 3:19); *"in their case the god of this world has blinded the minds of the unbelievers"* (2 Cor. 4:4).

Before me (before my face). That is, figuratively in God's sight or presence. Even the secret imaginations of the heart are known to God. This is the third reason for the first commandment. It is as if God says: *"If you reject me in my presence, it is a heinous offence, therefore see that you do not do*

2. This is a logical syllogism. The three lines represent the three parts of the syllogism, namely: (1) major premise, (2) minor premise, and (3) conclusion. The major premise expresses a general truth, the minor brings a particular case into relationship with it, and the conclusion draws the two premises together.

it." In the same manner the Lord says: *"I am God Almighty; walk before me, and be blameless"* (Gen. 17:1).

The Affirmative Part: *Make a choice of Jehovah to be your God*

The **Duties** commanded here are these:

1. To acknowledge God, that is, to know and confess him to be the God who he has revealed himself to be in his word and creatures. *"And increasing in the knowledge of God"* (Col. 1:10). *"I will give them a heart to know that I am the LORD, and they shall be my people and I will be their God, for they shall return to me with their whole heart"* (Jer. 24:7). We must glory in this knowledge of God. *"But let him who boasts boast in this, that he understands and knows me, that I am the LORD who practices steadfast love, justice, and righteousness in the earth"* (Jer. 9:24).
2. A union with God, whereby a man is knit to God by his heart. *"You shall cling to the LORD your God just as you have done to this day"* (Josh. 23:8). *"When he came and saw the grace of God, he was glad, and he exhorted them all to remain faithful to the Lord with steadfast purpose"* (Acts 11:23).

Man **Cleaves to God** in three ways: in Reliance, in Love, and in the Fear of God.

Reliance is that whereby a man steadfastly rests himself in the power and mercy of God at work in him against all assaults whatsoever. *"Believe in the LORD your God, and you will be established; believe his prophets, and you will succeed"* (2 Chron. 20:20). *"The LORD is my light and my salvation; whom shall I fear? The LORD is the stronghold of my life; of whom shall I be afraid? .... Though an army encamp against me, my heart shall not fear; though war arise against me, yet I will be confident"* (Psalm 27:1, 3).

From this arises Patience and Alertness in present perils. *"I am mute; I do not open my mouth, for it is you who have done it"* (Psalm 39:9). *"But the king said, 'What have I to do with you, you sons of Zeruiah? If he is cursing because the LORD has said to him, "Curse David," who then shall say, 'Why have you done so?'"* (2 Sam. 16:10). *"And now do not be distressed or angry with yourselves because you sold me here, for God sent me before you to preserve life .... So it was not you who sent me here, but God"* (Gen. 45:5, 8). *"He said, 'Do not be afraid, for those who are with us are more than those who are with them'"* (2 Kings 6:16).

This Reliance engenders Hope, which is a patient expectation of God's presence and assistance in all things that are to come. *"Commit your way to the LORD; trust in him, and he will act .... Be still before the LORD and wait patiently for him"* (Psalm 37:5, 7). *"Commit your work to the LORD, and your plans will be established"* (Prov. 16:3).

The **Love of God** is that whereby man, acknowledging God's goodness and favour towards him, loves God above all things in return. *"You shall love the LORD your God with all your heart and with all your soul and with all your might"* (Deut. 6:5).

The marks of the true love of God are these:

1. To willingly hear his word.
2. To speak often of him.
3. To think often of him.
4. To do his will without being irksome.
5. To devote our body and all that we have to his cause.
6. To desire his presence above all, and to lament his absence.
7. To embrace all things pertaining to him.
8. To love and hate the things that he loves and hates.
9. To seek to please him in all things.
10. To draw others to the love of him.
11. To highly esteem whatever gifts and graces he gives.
12. To abide upon his counsels revealed in his word.
13. To call on his name with reliance.

The **Fear of God** is that whereby man, acknowledging both God's mercy and justice, fears to displease him. *"But with you there is forgiveness (mercy), that you may be feared"* (Psalm 130:4). *"I hear, and my body trembles; my lips quiver at the sound; rottenness enters into my bones;*

my legs tremble beneath me. Yet I will quietly wait for the day of trouble to come upon people who invade us" (Hab. 3:16). *"Tremble, and sin not"* (Psalm 4:4, Geneva Bible).

Hence arises the godly man's desire to be acceptable to his God in all things. *"Enoch walked with God, etc"* (Gen. 5:22). *"The LORD appeared to Abram and said to him, I am God Almighty; walk before me, and be blameless"* (Gen. 17:1).

Out of these three virtues (reliance, love, & fear) proceeds Humility, whereby a man acknowledges God's free bounty and prostrates himself before him, ascribing to him all praise and glory. *"Let the one who boasts, boast in the Lord"* (1 Cor. 1:31). *"Clothe yourselves, all of you, with humility toward one another, for 'God opposes the proud but gives grace to the humble.' Humble yourselves, therefore, under the mighty hand of God so that at the proper time he may exalt you"* (1 Pet. 5:5–6). *"Therefore David blessed the LORD in the presence of all the assembly. And David said: 'Blessed are you, O LORD, the God of Israel our father, forever and ever. Yours, O LORD, is the greatness and the power and the glory and the victory and the majesty, for all that is in the heavens and in the earth is yours' .... 'But who am I, and what is my people, that we should be able thus to offer willingly? For all things come from you, and of your own have we given you'"* (1 Chron. 29:10–11, 14).

The negative part: *Do not account anything as God that is not by nature God*

Here these are sins are forbidden:

1. **Ignorance** of the true God and his will, which refers not only to not knowing but also to doubting what God has revealed in his word, *"For my people are foolish; they know me not; they are stupid children; they have no understanding. They are 'wise'—in doing evil! But how to do good they know not"* (Jer. 4:22). *"For they proceed from evil to evil, and they do not know me, declares the LORD"* (Jer. 9:3).
2. **Atheism**, meaning when the heart denies either God or his attributes, such as his justice, wisdom, providence, or presence. *"The fool says in his heart, 'There is no God'"* (Psalm 14:1). *"Having no hope and without God in the world"* (Eph. 2:12). *"'I have loved you,' says the*

LORD. But you say, 'How have you loved us?'" (Mal. 1:2). *"You have said, 'It is vain to serve God. What is the profit of our keeping his charge or of walking as in mourning before the LORD of hosts?'"* (Mal. 3: 14).

3. **Errors** concerning God, the persons of the Deity, or his attributes. Here Hellenism[3] is to be censured, since it is the acknowledging and adoring of a multiplicity of gods.[4] Likewise, Judaism is condemned, which worships one God without Christ. The same may be said of the heresies of the Manicheans[5] and Marcionites[6] who deny God the Father, of Sabellius' denial of the distinction of three persons,[7] and of Arius, who says that Christ the Son of God is not 'very God.'[8]
4. To **withdraw the affections of the heart** from the Lord and set them upon other things. *"This people draw near with their mouth and honour me with their lips, while their hearts are far from me"* (Isa. 29:13). *"You are near in their mouth and far from their heart"* (Jer. 12:2).

The heart may withdraw from God in many ways:

a. By Distrust in God. *"But my righteous one shall live by faith, and if he shrinks back, my soul has no pleasure in him"* (Heb. 10:38). From this distrust arises:
   i. Impatience in suffering afflictions. *"Cursed be the day on which I was born! The day when my mother bore me, let it not be blessed! Cursed be the man who brought the news to my father, 'A son is born to you,' making him very glad. .... Why did I come out from the womb to see toil and sorrow, and spend my days in shame?"* (Jer. 20:14–15, 18).
   ii. Tempting God, as when those who distrust (or rather scorn)

3. *Hellenism* refers to ancient Greek polytheistic religion.
4. Augustine, *City of God*, 6.7.
5. *Manichaeans* taught that reality was fundamentally dualistic, a struggle between light and darkness.
6. *Marcionites* rejected the Old Testament for allegedly teaching a god of wrath in contrast to the New Testament's god of love. This dualistic theology set the Father and Son against one another.
7. Sabellius (early 3rd century) taught *Modalism*: the idea that the Father, Son, and Spirit were only three expressions of God, rather than the three distinct persons of the Trinity.
8. Arius (c.256–336) denied the full deity of Jesus, claiming that he was not eternal but came into existence at a point in time (thus this position became *Arianism*).

him seek signs of God's truth and power. *"You shall not put the Lord your God to the test"* (Matt. 4:7). *"We must not put Christ to the test, as some of them did and were destroyed by serpents, nor grumble, as some of them did and were destroyed by the Destroyer"* (1 Cor. 10:9–10).

iii. Desperation. *"My punishment is greater than I can bear"* (Gen. 4:13). *"That you may not grieve as others do who have no hope"* (1 Thess. 4:13).

iv. Doubtfulness concerning the truth of God's present benefits, or of those to come. *"I said in my alarm, 'All mankind are liars'"* (Psalm 116:11).

b. By Confidence in Creatures. Whether it be in their strength: *"Cursed is the man who trusts in man and makes flesh his strength, whose heart turns away from the LORD"* (Jer. 17:5). Or Riches: *"You cannot serve God and money"* (Matt. 6:24); *"For you may be sure of this, that everyone who is .... covetous (that is, an idolater), has no inheritance in the kingdom of Christ and God"* (Eph 5:5). Or strong defences: *"The horror you inspire has deceived you, and the pride of your heart, you who live in the clefts of the rock, who hold the height of the hill. Though you make your nest as high as the eagle's, I will bring you down from there, declares the LORD"* (Jer. 49:16). Or pleasure, as it is for those whose stomach is their God (Phil. 3:14). Or in physicians: *"In the thirty-ninth year of his reign Asa was diseased in his feet, and his disease became severe. Yet even in his disease he did not seek the LORD, but sought help from physicians"* (2 Chron. 16:12). Here should also be included that Devilish confidence which Magicians (and all who take advise from them) put in the Devil and his works: *"If a person turns to mediums and necromancers, whoring after them, I will set my face against that person and will cut him off from among his people"* (Lev. 20:6).

c. Love of the Creature above the love of God: *"Whoever loves father or mother more than me is not worthy of me, and whoever loves son or daughter more than me is not worthy of me"* (Matt. 10:37). *"For they loved the glory that comes from man more than the glory that comes from God"* (John 12:43). This includes self-love (2 Tim. 3:2).

d. Hatred and Contempt of God, as when man flies from God and his wrath when he punishes our offences: *"For the mind that is set on the flesh is hostile to God, for it does not submit to God's law; indeed, it cannot"* (Rom. 8:7). *"Haters of God, insolent, haughty, etc."* (Rom. 1:30).

e. Lack of Fear of God, *"Transgression speaks to the wicked deep in his heart; there is no fear of God before his eyes"* (Psalm 36:1).

f. Fear of the Creature more than the Creator: *"But as for the cowardly, the faithless, ... their portion will be in the lake that burns with fire and sulphur, which is the second death"* (Rev. 21:8). *"And do not fear those who kill the body but cannot kill the soul. Rather fear him who can destroy both soul and body in hell"* (Matt. 10:28). *"Learn not the way of the nations, nor be dismayed at the signs of the heavens because the nations are dismayed at them"* (Jer. 10:2).

g. Hardness of Heart (that is, carnal security) when a man neither acknowledges God's judgements or his own sins, and so dreams that he is safe from God's vengeance and from those perils that arise from sin. *"But because of your hard and impenitent heart you are storing up wrath for yourself on the day of wrath when God's righteous judgement will be revealed"* (Rom. 2:5). *"But watch yourselves lest your hearts be weighed down with dissipation and drunkenness and cares of this life, and that day come upon you suddenly like a trap"* (Luke 21:34).

All these jointly generate pride, whereby man ascribes all good that he has to his own merit and hard work, and entirely to his own credit, rather than to God. *"That you may learn by us not to go beyond what is written, that none of you may be puffed up in favour of one against another. For who sees anything different in you? What do you have that you did not receive? If then you received it, why do you boast as if you did not receive it?"* (1 Cor. 4:6–7). *"For God knows that when you eat of it your eyes will be opened, and you will be like God, knowing good and evil"* (Gen. 3:5). The highest stair of pride's ladder is that fearful presumption by which many rashly climb into God's seat of majesty as if they were gods. *"And the people were shouting, 'The voice of a god, and not of a man!' Immediately an angel of the Lord struck him down, because he did not give God the glory, and he was eaten by worms and breathed his last"* (Acts 12:22–23). *"Who opposes and exalts himself against every so-called god or object of worship, so that he takes his seat in the temple of God, proclaiming himself to be God"* (2 Thess. 2:4).

Chapter Twenty One

THE SECOND COMMANDMENT

Hitherto we have examined the first commandment, which teaches us to choose and to entertain only one God in our hearts. The other three commandments of the first table concern that holy profession which we must make towards this God. For first, it is necessary to make choice of the true God, then secondly to make profession of him.

We will now consider the parts of the **Profession of God** and the time appointed for this profession.

There are two parts: the **Solemn Worship of God** and the **Glorifying of Him**.

The second Commandment describes the holy and solemn worship which is due to God. The words of the commandment are these:

> *You shall not make for yourself a carved image, or any likeness of anything that is in heaven above, or that is in the earth beneath, or that is in the water under the earth. You shall not bow down to them or serve them, for I the LORD your God am a jealous God, visiting the iniquity of the fathers on the children to the third and the fourth generation of those who hate me, but showing steadfast love to thousands of those who love me and keep my commandments.* (Exod. 20:4–6)

The Resolution

You shall not make. This is the first part of the commandment, forbidding man from making an idol. An idol is not only a certain representation or image of some false god, but also of the true God. This may be proved against the Papists by these arguments.

1. *"Therefore watch yourselves very carefully. Since you saw no form on the day that the LORD spoke to you at Horeb out of the midst of*

the fire, beware lest you act corruptly by making a carved image for yourselves, in the form of any figure, the likeness of male or female" (Deut. 4:15–16). Out of the words uttered by Moses, a reason may be framed thus.

> If you saw no image (of God) you shall make none.
> You saw no image, but only heard a voice.
> Therefore you shall make no image of God.

2. The idolatry which the Israelites committed was the very same as that prohibited in this commandment. The Israelites' idolatry was the worship of God in an image, *"And in that day, declares the LORD, you will call me 'My Husband,' and no longer will you call me 'My Baal'"* (Hos. 2:16). The golden calf was an image of God, for when it was finished Aaron proclaimed that *"Tomorrow shall be a feast to the LORD"* (Exod. 32:5). And the same calf is termed an idol (Acts 7:41). Therefore, this passage prohibits the worshipping of God in an image.

Any carved image. Here a graven image stands for all counterfeit means worshipping God. The first part of the commandment is illustrated in two ways. The first is drawn from the material causes of idolatry: *"You shall not make the any idol, whether it is engraved in wood, or stone, or whether it be painted"*. The second is taken from its place in creation: *"You shall not make an idol of things in heaven, such as the stars or birds; or anything in the earth, such as of men or women, or animals: or under the earth, such as fish"*. This passage is expounded in this way by Moses (Deut. 4:14–20).

You shall not bow down to them. This is the second part of the commandment, forbidding all men from bowing before an idol.

For I. These words are a confirmation of this commandment, persuading to obedience, by four reasons.

1. ***The Lord, (who is strong).*** The first reason is that God is strong, and so able to take revenge on idolatry (Heb. 10:31).
2. ***A jealous God.*** This figure of speech is taken from the estate of marriage, for God is called the husband of his Church (Isa. 54:5; Eph. 5:26–27). Our spiritual worship is a kind of marriage of our souls, consecrated to the Lord. *"I remember the devotion of your*

youth, your love as a bride, how you followed me in the wilderness, in a land not sown" (Jer. 2:2). Here is another argument drawn from a comparison of things that are alike. God's people must worship him alone because they are linked to him, as a wife is to her husband, to whom alone she is bound. Therefore, if his people forsake him, betrothing themselves to idols, he will undoubtedly give them a bill of divorce and they will no longer be married to him.

3. ***Visiting***. To visit, is not only to punish the children for the fathers' offences but to include them in the same faults. They too are given over to commit their fathers' transgressions and will be punished for them. This is the third reason drawn from the effects of God's anger.

   Hate me. It may be that there is an implicit reason here, which may be framed thus: "What if we use idols to inflame and excite in ourselves a love and remembrance of you?" The answer is this: "You may think that you use idols to kindle love for me, but it is anything but that. All who use idols hate me."

4. ***Show mercy***. The fourth reason is derived from the effects of God's mercy toward those who observe this commandment. Here we observe that God's mercy exceeds his justice. *"The LORD is merciful and gracious, slow to anger and abounding in steadfast love .... But the steadfast love of the LORD is from everlasting to everlasting .... He will not always chide, nor will he keep his anger forever"* (Psalm 103:8, 17, 9). Secondly, we may not presume that this excellent promise is made to every individual person who is born to faithful parents. For godly Isaac had godless Esau for his son, and godless Saul had godly Jonathan.

The negative part: *You shall neither worship false gods, nor the true God with false worship.*

Here many things are forbidden:

1. The representation of God by an image. For it is a lie. *"What profit is an idol when its maker has shaped it, a metal image, a teacher of lies?"* (Hab. 2:18). *"They are both stupid and foolish; the instruction of idols is but wood!"* (Jer. 10:8). The Council of Elvira (c.305) has this edict: *"We thought it not right to have images in Churches, least of all that what is worshipped and adored*

should be painted upon walls."[1] Clement: *"That serpent by others is wont to speak these words: We in honour of the invisible God, are accustomed to adore visible images, the which out of all controversy, is very false."*[2]

The image of the cross and Christ crucified also ought to be abolished out of Churches, as the brazen serpent was (2 Kings 18:4). Hezekiah is commended for breaking in pieces the bronze serpent to which the children of Israel burnt incense. Hezekiah did this, though at first this serpent was made by the Lord's appointment (Num. 21:8) and foreshadowed Christ's passion (John 3:14). Origen: *"We do not permit any to adore Jesus by images upon altars or church walls, for it is written: 'you shall have none other gods but me.'"*[3]

Epiphanius writes: *"It is against the custom of the Church, to see any image hanging in the Church, whether it be of Christ or any other saint. Therefore, he tore apart the veil as though with his own hands, wherein such an image was painted."*[4]

Some object to the sign which appeared to Constantine, declaring that he should overcome. But this was not the sign of the cross (as the Papists imagine) but of Christ's name: for it was made of these two Greek letters 'χρ' joined together.[5]

Neither do the cherubim which Solomon placed in the temple offer a defence of images, for they were only in the Holy of Holies where the people could not see them. And they were a foreshadowing of the glory of the Messiah, to whom the very angels were subject.

If any man reply that they do not worship the image but God in the image, let him know that the creature cannot comprehend the image of the Creator. Even if we could, God will not be worshipped in it, since it is a dead thing: the work of man's hands, *not of God*. Therefore, is more lowly than the smallest living creature of which we may lawfully say is the work *of God*. This shows that no kind of divine worship belongs to an image

1. Council of Elvira, Canon 36.
2. Augustine, *Treatise on Psalm 113*.
3. Origen, *Against Celsus*, bk. 7.
4. Epiphanius, letter to John, Bishop of Jerusalem
5. Eusebius, *Life of Constantine*, 1.22.25.

in any way, whatsoever the sophistic schoolmen argue to the contrary.

If any man desires images, he should hear in the preaching of the gospel a lively image of Christ crucified. *"O foolish Galatians! Who has bewitched you? It was before your eyes that Jesus Christ was publicly portrayed as crucified"* (Gal. 3:1). The same may be said of the two sacraments. And that saying of Clement is true: *"If you will truly adore the image of God, do good to man, and you shall worship his true image: for man is the image of God."*[6]

2. The least praise of idolatry. *"It is said of them, 'Those who offer human sacrifice kiss calves!'"* (Hos. 13:2). Now a kiss is an external sign of some allowance of a thing (Gen. 48:11).

   Therefore, it is unlawful to be present at Mass or any idolatrous service, even if our minds are absent. *"For you were bought with a price. So glorify God in your body"* (1 Cor. 6:20). *"But what is God's reply to him? 'I have kept for myself seven thousand men who have not bowed the knee to Baal'"* (Rom. 11:4). *"TThe Martyrs, when they were hauled into the temples of idols, cried out, with a loud voice in the midst of their tortures testified that they were not idolatrous sacrificers, but professed and constant Christians, rejoicing greatly that they might make such a confession."*[7]

   This provides an answer to criticism of Naaman the Syrian who worshipped in the temple of Rimmon. He didn't do it with intent to commit idolatry, but to perform that civil honour which was to be exhibited before the king's majesty (2 Kings 5:17–18).

   For this reason all such processions, plays, feasts consecrated to the memorial, and honour of idols are utterly forbidden. *"And they rose up early the next day and offered burnt offerings and brought peace offerings. And the people sat down to eat and drink and rose up to play"* (Exod. 32:6). *"Do not be idolaters as some of them were; as it is written, etc."* (1 Cor. 10:7). Paul earnestly discouraged the Corinthians from sitting at table in the idols temple, even though we know that *"an idol has no real existence"* (1 Cor. 8:4ff). The *Tripartite History* reports that certain *"soldiers refused to adore, as the custom was, the banner*

6. Pseudo-Clement, *The Recognitions of Clement of Alexandria*, bk. 5.
7. Eusebius, *Ecclesiastical History*, 8.3.

of Julian, in which were painted the images of Jupiter, Mercury, and Mars: others bring again the rewards, which they, after they had burned incense on an altar in the Emperors presence, had received: Crying, that they were Christians, and would live and die in that profession: and as for their former fact, it was of ignorance: yea though they had polluted hands with idolatry of the Painims, yet they kept their consciences clean."[8]

3. All relics and monuments of idols. For after the idols themselves are once abolished, they must be erased out of all memory. *"Pay attention to all that I have said to you, and make no mention of the names of other gods, nor let it be heard on your lips"* (Exod. 23:13). *"Then you will defile your carved idols overlaid with silver and your gold-plated metal images. You will scatter them as unclean things. You will say to them, 'Be gone!'"* (Isa. 30:22).
4. Relationships with unbelievers are unlawful. These serve to maintain concord and to join men in brotherly love. There are many kinds of such relationships:
    a. Marriage with unbelievers. *"The sons of God saw that the daughters of man were attractive. And they took as their wives any they chose"* (Gen. 6:2). *"Judah has been faithless, and abomination has been committed in Israel and in Jerusalem. For Judah has profaned the sanctuary of the LORD, which he loves, and has married the daughter of a foreign god"* (Mal. 2:11). *"Shall we break your commandments again and intermarry with the peoples who practice these abominations?"* (Ezra 9:14). *"And he walked in the way of the kings of Israel, as the house of Ahab had done, for the daughter of Ahab was his wife. And he did what was evil in the sight of the LORD"* (2 Kings 8:18).
    b. Allying in war: a mutual confederacy to assist one another in war, and to have one and the same enemies. This is impious in many ways:
        i. If it is unlawful to crave the assistance of God's enemies, it is likewise unlawful to agree that we will assist them.
        ii. It obscures God's glory, as though he either would not, or could not, aid his Church.

8. Cassiodorus (ed.), *The Tripartite History*, 6.30.

iii. We may be infected with their idolatry and other impious practices.

iv. It puts us in danger of sharing in their punishments. *"But Jehu the son of Hanani the seer went out to meet him and said to King Jehoshaphat, "Should you help the wicked and love those who hate the LORD? Because of this, wrath has gone out against you from the LORD"* (2 Chron. 19:2).

c. Trade, as when a man wittingly and willingly sells things which he knows will serve an idolatrous use, in hope of enriching himself. This condemns all merchants who transport wares to idolaters, and sell them frankincense, wax, cloth, or other such things as help them in the service of their idols.

d. Legal suites before judges who are unbelievers, when Christian courts may be frequented (though if they cannot, and we have to deal with unbelievers, we may appeal to unbelievers).[9] *"Brother goes to law against brother, and that before unbelievers?"* (1 Cor. 6:6). *"(Paul said) I appeal to Caesar"* (Acts 25:11).

e. Worshipping of the beast and receiving his mark. *"And another angel, a third, followed them, saying with a loud voice, "If anyone worships the beast and its image and receives a mark on his forehead or on his hand, he also will drink the wine of God's wrath, poured full strength into the cup of his anger, and he will be tormented with fire and sulphur in the presence of the holy angels and in the presence of the Lamb"* (Rev. 14:9–10). This beast is the Church of Rome, meaning this new Rome which is now no better than a heretical synagogue.

5. Will worship, where God is worshipped with good intention, but in ways not warranted by the word of God. *"These have indeed an appearance of wisdom in promoting self-made religion and asceticism and severity to the body, but they are of no value in stopping the indulgence of the flesh"* (Col. 2:23). *"So Saul said, 'Bring the burnt offering here to me, and the peace offerings.' And*

---

9. Perkins believed that England was a Christian nation in covenant with God. Its courts were (at least in principle) presided over by Christian judges.

he offered the burnt offering. As soon as he had finished offering the burnt offering, behold, Samuel came. And Saul went out to meet him and greet him .... And Samuel said to Saul, "You have done foolishly. You have not kept the command of the LORD your God, with which he commanded you" (1 Sam. 13:9–10, 13). Here may we add Popish superstitions of sacrifices, meats, holidays, apparel, the rosary, indulgences, austere life, whipping, ceremonies, gestures, gait, conversation, pilgrimage, building of altars, pictures, churches, and all the rest of that rabble. To these may be added consort in music in divine service, feeding the ears but not edifying the mind. *"What am I to do? I will pray with my spirit, but I will pray with my mind also; I will sing praise with my spirit, but I will sing with my mind also"* (1 Cor. 14:15). Justin Martyr says: *"It is not the custom of the Churches, to sing their meters with any such kind of instruments, &c. but their manner is only to use plain song."*[10]

Lastly Monastic Vows, which:

a. Reject the law of God, as that unchaste vow of single life and proud promise of poverty plainly attest. As Paul says: *"If anyone is not willing to work, let him not eat"* (2 Thess. 3:10); *"For it is better to marry than to burn with passion"* (1 Cor. 7:9).

b. Are greater than man's nature can perform, for example to live a single life of perpetual chastity.

c. They compromise Christian liberty, making such things necessary which are properly indifferent.

d. They renew Judaism.

e. They are idolatrous, because they make them parts of God's worship and esteem them as meritorious.

f. Hypocrisy, which gives painted worship to God: great outward sincerity, but completely devoid of inward and hearty affections. *"You hypocrites! Well did Isaiah prophesy of you, when he said: 'This people honours me with their lips, but their heart is far from me'"* (Matt. 15:7–8). *"In the pride of his face the wicked does not seek him; all his thoughts are,*

10. Justin Martyr, *Christian Questions*, 107.

'There is no God'" (Psalm 10:4).

The effects of hypocrisy are these:

i. To seek the pomp and glory of the world, and to enrich itself by all means, even by making a glorious show of serving God.

ii. It is sharp sighted and has eagles' eyes to observe other's behaviour but is blind as a beetle in the regard to its own.

iii. To be more curious in the observation of ancient traditions than the statutes and commandments of almighty God.

iv. To stumble at a straw and skip over a block, that is, to omit serious affairs and hunt after trifles. (Matt. 23:4).

v. To do all things in order to be seen by men (Matt. 6:5).

Popish fasting is sheer hypocrisy since it consists in the distinction of foods and is used with respect to merit. It merely involves external abstinence from food without internal and spiritual fasting from sin and unlawful desires. *"Is such the fast that I choose, a day for a person to humble himself? Is it to bow down his head like a reed, and to spread sackcloth and ashes under him? Will you call this a fast, and a day acceptable to the LORD? "Is not this the fast that I choose: to loose the bonds of wickedness, to undo the straps of the yoke, to let the oppressed go free, and to break every yoke?"* (Isa. 58:5–6).

6. Contempt and neglect of God's service. *"I know your works: you are neither cold nor hot. Would that you were either cold or hot! So, because you are lukewarm, and neither hot nor cold, I will spit you out of my mouth"* (Rev. 3:15–16).

7. Corrupting God's worship and the order of government which he has ordained for his Church. This is done when anything is added to, subtracted from, or distorts his prescripts in any way. *"Everything that I command you, you shall be careful to do. You shall not add to it or take from it"* (Deut. 12:32). This condemns that Popish elevation of bread in the Lord's Supper, and the administration of it alone to the people without wine, together with that fearful abomination of the Mass.

By this we may learn to reject all popish traditions, *"In vain do they worship me, teaching as doctrines the commandments of men"* (Matt. 15:9). Now it is clear that all popish traditions, either by their own nature or by others abusing them, promote superstition and false worship as well as they enrich that covetous and proud hierarchy. In contrast, the Scriptures contained in the Old and New Testament are sufficient not only to confirm doctrines, but also to reform manners. *"All Scripture is breathed out by God and profitable for teaching, for reproof, for correction, and for training in righteousness, that the man of God may be competent, equipped for every good work"* (2 Tim. 3:16–17).

The Romish hierarchy is also condemned here, from their lowest church officials all the way up to the Pope. This government is an express image of the old Roman Empire, whether we consider the governance itself, or the place of the Empire, or the vast scale of that government. *"And it was allowed to give breath to the image of the beast, so that the image of the beast might even speak and might cause those who would not worship the image of the beast to be slain"* (Rev. 13:15).

8. Religious reverence of the creature, such as when we attribute more to it than we ought. *"And when I heard and saw them, I fell down to worship at the feet of the angel who showed them to me, but he said to me, 'You must not do that! I am a fellow servant with you and your brothers the prophets, and with those who keep the words of this book. Worship God'"* (Rev. 22:8). *"When Peter entered, Cornelius met him and fell down at his feet and worshipped him"* (Acts 10:25).

If it is so heinous to reverence a creature, then it is much worse to pray to one, whether saint or angel. *"How then will they call on him in whom they have not believed?"* (Rom. 10:14). *"You shall worship the Lord your God and him only shall you serve"* (Matt. 4:10).

Neither may we pray to Christ in his humanity alone, but only as he is God and man. For we do not direct our prayers to the humanity, but to the deity, to which his humanity is knit by hypostatic union.

This teaches us plainly that praying to any creature is

unlawful. For we must pray to he who is able to know the secrets of the heart and discern the wisdom of the Spirit. None is able to do that, except one with a nature which is omnipotent. *"And he who searches hearts knows what is the mind of the Spirit, because the Spirit intercedes for the saints according to the will of God"* (Rom. 8:27).

Nevertheless, those who are saints are to be honoured by an admiration of God's gifts in them, by honourable mention of them, and by imitation of their manners and lives, which are patterns for us to walk after.

9. Worship of Devils, which is either Magic or Consulting Magicians.

    Magic is a mischievous art of accomplishing wonders by Satan's assistance. It is appropriate to God alone to do miracles; for he alone does wonderful things, both beyond and against the course of nature. The instruments which God uses in producing miracles are only those of the true Church of God who make profession of the faith.

    Although the devils cannot work miracles, yet they can cause marvels or wonders. They don't do this by making a new thing (something which previously did not exist), but rather by manipulating natural things in diverse ways, such as by causing a thin body such as the air to be thick and foggy, and also by bewitching the senses of men.

    The Foundation of Magic is a Covenant with Satan, which is a contract by which Magicians engage with the Devil.[11] In this observe:

    a. The Origin of this mutual contract:

        i. Satan chooses people to be his servants, from among those who are by nature either notoriously bad persons, or very silly souls.

        ii. He offers diverse means to them, either by other magicians or by books written by them. I label as 'satanic means' anything which is used to produce

11. For Perkins' fuller discussion of witchcraft, see his *A Discourse of the Damned Art of Witchcraft* (1608) in *The Works of William Perkins: Volume 9*. (ed. J. Stephen Yuille; Grand Rapids: Reformation Heritage Books, 2020).

an effect not of its own nature, and which was not ordained by an express rule out of God's word. This includes alleged hidden messages concealed in Scripture which are abusively wrested from it, to the great disgrace of the Lord God. Likewise, holy (or rather, unholy) water, sieves, seals, glass, images, bowing of the knee, and similar gestures.

iii. When the wicked see these means offered to them, they are greatly pleased, and assuredly believe that in those things there is virtue to work wonders by.

iv. They show this satanic confidence by their earnest desire, practising, and abusing of satanic means.

v. Then the Devil is at their elbows, that he may both assist them and in them show diverse tricks of his craftiness. For he alone causes that which his wicked instrument intended by such means.

b. Satan's counterfeiting of God. He is God's ape and conducts himself as though he were God.

i. As God has his word, his sacraments, and faith due to him, so the Devil has his word. To seal it to the wicked, he joins certain signs (characters, gestures, sacrifices, and so on) as if they were sacraments, both so that he may show his devilish pleasure to his magicians, and so that they may again testify their satanic obedience and confidence to him.

ii. As God hears those who call upon, trust in, and obey him; so the Devil is greatly delighted with magical ceremonies and invocations. For by them God is dishonoured, and the Devil magnified. Therefore, with the limits set by God, the Devil is ready to assist those who use such ceremonies or invocations.

The covenant is either Secret or Express:

i. Secret, or implicit, when one does not expressly compact with Satan, yet in his heart believes that his means will cause that great wonder which he desires.

ii. Express, when one not only puts his confidence in Satan, but covenants with him upon conditions: that for giving himself wholly over to the Devil, he may accomplish his desires through observing certain ceremonies.

Magic is either Conjectural or Operative:

Conjectural Magic is that whereby things are prophesied by Satan's direction. Some prophesies are done with means, others without.

Prophesies done **with means** are these:

i. Soothsaying and divination (Deut. 18:11).

ii. The kind of divination, which is, by looking at animal entrails *"For the king of Babylon stands .... to use divination .... he looks at the liver"* (Ezek. 21:21).

iii. Necromancy, or conjuring: by which the Devil, in the form of some dead man, is sought to for counsel. *"Then the woman said, 'Whom shall I bring up for you?' He said, 'Bring up Samuel for me.' When the woman saw Samuel, she cried out with a loud voice. And the woman said to Saul, 'Why have you deceived me? You are Saul.' The king said to her, 'Do not be afraid. What do you see?' And the woman said to Saul, 'I see a god coming up out of the earth.' He said to her, 'What is his appearance?' And she said, 'An old man is coming up, and he is wrapped in a robe.' And Saul knew that it was Samuel, and he bowed with his face to the ground and paid homage. Then Samuel said to Saul, 'Why have you disturbed me by bringing me up?' Saul answered, 'I am in great distress, for the Philistines are warring against me,' etc."* (1 Sam. 28:11–15). This Samuel, was not that true Prophet of God, who anointed Saul King over Israel: for:

1. The souls of the Saints departed, are far from the Devils claws and dominion.
2. That good Samuel, if it had truly been him, would never have permitted Saul to worship him.

3. He says to wicked Saul, *"tomorrow you will be with me"* (verse 19). Neither could this be a bare illusion and craftiness of the witch. For he plainly foretold Saul's destruction, which an ignorant woman could not know, much less would she dare assert such a thing to the King. It remains then, that this Samuel was a mere illusion of Satan.

Divining **without means** is when those who are possessed with an unclean spirit use the help of that spirit to reveal secrets. *"We were met by a slave girl who had a spirit of divination and brought her owners much gain by fortune-telling"* (Acts 16:16). *"Your voice shall come from the ground like the voice of a ghost, and from the dust your speech shall whisper"* (Isa. 29:4).

Magic Operative has two parts: Juggling and Enchantments.

Juggling, whereby through the Devils assistance, many great and very difficult feats are displayed (Exod. 7:10–12). Aaron cast forth his rod before Pharaoh and his servants, and it was turned into a serpent. Then Pharaoh called also for his wise men and sorcerers, and those charmers of Egypt did likewise by their enchantments. For each man cast down his rod and they were turned into serpents; but Aaron's rod devoured their rods.

Enchantment, or charming, is that whereby creatures (but men especially) are infected, poisoned, hurt, bound, killed, and otherwise molested by God's permission. Or, contrarily, sometimes they are cured by Satan by mumbling up a few words, making certain characters and figures, framing circles, hanging amulets about their neck or other parts, by herbs, medicines, and other such trumpery. In this way the punishments of the faithless are increased in reposing their strength upon such rotten staves, and the faithful are tested as to whether they too will commit these abominations. *"The cords of death encompassed me; the torrents of destruction assailed me"* (Psalm 18:4). *"If the serpent bites before it is charmed, etc."* (Eccl. 10:11).

Thus, have we heard Magic described out of God's word, which is very common among those who are without God in the world, and whom Satan strongly deludes by every means. The lamentable experience of many men in most places sufficiently proves this to us.

> And surely, if a man will take but a glance at 'popery,' he shall easily see that it is mostly mere magic.[12]
>
> Some spread the teaching (by their writing or otherwise) that witches are nothing else but melancholic doting women who the Devil has deluded into believing that they themselves do what the Devil alone does. Such people may find themselves defending murder, adultery, and all manner of other sins.

Those who **Consult with Magicians** also worship the Devil. For however much they plaster up their impiety with untempered mortar, claiming that they seek God's help by the means of magicians, they revolt from God to the Devil. *"And the woman said to Saul, 'I see a god coming up out of the earth'"* (1 Sam. 28:13). *"If a person turns to mediums and necromancers, whoring after them, I will set my face against that person and will cut him off from among his people"* (Lev. 20:6). *"And when they say to you, 'Inquire of the mediums and the necromancers who chirp and mutter,' should not a people inquire of their God? Should they inquire of the dead on behalf of the living? To the teaching and to the testimony!"* (Isa. 8:19–20).

The affirmative part: *You shall worship God in spirit and truth*

"God is spirit, and those who worship him must worship in spirit and truth" (John 4:24). For as soon as any man begins to worship God in an unlawful manner, he adores an idol, however he appears to colour his impiety. Paul therefore says that, *"(they) exchanged the glory of the immortal God for images resembling mortal man and birds and animals and creeping things .... because they exchanged the truth about God for a lie and worshipped and served the creature rather than the Creator"* (Rom. 1:23, 25) and *"What pagans sacrifice they offer to demons and not to God. I do not want you to be participants with demons"* (1 Cor. 10:20).

The following relate to the holy and solemn service of God:

1. The true and ordinary means of God's worship, such as calling upon the name of the Lord by humble supplication and hearty thanksgiving,

12. Perkins is referring to Roman Catholic beliefs such as transubstantiation and the allegedly miraculous power of relics.

and the ministry of the word and sacraments. *"So those who received his word were baptized, and there were added that day about three thousand souls. And they devoted themselves to the apostles' teaching and the fellowship, to the breaking of bread and the prayers"* (Acts 2:41–42). *"I urge that supplications, prayers, intercessions, and thanksgivings be made for all people, for kings and all who are in high positions"* (1 Tim. 2:1–2). *"On the first day of the week, when we were gathered together to break bread, Paul talked with them, intending to depart on the next day, and he prolonged his speech until midnight"* (Acts 20:7). Tertullian: *"We come into the assembly and congregation, that with our prayers, as with an army, we might besiege God. This kind of violence offered to God is acceptable to him..."*.[13]

2. A holy use of the Means of Grace:[14]

    1. Through the ministers, who ought to administer things belonging to God's worship, according to his word. *"Teaching them to observe all that I have commanded you"* (Matt. 28:20). *"For I received from the Lord what I also delivered to you"* (1 Cor. 11:23).

    2. In the rest of the assembly, whose duty is praying to God, hearing the word preached and read, and receiving the sacraments with outward modesty and without offence. *"But all things should be done decently and in order"* (1 Cor. 14:40). Inwardly they must take heed that their hearts are well prepared to serve God. *"Guard your steps when you go to the house of God. To draw near to listen is better than to offer the sacrifice of fools, for they do not know that they are doing evil. Be not rash with your mouth, nor let your heart be hasty to utter a word before God, for God is in heaven and you are on earth. Therefore, let your words be few"* (Eccl. 5:1–2). Again, we must see to it that we approach near God in confidence of his mercy, together with a contrite and repentant heart for all our sins. *"But the message they heard did not benefit them, because they were not united by faith*

13. Tertullian, *Apology*, ch. 39.
14. The *Means of Grace* are created things through which God promises to nurture faith and obedience in his people by the Holy Spirit. These are principally Scripture (both read and preached), and the two sacraments: Baptism and the Lord's Supper (see ***chapters 31–34***).

with those who listened" (Heb. 4:2). *"I wash my hands in innocence and go around your altar, O LORD"* (Psalm 26:6).

3. The Aids to the true worship are two: Vows and Fasting. These are not to be regarded as the worship of God itself. For we may not impose anything upon God as good service, or as though it binds the conscience, except where he has ordained it for that end and purpose.

   In the New Testament, a **Vow** is a promise to God with a full intent to observe some external duties which a Christian has on his own accord, without injunction, imposed upon himself so as to be better excited to repentance, meditation, sobriety, abstinence, patience, and thankfulness towards God. *"Then Jacob made a vow, saying, 'If God will be with me and will keep me in this way that I go, and will give me bread to eat and clothing to wear, so that I come again to my father's house in peace, then the LORD shall be my God, and this stone, which I have set up for a pillar, shall be God's house. And of all that you give me I will give a full tenth to you'"* (Gen. 28:20-22).

   In vowing, we have these things to observe:

   a. We must not vow that which is unlawful.
   b. We ought not to vow the performance of anything that is contrary to our vocation.
   c. Vows must be of things which we can do.
   d. Vows must avoid so much as a hint of the conceit of earning merit, or being worship of God.
   e. We must so perform our vows that they do not encroach upon Christian freedom given us in Christ. For we are not bound to fulfil our vows beyond their proper scope. *"You shall not bring the fee of a prostitute or the wages of a dog into the house of the LORD your God in payment for any vow .... If you make a vow to the LORD your God, you shall not delay fulfilling it, for the LORD your God will surely require it of you, and you will be guilty of sin"* (Deut. 23:18, 21). *"I will perform my vows to you, that which my lips uttered and my mouth promised"* (Psalm 66:13–14).

Fasting is when a man (perceiving lack of some blessing or suspecting some imminent calamity upon himself or another) abstains not only from food for a season, but also from all delights and sustenance. He does this so that thereby he may make a more diligent search into his own sins, or offer humble prayers to God that he would withhold what his anger threatened, or bestow upon us some such good thing that we want. *"Can the wedding guests mourn as long as the bridegroom is with them?"* (Matt. 9:15). *"Do not deprive one another, except perhaps by agreement for a limited time, that you may devote yourselves to prayer"* (1 Cor. 7:5). *"'Yet even now,' declares the LORD, 'return to me with all your heart, ... rend your hearts and not your garments." Return to the LORD your God, for he is gracious and merciful, slow to anger, and abounding in steadfast love; and he relents over disaster. .... Blow the trumpet in Zion; consecrate a fast; call a solemn assembly; gather the people. Consecrate the congregation; assemble the elders; gather the children, even nursing infants. Let the bridegroom leave his room .... let the priests, the ministers of the LORD, weep and say, "Spare your people, O LORD"'"* (Joel 2:12–13, 15–17).

A fast, is sometime private, sometimes public. *"Then Jehoshaphat was afraid and set his face to seek the LORD, and proclaimed a fast throughout all Judah"* (2 Chron. 20:3). *"Go, gather all the Jews to be found in Susa, and hold a fast on my behalf, and do not eat or drink for three days, night or day. I and my young women will also fast as you do"* (Esth. 4:16).

A fast might be one or many days in duration. Each is (as occasion serves) abstinence from: food at dinner alone, or at supper alone, or at both dinner and supper. *"And the people of Israel went up and wept before the LORD until the evening, etc."* (Jdg. 20:23). *"I, Daniel, was mourning for three weeks. I ate no delicacies, no meat or wine entered my mouth, nor did I anoint myself at all, for the full three weeks"* (Dan. 10:2–3).

4. Associations of friendship among those who fear God according to his word are lawful. So too are contracts in matrimony and leagues in war, especially if the war be lawful and without confidence in the power of man (2 Chron. 19:2; Mal. 2:11).

To these may be added covenants which magistrate and people make among themselves and with God for the preservation of Christian religion. *"And they entered into a covenant to seek the LORD, the God of their fathers, with all their heart and with all their soul .... They swore an oath to the LORD with a loud voice and with shouting and with trumpets and with horns"* (2 Chron. 15:12).

Chapter Twenty Two

THE THIRD COMMANDMENT

The third commandment concerns the glorifying of God in the affairs of life apart from the solemn service of God.

> *You shall not take the name of the LORD your God in vain, for the LORD will not hold him guiltless who takes his name in vain* (Exod. 20:7)

The Resolution

Name. This word properly signifies God's title. Here it is used figuratively for anything by which God may be known, just as men are known by their names. So it is used for his word, works, and judgements, *"He is a chosen instrument of mine to carry my name before the Gentiles"* (Acts 9:15). *"O LORD, our Lord, how majestic is your name in all the earth!"* (Psalm 8:1) which sets your glory above the heavens.

Take. That is, usurp. This word relates to precious things which may not be touched without permission. And in truth, men (which are no better than worms creeping on the earth) are utterly unworthy to take, or so much as touch, the sacred name of God with mind or mouth. Nevertheless, God of his infinite kindness permits us to so do.

In vain. Namely for no reason or matter, nor upon any frivolous occasion.

For. The reason of this commandment is taken from the penalty attached to it. Whoever abuses God's name is guilty of sin before God's judgement seat, and therefore is most miserable. *"Blessed is the one whose transgression is forgiven, whose sin is covered. Blessed is the man against whom the LORD counts no iniquity"* (Psalm 32:1–2).

Guiltless. That is, he shall not be unpunished.

The negative part: *You shall not bereave God of that honour that is due to him.*

Here are included abuses of anything used in the course of our lives which lays outside of the solemn service of God:

1. **Perjury**, when a man does not perform that which he swore to do of his own accord. *"You shall not swear falsely, but shall perform to the Lord what you have sworn"* (Matt. 5:33).

   Perjury contains in it four capital sins:

   a. Lying.

   b. False invocation of God's name, since they called upon God to confirm a lie.

   c. Contempt of God's threatening that he will most grievously punish perjury.

   d. A lie in his covenant with God. For swearing binds one to God and lies to him.

2. **To Swear Falsely**. This is to make God and the Devil both alike. *"You are of your father the Devil, ... when he lies, he speaks out of his own character, for he is a liar and the father of lies"* (John 8:44). *"It shall enter the house of the thief, and the house of him who swears falsely by my name"* (Zec. 5:4).

3. To **swear in common talk**. *"Let what you say be simply 'Yes' or 'No'; anything more than this comes from evil"* (Matt. 5:37).

4. **To swear by that which is not God**. *"But I say to you, Do not take an oath at all, either by heaven, for it is the throne of God, or by the earth, for it is his footstool, or by Jerusalem, for it is the city of the great King"* (Matt. 5:34–35). *"Then Jezebel sent a messenger to Elijah, saying, 'So may the gods do to me and more also, if I do not make your life as the life of one of them by this time tomorrow'"* (1 Kings 19:2). *"Even as they taught my people to swear by Baal"* (Jer. 12:16). *"Your children have forsaken me and have sworn by those who are no gods"* (Jer. 5:7).

   This passage condemns that usual swearing by the mass, faith, and such like. *"And whoever swears by heaven swears by the throne of*

God and by him who sits upon it" (Matt. 23:22).

But for a man to swear by Christ's death, wounds, blood, and other parts of him, is most horrible. It is like crucifying Christ again along with the Jews, or accounting Christ's members if they are God himself.

5. **Blasphemy**, which is a reproach against God, or speech that shows contempt of his majesty. *"Whoever blasphemes the name of the LORD shall surely be put to death. All the congregation shall stone him. The sojourner as well as the native, when he blasphemes the Name, shall be put to death"* (Lev. 24:16). *"Thus shall you speak to Hezekiah king of Judah: 'Do not let your God in whom you trust deceive you by promising that Jerusalem will not be given into the hand of the king of Assyria'"* (2 Kings 19:10). Ajax, in the *Tragedy*, makes a blasphemous speech, claiming that every coward may overcome if he has God on his side, but that he can get the victory without God's assistance.[1] That sly taunt of the Pope is likewise blasphemous, wherein he calls himself "the servant of all God's servants", when as in truth he makes himself Lord of Lords, and God party to his vain fantasy.
6. **Cursing our Enemies**: "go with a vengeance" or "the Devil go with you". Or cursing ourselves: "I wish I were dead" or, "as God shall condemn me". And so on. (Job 3; Jer. 15).
7. To **use the Name of God carelessly** in our common talk. For example, when we say "Good God!", "good Lord!", "O Jesus!", "Jesus God!", and so on. *"So that at the name of Jesus every knee should bow, in heaven and on earth and under the earth"* (Phil. 2:10). *"To me every knee shall bow, every tongue shall swear allegiance"* (Isa. 45:23).
8. **Abusing God's Creatures**: such as when we either mock the workmanship of God, or their manner of working. Also when we debase the excellence of the work, obscure God's gifts in our brother, or disapprove of such food as God has given us to eat. Finally, when we, in the contemplation of any of God's creatures, do not give him the due praise and glory. *"So, whether you eat or drink, or whatever you do, do all to the glory of God"* (1 Cor. 10:31). *"The heavens declare the glory of God, and the sky above proclaims his handiwork"* (Psalm 19:1).

1. Sophocles, *The Ajax*.

9. **Lots**, as when we search what (they claim) must be our fortune, by dice, bones, books, or similar. For we are not to use lots, except with great reverence, where the disposition to use them comes immediately from the Lord, and as reflects their proper use in deciding great controversies. *"The lot is cast into the lap, but its every decision is from the LORD"* (Prov. 16:33). *"The lot puts an end to quarrels and decides between powerful contenders"* (Prov. 18:18). For this reason, the land of Canaan was divided by lots (Joshua 14–15). So likewise the high priests and the kings were elected, such as Saul (1 Sam. 10), and Matthias was chosen to fill the place of Judas Iscariot (Acts 1:23).

10. **Superstition**, which is an opinion regarding the works of God's providence, the reason for which cannot be drawn out of the word of God, nor from the whole course of nature. For example, that it is unlucky for one in the morning to put on the left shoe on the right foot, to sneeze whilst putting on his shoes, to have salt fall toward him, to have a hare cross his path, to bleed a few drops of blood, or to burn on the right ear. Alternatively, that it is good luck to find old iron, to have drink spilled on him, for the left ear to burn, to trim our nails on a particular day of the week, or to dream of certain things. A similar superstition is to deduce that beasts may be tamed by verses, prayers, or the like; that the repetition of the Creed or the Lord's Prayer can infuse a faculty of healing diseases into herbs (Deut. 18:11). Here too palm reading is condemned, as when by the inspection of the hand our fortune is foretold.

    We are not to give credence to such things, even when they appear to cause true events. For God permits them to have such success, so that those who see and hear such things may be tested, and it may appear what confidence they have in God (Deut. 13).

11. **Astrology**, whether it be in casting of births or the making of prognostications (horoscopes). This counterfeit art is nothing else but an abuse of the heavens and of the stars.
    a. The twelve houses, which are the basis of all figures, are made of the false signs of a supposed zodiac in the highest sphere commonly called the "first movable" sphere. To these houses a man cannot truly ascribe any influence or virtue.
    b. This art does not arise from experience since we never observe

all stars in the same position more than once. And even if we did, no certainty could arise from it since the efficacy and influence of the stars cannot be isolated from that of the air and the earth. It is like when many herbs are mingled together in one vessel.

c. This art withdraws men's minds away from the contemplation of God's providence when as they hear that all things occur by the motion and disposition of the stars.
d. Stars were not ordained to foretell things to come, but to distinguish days, months, and years. *"Let there be lights in the expanse of the heavens to separate the day from the night. And let them be for signs and for seasons, and for days and years"* (Gen. 1:14). *"You are wearied with your many counsels; let them stand forth and save you, those who divide the heavens, who gaze at the stars, who at the new moons make known what shall come upon you. Behold, they are like stubble; the fire consumes them; they cannot deliver themselves from the power of the flame, etc."* (Isa. 47:13–14). *"Then the king commanded that the magicians, the enchanters, the sorcerers, and the Chaldeans be summoned to tell the king his dreams"* (Dan. 2:2). *"And a number of those who had practised magic arts brought their books together and burned them in the sight of all"* (Acts 19:19).
e. Astrological predictions make claims about things which either simply depend on the will and disposition of God (and not on the stars), or else depend upon man's free-will. Neither be foreseen, nor foretold.
f. It is impossible to precisely determine the precise effects by bare knowledge of a cause that is both common to many and far distant from the things that it works in. Yet the stars are causes which are both common to many and far distant from all things done upon earth. Therefore, a man can no more surely foretell what shall ensue by the contemplation of the stars than he who sees a hen sitting can tell what kind of chickens shall be in every egg.

Question: Have then the stars no force on earthly things?

Answer: Undoubtedly, the stars have a very great force, but only as relates to the four principle qualities of natural things, namely heat, cold, moisture, and dryness. Thus, in altering the state and disposition of the air, and in variously affecting compound bodies, the stars have no small effect. But they are so far from enforcing the will to do anything that they cannot so much as give to it the least inclination. Now to define how great a force the stars have is beyond any man's reach. For although the effects of the sun in the constitution of the four seasons of the year are apparent to all, and the operation of the moon is not too obscure, yet the force and nature of the planets and fixed stars (which appear to us innumerable) is not so clear. Therefore, since man can only know some stars and a few things regarding their operation, he cannot foretell future events even if they did depend on the stars. For what if the position of such and such a star demonstrates that such an effect will ensue? Might not things of which you do not know possibly hinder that, and produce the contrary effect?

Question: Is the use of Astrology utterly impious?

Answer: That part of Astrology which concerns the alteration of the air is almost all both false and frivolous. Therefore, all predictions grounded upon that doctrine are idle fancies by which silly and ignorant people are deluded. As for that other part of astrology—concerning births, revolutions, progressions, directions of births, election of times, and finding things lost—it is very wicked. It is also likely that it is of the same brood as magic. My reasons are these:

i. The word of God reckons astrologers among magicians, and these are given one and the same punishment.

ii. But the astrologer says that he foretells many things which come to pass as he said. This may be so, but how? By what means? He says by art, but that I deny. For to those who read them without prejudice, the precepts of his art appear ridiculous. From where, I ask, does this curious diviner bring forth the truth, but by an inward and secret instinct and from the Devil? This is Augustine's opinion: *"If we weigh all those things, he said, we will not without cause believe, that Astrologers, when they do wonderfully declare many truths, work by some secret instinct of evil*

> *spirits, which desire to fill men's brains with erroneous and dangerous opinions of starry destinies, and not by any art, derived from the inspection and consideration of the Horoscope, which indeed is none."*[2]

12. Popish consecration of water and salt to restore the mind to health, and to chase away Devils.[3]

13. To make jests of Scriptural expressions. *"But this is the one to whom I will look: he who is humble and contrite in spirit and trembles at my word"* (Isa. 66:2). We have an example of such scoffing in the *Tripartite History*: *"The heathen did grievously oppress the Christians, and inflicted sometimes upon their bodies corporal punishments. The which when the Christians signified to the Emperor, he disdained to assist them, and sent them away with this scoff: you are to suffer injuries patiently, for so are you commanded of your God."*[4]

14. To pass over lightly God's judgements witnessed in the world. *"Jesus said to him, "Truly, I tell you, this very night, before the rooster crows, you will deny me three times." Peter said to him, "Even if I must die with you, I will not deny you!" And all the disciples said the same"* (Matt. 26:34–35). *"There were some present at that very time who told him about the Galileans whose blood Pilate had mingled with their sacrifices. And he answered them, "Do you think that these Galileans were worse sinners than all the other Galileans, because they suffered in this way? No, I tell you; but unless you repent, you will all likewise perish"* (Luke 13:1–3).

15. Depraved conduct. *"Let your light shine before others, so that they may see your good works and give glory to your Father who is in heaven"* (Matt. 5:16). *"by this deed you have given great occasion to the enemies of the LORD to blaspheme, the child also who is born to you shall surely die"* (2 Sam. 12:14, NKJV).

---

2. Augustine, *The City of God*, 5.7.
3. *The Reformed Missal*, p. 96.
4. Cassiodorus (ed.), *The Tripartite History*, 36.6.

The affirmative part: *In all things give God his due glory* (1 Cor. 10:13)

To this pertain:

1. Zeal for God's glory above all else in the world. *"When Phinehas the son of Eleazar, son of Aaron the priest, saw it, he rose and left the congregation and took a spear in his hand and went after the man of Israel into the chamber and pierced both of them, the man of Israel and the woman through her belly"* (Num. 25:7–8). *"For zeal for your house has consumed me, and the reproaches of those who reproach you have fallen on me"* (Psalm 69:9).
2. To use God's titles only in serious affairs, and with all reverence. *"If you are not careful to do all the words of this law that are written in this book, that you may fear this glorious and awesome name, the LORD your God"* (Deut. 28:58). *"To them belong the patriarchs, and from their race, according to the flesh, is the Christ who is God over all, blessed forever. Amen"* (Rom. 9:5).
3. A holy commemoration of the creature, whereby we recognise the dignity and excellence of human achievements, name them with admiration, and celebrate the praise of God brightly shining in them. *"Then all mankind fears; they tell what God has brought about and ponder what he has done. Let the righteous one rejoice in the LORD and take refuge in him! Let all the upright in heart exult!"* (Psalm 64:9–10). *"And all who heard it wondered at what the shepherds told them. But Mary treasured up all these things, pondering them in her heart"* (Luke 2:18–19). *"They have spoken falsely of the LORD and have said, 'He will do nothing; no disaster will come upon us, nor shall we see sword or famine'" "Do you not fear me? declares the LORD. Do you not tremble before me? I placed the sand as the boundary for the sea, a perpetual barrier that it cannot pass; though the waves toss, they cannot prevail; though they roar, they cannot pass over it"* (Jer. 5:22).
4. An **Oath**, in which we must regard:

    a. How an oath is to be taken.

    b. How it is to be performed.

    In taking an oath, four Circumstances must be observed:

    a. The parts of an oath:

i. Confirmation of a truth.

ii. Calling on God alone as a witness to the truth, and as avenger of lies.

iii. Confession that God punishes perjury, when he is brought in as a false witness.

iv. An obligation that we will undergo the punishment at God's hand if we do not perform the condition.

b. The form. We must swear:

i. Truly, lest we swear falsely.

ii. Justly, lest we commit impiety.

iii. With earnest reflection, for fear of rashness. *"And if you swear, 'As the LORD lives,' in truth, in justice, and in righteousness"* (Jer. 4:2). *"Who swear by the name of the LORD and confess the God of Israel, but not in truth or right, etc."* (Isa. 48:1). Therefore, the oath of drunken, angry, and frantic men—also oaths of children—do not impose an observation of them, and by law are not oaths.

iv. The end goal, namely to confirm some necessary truth in question. *"For people swear by something greater than themselves, and in all their disputes an oath is final for confirmation"* (Heb. 6:16). I call it a necessary truth when a doubt which must necessarily be alleviated, cannot be alleviated in any way except by an oath. For example, when God's glory, our neighbours' body or goods, or the good name of the party for whom the oath is administered, are necessarily called into question. *"For God is my witness, whom I serve with my spirit in the gospel of his Son, that without ceasing I mention you always in my prayers"* (Rom. 1:9). *"But I call God to witness against me—it was to spare you that I refrained from coming again to Corinth"* (2 Cor. 1:23).

c. The diverse kinds or sorts of oaths. An oath is Public or Private:

Public, when the Magistrate, without any peril to him that swears and upon just cause, exacts a testimony together with an oath.

A Private Oath is one which two or more persons take privately. This is lawful, so long as it is sparingly and warily used. For if it is lawful in private to call upon God as a Judge in serious affairs and matters of great importance, why should he not as well be called to witness? Again, the examples of holy men show the practise of private oaths was not unlawful. Jacob and Laban confirmed their covenant one with another by a private oath, as did Boaz in his contract with Ruth.

This should be distinguished from a Solemn Affirmation or Asseveration (which bears similarities to an oath, but isn't one), which is a firm assertion of our mind, sometimes invoking the name of a creature. Such was Christ's assertion, *"Truly, truly, I say to you".* And Paul's, *"I call God to witness against me"* is both an oath and a solemn affirmation (2 Cor. 1:23). *"By your rejoicing which I have in Jesus Christ, I die daily"* (1 Cor. 15:31). *"Indeed, as the Lord lives, and as my soul lives, there is but a step between me and death."* (1 Sam. 20:3) And surely in such a kind of solemn affirmation there is great equity. For though it is unlawful to swear by creatures lest God's honour and power should be attributed to them, yet we may use them thus far in an oath or to make pledges, with due consideration of God's glory.

An oath is performed in this way. If the oath made is of a lawful thing, it must be performed, whether of great difficulty, damage, or extorted by force of him that made it. *"Who swears to his own hurt and does not change"* (Psalm 15:4). Yet the Magistrate may, as it shalt seem right and convenient, either annul or moderate such oaths.

On the other hand, if a man swears to perform things that are unlawful (whether by ignorance, error, or infirmity, or any other way), his oath is to be annulled. For we may not add sin to sin. *"Now David had said, 'Surely in vain have I guarded all that this fellow has in the wilderness, so that nothing was missed of all that belonged to him, and he has returned me evil for good. God do so to the enemies of David and more also, if by morning I leave so much as one male of all who belong to him' .... And David said to Abigail, "Blessed be the LORD, the God of Israel, who sent you this day to meet me! Blessed be your discretion, and blessed be you, who have kept me this day from bloodguilt and from avenging myself with my own hand!"* (1 Sam. 25:21–22, 32–33; 2 Sam. 19:23). David promises that Shimei would not die, but *"do not hold him guiltless, for you are a wise man. You will know what you ought to do to him, and you shall bring his gray head down with blood to Sheol"* (1 Kings 2:8–9).

5. **Sanctification** of God's creatures and ordinances, which is a separation of them for a holy use. Thus, we ought to sanctify our food and drink, the works of our vocation, and marriage.

The means of this sanctification are two: God's word and prayer. *"For everything created by God is good, and nothing is to be rejected if it is received with thanksgiving"* (1 Tim. 4:4).

By the word we are instructed:

a. Whether God allows the use of such things, or not.
b. About the manner, in what place, at what time, with what affection, and to what end we must use them. *"And without faith it is impossible to please him"* (Heb. 11:6). *"Your testimonies are my delight; they are my counsellors"* (Psalm 119:24). See also Josh. 22:19, 29 and 1 Sam. 15:23.

Prayer, which sanctifies, is Petition and Thanksgiving.

By **Petition** we obtain assistance, by God's grace, to make a holy use of his creatures and ordinances. *"And whatever you do, in word or deed, do everything in the name of the Lord Jesus, giving thanks to God the Father through him"* (Col. 3:17). *"Then David said to the Philistine, "You come to me with a sword and with a spear and with a javelin, but I come to you in the name of the LORD of hosts, the God of the armies of Israel, whom you have defied"* (1 Sam. 17:45). *"We will walk in the name of the LORD our God forever and ever"* (Mic. 4:5). Here may we observe prayer made upon particular occasion:

d. For a prosperous journey. *"When our days there were ended, we departed and went on our journey, and they all, with wives and children, accompanied us until we were outside the city. And kneeling down on the beach, we prayed"* (Acts 21:5).
e. For a blessing upon food at the table. *"Jesus then took the loaves, and when he had given thanks, he distributed them to those who were seated. So also the fish, as much as they*

wanted" (John 6:11). *"And when he had said these things, he took bread, and giving thanks to God in the presence of all he broke it and began to eat"* (Acts 27:35).

f. For issue in childbirth. Hannah did this (1 Sam. 1:14) as did Zachariah (Luke 1:13–14).

g. For good success in business. (Gen. 24:12). Abraham's servant prayed.

Thanksgiving is the magnifying of God's name, namely of the Father through Christ, for his grace, aid, and blessing in the lawful use of the creation. *"But in everything by prayer and supplication with thanksgiving let your requests be made known to God"* (Phil. 4:6). *"Give thanks in all circumstances; for this is the will of God in Christ Jesus for you"* (1 Thess. 5:18). In Scripture may be observed the following uses:

a. After food. *"And you shall eat and be full, and you shall bless the LORD your God for the good land he has given you"* (Deut. 8:10).

b. After the loss of outward wealth. *"And he said, 'Naked I came from my mother's womb, and naked shall I return. The LORD gave, and the LORD has taken away; blessed be the name of the LORD'"* (Job 1:21).

c. For deliverance out of slavery or servitude. *"Jethro said, "Blessed be the LORD, who has delivered you out of the hand of the Egyptians and out of the hand of Pharaoh and has delivered the people from under the hand of the Egyptians"* (Exod. 18:10).

d. For children. *"And she conceived again and bore a son, and said, 'This time I will praise the LORD.' Therefore she called his name Judah. Then she ceased bearing"* (Gen. 29:35).

e. For victory. *"And David spoke to the LORD the words of this song on the day when the LORD delivered him from the hand of all his enemies, and from the hand of Saul. He said, "The LORD is my rock and my fortress and my deliverer, etc."* (2 Sam. 22:1).

f. For good success in domestic affairs. Abraham's servant said: *"O LORD, God of my master Abraham, please grant me success today and show steadfast love to my master Abraham"* (Gen. 24:12).

Chapter Twenty Three

THE FOURTH COMMANDMENT

The fourth Commandment concerns the Sabbath: that holy time consecrated to the worship and glorifying of God. The words are these:

> *Remember the Sabbath day, to keep it holy. Six days you shall labour, and do all your work, but the seventh day is a Sabbath to the LORD your God. On it you shall not do any work, you, or your son, or your daughter, your male servant, or your female servant, or your livestock, or the sojourner who is within your gates. For in six days the LORD made heaven and earth, the sea, and all that is in them, and rested on the seventh day. Therefore the LORD blessed the Sabbath day and made it holy.* (Exod. 20:8–11)

The Resolution

Remember. This clause implies that in times past there was great neglect in the observation of the Sabbath, that God intends that all degrees and conditions of men should prepare themselves to sanctify this day, especially those who are governors of families, corporations, and cities, to whom this commandment is directed.

To Keep it holy, or to sanctify it. To sanctify is to sever a thing from common use and consecrate it for the service of God. Here are described the two parts of this commandment: the first being rest from labour, and the second, sanctification of that rest.

Six days. These words contain an answer to the objection that it is too much to cease from our callings for one whole day.[1] The answer is in

1. For Perkins's fuller discussion of vocation, see his *Treatise on the Vocations or Callings of Men* (1603) in *The Works of William Perkins: Volume 10* (ed. Joseph A. Pipa & J. Stephen Yuille; Grand Rapids: Reformation Heritage Books, 2020).

these words: *If I permit you to follow your calling six whole days, you must leave one only to serve me.* The first is true, therefore the second also.

Here we see that God has given us freedom to work all the six days. No man can annihilate this freedom. Nevertheless, upon extraordinary occasions, the Church of God is permitted to separate one day or more of the seven, as need be, either for fasting, or for a solemn day of rejoicing for some benefit received (Joel 2:15).

The seventh day. The second reason of this commandment taken from its end:

> If the Sabbath is consecrated to God and his service, we must abstain from our labours for that day. It was consecrated to God, and his service. Therefore we must then abstain from our labours.

The assumption in these words is that God alone has the privilege of having a Sabbath consecrated to him. Therefore, all holy days dedicated to any angel or saint whatsoever are unlawful, though the Church of Rome has imposed the observation of them upon many people.

On it you shall not do. This is the conclusion of the second reason, illustrated with examples. *You, or your son, or your daughter, your male servant, or your female servant, or your livestock, or the sojourner, shall cease that day from your work.*

Your work. This refers to ordinary work of your vocation which is able to be done the day before or left undone till the day after. Yet we are not forbidden, even on this day, to perform whatever works are both holy and of present necessity.

Such are those works which preserve and maintain the service and glory of God upon that day, such as:

1. A Sabbath day's journey. *"Then they returned to Jerusalem from the mount called Olivet, which is near Jerusalem, a Sabbath day's journey away"* (Acts 1:12).
2. The killing and dressing of sacrificial animals in the time of the law. *"Or have you not read in the Law how on the Sabbath the priests in the temple profane the Sabbath and are guiltless?"* (Matt. 12:5).

3. Journeys to the prophets and places appointed for the worship of God. *"And he said, 'Why will you go to him today? It is neither new moon nor Sabbath'"* (2 Kings 4:23). *"They go from strength to strength; each one appears before God in Zion"* (Psalm 84:7).

So also are the works of mercy, whereby the safety of life or goods is procured:

1. As that which Paul did, *"And a young man named Eutychus, sitting at the window, sank into a deep sleep as Paul talked still longer. And being overcome by sleep, he fell down from the third story and was taken up dead .... And they took the youth away alive, and were not a little comforted"* (Acts 20:9, 12).
2. To help out of a pit. *"Which of you, having a son or an ox that has fallen into a well on a Sabbath day"* (Luke 14:5).
3. Provision of food and drink. *"At that time Jesus went through the grainfields on the Sabbath. His disciples were hungry, and they began to pluck heads of grain and to eat"* (Matt. 12:1). In provision, we must ensure that our cooks, and household servants keep the Sabbath. This is reasoned from the lesser to the greater, out of this passage: *"And David said longingly, "Oh, that someone would give me water to drink from the well of Bethlehem that is by the gate!" Then the three mighty men broke through the camp of the Philistines and drew water out of the well of Bethlehem that was by the gate and carried and brought it to David. But he would not drink of it. He poured it out to the LORD and said, "Far be it from me, O LORD, that I should do this. Shall I drink the blood of the men who went at the risk of their lives?" Therefore he would not drink it. These things the three mighty men did"* (2 Sam 23:15–17). If David would not have his servants risk their lives for his provision, nor drink the water when they had provided it, much less ought we to enforce our servants breaking of the Sabbath for our food.
4. Watering of cattle. *"Then the Lord answered him, "You hypocrites! Does not each of you on the Sabbath untie his ox or his donkey from the manger and lead it away to water it?"* (Luke 13:15). Upon similar present and holy necessity, upon the Sabbath day physicians may take a journey to visit the diseased, mariners their voyage, shepherds may tend their flock, and midwives may

help women with child. *"The Sabbath was made for man, not man for the Sabbath"* (Mark 2:27).

Within your gates. This word 'gate' signifies jurisdiction and authority. *"The gates of hell shall not prevail against it"* (Matt. 16:18). Let this be a point of reflection by which all innkeepers and entertainers of strangers may examine themselves and recognise their duty.

For in six days. The third reason of this commandment is from its example:

> That which I did, you also must do.
> I rested the seventh day and hallowed it.
> Therefore you must do the same.

God sanctified the Sabbath when he consecrated it to his service; men sanctify it when they worship God upon it. In this passage we are to consider to what extent the Sabbath is Ceremonial and to what extent Moral.[2]

The Sabbath is **Ceremonial** with respect to its strict observation, which was a foreshadowing of the internal sanctification of the people of God, meaning a continual resting from the work of sin. *"You are to speak to the people of Israel and say, 'Above all you shall keep my Sabbaths, for this is a sign between me and you throughout your generations, that you may know that I, the LORD, sanctify you"* (Exod. 31:13). The same is recorded in Ezekiel 20:12.

It also signified the blessed rest of the faithful in the kingdom of heaven. *"From new moon to new moon, and from Sabbath to Sabbath, all flesh shall come to worship before me, declares the LORD"* (Isa. 66:23). *"For if Joshua had given them rest, etc."* (Heb. 4:8–10).

The Sabbath is also ceremonial in that it was observed on the seventh day after the creation of the world and was previously solemnised with ceremonies. *"On the Sabbath day, two male lambs a year old without*

2. Like other Reformed theologians, Perkins delineated the Old Testament Law into its *Moral*, *Civil*, and *Ceremonial* elements. The Moral Law represents timeless moral principles which Christians are bound by, whereas the civil and ceremonial precepts of the Old Testament Law have been superseded by the gospel.

blemish, and two tenths of an ephah of fine flour for a grain offering, mixed with oil, and its drink offering: this is the burnt offering of every Sabbath, besides the regular burnt offering and its drink offering" (Num. 28:9–10).

But now in the light of the gospel which the Churches profess, the ceremony of the Sabbath is ceased. *"Therefore let no one pass judgment on you in questions of food and drink, or with regard to a festival or a new moon or a Sabbath. These are a shadow of the things to come, but the substance belongs to Christ"* (Col. 2:16–17). The observation of the Sabbath was translated by the Apostles from the seventh day, to the day following. *"On the first day of the week, when we were gathered together to break bread, Paul talked with them"* (Acts 20:7). *"Now concerning the collection for the saints: as I directed the churches of Galatia, so you also are to do. On the first day of every week, each of you is to put something aside and store it up, as he may prosper, so that there will be no collecting when I come"* (1 Cor. 16:1–2). This day is called the Lord's day since on it our Saviour rose again: *"I was in the Spirit on the Lord's day"* (Rev. 1:10).

The observation of the Sabbath continued by the Apostles, was nevertheless neglected by those churches which came after them. However, it was afterwards revived and established by Christian emperors as a day most fitting to celebrate the remembrance of the creation of the world, and to make serious meditation upon the redemption of mankind.[3]

The observation of the Sabbath is **Moral** inasmuch as it is a fixed seventh day, and it preserves and conserves the ministry of the word and the solemn worship of God, especially in the assemblies of the Church. In this respect we are commanded to rest from our vocations upon this day, just as the Jews were. *"If you turn back your foot from the Sabbath, from doing your pleasure on my holy day, and call the Sabbath a delight and the holy day of the LORD honourable; if you honour it, not going your own ways, or seeking your own pleasure, etc."* (Isa. 58:13).

Finally, it is moral in that it frees servants and cattle from their labours, which serve their owner on other days.

3. Leo and Anton, *Edict. on Holy Days.*

The affirmative part: *Keep holy the Sabbath day*

We do this when we cease from the works of sin and our ordinary calling: performing those spiritual works which are commanded in the second and third commandments.

1. To arise early in the morning so that so we may prepare ourselves for the better sanctifying of the Sabbath. This preparation consists in private prayers and taking account of our sins. *"And rising very early in the morning, while it was still dark, he departed and went out to a desolate place, and there he prayed .... And he went throughout all Galilee, preaching in their synagogues and casting out demons"* (Mark 1:35, 39). *"And Aaron made proclamation and said, 'Tomorrow shall be a feast to the LORD.' And they rose up early the next day and offered burnt offerings and brought peace offerings. And the people sat down to eat and drink and rose up to play"* (Exod. 32:5–6). *"Guard your steps when you go to the house of God"* (Eccl. 5:1).
2. To be present at public assemblies in order to hear the word preached and read reverently and attentively, to receive the Lord's Supper, and to call upon and celebrate the name of the Lord publicly with the congregation (1 Tim. 1:1-3; Acts 20:7; 2 Kings 4:22-23). *"But they went on from Perga and came to Antioch in Pisidia. And on the Sabbath day they went into the synagogue and sat down. After the reading from the Law and the Prophets, the rulers of the synagogue sent a message to them, saying, 'Brothers, if you have any word of encouragement for the people, say it'"* (Act 13:14-15).
3. When public meetings are over, to spend the rest of the Sabbath in meditation upon God's word and his creatures (Psalm 29), *"Now these Jews were more noble than those in Thessalonica; they received the word with all eagerness, examining the Scriptures daily to see if these things were so"* (Act 17:11). At this time we must also exercise the works of charity, such as to visit the sick, give alms to the needy, admonish those who fall, reconcile those who dispute amongst themselves, and so on. *"And all the people went their way to eat and drink and to send portions and to make great rejoicing"* (Neh. 8:12).

The negative part: *Pollute not the Sabbath of the Lord*

This is a grievous sin. *"Pray that your flight may not be in winter or on a Sabbath"* (Matt. 24:20). *"You shall keep my Sabbaths and reverence my sanctuary: I am the LORD"* (Lev. 19:30). These things are here forbidden:

1. The works of our calling. If we engage in them at all, then it must be entirely for the sake of charity, and not for our own private gain.
2. Unnecessary journeys. *"Remain each of you in his place; let no one go out of his place on the seventh day"* (Exod. 16:29). For this reason, the master of the family must remain at home that day, so as to sanctify the Sabbath with his household.
3. Fairs upon the Sabbath days. *"As soon as it began to grow dark at the gates of Jerusalem before the Sabbath, I commanded that the doors should be shut and gave orders that they should not be opened until after the Sabbath. And I stationed some of my servants at the gates, that no load might be brought in on the Sabbath day"* (Neh. 13:19; cf. 13:15–18).
4. All kind of farming, such as ploughing, sowing, reaping, mowing, bringing home harvest, and so on. *"Six days you shall work, but on the seventh day you shall rest. In ploughing time and in harvest you shall rest"* (Exod. 34:21).
5. To use jests, sports, banqueting, or any other thing which hinders or withdraws the mind from serious attention to God's service. For if the works of our calling must not be exercised, much less may these in which the mind is as distracted from God's service, as it would be by the greatest labour.
6. An external observation of the Sabbath, without an internal regard of godliness. *"Your new moons and your appointed feasts my soul hates; they have become a burden to me; I am weary of bearing them. When you spread out your hands, I will hide my eyes from you; even though you make many prayers, I will not listen; your hands are full of blood"* (Isa. 1:14–15). *"Having the appearance of godliness, but denying its power. Avoid such people"* (2 Tim. 3:5).
7. Overt profanation of the Sabbath, for example in pampering the belly, feasting, adultery, and other profane acts. Such things are nothing else but to celebrate a Sabbath to the Devil and not to God.

Chapter Twenty Four

THE FIFTH COMMANDMENT

Thus far we have spoken of the commandments of the first Table of the Law. Now follows the second Table, which concerns the love of our neighbour. *"For the commandments, "You shall not commit adultery, You shall not murder, You shall not steal, You shall not covet,' and any other commandment, are summed up in this word: 'You shall love your neighbour as yourself'"* (Rom. 13:9).

Our neighbour is everyone who is a fellow human being. *"When you see the naked, to cover him, and not to hide yourself from your own flesh?"* (Isa. 58:7).

The manner of loving is to love our neighbour as ourselves, truly and sincerely. In contrast, the true manner of loving God is to do so without measure.

The second Table contains six commandments. The first of these (the fifth commandment) concerns the preservation of the dignity and excellence of our neighbour.

The words are these:

> *Honour your father and your mother, that your days may be long in the land that the LORD your God is giving you.* (Exod. 20:12)

The Resolution

Honour. This word signifies all those duties by which our neighbour's dignity is preserved, and especially that of our superiors. The basis of this dignity is that every man bears some part of the image of God with respect to the outward order and decency which is observed in the Church and commonwealth. In the Magistrate there is a certain image of the power and glory of God. *"You, O king, the king of kings, to whom the God of heaven has given the kingdom, the power, and the might, and the glory"* (Dan. 2:37). Hence is it, that Magistrates are called God's (Psalm 82:6). An old man represents the eternity of God, and a father is the likeness of God's fatherhood. *"And call no man your father on earth, for you have one Father, who is in heaven"* (Matt. 23:9). In a man is the image of God's providence and authority. *"For a man ought not to cover his head, since he is the image and glory of God, but woman is the glory of man"* (1 Cor. 11:7). Finally, in a learned man, there is the likeness of the knowledge and wisdom of God. Therefore, any person in whom even the least title of the image of God appears is to be honoured and reverenced.

Your Father. We must understand this as including all who are our superiors, such as parents, magistrates, ministers, our elders, and those who excel us in any gifts whatsoever. The Kings of Gerar were called Abimelech, my Father the king (Gen. 20:2). *"He has made me a father to Pharaoh, and lord of all his house and ruler over all the land of Egypt"* (Gen. 45:8). *"For though you have countless guides in Christ, you do not have many fathers. For I became your father in Christ Jesus through the gospel"* (1 Cor. 4:15). *"But his servants came near and said to him, "My father, it is a great word the prophet has spoken to you; will you not do it? Has he actually said to you, 'Wash, and be clean'?""* (2 Kings 5:13). *"And Elisha saw it and he cried, 'My father, my father! The chariots of Israel and its horsemen!'"* (2 Kings 2:12).

And your mother. This is added lest we should despise our mothers for their infirmities. *"Listen to your father who gave you life, and do not despise your mother when she is old"* (Prov. 23:22).

We are to keep in mind to perform due honour to our stepmothers and fathers-in-law, as if they were our natural parents. *"Then Naomi her mother-in-law said to her, 'My daughter, should I not seek rest for you, that it may be well with you?' .... And she replied, 'All that you say I will do'"* (Ruth 3:1, 5). *"Moses' father-in-law said to him, 'What you are doing is not good' .... Now obey my voice; I will give you advice, and God be with you!' .... So Moses listened to the voice of his father-in-law and did all that he had said"* (Exod. 18:17, 19, 24). *"For the son treats the father with contempt, the daughter rises up against her mother, the daughter-in-law against her mother-in-law"* (Mic. 7:6).

That your days may be long. Parents are said to prolong the lives of their children because they are God's instruments, by which their children's lives are prolonged. For often the name of the action is attributed to the instrument by which the action is performed. *"And I tell you, make friends for yourselves by means of unrighteous wealth, so that when it fails they may receive you into the eternal dwellings"* (Luke 16:9). *"For by so doing you will save both yourself and your hearers"* (1 Tim. 4:16).

Parents prolong the lives of their children by commanding them to walk in the ways of the Lord, and by exercising justice and judgement (Gen. 18:19). For becoming godly has promise both for this life, and for the life to come (1 Tim. 4:8).

Further, they do the same thing by their prayers made on behalf of their children. By this it is clear that the custom of children seeking their parents blessing is no vain or pointless thing.

Moreover, in these words, the reason to move us to obey this commandment comes at the end. This reason is also a promise, yet a special promise. *"Honour your father and mother (this is the first commandment with a promise)"* (Eph. 6:2). I say 'special' because the promise of the second commandment is general, and belongs to all the rest of the commandments.

God promises long life not absolutely, but insofar as it is a blessing. *"That it may go well with you and that you may live long in the land"* (Eph. 6:3). For long life is not always a blessing, and sometimes it is better to die than to live. *"The righteous man perishes, and no one lays it to heart; devout men are taken away, while no one understands. For the righteous man is taken away from calamity"* (Isa. 57:1).

But if at any time the Lord gives a short life to obedient children, he rewards them again with eternal life in heaven, so the promise does not fail but changes for the better.

The affirmative part: *Preserve the dignity of your neighbour*

Under this part is commanded:

1. **Reverence** towards all our superiors. The actions of this are: to reverently to rise up before any man which pass by us. *"You shall*

stand up before the grey head and honour the face of an old man, and you shall fear your God: I am the LORD" (Lev. 19:32). To meet him that comes towards us: *"He lifted up his eyes and looked, and behold, three men were standing in front of him. When he saw them, he ran from the tent door to meet them and bowed himself to the earth"* (Gen. 18:2). *"So Bathsheba went to King Solomon to speak to him on behalf of Adonijah. And the king rose to meet her and bowed down to her"* (1 Kings 2:19). To bow the knee: *"And as he was setting out on his journey, a man ran up and knelt before him"* (Mark 10:17). *"When he saw them, he ran from the tent door to meet them and bowed himself to the earth"* (Gen. 18:2). To stand beside those that sit down: *"Then he took curds and milk and the calf that he had prepared, and set it before them. And he stood by them under the tree while they ate"* (Gen. 18:8). *"The next day Moses sat to judge the people, and the people stood around Moses from morning till evening"* (Exod. 18:13). To give the chief seat: *"Then he sat on his throne and had a seat brought for the king's mother, and she sat on his right"* (1 Kings 2:19). *"Now he told a parable to those who were invited, when he noticed how they chose the places of honour, saying to them, "When you are invited by someone to a wedding feast, do not sit down in a place of honour, lest someone more distinguished than you be invited by him, and he who invited you both will come and say to you, 'Give your place to this person,' and then you will begin with shame to take the lowest place"* (Luke 14:7–9). *"And they sat before him, the firstborn according to his birthright and the youngest according to his youth. And the men looked at one another in amazement"* (Gen. 43:33). To let our superiors speak before us (Job 32:6–7, 17). To Keep silence in courts and judgement places until we be bid to speak. *"And when the governor had nodded to him to speak, Paul replied"* (Acts 24:10). To use others' proper titles, which declares our reverence when we speak to them. *"As Sarah obeyed Abraham, calling him lord. And you are her children, if you do good"* (1 Pet 3:6). *"Good Teacher, what must I do to inherit eternal life? .... And he said to him, 'Teacher, all these I have kept from my youth'"* (Mark 10:17, 20). *"And Eli said to her, 'How long will you go on being drunk? Put your wine away from you.' But Hannah answered, 'No, my lord, I am a woman troubled in spirit. I have drunk neither wine nor strong drink, but I have been pouring out my soul before the LORD'"* (1 Sam. 1:14–15).

2. Towards those who are our superiors in authority, and quick obedience to their commandments. *"Let every person be subject to the governing authorities .... those that exist have been instituted by God"* (Rom. 13:1).

We are to be admonished to obedience: because every higher power is the ordinance of God, and the obedience which we perform to them, God accepts it as though it were done to himself and to Christ. *"Therefore whoever resists the authorities resists what God has appointed, and those who resist will incur judgment"* (Rom. 13:2). *"Whatever you do, work heartily, as for the Lord and not for men, knowing that from the Lord you will receive the inheritance as your reward. You are serving the Lord Christ"* (Col. 3:23–24). Obedience is to be performed to our superiors with diligence and faithfulness. *"And Abraham said to his servant, the oldest of his household, who had charge of all that he had, "Put your hand under my thigh, that I may make you swear by the LORD, the God of heaven and God of the earth, that you will not take a wife for my son from the daughters of the Canaanites, among whom I dwell .... Then the servant took ten of his master's camels and departed .... And he said, 'O LORD, God of my master Abraham, please grant me success today and show steadfast love to my master Abraham' .... Then food was set before him to eat. But he said, 'I will not eat until I have said what I have to say.' He said, 'Speak on' .... But he said to them, 'Do not delay me, since the LORD has prospered my way. Send me away that I may go to my master'"* (Gen. 24:2–3, 10, 12, 33, 56). *"These twenty years I have been with you. Your ewes and your female goats have not miscarried, and I have not eaten the rams of your flocks .... There I was: by day the heat consumed me, and the cold by night, and my sleep fled from my eyes"* (Gen. 31:38, 40).

Furthermore, we must yield obedience to our superiors, indeed even if they are cruel and wicked, but not in wickedness. *"Servants, be subject to your masters with all respect, not only to the good and gentle but also to the unjust"* (1 Pet. 2:18). *"But Peter and John answered them, 'Whether it is right in the sight of God to listen to you rather than to God, you must judge'"* (Acts 4:19).

Subjection in suffering the punishments inflicted by our superiors. *"But Abram said to Sarai, 'Behold, your servant is in your power; do to her as you please.' Then Sarai dealt harshly with her, and she fled from her .... The angel of the LORD said to her, 'Return to your mistress and submit to her'"* (Gen. 16:6, 9).

And although a punishment might be unjust, yet we must endure it until we can attain some lawful remedy for it. *"For this is a gracious thing, when, mindful of God, one endures sorrows while suffering unjustly. For what credit is it if, when you sin and are beaten for it, you endure? But if when you do good and suffer for it you endure, this is a gracious thing in the sight of God"* (1 Pet. 2:19–20).

Thankfulness in our prayers. *"First of all, then, I urge that supplications, prayers, intercessions, and thanksgivings be made for all people, for kings and all who are in high positions, that we may lead a peaceful and quiet life, godly and dignified in every way"* (1 Tim. 2:1-2). *"Let the elders who rule well be considered worthy of double honour"* (1 Tim. 5:17). *"Hurry and go up to my father and say to him, 'Thus says your son Joseph, God has made me lord of all Egypt. Come down to me; do not tarry. You shall dwell in the land of Goshen, and you shall be near me, you and your children and your children's children, and your flocks, your herds, and all that you have. There I will provide for you, for there are yet five years of famine to come, so that you and your household, and all that you have, do not come to poverty'"* (Gen. 45:9-11).

3. Towards those who excel us in gifts. Our duty is to acknowledge their gifts and speak of them to their praise. 2 Cor. 8:22-23.
4. Toward all our equals: to think reverently of them. *"Do nothing from rivalry or conceit, but in humility count others more significant than yourselves"* (Phil. 2:3).

In giving honour, to outdo one another in giving it rather than receiving it (Rom. 12:10). Submitting yourselves to one another in the fear of God. To greet one another with holy signs, by which we show the love which we have one to another in Christ. *"Greet one another with the kiss of love. Peace to all of you who are in Christ"* (1 Pet. 5:14). *"Greet one another with a holy kiss"* (Rom. 16:16). *"Moses went out to meet his father-in-law and bowed down and kissed him"* (Exod. 18:7). *"And behold, Boaz came from Bethlehem. And he said to the reapers, 'The LORD be with you!' And they answered, 'The LORD bless you.'"* (Ruth 2:4).

5. The duties of all superiors towards their inferiors:

    a. To yield to them in good matters, since thy are our brethren. *"That his heart may not be lifted up above his brothers, and that he may not turn aside from the commandment, either to the right hand or to the left"* (Deut. 17:20). *"If I have rejected the cause of my manservant or my maidservant, when they brought a complaint against me"* (Job 31:13). *"But his servants came near and said to him, ... So he went down and dipped himself seven times in the Jordan, etc."* (2. Kings 5:13–14).

    b. To shine before their inferiors by setting an example of a blameless life. *"Older men are to be sober-minded, dignified, self-controlled, sound in faith, in love, and in steadfastness. Older women likewise are to be reverent in behaviour, not slanderers or slaves to much wine. They are to teach what is good"* (Titus 2:2–3). *"Not domineering over those in your charge, but being examples to the flock"* (1 Pet. 5:3; Phil. 4:9).

    c. To exude gravity and dignity by their countenance, gesture, deeds, and words. *"The young men saw me and withdrew, and the aged rose and stood"* (Job 29:8; Titus 2:3–6).

6. Towards their subjects:

    a. To rule them in the Lord, that they do not offend. *"Be subject for the Lord's sake to every human institution, whether it be to the emperor as supreme, or to governors as sent by him to punish those who do evil and to praise those who do good"* (1 Pet. 2:13–14). *"And it shall be with him, and he shall read in it all the days of his life, that he may learn to fear the LORD his God by keeping all the words of this law and these statutes, and doing them"* (Deut. 17:19). *"Masters, treat your slaves justly and fairly, knowing that you also have a Master in heaven"* (Col. 4:1).

    b. To provide such things as shall be to the good of their subjects, whether they belong to the body or to the soul. *"For he is God's servant for your good"* (Rom. 13:4). *"Kings shall be your foster fathers, and their queens your nursing mothers"* (Isa. 49:23). *"Remember, O LORD, in David's favour, all the hardships he endured, how he swore to the LORD and vowed to the Mighty One of Jacob, 'I will not enter my house or get into my bed, I will not give sleep to my eyes or slumber to my eyelids, until I find a place for the LORD, a dwelling place for the Mighty One of Jacob"'* (Psalm 132:1-5).

c. To punish their faults: the lesser by rebuke and the greater by correction (that is, by inflicting bodily punishment).

The holy manner of punishing the guilty is:

i. To be assured of the crime committed after diligent and wise examination.

ii. To show the offence of the sin from God's word so that the conscience of the offender may be touched.

iii. It is appropriate to defer or omit the punishment, if thereby any hope of amendment may appear. *"Do not take to heart all the things that people say, lest you hear your servant cursing you. Your heart knows that many times you yourself have cursed others"* (Eccl. 7:21-22). *"But some worthless fellows said, 'How can this man save us?' And they despised him and brought him no present. But he held his peace"* (1 Sam. 10:27).

iv. To inflict the deserved punishment in God's name, not in his own, and with holiness and reverence. *"Then Joshua said to Achan, 'My son, give glory to the LORD God of Israel and give praise to him. And tell me now what you have done; do not hide it from me.' And Achan answered Joshua, 'Truly I have sinned against the LORD God of Israel, and this is what I did' .... And Joshua said, 'Why did you bring trouble on us? The LORD brings trouble on you today.' And all Israel stoned him with stones. They burned them with fire and stoned them with stones"* (Josh. 7:19-20, 25).

v. When you punish, aim for one thing only: that the evil may be purged and amended, and the offender (by sorrowing for his sin) may honestly repent. *"Blows that wound cleanse away evil; strokes make clean the innermost parts"* (Prov. 20:30).

7. Lastly, a man has a certain duty toward himself, which is to preserve and maintain with modesty the dignity and worthiness which is inherent in his own person. *"Finally, brothers, whatever is true, whatever is honourable, whatever is just, whatever is pure, whatever is lovely, whatever is commendable, if there is any excellence, if there is*

anything worthy of praise, think about these things" (Phil. 4:8).

The negative part: *Do not diminish the dignity of your neighbour*

To this belong the following sins:

First, against our superiors:

1. Irreverent behaviour and contempt of them. These sins deride our superiors. *"And Ham, the father of Canaan, saw the nakedness of his father and told his two brothers outside"* (Gen. 9:22). *"The eye that mocks a father and scorns to obey a mother will be picked out by the ravens of the valley and eaten by the vultures"* (Prov. 30:17). *"Whoever curses his father or his mother shall be put to death"* (Exod. 21:17).
2. Disobedience, by which we show contempt toward their just commandments. *"Disobedient to parents"* (Rom. 1:30). *"Without self-control, brutal, not loving good"* (2 Tim. 3:3). The sins here include:

    a. To marry without the counsel and consent of parents. *"The sons of God saw that the daughters of man were attractive. And they took as their wives any they chose"* (Gen. 6:2). *"Now Esau saw that Isaac had blessed Jacob and sent him away to Paddan-aram to take a wife from there, and that as he blessed him he directed him, 'You must not take a wife from the Canaanite women' .... Esau went to Ishmael and took as his wife, besides the wives he had, Mahalath the daughter of Ishmael, Abraham's son, the sister of Nebaioth"* (Gen. 28:6, 9).

    b. The 'eye-service' of servants. *"Slaves, obey in everything those who are your earthly masters, not by way of eye-service, as people-pleasers, but with sincerity of heart, fearing the Lord"* (Col. 3:22). *"Not by the way of eye-service, as people-pleasers"* (Eph. 6:6).

    c. Answering back when reprimanded. *"Slaves are to be submissive to their own masters in everything; they are to be well-pleasing, not argumentative"* (Titus 2:9).

d. Deceitfulness and wasting of their master's goods. *"Not pilfering, but showing all good faith"* (Titus 2:10).

e. To flee from the power of their superior. *"Then Sarai dealt harshly with her, and she fled from her"* (Gen. 16:6).

f. To resist the lawful authority of their superiors (1 Pet. 2:20).

g. To obey them in things unlawful (Acts 4:19).

h. To set themselves above their superiors: this is the sin of Antichrist. *"The man of lawlessness .... who opposes and exalts himself against every so-called god or object of worship"* (2 Thess. 2:3–4).

i. Lastly, the freedom of the Papists, by which they free children from the rule of their parents and subjects from the authority of their princes, so that they make it lawful for them to seek their own deaths. *"Then said Abishai to David, 'God has given your enemy into your hand this day. Now please let me pin him to the earth with one stroke of the spear, and I will not strike him twice.' But David said to Abishai, 'Do not destroy him, for who can put out his hand against the LORD's anointed and be guiltless?'"* (1 Sam. 26:8–9).

3. Ingratitude and lack of loving affection towards parents. *"But you say, 'If anyone tells his father or his mother, "What you would have gained from me is given to God," he need not honour his father.' So for the sake of your tradition you have made void the word of God."* (Matt. 15:5–6. See also 1 Tim. 5:4).

Secondly, we offend against our equals in preferring ourselves before them, in talking or in sitting down. *"Then the mother of the sons of Zebedee came up to him with her sons, and kneeling before him she asked him for something. And he said to her, 'What do you want?' She said to him, 'Say that these two sons of mine are to sit, one at your right hand and one at your left, in your kingdom' .... And when the ten heard it, they were indignant at the two brothers"* (Matt. 20:20-21, 24).

Thirdly, toward our inferiors:

1. Through negligence in governing them and providing for their wellbeing. *"Is it a time for you yourselves to dwell in your panelled*

houses, while this house lies in ruins?" (Hag. 1:4, Dan. 3:28). This condemns those mothers who give their children to be nursed by others, though they have both sufficient strength and store of milk themselves. *"If she has brought up children"* (1 Tim. 5:10).

2. By too much gentleness and leniency in correcting them. *"Now Adonijah the son of Haggith exalted himself, saying, "I will be king." And he prepared for himself chariots and horsemen, and fifty men to run before him. His father had never at any time displeased him by asking, 'Why have you done thus and so?'"* (1 Kings 1:5–6) *"Now Eli was very old, and he kept hearing all that his sons were doing to all Israel, and how they lay with the women who were serving at the entrance to the tent of meeting. And he said to them, 'Why do you do such things? For I hear of your evil dealings from all the people. No, my sons; it is no good report that I hear the people of the LORD spreading abroad. If someone sins against a man, God will mediate for him, but if someone sins against the LORD, who can intercede for him?' But they would not listen to the voice of their father, for it was the will of the LORD to put them to death."* (1 Sam. 2:22–25).
3. By overt cruelty and threats. *"Fathers, do not provoke your children to anger .... Masters, do the same to them, and stop your threatening"* (Eph. 6:4, 9).

Fourthly (and lastly), a man offends against himself when through his wicked behaviour he obscures and almost extinguishes those gifts which God has given him (Matt. 25:2, 16). Or, on the contrary, when he is conceited and too wise in his eyes. *"For by the grace given to me I say to everyone among you not to think of himself more highly than he ought to think, but to think with sober judgement"* (Rom. 12:3).

Chapter Twenty Five

THE SIXTH COMMANDMENT

Thus far we have spoken of the commandments of the first Table of the Law. Now follows the second Table, which concerns the love of our neighbour.

> *You shall not murder.* (Exod. 20:13)

The Resolution

Murder. Here part of the matter stands for the whole, for killing signifies any kind of injury to our neighbour.

The justice of this commandment appears by this, that man was created after the likeness of God. *"Whoever sheds the blood of man, by man shall his blood be shed, for God made man in his own image"* (Gen. 9:6). Again, all men are the same flesh. *"When you see the naked, to cover him, and not to hide yourself from your own flesh?"* (Isa. 58:7).

Neither ought we to be ignorant that it is unlawful for any private person to kill another, though a public officer may if it is warranted by a calling. Thus Moses, *"He looked this way and that, and seeing no one, he struck down the Egyptian and hid him in the sand"* (Exod. 2:12). *"He supposed that his brothers would understand that God was giving them salvation by his hand, but they did not understand"* (Acts 7:25). And Phineas. *"And went after the man of Israel into the chamber and pierced both of them, the man of Israel and the woman through her belly. Thus the plague on the people of Israel was stopped .... Phinehas the son of Eleazar, son of Aaron the priest, has turned back my wrath from the people of Israel, in that he was jealous with my jealousy among them, so that I did not consume the people of Israel in my jealousy"* (Num. 25:8, 11). And Elijah, *"And Elijah said to them, "Seize the prophets of Baal; let not one of them escape." And they seized them. And Elijah brought them down to the brook Kishon and slaughtered them there"* (1 Kings 18:40). And soldiers in battles waged upon just causes. *"Do not be afraid and do not be dismayed at this great horde, for the battle is not yours but God's."* (2 Chron. 20:15).

The negative part: *You shall not hurt or hinder either your own or your neighbour's life.*

The sins relating to this commandment are such as are committed against our neighbour, or against ourselves.

Against our neighbour are the following:

1. In heart:
   a. Hatred against him. *"Everyone who hates his brother is a murderer"* (1 John 3:15).
   b. Unadvised anger. *"But I say to you that everyone who is angry with his brother will be liable to judgement"* (Matt. 5:22).
   c. Envy. *"They are full of envy, murder, strife, deceit, maliciousness"* (Rom. 1:29).
   d. Grudges. *"But if you have bitter jealousy and selfish ambition in your hearts, do not boast and be false to the truth"* (James 3:14).
   e. Lack of compassion or sorrow at our neighbours' calamities. *"Who sing idle songs to the sound of the harp, etc. .... but are not grieved over the ruin of Joseph!"* (Amos 6:5-6).
   f. Stubbornness, when we will not be reconciled to our neighbour. *"unforgiving, unmerciful"* (Rom. 1:31 NJKV).
   g. Desire of revenge. *"The LORD abhors the bloodthirsty and deceitful man"* (Psalm 5:6).
2. In words:
   a. Bitterness in speaking. *"There is one whose rash words are like sword thrusts, but the tongue of the wise brings healing"* (Prov. 12:18).
   b. Reproach and railing, which is a casting of a man's sins which he has committed in his teeth, or an objecting to some inherent infirmities in him, *"But I say to you that*

everyone who is angry with his brother will be liable to judgment; whoever insults his brother will be liable to the council; and whoever says, 'You fool!' will be liable to the hell of fire" (Matt. 5:22). *"As the ark of the LORD came into the city of David, Michal the daughter of Saul looked out of the window and saw King David leaping and dancing before the LORD, and she despised him in her heart .... But Michal the daughter of Saul came out to meet David and said, 'How the king of Israel honoured himself today, uncovering himself today before the eyes of his servants' female servants, as one of the vulgar fellows shamelessly uncovers himself!'"* (2 Sam. 6:16, 20).

c. Contention when two or more argue with one another for any kind of superiority.

d. Brawling in any meeting.

e. Shouting, which is an unseemly elevation of the voice against one's adversary. *"Now the works of the flesh are evident: sexual immorality, impurity, sensuality"* (Gal. 5:19). *"Let all bitterness and wrath and anger and clamour and slander be put away from you, along with all malice. Be kind to one another, tenderhearted, forgiving one another, as God in Christ forgave you"* (Eph. 4:31–32). *"[Ishmael] shall be a wild donkey of a man, his hand against everyone and everyone's hand against him, and he shall dwell over against all his kinsmen."* (Gen. 16:12)

f. Complaints against everyone who offer us injuries. *"Do not grumble against one another, brothers, so that you may not be judged"* (James 5:9).

3. All signs of countenance and gesture that express malicious affections lurking in the heart. *"So Cain was very angry, and his face fell. The LORD said to Cain, 'Why are you angry, and why has your face fallen?'* (Gen. 4:5–6). *"And those who passed by derided him, wagging their heads"* (Matt. 27:39). Hence, derision is termed persecution. *"But Sarah saw the son of Hagar the Egyptian, whom she had borne to Abraham, laughing"* (Gen. 21:9). *"He who was born according to the flesh persecuted him who was born according to the Spirit"* (Gal. 4:29).

4. In deeds:
   a. To fight with, or to beat and maim our neighbour. *"If anyone injures his neighbour, as he has done it shall be done to him, fracture for fracture, eye for eye, tooth for tooth; whatever injury he has given a person shall be given to him"* (Lev. 24:19–20).
   b. To procure the death of our neighbour in any way, whether by the sword, famine, or poison. *"Cain rose up against his brother Abel and killed him"* (Gen. 4:8).
   c. To exercise tyrannous cruelty in inflicting punishments, *"Forty stripes may be given him, but not more, lest, if one should go on to beat him with more stripes than these, your brother be degraded in your sight"* (Deut. 25:3). *"Five times I received at the hands of the Jews the forty lashes less one"* (2 Cor. 11:24).
   d. To treat any of God's creatures harshly. *"Whoever is righteous has regard for the life of his beast, but the mercy of the wicked is cruel"* (Pro. 12:10). *"If you come across a bird's nest in any tree or on the ground, with young ones or eggs and the mother sitting on the young or on the eggs, you shall not take the mother with the young. You shall let the mother go, but the young you may take for yourself, that it may go well with you, and that you may live long"* (Deut. 22:6–7).
   e. To take opportunity offered by our neighbours infirmities to treat him discourteously, to make him our laughing stock, or to make recreation of taunting him, *"You shall not curse the deaf or put a stumbling block before the blind, but you shall fear your God: I am the LORD"* (Lev. 19:14). *"And while he was going up on the way, some small boys came out of the city and jeered at him, saying, 'Go up, you baldhead! Go up, you baldhead!'"* (2 Kings 2:23).
   f. To injure the impotent, feeble, poor, strangers, fatherless, or widows. *"You shall not wrong a sojourner or oppress him, for you were sojourners in the land of Egypt. You shall not mistreat any widow or fatherless child .... and you shall not exact interest from him"* (Exod. 22:21–22, 25).

We injure in these ways:

i. If we refuse to pay the labourer his wages. *"You shall not oppress a hired servant who is poor and needy, whether he is one of your brothers or one of the sojourners who are in your land within your towns. You shall give him his wages on the same day, before the sun sets (for he is poor and counts on it), lest he cry against you to the LORD, and you be guilty of sin"* (Deut. 24:14–15).

ii. If we do not fulfil a pledge of the poor. *"If ever you take your neighbour's cloak in pledge, you shall return it to him before the sun goes down, for that is his only covering, and it is his cloak for his body; in what else shall he sleep? And if he cries to me, I will hear, for I am compassionate"* (Exod. 22:26–27).

iii. If we take food from the poor. *"The people curse him who holds back grain, but a blessing is on the head of him who sells it"* (Prov. 11:26).

Again, this law is as effectively transgressed by not killing—as when the law charges to kill but we pardon the punishment due to murder—as by killing when we should not. *"But if he struck him down with an iron object, so that he died, he is a murderer. The murderer shall be put to death .... no atonement can be made for the land for the blood that is shed in it, except by the blood of the one who shed it"* (Num. 35:16, 33).

This passage also makes dueling or hand to hand combat for the deciding of controversies utterly unlawful:

1. Because this is not a means ordained by God to determine controversies.
2. Because it often happens in such contests that the conqueror before man is the one who is guilty before God.

This also condemns Popish sanctuaries and places of privilege, such as churches and the like, where murderers shelter and shroud themselves from the danger of the law. For God expressly commands: *"But if a man wilfully attacks another to kill him by cunning, you shall take him from my altar, that he may die"* (Exod. 21:14) And Joab, *"Joab has fled to the tent of the LORD, and behold, he is beside the altar ... Benaiah the son of*

Jehoiada went up and struck him down and put him to death. And he was buried in his own house in the wilderness" (1 Kings 2:29, 34)

Likewise, such things as concern the soul of our neighbour belong here:

1. To be a scandal or offence to the soul of our neighbour, either in life or doctrine. *"Woe to the world because of offences! For offences must come, but woe to that man by whom the offence comes!"* (Matt. 18:7 NKJV).
2. To produce occasions of strife and discord. We do this when:
   a. We cannot be brought to forego some of our own rights.
   b. We return snappish and crooked answers.
   c. We interpret everything amiss and take them in the worst part. *"Nabal is his name, and folly is with him"* (1 Sam. 25:25). *"But the princes of the Ammonites said to Hanun their lord, "Do you think, because David has sent comforters to you, that he is honouring your father? Has not David sent his servants to you to search the city and to spy it out and to overthrow it?" So Hanun took David's servants and shaved off half the beard of each and cut off their garments in the middle, at their hips, and sent them away"* (2 Sam. 10:3).
3. The minister's sin against their neighbours is this: to not preach the word of God to those charged to them, that they might thereby be instructed in the ways of life. *"Where there is no prophetic vision the people cast off restraint, but blessed is he who keeps the law"* (Prov. 29:18). *"His watchmen are blind; they are all without knowledge; they are all silent dogs; they cannot bark, dreaming, lying down, loving to slumber. The dogs have a mighty appetite; they never have enough. But they are shepherds who have no understanding; they have all turned to their own way, each to his own gain, one and all"* (Isa. 56:10–11). *"If I say to the wicked, 'You shall surely die,' and you give him no warning, nor speak to warn the wicked from his wicked way, in order to save his life, that wicked person shall die for his iniquity, but his blood I will require at your hand"* (Ezek. 3:18).

   It is not only sinful to not preach at all, but also to preach negligently. *"Cursed is he who does the work of the LORD with slackness, and cursed is he who keeps back his sword from bloodshed"* (Jer. 48:10). *"So, because you are lukewarm, and neither hot nor cold, I will spit you out of my mouth"* (Rev. 3:16). This condemns the non-residency of ministers from the particular congregation committed to him. *"On your walls, O Jerusalem, I have set watchmen; all the day and all the night they shall never be silent. You who put the LORD in remembrance, take no rest, and give him no rest until he establishes Jerusalem and makes it a praise in the earth"* (Isa. 62:6). *"Pay careful attention to yourselves and to all the flock, in which the Holy Spirit has made you overseers, to care for the church of God, which he obtained with his own blood. I know that after my departure fierce wolves will come in among you, not sparing the flock; and from among your own selves will arise men speaking twisted things, to draw away the disciples after them. Therefore be alert, remembering that for three years I did not cease night or day to admonish everyone with tears"* (Act 20:28–31). *"Shepherd the flock of God that is among you, exercising oversight, not under compulsion, but willingly, as God would have you; not for shameful gain, but eagerly; not domineering over those in your charge, but being examples to the flock"* (1 Pet. 5:2–3; Ezek. 34:4, 33).

Likewise, the judgement of many church councils. The Council of Antioch: *"If any Bishop is inducted into a charge by imposition of hands, and appointed to govern a people, and if he neglects to take that office upon himself, but delays to go to the congregation allotted to him, such a man shall be prohibited from the Lord's table until he attends upon his charge, or otherwise as shall be determined by a complete assembly of the Ministers of that province."*[1] The Council of Sardice: *"We remember that our brethren in a former assembly decreed that if any layman remaining three Sabbaths or Lord's days (three weeks) in a city did not frequent the church assemblies in that city, he should be excommunicated. If then such things are not allowable in laymen, much less in ministers, for whom it is neither lawful nor appropriate to be absent from his parish Church longer then the time above mentioned (without urgent necessity). Not one man was*

1. The Council of Antioch, canon 17.

displeased with this decree, but every one said, 'it likes us well'."[2] The council held at Constantinople decreed that: *"ministers ought not to have substitutes or vicars, but should themselves perform all duties that are required of them in the service of God with fear and cheerfulness."*[3] The Canon Law concludes the same thing: *"The Bishops* (says the Canon) *ought to be continually resident in God's tabernacle so that they may learn somewhat of God and his people, whilst they read often and meditate upon God's word."*[4] Again, in the canons entitled 'Pontifices': *"The Bishops which take upon them to feed God's flock, ought not to depart from their duty, lest they lose that excellent talent which God has bestowed upon them. Rather they must strive with that one talent, to get three more."*[5] And in those which are termed the 'Canons of the Apostles', there is an express mandate: *"whether Bishop or Senior, anyone who does not attend upon their office in the Church shall forthwith be removed from that place."*[6] The Chalcedonian Council: *"Let no man be ordained a minister of two churches in two different cities, but let him remain in that to which he was first called. And if for vainglory he shall afterwards go to a greater congregation, let him immediately be recalled to his first charge and exercise his ministry in that only. But if he is called to another charge, let him simply give over the former and have no further position in it..."*.[7]

These testimonies notwithstanding, there are some cases in which it is permitted for the minister to be absent, if by his absence the congregation will not be damaged:

a. Sickness: *"If a Bishop is not at home, or is sick, or cannot be present at his parish, let him procure someone qualified to preach to his charge upon Sabbaths and festival days."*[8] Augustine testifies that he was absent on such an occasion.[9]

---

2. The Council of Sardice, canon 34.
3. The Council of Constantinople, canon 24.
4. Canon 36.
5. Canons entitled *Pontifices*.
6. *Canons of the Apostles*, canon 80.
7. The Chalcedon Council, canon 10. See further the Decrees of Damascus, and the Council of Trent, 7.8.
8. Counsel of Mentz, canon 25.
9. Augustine, Letter 138.

b. Allowance by the Church to be absent for a time for some necessary and public service. *"Epaphras our beloved fellow servant. He is a faithful minister of Christ on your behalf"* (Col. 1:7), but being absent he *"greets them"* (4:12). And Ambrose, whilst he was Bishop of Milan, went to France twice as an ambassador to make agreement between Maximus and Valentinian.[10]

c. If he is forced to flee persecution and sees no hope to procure the safety of his people. This led Cyprian to be absent from Carthage, as he testifies in his epistles.

Thus much concerning sins against our neighbour.

Now follow Sins which a Man Commits Against his own Person, as when he hurts, kills, or endangers himself. *"If anyone would come after me, let him deny himself and take up his cross and follow me"* (Matt. 16:24). *"(He) said to him, 'If you are the Son of God, throw yourself down, for it is written,' 'He will command his angels concerning you,' and 'On their hands they will bear you up, lest you strike your foot against a stone.' Jesus said to him, 'Again it is written, 'You shall not put the Lord your God to the test'"* (Matt. 4:6–7). Therefore, for a man to commit suicide—even to escape a most shameful death—is utterly unlawful and ungodly.

The affirmative part: *You shall preserve the life of your neighbour*

Here may we refer these duties:

1. Such as appertain to the person of our neighbour. These concern:
   a. His welfare, both of body and mind, such as to rejoice with them who rejoice. *"And he said to him, "Teacher, all these I have kept from my youth." And Jesus, looking at him, loved him, and said to him, 'You lack one thing: go, sell all that you have and give to the poor, and you will have treasure in heaven; and come, follow me.'"* (Mark 10:20-21).
   b. His miseries, to be grieved for with them. *"Rejoice with those who rejoice, weep with those who weep"* (Rom. 12:15). *"But I*

10. Ambrose, 5.27 (Letter to Valentinian).

say, 'I waste away, I waste away. Woe is me! For the traitors have betrayed, with betrayal the traitors have betrayed'" (Isa. 24:16). *"My eyes shed streams of tears, because people do not keep your law"* (Psalm 119:136). Again, we must help him as much as we are able. *"I was eyes to the blind and feet to the lame"* (Job 29:15). *"For they gave according to their means, as I can testify, and beyond their means, of their own accord"* (2 Cor. 8:3). And we must do this speedily. *"Do not say to your neighbour, 'Go, and come again, tomorrow I will give it'—when you have it with you"* (Prov. 3:28). *"You shall reason frankly with your neighbour, lest you incur sin because of him"* (Lev. 19:17).

c. Concerning such injuries as he does to us:

   i. You shall not be angry against him, except upon a small occasion. *"Now the man Moses was very meek, more than all people who were on the face of the earth"* (Num. 12:3). *"Good sense makes one slow to anger, and it is his glory to overlook an offence"* (Prov. 19:11).

   ii. You must be slow to wrath and never angry, except for a most just cause. *"And he looked around at them with anger, grieved at their hardness of heart"* (Mark 3:5). *"Whoever is slow to anger has great understanding, but he who has a hasty temper exalts folly"* (Prov. 14:29).

   iii. Your anger must only be but for a while. *"Be angry and do not sin; do not let the sun go down on your anger"* (Eph. 4:26).

   iv. Forgive an injury freely and do not take revenge. *"Be kind to one another, tenderhearted, forgiving one another, as God in Christ forgave you"* (Eph. 4:32).

d. His lack and infirmities:

   i. Avoid occasions by which they may be stirred and laid open. *"Then Abram said to Lot, 'Let there be no strife between you and me, and between your herdsmen and my herdsmen, for we are kinsmen. Is not the whole land before you? Separate yourself from me. If you take the left hand, then I will go to the right, or if you take the right hand, then I will go to the left'"* (Gen. 13:8–9). *"And stay with him a while, until your brother's fury turns away—until your brother's anger turns away from you, and he forgets what you have done to him. Then I will send and bring you from there. Why should I be bereft of you both in one day?"* (Gen. 27:44–45).

ii. Forego your own rights sometimes. *"'What do you think, Simon? From whom do kings of the earth take toll or tax? From their sons or from others?' And when he said, 'From others,' Jesus said to him, 'Then the sons are free.' However, not to give offense to them, go to the sea and cast a hook and take the first fish that comes up, and when you open its mouth you will find a shekel. Take that and give it to them for me and for yourself"* (Matt. 17:25–26).

iii. To appease anger when it is kindled, which is done:

1. By overcoming evil with goodness. *"Do not be overcome by evil, but overcome evil with good"* (Rom. 12:21).
2. By seeking peace. *"Let him turn away from evil and do good; let him seek peace and pursue it"* (1 Pet. 3:11).
3. By courteous answers. *"A soft answer turns away wrath, but a harsh word stirs up anger"* (Prov. 15:1). *"And Eli said to her, 'How long will you go on being drunk? Put your wine away from you.' But Hannah answered, 'No, my lord, I am a woman troubled in spirit. I have drunk neither wine nor strong drink, but I have been pouring out my soul before the LORD'"* (1 Sam. 1:14–15). *"For this perhaps is why he was parted from you for a while, that you might have him back forever"* (Philem. 15).
4. By overlooking some deficiencies and frailness in mens' words and deeds. *"And it is his glory to overlook an offence"* (Prov. 19:11).
5. By covering them with silence. *"Above all, keep loving one another earnestly, since love covers a multitude of sins"* (1 Pet. 4:8). *"Whoever covers an offense seeks love, but he who repeats a matter separates close friends"* (Prov. 17:9).

6. By taking everything (if it is possible) in the best part. *"(Love) thinks no evil"* (1 Cor. 13:5 NKJV).

This shows the lawfulness of truces, covenants, and other agreements concerning peace which are made to avoid injuries, maintain ancient boundaries, procure security in traffic, possessions, and journeys, set pensions, commons for cattle, liberties of hunting, fishing, or fowling, or other necessities for the public good (so long as there be no unlawful conditions joined to them). And we may make this covenant not only with Christians but, for the maintenance of peace, with unbelievers also. For whatever is godly to be performed is no less godly to be promised. But it is a mark of true godliness to be at peace with all men as much as is possible. Therefore, to promise peace by covenant is very godly. We may see the experience of this in the lives of holy men. *"At that time Abimelech and Phicol the commander of his army said to Abraham, 'God is with you in all that you do. Now therefore swear to me here by God that you will not deal falsely with me or with my descendants or with my posterity, etc.' And Abraham said, 'I will swear.' .... So Abraham took sheep and oxen and gave them to Abimelech, and the two men made a covenant"* (Gen. 21:22–24, 27). *"Come now, let us make a covenant, you and I. And let it be a witness between you and me." So Jacob took a stone and set it up as a pillar .... Then Laban said to Jacob, "See this heap and the pillar, which I have set between you and me .... The God of Abraham and the God of Nahor, the God of their father, judge between us." So Jacob swore by the Fear of his father Isaac"* (Gen. 31:44–45, 51, 53).

2. Concerning his **Body**, we are to have due regard to it whether alive or dead. Being alive, if need be we ought:

    a. To minister to it food and clothing. *"Then he will say to those on his left, 'Depart from me, you cursed, into the eternal fire prepared for the Devil and his angels. For I was hungry and you gave me no food, I was thirsty and you gave me no drink,' etc. .... 'Truly, I say to you, as you did not do it to one of the least of these, you did not do it to me'"* (Matt. 25:41–42, 45).

    b. To lend our helping hand when our neighbour's body is in any danger. *"By this we know love, that he laid down his life for us, and we ought to lay down our lives for the brothers"* (1 John 3:16).

When a man is dead we ought to commit the dead corpse to the grave, as may appear by these arguments:

a. The instinct of nature itself.

b. The examples of the patriarchs and other holy persons. Abraham buried Sarah (Gen. 23:19), Jacob is buried by his sons (Gen. 50:12), Stephen by religious and devout men (Acts 8:2).

c. The Lord's own use of burial, in that he numbered it among his benefits. For lack of burial is a curse. *"Thus says the LORD concerning Jehoiakim ... 'with the burial of a donkey he shall be buried, dragged and dumped beyond the gates of Jerusalem'"* (Jer. 22:18–19). Therefore, rather than Moses not being buried, the Lord buried him: *"So Moses the servant of the LORD died there in the land of Moab, according to the word of the LORD, and he buried him in the valley in the land of Moab opposite Beth-peor; but no one knows the place of his burial to this day"* (Deut. 34:5–6).

d. There is no dead carcass so loathsome as man is. This proves both how necessary burial is, and how ugly we are in the sight of God because of sin.

e. The body must rise again out of the earth so that it may be made a perpetual dwelling for the soul to dwell in.

f. The bodies of the faithful are the temples of the Holy Spirit, and therefore must rise again to glory.

g. Burial is a testimony of the love and reverence we bear to the deceased.

A funeral ought to be conducted in an honest and civil manner: agreeable to those who remain alive, and honouring to them who is dead. Concerning the living, they must ensure that:

a. Their mourning is moderate, and such as expresses their affection and love to the party departed. *"And he said, 'Where have you laid him?' They said to him, 'Lord, come and see.' Jesus wept. So the Jews said, 'See how he loved him!'"* (John 11:34-36).

b. They must avoid superstition and not seek ceremonies for the dead. Such are the rites of the Church of Rome, such as to be buried in a Church, especially under the altar.

c. They ought to avoid superfluous pomp and solemnities. For of all exhibitions of pride, the most foolish is to boast of a loathsome and deformed corpse. *"Thus says the Lord God of hosts, "Come, go to this steward, to Shebna, who is over the household, and say to him: What have you to do here, and whom have you here, that you have cut out here a tomb for yourself, you who cut out a tomb on the height and carve a dwelling for yourself in the rock?"* (Isa. 22:15-16).

To this commandment belongs these duties:

a. Before vintage or harvest we ought to permit any man to gather grapes, or pluck off the ears of grain in the field for the repressing of hunger. *"If you go into your neighbour's vineyard, you may eat your fill of grapes, as many as you wish, but you shall not put any in your bag. If you go into your neighbour's standing grain, you may pluck the ears with your hand, but you shall not put a sickle to your neighbour's standing grain"* (Deut. 23:24-25). *"At that time Jesus went through the grainfields on the Sabbath. His disciples were hungry, and they began to pluck heads of grain and to eat, etc."* (Matt. 12:1).

b. In the vintage and time of harvest, we ought neither to leave the trees naked of grapes, nor rake up ears of corn after the reaping, but leave the gleanings for the poor. *"And when you reap the harvest of your land, you shall not reap your field right up to its edge, nor shall you gather the gleanings after your harvest. You shall leave them for the poor and for the sojourner: I am the LORD your God"* (Lev. 23:22). *"Then Boaz said to Ruth, "Now, listen, my daughter, do not go to glean in another field or leave this one, but keep close to my young women"* (Ruth 2:8).

3. Concerning the **Soul** of our neighbour:

   i. We must seek to win him to the profession of Christian religion by all means. *"Just as I try to please everyone in everything I do, not seeking my own advantage, but that of many, that they may be saved"* (1 Cor. 10:33). *"And let us consider how to stir up one another to love and good works"* (Heb. 10:24).

   ii. We must live among others without offence. *"Give no offence to Jews or to Greeks or to the church of God"* (1 Cor. 10:32). *"Therefore, if food makes my brother stumble, I will never eat meat, lest I make my brother stumble"* (1 Cor. 8:13).

   iii. The light of our good life must be as a lantern to direct the ways of our neighbours. *"But this I confess to you, that according to the Way, which they call a sect, I worship the God of our fathers, believing everything laid down by the Law and written in the Prophets, having a hope in God, which these men themselves accept, that there will be a resurrection of both the just and the unjust. So I always take pains to have a clear conscience toward both God and man"* (Acts 24:14).

   iv. If our neighbour offends, we are to admonish him. *"And we urge you, brothers, admonish the idle, encourage the fainthearted, help the weak, be patient with them all"* (1 Thess. 5:14).

   v. If our neighbour runs well in the ways of God's commandment (as David speaks) we ought to encourage him to thus continue.

4. This commandment also relates to things relating to the **Preservation** of each and every man's life:

   i. Recreation, which is an exercise joined with the fear of God and relating to activities indifferent,[11] for the preservation of

11. The term 'things indifferent' (*adiaphora*) referred to matters about which the Bible makes no explicit commands or prohibitions. In the realm of personal affairs they were therefore areas for freedom of conscience. However, in the realms of political and ecclesiastical affairs, *adiaphora* meant that those in authority could regulate as seemed best to them and that subjects were expected to conform.

bodily strength and confirmation of the mind in holiness. *"I said of laughter, 'It is mad,' and of pleasure, 'What use is it?'"* (Eccl. 2:2). *"They have lyre and harp, tambourine and flute and wine at their feasts, but they do not regard the deeds of the LORD, or see the work of his hands"* (Isa. 5:12). *"Do not be idolaters as some of them were; as it is written, 'The people sat down to eat and drink and rose up to play'"* (1 Cor. 10:7). *"Woe to you who laugh now, for you shall mourn and weep."* (Luke 6:25). *"And there you shall eat before the LORD your God, and you shall rejoice, you and your households, in all that you undertake, in which the LORD your God has blessed you"* (Deut. 12:7). To this end has the word of God permitted hunting. *"Also he bade them teach the children of Judah the use of the bow: behold, it is written in the book of Jasher"* (2 Sam. 1:18, KJV). And musical comfort. *"Besides their male and female servants, of whom there were 7,337. And they had 245 singers, male and female"* (Neh. 7:67). And putting forth of riddles. *"And Samson said to them, 'Let me now put a riddle to you. If you can tell me what it is, within the seven days of the feast, and find it out, then I will give you thirty linen garments and thirty changes of clothes, but if you cannot tell me what it is, then you shall give me thirty linen garments and thirty changes of cloThess.' And they said to him, 'Put your riddle, that we may hear it.' And he said to them, 'Out of the eater came something to eat. Out of the strong came something sweet.' And in three days they could not solve the riddle"* (Judges 14:12–14). *"Catch the foxes for us, the little foxes that spoil the vineyards, for our vineyards are in blossom"* (Song 2:15). Lastly, the contemplation of the works of God. *"He (Solomon) spoke of trees, from the cedar that is in Lebanon to the hyssop that grows out of the wall. He spoke also of beasts, and of birds, and of reptiles, and of fish"* (1 Kings 4:33).

ii. Medicine, the use of which is holy if, before receiving it, a person desires forgiveness of their sins and places their confidence in God alone and not upon the means. *"And behold, some people brought to him a paralytic, lying on a bed. And when Jesus saw their faith, he said to the paralytic,*

'Take heart, my son; your sins are forgiven.' .... Jesus said to him, 'Get up, take up your bed, and walk.' .... But that you may know that the Son of Man has authority on earth to forgive sins"—he then said to the paralytic—'Rise, pick up your bed and go home'" (Matt. 9:2, 6). *"One man was there who had been an invalid for thirty-eight years .... Afterwards Jesus found him in the temple and said to him, 'See, you are well! Sin no more, that nothing worse may happen to you'"* (John 5:5, 8, 14) *"In the thirty-ninth year of his reign Asa was diseased in his feet, and his disease became severe. Yet even in his disease he did not seek the LORD, but sought help from physicians"* (2 Chron. 16:12).

iii. Avoiding of an injury offered by some private person. If this is against an unruly and reckless adversary, and the defence is faultless, it is very lawful and so far from a private revenge that it is to be accounted a just defence. Thus, the defence is without fault when a man so assaults his adversary as has no intention for revenge or his enemy's harm, but only his safety from danger.

Question: May a man flee in a time of plague?[12]

Answer: Those who are hindered by their vocation may not, for example magistrates and pastors (who have charge of souls), yet free men who are not bound by the duties of their calling may flee. Reasons:

a. A man may provide for his own safety if it does not hinder another.

b. A man may flee wars, famine, floods, fire, and other such dangers, and therefore the plague also.

c. There is less danger of sickness when the number of people is diminished.

12. Outbreaks of plague occurred very regularly during the medieval and early modern periods. How Christians (and particularly Christian leaders) were to respond was an important pastoral question.

Objection 1: To flee is a sign of distrust.

> *Answer*: This confuses action and motive. In itself, fleeing is not a sign or distrust. Some will have good motives, others bad.

Objection 2: It is offensive.

> *Answer*: The offence is given, not taken.

Objection 3: To flee forsakes our neighbour and the rule of love.

> *Answer*: Not if others remain to help, such as kinsfolk and magistrates.

Objection 4: Men are to visit the sick by God's appointment.

> *Answer*: Lepers were an exception among the Jews, so likewise those infected with dangerous and contagious diseases today.

Chapter Twenty Six

THE SEVENTH COMMANDMENT

The seventh commandment shows how we may preserve our chastity and that of our neighbour. The words are these:

> *You shall not commit adultery*. (Exod. 20:14)

The Resolution

Adultery. To commit adultery means to do anything whereby the chastity of ourselves or our neighbours may be stained (Matt. 5:28).

The negative part: *You shall not hurt or hinder you neighbour's chastity in any way*

In this passage, the following are prohibited:

1. The lust of the heart, or the evil concupiscence[1] of the flesh. *"But I say to you that everyone who looks at a woman with lustful intent has already committed adultery with her in his heart"* (Matt. 5:28). *"Put to death therefore what is earthly in you: sexual immorality, impurity, passion, evil desire, and covetousness"* (Col. 3:5).
2. Inward fervent lust, whereby the godly motions of the heart are hindered, overwhelmed, and, as it were burnt up with contrary fire, *"But if they cannot exercise self-control, they should marry. For it is better to marry than to burn with passion"* (1 Cor. 7:9).
3. Strange sexual practices which are prohibited in the word of God, of which there are many:

---

1. Concupiscence refers to the sinful desire which in all human beings, as a result of Adam's Fall. It essentially means the same thing as Paul's use of the word 'flesh' (e.g. Romans 7; Galatians 5). See ***chapters 12 & 29***.

a. With animals. *"And you shall not lie with any animal and so make yourself unclean with it"* (Lev. 18:23).
b. With the Devil, as witches do by their own confession (since spirits eat with witches, we should assume that they also engage in such practices with them).
c. With one of the same sex. *"You shall not lie with a male as with a woman; it is an abomination"* (Lev. 18:22). This is a sin which those commit, whom God has given over to reprobate senses. *"For this reason God gave them up to dishonourable passions. For their women exchanged natural relations for those that are contrary to nature; and the men likewise gave up natural relations with women and were consumed with passion for one another, men committing shameless acts with men and receiving in themselves the due penalty for their error"* (Rom. 1:26–27). It was the sin of Sodom where it was so common that to this day it is termed 'sodomy' (Genesis 19).
d. With those who are within the degrees of blood relation prohibited in the word of God. *"None of you shall approach any one of his close relatives to uncover nakedness. I am the LORD"* (Lev. 18:6).
e. With unmarried persons. This sin is termed fornication. *"If a man meets a virgin who is not betrothed, and seizes her and lies with her, and they are found, then the man who lay with her shall give to the father of the young woman fifty shekels of silver, and she shall be his wife, because he has violated her. He may not divorce her all his days"* (Deut. 22:28–29). *"We must not indulge in sexual immorality as some of them did, and twenty-three thousand fell in a single day"* (1 Cor. 10: 8).
f. With one who is married or betrothed. This sin is called adultery. God has inflicted by his word the same punishment upon them who commit this sin after they are betrothed, as he does upon those who are already married. *"If a man is found lying with the wife of another man, both of them shall die, the man who lay with the woman, and the woman. So you shall purge the evil from Israel. "If there is a betrothed virgin, and a man meets her in the city and lies with her, then you shall bring them both out to the gate of that city, and you shall stone them to death with stones, the young woman because she did not cry for help though she was in*

the city, and the man because he violated his neighbour's wife. So you shall purge the evil from your midst" (Deut. 22:22–24).

That this is a very great sin is clear in that it shares the same punishment as idolatry. *"(They) exchanged the glory of the immortal God for images resembling mortal man, etc. .... Therefore God gave them up in the lusts of their hearts to impurity"* (Rom. 1:23–24). Indeed, this sin is more heinous than theft. *"People do not despise a thief if he steals to satisfy his appetite when he is hungry .... He who commits adultery lacks sense; he who does it destroys himself"* (Prov. 6:30, 32). Again, the adulterer breaks the covenant of marriage, which is God's covenant. *"Who forsakes the companion of her youth and forgets the covenant of her God"* (Prov. 2:17). Adulterers dishonour their own bodies. *"Flee from sexual immorality. Every other sin a person commits is outside the body, but the sexually immoral person sins against his own body"* (1 Cor. 6:18). They also bereave their neighbours of a great and unrecoverable benefit, namely their chastity.

As for children which are begotten in this way, they are shut out from that place which they might otherwise have obtained in the church. *"No one born of a forbidden union may not enter the assembly of the LORD. Even to the tenth generation, none of his descendants may enter the assembly of the LORD"* (Deut. 23:2). He makes his family a stench, as appears in David, whose adultery was punished by Absalom's lying with his father's concubines. *"Ahithophel said to Absalom, 'Go in to your father's concubines, whom he has left to keep the house, and all Israel will hear that you have made yourself a stench to your father, and the hands of all who are with you will be strengthened'"* (2 Sam. 16:21). *""If my heart has been enticed toward a woman, and I have lain in wait at my neighbour's door, then let my wife grind for another, and let others bow down on her"* (Job 31:9–10). Man's descendants feel the pain of this sin. *"For that (adultery) would be a fire that consumes as far as Abaddon, and it would burn to the root all my increase"* (Job 31:12). To conclude, though this sin might be committed ever so secretly, God will reveal it (Num. 5:12–23). And it usually has one of these two as companions: dullness of heart or a terrible horror of conscience. *"Whoredom, wine, and new wine, which take away the understanding"* (Hos. 4:11).

As for the patriarchs' polygamy, or marrying of many wives: although it cannot be defended, it may be excused, either because it served to the enlarging of the number of mankind when there were but few, or at the least to the propagation of the Church of God.

g. With man and wife. They abuse their freedom if they know each other when the woman is menstruating. *"In you men uncover their fathers' nakedness; in you they violate women who are unclean in their menstrual impurity"* (Ezek. 22:10). *"You shall not approach a woman to uncover her nakedness while she is in her menstrual uncleanness"* (Lev. 18:19), *"or approach a woman in her time of menstrual impurity"* (Ezek. 8:6). Ambrose says that he who uses wedlock without regard for decency and honesty commits adultery with his wife.[2] Jerome says: *"A wise man ought to rule his wife in judgement, not in affection. He will not give the bridle to headstrong pleasure, not headily company with his wife. Nothing* (he says) *is more shameless than to treat his wife as a prostitute."*[3]

h. Nocturnal emissions, which arise from immoderate diet or previous unchaste thoughts (Deut. 23:10). Onan's sin (Gen. 38:8) was not unlike these.

i. Self-abandonment to passions, by which occasions are sought to stir up lust. *"Now the works of the flesh are evident: sexual immorality, impurity, sensuality"* (Gal. 5:19). Of this kind are:

    i. Eyes full of adultery. *"They have eyes full of adultery, insatiable for sin"* (2 Pet. 2:14).

    ii. Idleness. *"It happened, late one afternoon, when David arose from his couch and was walking on the roof of the king's house, that he saw from the roof a woman bathing; and the woman was very beautiful. And David sent and inquired about the woman. And one said, "Is not this Bathsheba, the daughter of Eliam, the wife of Uriah the Hittite?" So David sent messengers and took her, and she came to him, and he lay with her"* (2 Sam. 11:2–4).

2. Ambrose, *Book of Philosophy*. Perkins notes that Augustine cites in his *Against Julian*, bk. 2.
3. Jerome, *Against Jovianus*, bk. 1.

iii. Extravagant and arousing attire. *"Likewise also that women should adorn themselves in respectable apparel, with modesty and self-control, not with braided hair and gold or pearls or costly attire, but with what is proper for women who profess godliness—with good works"* (1 Tim. 2:9–10). *"The LORD said: Because the daughters of Zion are haughty and walk with outstretched necks, glancing wantonly with their eyes, mincing along as they go, tinkling with their feet, therefore the Lord will strike with a scab the heads of the daughters of Zion, and the LORD will lay bare their secret parts. In that day the Lord will take away the finery of the anklets, the headbands, and the crescents; the pendants, the bracelets, and the scarves; the headdresses, the armlets, the sashes, the perfume boxes, and the amulets; the signet rings and nose rings; the festal robes, the mantles, the cloaks, and the handbags; the mirrors, the linen garments, the turbans, and the veils"* (Isa. 3:16–23). It is no wonder that the prophet is so firmly against excessive and wanton apparel, for it is:

1. A lavish and wasteful use of God's gifts, which might well have been put to better uses.
2. A testimony to pride, whereby a man would have himself be of greater reputation than another.
3. A sign of great idleness and sloth. For typically, those who spend much time in tricking and trimming themselves neglect other business.
4. Frivolous, in devising some new fashion every day, or imitating those fashions which others devise.
5. It makes a confusion of such degrees and callings as God has ordained whereby men of inferior degree and calling cannot be discerned from men of higher estate by their attire.[4]

iv. Excessive food, which provoke lust. *"Behold, this was the guilt of your sister Sodom: she and her daughters had pride,*

4. In early modern English society, clothing expressed a person's social rank and vocation. As such, dressing in fitting attire was regarded as part of maintaining peaceful social order, against radicals and revolutionaries. See further under 'Modesty', on page 207.

excess of food, and prosperous ease" (Ezek. 16:49). *"There was a rich man who was clothed in purple and fine linen and who feasted sumptuously every day"* (Luke 16:19). *"Let us walk properly as in the daytime, not in orgies and drunkenness, not in sexual immorality and sensuality, not in quarrelling and jealousy"* (Rom. 13:13).

v. Corrupt, dishonest and unseemly talk. *"Do not be deceived: "Bad company ruins good morals.""* (1 Cor. 15:33). Such are vain love songs, ballads, interludes, and amorous books. We must carefully shun this in the reading of poets, just as mariners do in navigation: they do not forsake not the sea, but flee from the rocks.

vi. Arousing representations of matters relating to love, as in plays and comedies. *"But sexual immorality and all impurity or covetousness must not even be named among you, as is proper among saints. Let there be no filthiness nor foolish talk nor crude joking, which are out of place"* (Eph. 5:3–4).

vii. Indecent and unseemly pictures (i.e. pornography). *"Abstain from every form of evil"* (1 Thess. 5:22).

viii. Arousing dancing of man and woman together. *"For when Herodias's daughter came in and danced, she pleased Herod and his guests"* (Mark 6:22).

ix. Company with self-indulgent persons. *"Let not your heart turn aside to her ways; do not stray into her paths"* (Prov. 7:25).

4. To appoint only light punishment for adultery, such as Romish Catholic judiciary does. For this is nothing else but to open a way for other lewd persons to run headlong into similar impiety.

The Affirmative part: *You shall preserve the chastity of your neighbour*

Chastity is the purity of soul and body in matters relating to sexuality. The mind is chaste when it is free, or at least freed from fleshly concupiscence. The body is chaste when it does not obey the concupiscence of the flesh.

"For this is the will of God, your sanctification: that you abstain from sexual immorality; that each one of you know how to control his own body in holiness and honour, not in the passion of lust like the Gentiles who do not know God" (1 Thess. 4:3–5). *"The unmarried or betrothed woman is anxious about the things of the Lord, how to be holy in body and spirit."* (1 Cor. 7:34).

There are two special virtues which preserve chastity: Modesty and Sobriety.

Modesty is a virtue which keeps a holy decorum or decency in each work. It is seen:

1. In the countenance and eyes, namely when they neither express nor excite the concupiscence of the heart. *"I have made a covenant with my eyes; how then could I gaze at a virgin?"* (Job 31:1). *"And Rebekah lifted up her eyes, and when she saw Isaac, she dismounted from the camel and said to the servant, "Who is that man, walking in the field to meet us?" The servant said, "It is my master." So she took her veil and covered herself"* (Gen. 24:64–65). *"She seizes him and kisses him, and with bold face she says to him, etc."* (Prov. 7:13).
2. In words: when a man's talk is decent when speaking of such things as we cannot but be ashamed of *"Now Adam knew Eve his wife, etc."* (Gen. 4:1). *"A Psalm of David, when Nathan the prophet went to him, after he had gone in to Bathsheba"* (Psalm. 51:1). *"In that day the Lord will shave with a razor that is hired beyond the River—with the king of Assyria—the head and the hair of the feet, and it will sweep away the beard also"* (Isa. 7:20). *"When he had gone, the servants came, and when they saw that the doors of the roof chamber were locked, they thought, 'Surely he is relieving himself in the closet of the cool chamber'"* (Jug. 3:24). Again, a man's words should be few and moderate. *"Behold, my servant whom I have chosen .... He will not quarrel or cry aloud, nor will anyone hear his voice in the streets"* (Matt. 12:18–19). *"When words are many, transgression is not lacking, but whoever restrains his lips is prudent"* (Prov. 10:19). It is a note of a harlot to be lewd and loud tongued. *"She is loud and wayward"* (Prov. 7:11). In apparel, we must observe a holy decency. *"Older women likewise are to be reverent in behaviour"* (Titus 2:3). Holy

Decency is that which expresses to the eye the sincerity of a man or woman, that is, their godliness, temperance, and gravity. This decency will more plainly appear if we consider the purposes of apparel, which number five:

a. Necessity, to the end that our body may be defended against the extremities of parching heat and pinching cold.
b. Honesty, that the deformity of our naked bodies might be covered, which immediately followed the transgression of our first parents.
c. Commodity, whereby men apparel themselves as befits their calling, work, and trade of life. Hence it is that some apparel is more decent for certain estates of men, than other.
d. Frugality, when a man's attire is proportionate to his ability and calling.
e. Distinction of persons, as of sex, ages, offices, times, and actions. For a man has his set attire, a woman hers, a young man apparelled on this fashion, an old man on that. Therefore, it is unseemly for a man to put on a woman's apparel, or a woman that of men. *"A woman shall not wear a man's garment, nor shall a man put on a woman's cloak, for whoever does these things is an abomination to the LORD your God"* (Deut. 22:5).

To set down precisely out of God's word what apparel is decent is very hard. Therefore, in this case, the judgement and practice of modest and sincere men, of every particular estate, is most to be followed. Men are better off to keep too far within such bounds than to step outside its precincts. Concerning the purging of excrement of nature, care must be had that they be set out some separate and secret place, and are also covered there. *""You shall have a place outside the camp, and you shall go out to it. And you shall have a trowel with your tools, and when you sit down outside, you shall dig a hole with it and turn back and cover up your excrement. Because the LORD your God walks in the midst of your camp, to deliver you and to give up your enemies before you, therefore your camp must be holy, so that he may not see anything indecent among you and turn away from*

> *you"* (Deut. 23:12–14). *"And he came to the sheepfolds by the way, where there was a cave, and Saul went in to relieve himself"* (1 Sam. 24:3).

Sobriety is a virtue, which concerns the use of our diet in holiness. For the better observation thereof, these rules may serve:

1. Let the head of the banquet consecrate the meal to God by saying grace. *"For the people will not eat till he (Samuel) comes, since he must bless the sacrifice; afterwards those who are invited will eat"* (1 Sam. 9:13). *"Then he commanded them all to sit down in groups on the green grass, etc. .... and taking the five loaves and the two fish he looked up to heaven and said a blessing"* (Mark 6:39, 41). *"And when he (Paul) had said these things, he took bread, and giving thanks to God in the presence of all he broke it and began to eat"* (Acts 27:35).
2. It is lawful to furnish a table with store of dishes, not only for necessity, but also for the good entertainment of a friend, and for delight. *"And Levi made him a great feast in his house, and there was a large company of tax collectors and others reclining at table with them"* (Luke 5:29). *"(The LORD gives) wine to gladden the heart of man, oil to make his face shine and bread to strengthen man's heart"* (Psalm 104:15). *"So they gave a dinner for him there. Martha served, and Lazarus was one of those reclining with him at table. Mary therefore took a pound of expensive ointment made from pure nard, and anointed the feet of Jesus and wiped his feet with her hair. The house was filled with the fragrance of the perfume"* (John 12:2–3).
3. Choose the lower place at a banquet, and sit as the master of the feast assigns you rather than be troublesome. *"Now he told a parable to those who were invited, when he noticed how they chose the places of honour, saying to them, "When you are invited by someone to a wedding feast, do not sit down in a place of honour, lest someone more distinguished than you be invited by him, and he who invited you both will come and say to you, 'Give your place to this person,' and then you will begin with shame to take the lowest place. But when you are invited, go and sit in the lowest place, so that when your host comes he may say to you, 'Friend, move up higher.' Then you will be honoured in the presence of all who sit at table with you"* (Luke 14:7–10). *"Do not put yourself forward in the king's presence or stand in the place of the great"* (Prov. 25:6).

4. Man must eat at due times, not at unseasonable hours. *"Woe to you, O land, when your king is a child, and your princes feast in the morning! Happy are you, O land, when your king is the son of the nobility, and your princes feast at the proper time, for strength, and not for drunkenness!"* (Eccl. 10:16–17).
5. Man must eat and drink moderately so that the body may thereby receive strength, and the soul be more fresh and lively to perform the actions of godliness. *"But watch yourselves lest your hearts be weighed down with dissipation and drunkenness and cares of this life"* (Luke 21:34). *"Who has woe? Who has sorrow? .... Do not look at wine when it is red, when it sparkles in the cup and goes down smoothly, etc."* (Prov. 23:29, 31). *"If you have found honey, eat only enough for you, lest you have your fill of it and vomit it"* (Prov. 25:16). *"It is not for kings, O Lemuel, it is not for kings to drink wine, or for rulers to take strong drink, lest they drink and forget what has been decreed and pervert the rights of all the afflicted"* (Prov. 31:4–5).
6. We must especially observe these things when we eat at great men's tables. *"When you sit down to eat with a ruler, observe carefully what is before you, and put a knife to your throat if you are given to appetite. Do not desire his delicacies, for they are deceptive food"* (Prov. 23:1–3).
7. Godly enjoyment at meals is permissible. *"They received their food with glad and generous hearts"* (Acts 2:46).
8. Table talk, as occasion offers, must be edifying. Such was Christ's talk at the Pharisees table (Luke 14:1–16).
9. See that after the banquet ends, the broken food is not lost but kept for later. *"And when they had eaten their fill, he told his disciples, 'Gather up the leftover fragments, that nothing may be lost'"* (John 6:12).
10. At a feast, leave some food for later. *"And she ate until she was satisfied, and she had some left over"* (Ruth 2:14).

Chastity is twofold: one of single life, another in wedlock.

They who are Single must:

1. Take great care to keep their affections and bodies in holiness. *"How can a young man keep his way pure? By guarding it according to your word"* (Psalm 119:9). *"I am writing to you, fathers, because you know him who is from the beginning. I am writing to you, young*

men, because you have overcome the evil one. I write to you, children, because you know the Father. I write to you, fathers, because you know him who is from the beginning. I write to you, young men, because you are strong, and the word of God abides in you, and you have overcome the evil one" (1 John 2:13–14). *"Remember also your Creator in the days of your youth, before the evil days come and the years draw near of which you will say, 'I have no pleasure in them'"* (Eccl. 12:1).

2. They must fast often. *"But I discipline my body and keep it under control, lest after preaching to others I myself should be disqualified"* (1 Cor. 9:27).
3. They must take heed not to burn in lust *"for it is better to marry than to burn with passion"* (1 Cor. 7:9).

Chastity in wedlock is when the holy and pure use of wedlock is observed. *"Let marriage be held in honour among all, and let the marriage bed be undefiled, for God will judge the sexually immoral and adulterous"* (Heb. 13:4). To preserve purity in wedlock, these cautions are profitable:

1. Marriage must be "in the Lord," and with a fellow believer only. *"Judah has been faithless, and abomination has been committed in Israel and in Jerusalem. For Judah has profaned the sanctuary of the LORD, which he loves, and has married the daughter of a foreign god"* (Mal. 2:11). *"But if her husband dies, she is free to be married to whom she wishes, only in the Lord"* (1 Cor. 7:39).
2. Both parties must separate themselves in the time of a woman's menstruation, and at appointed fasts (Ezek. 18:6), *"Do not deprive one another, except perhaps by agreement for a limited time, that you may devote yourselves to prayer; but then come together again, so that Satan may not tempt you because of your lack of self-control"* (1 Cor. 7:5).
3. Wedlock must be used to suppress, rather than to satisfy corrupt concupiscence of the flesh, and especially to enlarge the Church of God. *"But put on the Lord Jesus Christ, and make no provision for the flesh, to gratify its desires"* (Rom. 13:14).
4. It must be used with prayer and thanksgiving (1 Tim. 4:3–4).

Chapter Twenty Seven

THE EIGHTH COMMANDMENT

This Commandment concerns the preservation of our neighbour's goods. The words are these:

> *You shall not steal. (Exod. 20:15)*

The Resolution

Steal. To steal is to secretly take away anything from another. *"And Jacob stole away, unknown to Laban the Syrian"* (Gen. 31:20 NKJV*)*. In this passage it signifies the desire for that which belongs to another, to get it by fraud, and any way to impair his wealth.

The negative part: *You shall not fail to preserve, nor hinder or hurt your neighbour's goods*

In this passage these sins are forbidden:

1. Laziness, whether it be in no set vocation, or in idleness, wherein by neglecting their duties such persons misspend their time, goods, and revenues. *"For we hear that there are some which walk among you disorderly, working not at all, but are busybodies"* (2 Thess. 3:11). *"By the sweat of your face you shall eat bread, till you return to the ground, for out of it you were taken"* (Gen. 3:19). *"But if anyone does not provide for his relatives, and especially for members of his household, he has denied the faith and is worse than an unbeliever"* (1 Tim. 5:8).
2. Unjust dealing, which is either in Heart or Deed.

   Unjust dealing in heart is named covetousness. *"For out of the heart come evil thoughts, murder, adultery, sexual immorality, theft, false witness, slander, etc"* (Matt. 15:19). Covetousness is idolatry. *"For you may be sure of this, that everyone who is sexually immoral or impure, or who is covetous (that is, an idolater), has no inheritance in the kingdom of Christ and God"* (Eph. 5:5). Indeed, it is the very root of all kinds of evil, *"For the love of money is a root of all kinds of evils. It is through this craving that some have wandered away from the faith and pierced themselves with many pangs"* (1 Tim. 6:10).

Unjust dealing in Deed is within bargaining, or outside it. Unjust dealing in bargaining, has many branches. *"That no one transgress and wrong his brother in this matter, because the Lord is an avenger in all these things"* (1 Thess. 4:6).

a. To sell or bargain for what is not saleable. Of this kind:
    i. Is the gift of the Holy Spirit, which cannot be bought with money: *"Now when Simon saw that the Spirit was given through the laying on of the apostles' hands, he offered them money, saying, "Give me this power also, so that anyone on whom I lay my hands may receive the Holy Spirit." But Peter said to him, "May your silver perish with you, because you thought you could obtain the gift of God with money!"* (Acts 8:18–20).
    ii. Church goods are not for sale as private property. Therefore, it is not to be allowed for men to sell or alienate goods from the Church. *"It is a snare to say rashly, "It is holy," and to reflect only after making vows"* (Prov. 20:25; cf. Malachi 3:8). Church goods are the possession of the Lord.
    iii. Whatever is unprofitable either to the Church or commonwealth must not be sold.
b. All misrepresentation and deceit in bargaining. *"And Zacchaeus stood and said to the Lord, 'Behold, Lord, the half of my goods I give to the poor. And if I have defrauded anyone of anything, I restore it fourfold'"* (Luke 19:8). This deceit is used:
    i. When men sell that which is counterfeit for something good (e.g. copper for gold), and mingle bad with good whilst making show only of the good. *'Hear this, you who trample on the needy and bring the poor of the land to an end, etc. .... and sell the chaff of the wheat?'* (Amos 8:4–6).

   ii. When men falsify measures and weights. *""You shall not have in your bag two kinds of weights, a large and a small. You shall not have in your house two kinds of measures, a large and a small"* (Deut. 25:13–14). *""You shall do no wrong in judgment, in measures of length or weight or quantity. You shall have just balances, just weights, a just ephah, and a just hin"* (Lev. 10:35–36). *"Hear this, you who (are) 'When will the new moon be over, that we may sell grain? And the Sabbath, that we may offer wheat for sale, that we may make the ephah small and the shekel great and deal deceitfully?'"* (Amos 8:4–6).

c. When the buyer conceals the goodness of the thing, or the seller the faults of it, and covers over the truth with counterfeit speech. *"So whatever you wish that others would do to you, do also to them, for this is the Law and the Prophets"* (Matt. 7:12). *"Bad, bad," says the buyer, but when he goes away, then he boasts"* (Prov. 20:14).

d. When people are oppressed in buying and selling. And this is:

   i. When the just price of things is raised. For in bargaining, it is not lawful to take one penny without the giving of a penny's worth.

   ii. Sale upon a set day in order that the price may be raised. For what is this, I pray you, but to sell time, and to take more from our neighbour than is right?

   iii. To monopolise, which is to buy up all of one commodity into your own hands, so that when nobody has any, you may sell it at your own price.

   iv. To become bankrupt so that you may be enriched by the damages, and goods of other men.

   v. Not to return what was loaned to one, pledged to him, or found by him. *"(He) does not oppress anyone, but restores to the debtor his pledge, commits no robbery, etc."* (Ezek. 18:7).

vi. To delay any kind of restitution from one day to another. *"Do not say to your neighbour, "Go, and come again, tomorrow I will give it"—when you have it with you"* (Prov. 3:28). *"The wicked borrows but does not pay back, but the righteous is generous and gives"* (Psalm 37:21).

vii. To practise usury (Psalm 15:5) with those who have not put their money to usury. *"If you lend money to any of my people with you who is poor, you shall not be like a moneylender to him, and you shall not exact interest from him"* (Exod. 22:25).

Usury is a gain exacted by covenant, above the principle only in lieu, and recompense of the lending of it. Usury, considered as thus described, is contrary to God's word and may very fitly be termed harmful gain. *""If a man borrows anything of his neighbour, and it is injured or dies, the owner not being with it, he shall make full restitution. If the owner was with it, he shall not make restitution; if it was hired, it came for its hiring fee"* (Exod. 22:14–15). *"(He) does not lend at interest or take any profit, withholds his hand from injustice, executes true justice between man and man"* (Ezek. 18:8). *"For I do not mean that others should be eased and you burdened, but that as a matter of fairness your abundance at the present time should supply their need, so that their abundance may supply your need, that there may be fairness"* (2 Cor. 8:13). Positive laws not only restrain such usury but disallow it.

Question: Is it ever lawful to loan money at interest?

Answer: Yes, with these conditions:

1. If a man heeds that he exacts no repayment beyond what his debtor may attain by good and lawful means.
2. He may not take more than the gain, nor all the gain, nor that part of the gain which drinks up the living of him that uses the money.

3. He must sometimes be so far from taking gain that he must not require the principle, if his debtor is brought behind by inevitable and just casualties, and it is also plain that he could not make, even by great diligence, any commodity of the money borrowed.

The reasons why a man may take sometimes above the principle, are:

1. The creditor may safely receive where the debtor is able to give, having himself an honest gain besides what is repaid, and no man is disadvantaged in any way.
2. It is fitting that he who gains by money loaned to him should show all possible gratitude to him to his creditor by whom he has been enriched.
3. It is often to the benefit of the creditor to have the goods in his own hands which he loaned.

Objection: Money is not productive in itself, therefore it is unlawful to receive more then we loaned.

Answer: Although money is not productive in itself, yet it is made very fruitful by the borrower's good use of it, just as ground is not fruitful unless it is tilled.

viii. Last of all, when a man withholds the labourers wages. *"Behold, the wages of the labourers who mowed your fields, which you kept back by fraud, are crying out against you, and the cries of the harvesters have reached the ears of the Lord of hosts"* (James 5:4).

Unjust Dealing outside of bargaining is likewise manifold:

a. To pronounce false sentence or judgement for reward. *"Your princes are rebels and companions of thieves. Everyone loves a bribe and runs after gifts. They do not bring justice to the fatherless, and the widow's cause does not come to them"* (Isa. 1:23). This is the lawyers' and judges' sin.

b. To feed or clothe able-bodied rogues or beggars. *"For even when we were with you, we would give you this command: If anyone is not willing to work, let him not eat"* (2 Thess. 3:10). What then shall we think of those rogues and beggars licensed by authority, meaning all idle monks and abbey-lubbers? The *Tripartite History* says plainly that that the monk who does not labour with his hands is no better than a thief.

c. Gaming for money and gain. For you may not enrich yourself by impoverishing your brother. This gaming is far worse than usury, and far more greatly enriches a man in a short while.

d. To gain money by unlawful arts: magic, judicial astrology, stage-players, and similar. *"Let the thief no longer steal, but rather let him labour, doing honest work with his own hands, so that he may have something to share with anyone in need"* (Eph. 4:28). *"Abstain from every form of evil"* (1 Thess. 5:22). See also Deuteronomy 18:11, Ephesians 5:3.

e. To steal or pilfer the least pin or point from another. *"Do not steal, ... do not defraud"* (Mark 10:19). *"And why not do evil that good may come?—as some people slanderously charge us with saying. Their condemnation is just"* (Rom. 3:8).

f. To steal by moving land boundaries. *"Do not move the ancient landmark that your fathers have set"* (Prov. 22:28). *"The princes of Judah have become like those who move the landmark"* (Hos. 5:8).

g. To steal other men's servants or children, or to commit sacrilege or robbery. *"The sexually immoral, men who practice homosexuality, enslavers"* (1 Tim. 1:10). Achan's theft (Josh. 7:19). *"Nor thieves, nor the greedy, nor drunkards, nor revilers, nor swindlers will inherit the kingdom of God"* (1 Cor. 6:10). For robbery, these sorts of men especially are famous: thieves by the Queen's highways, pirates upon the seas, soldiers not content with their pay, and whosoever that by force takes that which is not their own. *"Soldiers also asked him, 'And we, what shall we do?' And he said to them, 'Do not extort money from anyone by threats or by false accusation, and be content with your wages'"* (Luke 3:14).

h. To conspire with a thief, whether by giving advice how he may accomplish his enterprise, or by sheltering him that he would not be punished. *"The partner of a thief hates his own life; he hears the curse, but discloses nothing"* (Prov. 29:24).

The punishment of the theft may sometimes be increased at the discretion of the Judge, as he sees the quality of the offence to be. Therefore, thieves are sometimes punished with death.

Now if any man objects that the judicial law of God only requires a fourfold restitution for such an offence, I answer that the civil magistrate, when he sees one or many offences increase, may by his authority increase the civil punishment due to that sin. Now it is clear that the sin of theft is far more grievous in our commonwealth than it was among the Jews. For first, the inhabitants of this commonwealth are generally far poorer than the Jews were. Therefore, to steal a thing even of some small value, does more harm to someone in this country than a thing of great value would have done the Jews.

Again, the people of this country are of a more stirring and fierce disposition. This makes thieves more outrageous, with their robbery joined with violence and the disturbance of the peace of the country. More regard is warranted, therefore, than one man's life alone.

The affirmative part: *You shall preserve and increase your neighbour's goods*

To this end, the following are required:

1. A certain vocation, wherein every man must invest himself honestly to his own and his neighbour's good, according to that gift which God has given him. *"So, brothers, in whatever condition each was called, there let him remain with God"* (1 Cor. 7:24; cf. Eph. 4:28). *"As each has received a gift, use it to serve one another, as good stewards of God's varied grace"* (1 Pet. 4:10). *"Through love serve one another"* (Gal. 5:13).
2. The true use of riches and all the goods a man has, to which belong two virtues: Contentment and Thrift.

   Contentment is a virtue whereby a man is well pleased with that estate in which he is placed. *"Now there is great gain in godliness with* *contentment, for we brought nothing into the world, and we cannot take anything out of the world. But if we have food and clothing, with these we will be content"* (1 Tim. 6:6–8). *"Not that I am speaking of being in need, for I have learned in whatever situation I am to be content"* (Phil. 4:11). *"Give us this day our daily bread"* (Matt. 6:11). *"Keep your life free from love of money, and be content with what you have, for he has said, "I will never leave you nor forsake you"* (Heb. 13:5).

Thrift (or frugality) is a virtue whereby a man carefully keeps his goods which he has gotten and employs them to such uses as are both necessary and profitable. *"Drink water from your own cistern, flowing water from your own well. Should your springs be scattered abroad, streams of water in the streets? Let them be for yourself alone, and not for strangers with you"* (Prov. 5:15–17). *"The plans of the diligent lead surely to abundance, ... Whoever loves pleasure will be a poor man; he who loves wine and oil will not be rich"* (Prov. 21:5, 17). *"Whoever is slothful will not roast his game, but the diligent man will get precious wealth"* (Prov. 12:27). See also John 6:12.

3. To speak the truth from the heart and to use a harmless simplicity in all affairs. *"He who walks blamelessly and does what is right and speaks truth in his heart"* (Psalm 15:2). *""My lord, listen to me: a piece of land worth four hundred shekels of silver, what is that between you and me? Bury your dead." Abraham listened to Ephron, and Abraham weighed out for Ephron the silver that he had named in the hearing of the Hittites, four hundred shekels of silver, according to the weights current among the merchants"* (Gen. 23:15–16).
4. Just dealings (1 Thess. 4:6). Of this there are many kinds:
   a. In buying and selling; in letting and hiring of farms, tenements, lands; in merchandise, and all manner of commodities: men must keep a just price. A just price is where the things prized and the price given for them are equal, as near as may be. For the observation of this equality, these four rules are to be considered, for by them all bargains must be ordered:
      i. There must be a proportion and equality in all contracts. Such will be the case when the seller only values the thing according to his own pains and costs bestowed upon it, but also sees what profit it may be to the buyer and in what need

he has of it. *"And if you make a sale to your neighbour or buy from your neighbour, you shall not wrong one another. You shall pay your neighbour according to the number of years after the jubilee, and he shall sell to you according to the number of years for crops. If the years are many, you shall increase the price, and if the years are few, you shall reduce the price, for it is the number of the crops that he is selling to you"* (Lev. 25:14–16).

ii. They must be in step with the law of nature, the sum thereof Christ propounds in these words: *"whatever you want others to do to you, do the same to them."*

iii. The bond of nature must be kept, which binds him that receives a benefit and makes a lawful gain of another man's goods, that being enriched he shall make a proportionate and natural recompense, even above the principle.

iv. Men must trade and make use of their goods with that caveat which Paul gives: not so as *"others should be eased and you burdened"*, nor the reverse (2 Cor. 8:13).

b. Men must only make sale of such things as are of value.

c. They must use just weights and measures. *"You shall not have in your bag two kinds of weights, a large and a small"* (Deut. 25:13). *"You shall have just balances, a just ephah, and a just bath"* (Ezek. 55:10). *"Shall I acquit the man with wicked scales and with a bag of deceitful weights?"* (Mic. 6:11).

d. He that hires anything must not only pay the appointed hire, but make that which he hired good, even by his default if necessary. *""If a man borrows anything of his neighbour, and it is injured or dies, ... he shall make full restitution, etc"* (Exod. 22:14–15).

e. The pledge ought to be redeemed. If it is of importance or necessity as something that preserves the life of our neighbour, it must be restored to him without condition. *"If ever you take your neighbour's cloak in pledge, you shall return it to him before the sun goes down, for that is his only covering"* (Exod. 22:26–27). *"No one shall take a mill or an upper millstone in pledge, for that would be taking a life (or living) in pledge"* (Deut. 24:6). Neither may a man in a pledge choose for himself, but he must take what is offered. *"When you make your neighbour a loan of any sort, you shall not go into his house to collect his pledge. You shall stand outside, and the man to whom you make the loan shall bring the pledge out to you. And if he is a poor man, you shall not sleep in his pledge"* (Deut. 24:10-12).

f. Only men who are honest and very well-known may be guarantors of loans, and that warily with much deliberation. *"Whoever puts up security for a stranger will surely suffer harm, but he who hates striking hands in pledge is secure"* (Prov. 11:15). *"One who lacks sense gives a pledge and puts up security in the presence of his neighbour"* (Prov. 17:18, see also Prov. 22:26). But if a man has entangled himself by suretyship, the best way out is to seek his creditors favour, whether by his own humble suite and that of his friends. *"My son, if you have put up security for your neighbour, have given your pledge for a stranger, if you are snared in the words of your mouth, caught in the words of your mouth, then do this, my son, and save yourself, for you have come into the hand of your neighbour: go, hasten, and plead urgently with your neighbour. Give your eyes no sleep and your eyelids no slumber"* (Prov. 6:1-4).

g. All just covenants, contracts and promises—though they be to our disadvantage—must be performed. For a promise is binding, if it is lawful, so far as the one to whom we make the promise insists on it. *"Who swears to his own hurt and does not change"* (Psalm 15:4). *"Like clouds and wind without rain is a man who boasts of a gift he does not give"* (Prov. 25:14). *"And the spies saw a man coming out of the city, and they said to him, "Please show us the way into the city, and we will deal kindly with you." And he showed them the way into the city. And they struck the city with the edge of the sword, but they let the man and all his family go"* (Jug. 1:24–25). Therefore, if after a promise is made, a man sees that he shall be damaged by it or hindered in its fulfilment, he may crave release, and accept it if granted.

h. To lend freely. *"But love your enemies, and do good, and lend, expecting nothing in return, and your reward will be great"* (Luke 6:35). And when we borrow, we must be careful to make restitution, even with the sale of our own goods, if need be. In 2 Kings 4:2-7, the wife of the sons of the prophets sells her oil which God sent by the hand of Elisha, to pay her creditor.

i. To restore that which is committed to our custody without delay. *"He will put those wretches to a miserable death and let out the vineyard to other tenants who will give him the fruits in their seasons"* (Matt. 21:41; cf. Prov. 3:28). But if such a thing is lost for reasons not of our doing, we are not urged to repay it. *"If a man gives to his neighbour money or goods to keep safe, and it is stolen from the man's house, then, if the thief is found, he shall pay double. If the thief is not found, the owner of the house shall come near to God to show whether or not he has put his hand to his neighbour's property"* (Exod. 22:7–8).

j. That which a man finds may be kept by him if the true owner cannot be found. But if he is found, it must be restored. *""You shall not see your brother's ox or his sheep going astray and ignore them. You shall take them back to your brother. And if he does not live near you and you do not know who he is, you shall bring it home to your house, and it shall stay with you until your brother seeks it. Then you shall restore it to him. And you shall do the same with his donkey or with his garment, or with any lost thing of your brother's, which he loses and you find; you may not ignore it"* (Deut. 22:1–3).

k. To get our own we may sue our neighbour in law, if we cannot do otherwise. But we must conduct our suits in a holy manner, and with these circumstances:

    i. In all suits, we must not do anything that may defame the Christian religion. Therefore, all suitors in law offend when they trust more in man than in God, and make their religion a mockery to worldlings, partly by striving about things of little importance and partly by not allowing any conditions for reconciliation. *"When one of you has a grievance against another, does he dare go to law before the unrighteous instead of the saints?"* (1 Cor. 6:1).

    ii. Law must be the last remedy, as a desperate medicine is the last remedy the physician uses. We must consider all means possible before we use this, especially with a brother. *"To have lawsuits at all with one another is already a defeat for you. Why not rather suffer wrong? Why not rather be defrauded?"* (1 Cor. 6:7).

iii. In all suits of law we must be mindful of the law of charity, and not so much endeavour to maintain our own right as to recall our brother (who errs) to the right way.

Chapter Twenty Eight

THE NINETH COMMANDMENT

The ninth commandment belongs to the preservation of our neighbour's good name. The words are these:

> *You shall not bear false witness against your neighbour.* (Exod. 20:16)

The Resolution

You shall not bear. That is, answer when you are asked before a Judge. *"Then both parties to the dispute shall appear before the LORD, before the priests and the judges who are in office in those days. The judges shall inquire diligently, and if the witness is a false witness and has accused his brother falsely"* (Deut. 19:17).

Witness. This signifies every word whereby the credit and estimation of our neighbour is either impaired or diminished.

The negative part: *You shall not diminish or hurt the good name and estimation of your neighbour*

Here is forbidden:

1. Envy, disdain of others, desire of another man's glory. *"He is puffed up with conceit and understands nothing. He has an unhealthy craving for controversy and for quarrels about words, which produce envy, dissension, slander, evil suspicions"* (1 Tim. 6:4). *"So put away all malice and all deceit and hypocrisy and envy and all slander"* (1 Pet. 2:1). *"But when the chief priests and the scribes saw the wonderful things that he did, and the children crying out in the temple, "Hosanna*

to the Son of David!" they were indignant" (Matt. 21:15).

2. Evil suspicions (1 Tim. 6:4). *"Now Eliab his eldest brother heard when he spoke to the men. And Eliab's anger was kindled against David, and he said, 'Why have you come down? And with whom have you left those few sheep in the wilderness? I know your presumption and the evil of your heart, for you have come down to see the battle'"* (1 Sam. 17:28). *"When the native people saw the creature hanging from his hand, they said to one another, 'No doubt this man is a murderer. Though he has escaped from the sea, Justice has not allowed him to live'"* (Acts 28:4). Here hard censures and sinister judgements against our neighbour are condemned. *"Judge not, that you be not judged. For with the judgement you pronounce you will be judged, and with the measure you use it will be measured to you"* (Matt. 7:1–2). The judgements which Christ forbids here are private and reproachful or slanderous judgements, namely when either a good or indifferent action is interpreted to the worse part, or when a light offence is made heinous through evil will, without great desire either to amend or to cover it. *"But others mocking said, "They are filled with new wine." But Peter, standing with the eleven, lifted up his voice and addressed them: "Men of Judea and all who dwell in Jerusalem, let this be known to you, and give ear to my words. For these people are not drunk, as you suppose, since it is only the third hour of the day"* (Acts 2:13–15). *"Hannah was speaking in her heart; only her lips moved, and her voice was not heard. Therefore Eli took her to be a drunken woman"* (1 Sam. 1:13). But we must know that there are three kinds of judgements which are not forbidden by this commandment of Christ:

    a. The ministry of gospel which judges and reproves sin.

    b. The judgement of the Magistrate.

    c. The correction of a friend admonishing us, as when he says "abstain from the company of such a man, for I know him to be a drunkard...".

3. A relation of our neighbour's bare words only, and not of their sense and meaning. *"Now the chief priests and the whole Council were seeking false testimony against Jesus that they might put him to death, but they found none, though many false witnesses came forward. At last two came forward and said, "This man said, 'I am able to destroy the temple of God, and to rebuild it in three days'"* (Matt. 26:59-61).

Indeed, Christ said some such thing in words, for example: *"Jesus answered them, 'Destroy this temple, and in three days I will raise it up'"* (John 2:19).

4. A lie, which signifies every falsehood with purpose to deceive whether in words or in deeds, or concealing the truth, or any other way whatsoever, even if intended for the good of our neighbour.

5. To pronounce unjust sentence in judgement: to rely on a single witness, to accuse another falsely, or to betray a man's cause by collusion. *"They proclaimed a fast and set Naboth at the head of the people. And the two worthless men came in and sat opposite him. And the worthless men brought a charge against Naboth in the presence of the people, saying, 'Naboth cursed God and the king.' So they took him outside the city and stoned him to death with stones"* (1 Kings 21:12–13). *"On the evidence of two witnesses or of three witnesses the one who is to die shall be put to death"* (Deut. 17:6).

6. To openly raise invented and hurtful tales and reports of our neighbour, or privately to devise them. *"They are gossips, slanderers, haters of God, insolent, haughty, boastful, inventors of evil"* (Rom. 1:29–30). *"You shall not go around as a slanderer among your people, and you shall not stand up against the life of your neighbour: I am the LORD"* (Lev. 19:16). *"Besides that, they learn to be idlers, going about from house to house, and not only idlers, but also gossips and busybodies, saying what they should not"* (1 Tim. 5:13). To spread fanciful tales, or to add anything to them. *"For lack of wood the fire goes out, and where there is no whisperer, quarrelling ceases. As charcoal to hot embers and wood to fire, so is a quarrelsome man for kindling strife. The words of a whisperer are like delicious morsels; they go down into the inner parts of the body"* (Prov. 26:20-22). *"For I fear that perhaps when I come I may find you not as I wish, and that you may find me not as you wish—that perhaps there may be quarrelling, jealousy, anger, hostility, slander, gossip, conceit, and disorder"* (2 Cor. 12:20). To receive or believe those tales which we hear of others. *"You shall not spread a false report. You shall not join hands with a wicked man to be a malicious witness"* (Exod. 23:1). *"And David said to Saul, 'Why do you listen to the words of men who say, 'Behold, David seeks your harm'?"* (1 Sam. 24:9).

7. To accuse our neighbour for what is certain and true when motivated

by hatred, and with intent to hurt him. *"Then answered Doeg the Edomite, who stood by the servants of Saul, 'I saw the son of Jesse coming to Nob, to Ahimelech the son of Ahitub, and he inquired of the LORD for him and gave him provisions and gave him the sword of Goliath the Philistine'"* (1 Sam. 22:9–10). Of this deed David thus speaks: *"Why do you boast of evil, O mighty man? The steadfast love of God endures all the day. Your tongue plots destruction, like a sharp razor, you worker of deceit. You love evil more than good, and lying more than speaking what is right. Selah You love all words that devour, O deceitful tongue"* (Psalm 52:1-4).

8. To openly declare our neighbour's secret to any man, especially if he did it of infirmity. *"If your brother sins against you, go and tell him his fault, between you and him alone. If he listens to you, you have gained your brother"* (Matt. 18:15). *"Whoever goes about slandering reveals secrets, but he who is trustworthy in spirit keeps a thing covered"* (Prov. 11:13).

9. All babbling talk and bitter words. *"But sexual immorality and all impurity or covetousness must not even be named among you, as is proper among saints. Let there be no filthiness nor foolish talk nor crude joking, which are out of place, but instead let there be thanksgiving"* (Eph. 5:3–4). *"They answered him, 'You were born in utter sin, and would you teach us?' And they cast him out"* (John 9:34). Such jesting (or as it is now termed, *wit*), which Aristotle the philosopher makes a virtue, is accounted a vice by Paul the Apostle, and not without cause:

    a. Such quips that sting others are very offensive to those who are so targeted, though they be a great pleasure for some to hear.

    b. It is very hard to align such behaviour with Christian godliness and gravity.

    Objection: But sharp and stinging speeches are usual in the scriptures: Elijah mocked the Priests of Baal (1 Kings 18:27; cf. Isa. 14:9).

    Answer: Such speeches are not spoken to please others but are sharp denouncements of God's enemies to his glory.

10. Flattery, whereby we praise our neighbour beyond what we know is true. *"Faithful are the wounds of a friend; profuse are the kisses of*

an enemy .... Whoever blesses his neighbour with a loud voice, rising early in the morning, will be counted as cursing" (Prov. 27:6, 14). *"And the people were shouting, 'The voice of a god, and not of a man!'"* (Acts 12:22). This is a grievous sin in the Ministers of the word. *"For we never came with words of flattery, as you know, nor with a pretext for greed—God is witness"* (1. Thess. 2:5). *"For from the least to the greatest of them, everyone is greedy for unjust gain; and from prophet to priest, everyone deals falsely. They have healed the wound of my people lightly, saying, 'Peace, peace,' when there is no peace"* (Jer. 6:13–14). *"For such persons do not serve our Lord Christ, but their own appetites, and by smooth talk and flattery they deceive the hearts of the naive"* (Rom. 16:18).

11. Foolish and overconfident boasting. *"Do not boast about tomorrow, for you do not know what a day may bring. Let another praise you, and not your own mouth; a stranger, and not your own lips"* (Prov. 27:1–2).
12. To accuse or witness against one falsely. *"Naboth cursed God and the king"* (1 Kings 21:13).

The affirmative part: *Preserve the good name of your neighbour*

"A good name is better than precious ointment" (Eccl. 7:1). Here is commanded:

1. A rejoicing for the credit and good estimation of your neighbour. *"But the fruit of the Spirit is love, joy, peace, patience, kindness, goodness, faithfulness"* (Gal. 5:22). *"First, I thank my God through Jesus Christ for all of you, because your faith is proclaimed in all the world"* (Rom 1:8).
2. To willingly acknowledge the goodness that we see in any man whatsoever, and only to speak of the same. *"To speak evil of no one, to avoid quarrelling, to be gentle, and to show perfect courtesy toward all people"* (Titus 3:2). Moreover, we must with all desire receive and believe reports of our neighbour's good. *"Paul came also to Derbe and to Lystra. A disciple was there, named Timothy, the son of a Jewish woman who was a believer, but his father was a Greek. He was well spoken of by the brothers at Lystra and Iconium. Paul wanted Timothy*

to accompany him, and he took him and circumcised him" (Acts 16:1–3). This must be done by us in such a way that we do not approve or allow the vices and faults of men. *"And he did what was right in the eyes of the LORD, yet not with a whole heart"* (2 Chron. 25:2) and *"And he did what was right in the eyes of the LORD according to all that his father Uzziah had done, except he did not enter the temple of the LORD. But the people still followed corrupt practices"* (2 Chron. 27:2).

3. To assume the best when interpreting a possible evil. *"Love thinks no evil .... believes all things, hopes all things"* (1 Cor. 13:5, 7 NKJV). *"Then they took Joseph's robe and slaughtered a goat and dipped the robe in the blood. And they sent the robe of many colours and brought it to their father and said, 'This we have found; please identify whether it is your son's robe or not.' And he identified it and said, 'It is my son's robe. A fierce animal has devoured him. Joseph is without doubt torn to pieces'"* (Gen. 37:31–33).

   And here observe the religion of Joseph, betrothed to Mary, who when he saw that Mary was with child was more ready to conclude that she was with child before her betrothing by committing fornication, then after, by committing adultery (Matt. 1:19). But for all this, men must not be gullible. *"But Jesus on his part did not entrust himself to them, because he knew all people"* (John 2:24).

4. Not to believe an evil report running abroad among the common people by the whispers of talebearers, as if by conduit pipes. *"Who does not slander with his tongue and does no evil to his neighbour, nor takes up a reproach against his friend"* (Psalm 15:3). *"And said to him, 'Do you know that Baalis the king of the Ammonites has sent Ishmael the son of Nethaniah to take your life?' But Gedaliah the son of Ahikam would not believe them .... But Gedaliah the son of Ahikam said to Johanan the son of Kareah, 'You shall not do this thing, for you are speaking falsely of Ishmael'"* (Jer. 40:14, 16). We also ought to be angry at such whispering. *"The north wind brings forth rain, and a backbiting tongue, angry looks."* (Prov. 25:23).

5. To keep the offence of our neighbour secret unless it must necessarily be revealed. *"Hatred stirs up strife, but love covers all offences"* (Prov. 10:12). *"And her husband Joseph, being a just man and unwilling to put her to shame, resolved to divorce her quietly"* (Matt. 1:19).

A man might suppose that by this means we would be partakers of other men's sins. However, we ought to conceal our neighbour imperfections lest he should be provoked to offence. Yet, in due season, he must be admonished that he may amend (Gal. 6:1), *"My brothers, if anyone among you wanders from the truth and someone brings him back, let him know that whoever brings back a sinner from his wandering will save his soul from death and will cover a multitude of sins"* (James 5:19–20).

But if the sin which is concealed cannot be taken away in this way, then in love and charity we must declare it to those who may remove and amend it. *"These are the generations of Jacob. Joseph, being seventeen years old, was pasturing the flock with his brothers. He was a boy with the sons of Bilhah and Zilpah, his father's wives. And Joseph brought a bad report of them to their father"* (Gen. 37:2). *"For it has been reported to me by Chloe's people that there is quarrelling among you, my brothers"* (1 Cor. 1:11). *"But if he does not listen, take one or two others along with you, that every charge may be established by the evidence of two or three witnesses"* (Matt. 18:16).

To get a good name and estimation among men, and to keep it when we have gotten it. *"Finally, brothers, whatever is true, whatever is honourable, whatever is just, whatever is pure, whatever is lovely, whatever is commendable, if there is any excellence, if there is anything worthy of praise, think about these things"* (Phil. 4:8).

A good name is attained:

a. If we, seeking the kingdom of God before all things, repent of all our sins, and with an earnest desire, embrace and follow after righteousness. *"The memory of the righteous is a blessing, but the name of the wicked will rot"* (Prov. 10:7). *"And truly, I say to you, wherever the gospel is proclaimed in the whole world, what she has done will be told in memory of her"* (Mark 14:9).

b. We must take care both to judge and speak well of others. *"For with the judgement you pronounce you will be judged"* (Matt. 7:2). *"Do not take to heart all the things that people say, lest you hear your servant cursing you. Your heart knows that many times you yourself have cursed others"* (Eccl. 7:21–22).

c. We must abstain from all kind of wickedness, for even one vice or sin obscures and darkens a man's good name. *"Dead flies make the perfumer's ointment give off a stench; so a little folly outweighs wisdom and honour"* (Eccl. 10:1).

d. In all things we must earnestly seek the glory of God only, and not our own. *"And when you pray, you must not be like the hypocrites. For they love to stand and pray in the synagogues and at the street corners, that they may be seen by others. Truly, I say to you, they have received their reward"* (Matt. 6:5–6).

But if, when we seek the glory of God, honest and godly men praise and testify well of us, we must not despise their testimony and commendation. And if they neither praise us nor testify of us at all, we must take it in good part. *"For our boast is this, the testimony of our conscience, that we behaved in the world with simplicity and godly sincerity, not by earthly wisdom but by the grace of God, and supremely so toward you"* (2 Cor. 1:12), and *"But we will not boast beyond limits, but will boast only with regard to the area of influence God assigned to us, to reach even to you"* (2 Cor. 10:13). *"The LORD is my chosen portion and my cup; you hold my lot. The lines have fallen for me in pleasant places; indeed, I have a beautiful inheritance"* (Psalm 16:5–6). *"Let the one who boasts, boast in the Lord"* (1 Cor. 1:31).

Chapter Twenty Nine

THE TENTH COMMANDMENT

The tenth commandment concerns **Concupiscence** (sinful desire) committed against our neighbour. The words are these:

> *You shall not covet your neighbour's house; you shall not covet your neighbour's wife, or his male servant, or his female servant, or his ox, or his donkey, or anything that is your neighbour's.* (Exod. 20:17)

The Resolution

Covet. This motion of the heart is of three sorts:

1. Some sudden or temporary thought, suggested to the mind by Satan, which suddenly vanishes away and is not actively received by the mind. This is not sin. For such was in Christ when he was tempted by the Devil (Matt. 4:1).
2. A more permanent and settled thought which tickles and deceives the mind with some inward joy.
3. A thought which draws full agreement to sin from the will and affections.

We are to understand this commandment of the second sort of motions only, not of the first (which is not sinful), or of the last, to which the five former commandments do belong.

Now then, to covet is to think inwardly and desire anything by which our neighbour may be hindered (providing that there follows no agreement of the will to actually commit that evil). For even the ancient philosophers condemn covetousness of the heart, and good men prohibit it if it is done with a clear purpose to do evil. And as for the concupiscence forbidden here we think it is more hidden and secret, because Paul, who knew the law, seems ignorant of it. *"For I would not have known what it is to covet if the law had not said, 'You will not covet.'"* (Rom. 7:7). Again, if that concupiscence immediately going before the consent were not what was prohibited in this passage, then there must be a great confusion in the Decalogue. For the seventh commandment forbids some kind of coveting of our neighbour's wife.

House. The commandment is illustrated by an argument drawn from the distribution of the objects of concupiscence. Here it is apparent that only evil concupiscence is condemned in this passage (cf. Col. 3:5). For there is a good concupiscence or desire, such as for food and drink, and that of the Spirit. *"The desires of the Spirit are against the flesh"* (Gal. 5:17).

The negative part: *You shall not covet that which is your neighbours'*

Here are prohibited:

1. Concupiscence itself, namely original corruption, in as much as it is hurtful to our neighbour (James 1:14).
2. Each corrupt thought and passion of the heart, springing out of the bitter root of concupiscence: *"The desires of the Spirit are against the flesh"* (Gal. 5:17). *"You shall love the Lord your God with all your heart and with all your soul"* (Luke 10:27). Likewise Satan's suggestion is of this sort if it is entertained and received in the heart.
3. The least thought and motion which, though it doesn't procure consent, delights and tickles the heart. Of this kind are these foolish wishes: "if such a house were mine, such a living, such a thing," and so on. And likewise, all unchaste dreams arising from concupiscence.

The affirmative part: *Covet that only, which is to your neighbour's good*

Here are commended:

1. A pure heart towards our neighbour. *"The aim of our charge is love that issues from a pure heart and a good conscience and a sincere*

faith" (1 Tim. 1:5).

2. Holy thoughts and motions of the Spirit. Paul prays that the Thessalonians may be holy, not only in body and soul but also in spirit (1 Thess. 5:23, cf. Eph. 4:23).

3. A conflict against the evil affections and lusts of the flesh. *"For I delight in the law of God, in my inner being, but I see in my members another law waging war against the law of my mind and making me captive to the law of sin that dwells in my members. Wretched man that I am! Who will deliver me from this body of death?"* (Rom. 7:22–24; cf. 2 Cor. 12:7–9).

Chapter Thirty

THE USE OF THE LAW

The **Use of the Law in Unregenerate** persons is threefold.

The First Use is to lay open sin and make it known. *"For by works of the law no human being will be justified in his sight, since through the law comes knowledge of sin"* (Rom. 3:20).

The Second Use is 'accidental,' in that it effects and augments sin by means of the flesh.[1] The flesh causes man to turn from that which is commanded and inclines him toward that which is prohibited. *"But sin, seizing an opportunity through the commandment, produced in me all kinds of covetousness. For apart from the law, sin lies dead. I was once alive apart from the law, but when the commandment came, sin came alive and I died. The very commandment that promised life proved to be death to me"* (Rom. 7:8–10).

The Third Use is to declare eternal damnation for the least disobedience, without offering any hope of pardon. This law pronounces against offenders, and by this means (partly by threatening, partly by terrifying) it reigns and rules over man. *"Now we know that whatever the law says it speaks to those who are under the law, so that every mouth may be stopped, and the whole world may be held accountable to God"* (Rom 3:19). *"For all who rely on works of the law are under a curse; for it is written, 'Cursed be everyone who does not abide by all things written in the Book of the Law, and do them'"* (Gal. 3:10). *"Now if the ministry of death, carved in letters on stone, came with such glory that the Israelites could not gaze at Moses' face because of its glory, which was being brought to an end, will not the ministry of the Spirit have even more glory? For if there was*

1. Perkins specifies that this use of the law is 'accidental', meaning that this outcome is not of the essence of the law, nor does it prove some kind of lack of goodness in the law itself. The reason that the law causes sinners to sin further is because the sinful nature (flesh, concupiscence) is at work in sinners.

glory in the ministry of condemnation, the ministry of righteousness must far exceed it in glory" (2 Cor. 3:7–9).

The purpose for which sin reigns in man is to urge sinners to flee to Christ. *"But the Scripture imprisoned everything under sin, so that the promise by faith in Jesus Christ might be given to those who believe .... So then, the law was our guardian until Christ came, in order that we might be justified by faith"* (Gal. 3:22, 24). See also Heb. 12:18–20.

The continuance of this power of the Law is unceasing, unless a sinner repents. The very first act of repentance so frees him that he shall no more be under the Law, but under grace. *"David said to Nathan, 'I have sinned against the LORD.' And Nathan said to David, 'The LORD also has put away your sin; you shall not die'"* (2 Sam. 12:13). *"For sin will have no dominion over you, since you are not under law but under grace"* (Rom. 6:14).

Therefore, if you seriously desire eternal life, first thoroughly examine yourself and the course of your life against the standard of God's law. Next, set before your eyes the curse that is due to sin, so that (bewailing your misery and utterly despairing of your own power to attain everlasting happiness) you may renounce yourself and be provoked to seek Christ Jesus.

The **Use of the Law in the Regenerate** is far different. It guides regenerate persons to new obedience through the whole course of their life. Such obedience is acceptable to God through Christ. *"Do we then overthrow the law by this faith? By no means! On the contrary, we uphold the law"* (Rom. 3:31). *"Your testimonies are my delight; they are my counsellors .... Your word is a lamp to my feet and a light to my path"* (Psalm 119:24, 105).

CHAPTER 31–34:

Covenant Admin

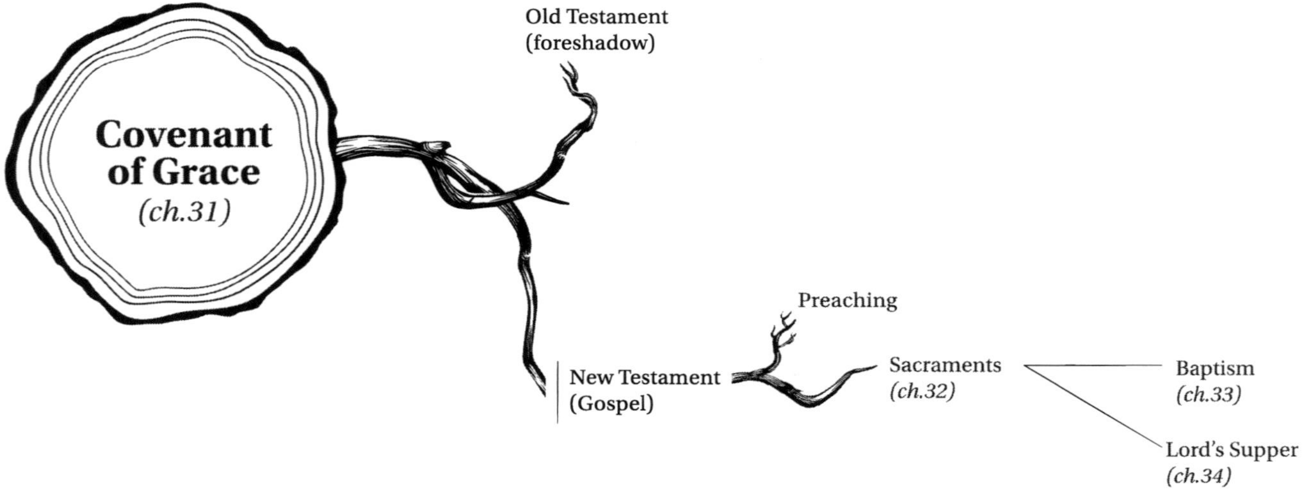

Chapter Thirty One

THE COVENANT OF GRACE

Hitherto concerning the Covenant of Works and the Law; now follows the Covenant of Grace.

The **Covenant of Grace** is that whereby God, freely promising Christ and his benefits, commands that man receive Christ by faith and repent of his sins. *"And I will make for them a covenant on that day with the beasts of the field, the birds of the heavens, and the creeping things of the ground. And I will abolish the bow, the sword, and war from the land, and I will make you lie down in safety. And I will betroth you to me forever. I will betroth you to me in righteousness and in justice, in steadfast love and in mercy. I will betroth you to me in faithfulness. And you shall know the LORD"* (Hos. 2:18–20). *"I will sprinkle clean water on you, and you shall be clean from all your uncleannesses, and from all your idols I will cleanse you. And I will give you a new heart, and a new spirit I will put within you. And I will remove the heart of stone from your flesh and give you a heart of flesh. And I will put my Spirit within you, and cause you to walk in my statutes and be careful to obey my rules"* (Ezek. 36:25–27). *"Behold, I send my messenger, and he will prepare the way before me. And the Lord whom you seek will suddenly come to his temple; and the messenger of the covenant in whom you delight, behold, he is coming, says the LORD of hosts"* (Mal. 3:1).

This Covenant is also named a Testament, for it partly has the nature and properties of a testament or will. First, it is confirmed by the death of the Testator. *"For where a will is involved, the death of the one who made it must be established. For a will takes effect only at death, since it is not in force as long as the one who made it is alive"* (Heb. 9:16). Secondly, in this covenant we do not so much offer or promise any great matter to God, but (in a particular way) only receive, just as the last will and testament of a man is not for the testator, but the heirs possession.

Though it is one in substance, the Covenant is distinguished into the Old and New Testaments. The Old Testament prefigured Christ to come by means of types and foreshadowings. The New Testament declares Christ already come in the flesh, as is shown in the gospel.

The **gospel** is that part of God's word which contains a most worthy and welcome message, namely that mankind is fully redeemed by the blood of Jesus Christ, the only begotten Son of God manifest in the flesh, so that now there is prepared a full remission of all sins (together with salvation and life everlasting) for all who repent and believe in Christ Jesus. *"And as Moses lifted up the serpent in the wilderness, so must the Son of Man be lifted up, that whoever believes in him may have eternal life"* (John 3:14–15). *"To him all the prophets bear witness that everyone who believes in him receives forgiveness of sins through his name"* (Acts 10:43).

The goal and use of the gospel is, firstly: to declare that righteousness in Christ by which the whole law is fully satisfied and salvation is attained. Secondly, it is the instrument and, as it were, the conduit pipe of the Holy Spirit by which he fashions and infuses faith into the soul. By this faith those who believe apprehend Christ's righteousness as though with a hand. *"For I am not ashamed of the gospel, for it is the power of God for salvation to everyone who believes, to the Jew first and also to the Greek. For in it the righteousness of God is revealed from faith for faith, as it is written, 'The righteous shall live by faith'"* (Rom. 1:16–17). *"It is the Spirit who gives life; the flesh is no help at all. The words that I have spoken to you are spirit and life"* (John 6:63). *"It pleased God through the folly of what we preach to save those who believe"* (1 Cor. 1:21).

When Christ's Church is flourishing, the gospel preached is the ordinary means by which God begets faith.[1] When the church is in a ruinous state—when its foundations are shaken by apostasy and the clear light of the word is darkened—then, when God's word is read or repeated, the very sound of it is extraordinarily effectual (by the assistance of God's Spirit) to them whom God will have called out of that great darkness into his exceeding light. *"How then will they call on him in whom they have not believed? And how are they to believe in him of whom they have never heard? And how are they to hear without someone preaching?"* (Rom. 10:14) *"Now those who were scattered because of the*

1. For Perkins' account of preaching, see his *The Art of Prophesying* (1607) in *The Works of William Perkins: Volume 10* (ed. Joseph A. Pipa & J. Stephen Yuille; Grand Rapids: Reformation Heritage Books, 2020).

persecution that arose over Stephen travelled as far as Phoenicia and Cyprus and Antioch, speaking the word to no one except Jews. But there were some of them, men of Cyprus and Cyrene, who on coming to Antioch spoke to the Hellenists also, preaching the Lord Jesus. And the hand of the Lord was with them, and a great number who believed turned to the Lord" (Acts 11:19–21). *"So the woman left her water jar and went away into town and said to the people, 'Come, see a man who told me all that I ever did. Can this be the Christ?' .... Many Samaritans from that town believed in him because of the woman's testimony, 'He told me all that I ever did' .... And many more believed because of his word. They said to the woman, 'It is no longer because of what you said that we believe, for we have heard for ourselves, and we know that this is indeed the Savior of the world'"* (John 4:28–29, 39, 41–42). *"But I ask, have they not heard? Indeed they have, for 'Their voice has gone out to all the earth, and their words to the ends of the world'"* (Rom. 10:18). Thus, we may see how many of our forefathers and ancestors obtained eternal life even in the midst of Popery. *"Then the dragon became furious with the woman and went off to make war on the rest of her offspring, on those who keep the commandments of God and hold to the testimony of Jesus"* (Rev. 12:17). *"But what is God's reply to him? 'I have kept for myself seven thousand men who have not bowed the knee to Baal'"* (Rom. 11:4).

Chapter Thirty Two

THE SACRAMENTS

Thus much concerning the preaching of the word. Now follow its attendants, namely the Sacraments.

A **Sacrament** is that whereby Christ and his saving graces are (by certain external rites) signified, exhibited, and sealed to a Christian man.[1] *"He received the sign of circumcision as a seal of the righteousness that he had by faith while he was still uncircumcised"* (Rom. 4:11). *"You shall be circumcised in the flesh of your foreskins, and it shall be a sign of the covenant between me and you"* (Gen. 17:11).

God alone is the author of a sacrament. For a sign cannot confirm anything except by the consent and promise of the one from whose hands the benefit of the promise must be received. Therefore, God alone appointed the signs of grace, and he alone is able to bestow grace.

God made sacraments by the sacramental word, as Augustine witnesses, saying: *"Let the word come to the element, and there is made a sacrament."* The **Sacramental Word** is the word of institution, which God has set down in each sacrament. Of this word there are two parts:

1. The **Commandment** is that by which Christ appoints the administration and reception of sacraments. In Baptism: *go into the whole world baptising them in the Name,* and so on. In the Lord's Supper. *Take, eat, drink, do this.*
2. The **Promise** is the other part of the institution, whereby God ordained elements that they might be instruments and seals of his grace.

1. This conventional sacramental terminology is used in the Church of England's doctrinal statement *The Articles of Religion* (1563, 1571) which Perkins was bound to uphold (see Articles 25–30). A sacrament was an outward *sign* of the grace which it symbolised. Thus, the sacraments *exhibited* the grace of the gospel for people to see. For those who rightly received them (that is, by faith), the reception of the sacraments *sealed*, or certified, that they truly were participants in the grace of the gospel.

a. In Baptism: *"baptise them in the name of the Father and of the Son and of the Holy Spirit".*

b. In the Supper: *"This is my body, which is given for you."* and *"This is the new covenant in my blood".*

Therefore this word in the administration of the sacrament ought to be pronounced distinctly and loudly. Indeed, it ought to be explained too, as occasion serves, so that all to whom the commandment and promise apply may know and understand them. Thus, it is very plain that a minister's impiety does not annul the sacrament that he administers. Neither does it hinder a worthy receiver any more than the piety of a good minister can profit an unworthy receiver. All the efficacy and worthiness of the sacraments depends upon God's institution alone.

The parts of a sacrament are the Sign and the Thing that it signifies.

The **Sign** is the observable matter of the sacrament, and the actions associated with its administration. The material element is called the sign.

There is no natural change in the matter of the sign (that is, to their substance), but only a change in their designated use. For they are severed from common to holy use. Therefore, the signs do not have any inherent force or efficacy to make us holy, as baths naturally purify diseases. Rather, all such efficacy is entirely from the Holy Spirit. Yet the Spirit's work in the sacraments is inseparably tied to true faith and repentance. He works together with the sign exhibited in those who turn to the Lord. Thus, by God's ordinance, the signification of grace and its sealing correspond to the sign.

The **Thing** signified in the Sacrament is either Christ and his Saving Graces, or the Action regarding Christ.

I say first Christ and then his Graces because no man receives grace from Christ unless he is first truly a partaker of his body and blood (just as no man has the right to reap fruit of the ground where he has no just title and interest).

The Action about Christ is spiritual, and is either the action of God, or of Faith. The action of God is either the offering of Christ, or the application of Christ and his graces to the faithful. The action of faith is the consideration, desire, apprehension, and receiving of Christ in the lawful use of the sacrament.

Thus much of the parts of a sacrament: Now follows the **Union of the Parts**. This sacramental union:

1. Is *not absolute or natural*: there is no change of the sign into the thing signed;[2] neither is the thing signed included within or fastened to the sign.[3]
2. Rather it is *relative or signifying*: there is a certain agreement and proportionate resemblance between the external sign with the thing signified, as also of the outward action and the inward act. Thus, it comes to pass that the signs (as visible words presented to the external senses) draw a Christian's mind to the consideration of the things signified, which are to be applied.

This mutual sacramental relation is the cause of so many figures of speech and similes in Scripture, which are used when the one thing is put for the other:

1. The sign is used for the thing signified. *"And you shall eat it in haste. It is the LORD's Passover"* (Exod. 12:11). *"I am the living bread that came down from heaven. If anyone eats of this bread, he will live forever. And the bread that I will give for the life of the world is my flesh"* (John 6:51). *"For Christ, our Passover lamb, has been sacrificed"* (1 Cor. 5:7). *"We who are many are one body, for we all partake of the one bread"* (1 Cor. 10:17).
2. The name of the thing signified is given to the sign. For example: The bread is Christ's body, the cup is Christ's blood (1 Cor. 11:24, Matt. 26:28).
3. The effect of the thing signified is given to the sign, as circumcision is a covenant (Gen. 17:10, Act 7:8). The cup is the new testament (covenant) in Christ's blood (Luke 22:16).

---

2. The Roman Catholic doctrine of Transubstantiation asserts that the *substance* of the elements allegedly transform into the body and blood of Jesus, but their *accidents* (their sensory characteristics) remain the same, such that the transformation cannot be perceived except by faith.
3. The Lutheran view of the Lord's Supper asserted that the body and blood of Christ were truly present in the sign.

Baptism is the washing of the new birth (Titus 3:5).

4. That which properly belongs to the sign is attributed to the thing signified. *"Circumcise therefore the foreskin of your heart, and be no longer stubborn"* (Deut. 10:16). *"Unless you eat the flesh of the Son of Man and drink his blood, you have no life in you"* (John 6:53).

The reason for which a sacrament was ordained is:

1. For the better confirmation of our faith. For by it God (of his great mercy) binds himself to us, as by certain pledges given. Now a sacrament confirms our faith, not by any inherent power in itself, but rather by reasoned use of the signs when the Holy Spirit frames in our hearts such a conclusion as this:
    a. *All those converted, rightly using the sacraments, shall receive Christ and his graces,*
    b. *I am converted, and do rightly use the sacraments,*
    c. *Therefore, I shall receive Christ and his graces.*
2. That it might be a badge and outward sign of that profession by which the true church of God is distinguished from others.
3. That it might be a means to preserve and spread the doctrine of the gospel.
4. It serves to bind the faithful to continue in both loyalty and gratitude to their Lord God.
5. It is the bond of mutual friendship between the faithful.

How a Sacrament is Necessary to Salvation

The Covenant of Grace is absolutely necessary to salvation. Christ Jesus is the very substance of the Covenant, and so all must necessarily either receive it or perish eternally. But a sacrament is not absolutely necessary, but only as it is a support and stay for faith to lean upon. It cannot entitle us to the inheritance of the sons of God, as the covenant does, but only seals that which was already bestowed upon us by faith. As we see in human contracts, the bond arises from the mutual consent of the parties. The instrument and setting of the seal don't make the agreement, but rather confirm the mutual bond previously made. Where mutual consent remains firm the contract stands, even without an instrument or seal.

Therefore, the lack of a sacrament does not condemn, but contempt of sacraments will condemn a man. The lack of a sacrament might occur because we are justly hindered from receiving it, as when one is prevented by death, or lives in such a place where he cannot receive the sacrament. As for the deliberate neglect of a sacrament, whilst it is a very grievous sin, yet it is one for which the heartily penitent man may well hope for pardon.

The holy use of a sacrament is when the truly converted use those rites which God has prescribed for their true purpose in the receiving of a sacrament. Therefore:

1. The Reprobate, though God offers the whole sacrament to them, receive the signs alone without the things signified. For the sign without its right use is not a sacrament to the receiver of it. So Paul says, *"For circumcision indeed is of value if you obey the law, but if you break the law, your circumcision becomes uncircumcision"* (Rom. 2:25). And Augustine has this saying, *"If you receive it carnally, yet ceases it not to be spiritual, though to the it be not so."*[4]
2. The Elect not yet converted similarly receive the bare signs without the thing signified, yet so as the sacrament shall afterwards have his good effect in them. For the sacrament received before a man's conversion is afterwards ratified and becomes profitable to the repentant, and the use of the sacrament which before was utterly unlawful then becomes very lawful.
3. The Elect already converted receive both the sign and the thing signified together (to their salvation), yet so that by their unworthy receiving (by reason of their many infirmities and relapses into sin) they are subject to temporal punishments.

The difference between a sacrament and a sacrifice is: in a sacrament God bestows his graces upon us, whereas in a sacrifice we offer faith and obedience to God.

There are many differences between the sacraments of the Old Testament and those of the New Testament:

1. They were many; these are but few.

4. Augustine, *Tractates on the Gospel According to St. John*, 26.18.

2. They pointed at Christ to come; these show that he is come.
3. They were appropriate to the descendants of Abraham; these are common to the whole Church, called out from among the Jews and the Gentiles.

CHAPTER 33:

Baptism

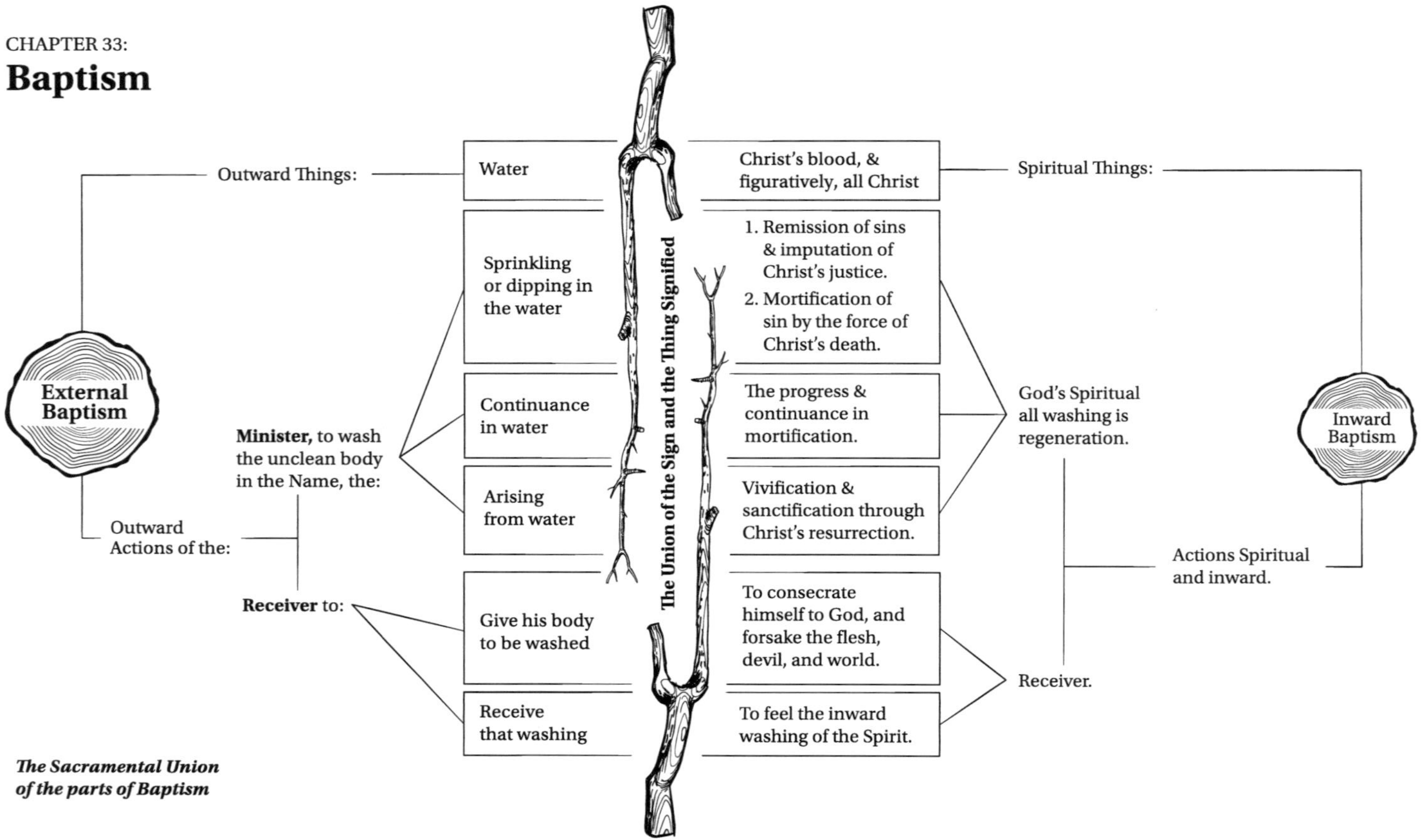

The Sacramental Union of the parts of Baptism

Chapter Thirty Three

BAPTISM

There are two Sacraments. *"For I want you to know, brothers, that our fathers were all under the cloud, and all passed through the sea, and all were baptized into Moses in the cloud and in the sea, and all ate the same spiritual food, and all drank the same spiritual drink. For they drank from the spiritual Rock that followed them, and the Rock was Christ"* (1 Cor. 10:1).[1] The first sacrament—Baptism—is that whereby Christians are initiated and admitted into the Church of God. The second sacrament —the Lord's Supper—is that whereby the Church is preserved and nourished.

Baptism is a sacrament by which those who are within the covenant are washed with water in the name of the Father, the Son, and the Holy Spirit, so that—being thus grafted into Christ—they may have perpetual fellowship with him. *"Go therefore and make disciples of all nations, baptizing them in the name of the Father and of the Son and of the Holy Spirit"* (Matt. 28:19). *"Whoever believes and is baptized will be saved, but whoever does not believe will be condemned"* (Mark 16:16). *"Is Christ divided? Was Paul crucified for you? Or were you baptized in the name of Paul? I thank God that I baptized none of you except Crispus and Gaius"* (1 Cor. 1:13–14).

Within the covenant are all the seed of Abraham, or the seed of the faithful. These are either of Riper Years or Infants.

Those of Riper Years (i.e. adults) within the covenant are all who join themselves to the visible Church, and do both testify their repentance of their sins and hold to the foundations of religion taught in the same Church.[2] *"And they were baptized by him in the river Jordan, confessing*

1. Tertullian, *Against Marcion*, bk. 4; Augustine, *On the Creed*, 4.6.
2. Perkins' expounds what he regarded as the foundational doctrines of the Christian faith in his catechetical works: *Foundation of Christian Religion Gathered into Six Principles* (1590), *Exposition of the Symbol or Creed of the Apostles* (1595),

their sins" (Matt. 3:6). *"And as they were going along the road they came to some water, and the eunuch said, 'See, here is water! What prevents me from being baptized?' And Philip said, 'If you believe with all your heart, you may.' And he replied, 'I believe that Jesus Christ is the Son of God.' And he commanded the chariot to stop, and they both went down into the water, Philip and the eunuch, and he baptized him"* (Acts 8:36-38). *"If a stranger shall sojourn with you and would keep the Passover to the LORD, let all his males be circumcised. Then he may come near and keep it; he shall be as a native of the land. But no uncircumcised person shall eat of it"* (Exod. 12:48).

Infants within the covenant are those who have at least one believing parent. *"For the unbelieving husband is made holy because of his wife, and the unbelieving wife is made holy because of her husband. Otherwise your children would be unclean, but as it is, they are holy"* (1 Cor. 7:14). *"If the dough offered as first fruits is holy, so is the whole lump, and if the root is holy, so are the branches"* (Rom. 11:16). *"And I will establish my covenant between me and you and your offspring after you throughout their generations for an everlasting covenant, to be God to you and to your offspring after you .... both he who is born in your house and he who is bought with your money, shall surely be circumcised. So shall my covenant be in your flesh an everlasting covenant"* (Gen. 17:7, 13). *"And they said, 'Believe in the Lord Jesus, and you will be saved, you and your household'"* (Acts 16:31).

Question: How are the children of faithful parents in the covenant?

Answer: Holy parents are to be considered in two ways.

First, as they were children of the first Adam and so are partly carnal. In this state they likewise beget their offspring as children of wrath. For the father begets a son, not as he is a good man, but simply as a man. Therefore being impure, he necessarily begets that which is impure.

Secondly, we must consider the parents as they are the sons of God, grafted into the second Adam. In this state they cannot impart faith to their descendants (for the sons of God are not made such by natural generation, but by the adoption of God the Father). Yet

---

and *Exposition of the Lord's Prayer* (1592) in *The Works of William Perkins: Volume 5* (ed. Ryan Hurd. Grand Rapids: Reformation Heritage Books, 2017).

they may believe both for themselves and others according to the tenor of the covenant of grace. Thus, Adam sinned both for himself and others, as in business parents covenant both for themselves and for their heirs after them. Hence Paul says that the parents are like the first fruits which sanctify the whole lump (Rom. 11:16). Thus, the faith of the parents makes their children to be accounted within the covenant even though, due to their age, they do not yet actually believe.

To be baptised into the name of the Trinity, receiving the outward sign of washing, is to be made one of God's family (his Church) and to share in its privileges. *"The Angel who has redeemed me from all evil, bless the boys; and in them let my name be carried on, and the name of my fathers Abraham and Isaac; and let them grow into a multitude in the midst of the earth"* (Gen. 48:16). *"And seven women shall take hold of one man in that day, saying, 'We will eat our own bread and wear our own clothes, only let us be called by your name; take away our reproach'"* (Isa. 4:1).

By this it is clear that a marvellous, solemn covenant and contract is sealed and set forth in this washing of baptism. This covenant is, first, of God with the baptised, whereby God the Father guarantees to receive him into favour, the Son to redeem him, the Holy Spirit to purify and regenerate him. Secondly, this covenant is of the baptised with God, whereby they promise to acknowledge, call upon, and worship no other God but the true Jehovah, who is the Father, Son, and Holy Spirit.

The **External and Visible Matter** used in baptism is water. The minister may not baptize with any other liquid, but only with natural water. This was the judgement of the primitive church. For example, when a *'certain minister, lacking water, took sand and baptized with that. The party thus 'sanded' was afterward baptized, the former event being considered as of no effect'.*[3]

The **External Form** of baptism is the minister's washing of the baptised according to the prescribed rule of God's word (Rom. 10:14).

The ancient custom of baptising was to dip the entire body of the

3. Nicephorus, *Ecclesiastical History*, 3.33.

baptised in the water.[4] But now, especially in cold countries, the Church only sprinkles the baptised, due to the weakness of infants (for very few of ripe years are baptised these days). We need not marvel at this alteration, seeing charity and necessity may dispense with ceremonies, or soften their sharpness.[5]

The **Sacramental Union** of the parts of Baptism is of this sort.

The element of water (by which the body is washed) stands for the blood of Christ (which itself stands for the whole Christ). *"And the blood of Jesus his Son cleanses us from all sin"* (1 John 1:7).

The **Action of the Minister** is his washing of the party baptised with the element of water. This seals and confirms a twofold action of God:

1. The grafting in, or incorporating of, the baptised into Christ. *"For as many of you as were baptized into Christ have put on Christ"* (Gal. 3:27). *"For in one Spirit we were all baptized into one body"* (1 Cor. 12:13).
2. Our spiritual regeneration. *"Not because of works done by us in righteousness, but according to his own mercy, by the washing of regeneration and renewal of the Holy Spirit"* (Titus 3:5).

Of **Washing** there are three parts: the putting into the water, the continuance in the water, and the coming out of the water.

The **putting into**, or the sprinkling of water, denotes:

1. The shedding of the blood of Christ for the remission of all our sins and the imputation of his righteousness to us. *"Rise and be baptized and wash away your sins, calling on his name"* (Acts 22:16). *"And such were some of you. But you were washed, you were sanctified, you were justified in the name of the Lord Jesus Christ and by the Spirit of our God"* (1 Cor. 6:11).
2. The mortification of sin by the power of Christ's death. *"Do you not know that all of us who have been baptized into Christ Jesus*

4. As seen in Romans 6, and attested by the Councils of Laodicea (c.363) and Neocaesarea (c.314).
5. Here Perkins echoes the preface to the *Book of Common Prayer* (1559) entitled 'Of Ceremonies, why some be abolished, and some retained'.

> *were baptized into his death? .... We know that our old self was crucified with him in order that the body of sin might be brought to nothing, so that we would no longer be enslaved to sin"* (Rom. 6:3, 6).

The **continuance in** the water denotes the burial of sin, namely a continual increase of mortification by the power of Christ death and burial: *"We were buried therefore with him by baptism into death"* (Rom. 6:4).

The **coming out** of the water confirms our spiritual rebirth to newness of life in all holiness and justice, which we attain to by the power of Christ's resurrection. *"Just as Christ was raised from the dead by the glory of the Father, we too might walk in newness of life. For if we have been united with him in a death like his, we shall certainly be united with him in a resurrection like his"* (Rom. 6:4–5).

The **Action of the Party to be Baptised** is twofold:

1. To offer himself to be baptised before the minister in the presence of the congregation. This signifies that he consecrates himself to the Lord, and that he utterly renounces the Flesh, the World, and the Devil. *"Baptism, which corresponds to this, now saves you, not as a removal of dirt from the body but as an appeal to God for a good conscience, through the resurrection of Jesus Christ"* (1 Pet. 3:21).
2. To receive the external washing by water. This signifies that the party baptised receives the internal washing which is by the blood of Christ, or at the least that it is offered to him.

Rebaptising is not to be permitted, for as man is born only once, so must it be with spiritual regeneration. Therefore, those who were baptised by a minister who is a heretic (but was not yet degraded from that calling), must not be baptised again in the Church of God (assuming that the external form of administration was previously observed). This is especially important if, after baptism, they have been made partakers of the Lord's Supper. They should instead be instructed in the true faith. As Eusebius reports: *'There was one in our province long considered a believer, and a member of our congregation before the appointment of my predecessor Heraclas. Once, whilst present at the baptism of others and hearing the questions they were asked and their answers, he came to me weeping. He confessed that he was baptized by a heretic, and that the administration of his baptism was full of blasphemies. He declared that he was deeply grieved for this offense, and that he didn't dare so much as to lift up his eyes to heaven. He earnestly begged that he might be baptised and purified with the baptism of our church, and so receive the gift of the Holy Spirit. However, I did not dare presume to do this. I said that it was sufficient that he had been so long a professing believer among us, and that at the receipt of the Lord's Supper he answered "Amen." ...I advised him to rest himself in his former faith with his conscience already sufficiently purified, especially in that he was so long a partaker with us in the Sacraments.'*[6]

The **Right Use** of baptism is this. When you feel inwardly in your heart that (through the heat of concupiscence) you are moved to commit some sin, then begin some holy meditation on that solemn vow which you made to God in baptism.

Again, if through infirmity you fall once or often into some sin, recall your baptism that there you may receive courage to your soul. For although baptism is administered but once, yet it testifies that all man's sins—past, present, and to come—are washed away (1 Pet. 3:20, Eph. 5:25-27). Therefore, baptism may be truly termed the *Sacrament of Repentance,* being as a board to swim upon whenever a man fears the shipwreck of his soul (Mark 1:4, 1 Tim. 1:19, Rom. 6:4, 6).

Last of all, see that you never rest until such a time as you have a feeling of the reviving power signified in baptism, namely the power of Christ's death mortifying sin, and the virtue of his resurrection in the renovation of the Spirit.

---

6. Eusebius, *Ecclesiastical History*, 7.9. See also: Augustine, *Answer to the Letters of Petilianus*, 3.2.

CHAPTER 34:

Lord's Supper

The Sacramental Relationship between the parts of the Lord's Supper

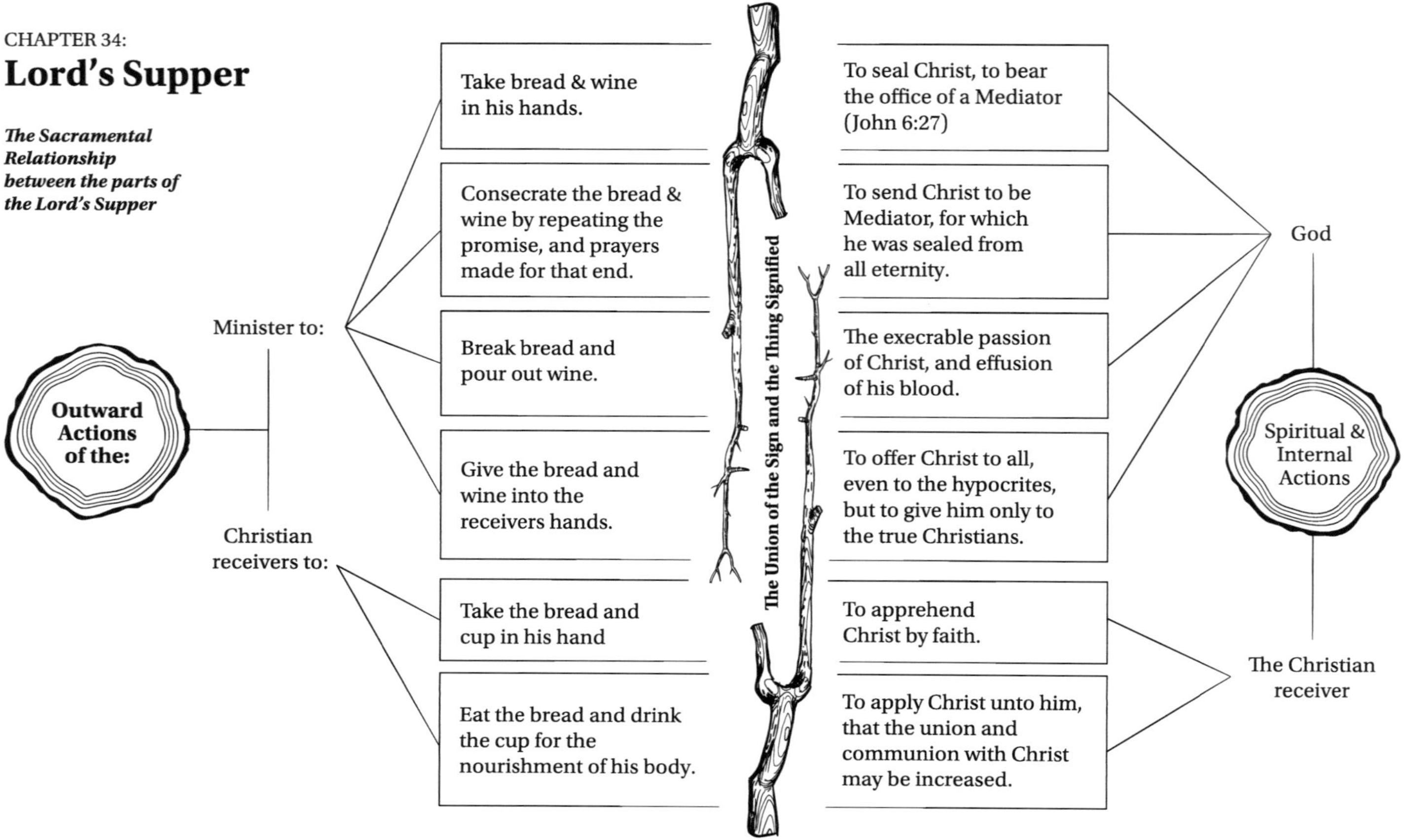

Chapter Thirty Four

THE LORD'S SUPPER

The **Lord's Supper** is a sacrament by which those who are grafted into Christ are daily, in a spiritual manner, nourished in Christ to eternal life, by means of the signs of bread and wine (1 Cor. 11:23–25; Rom. 6:5).

The parts of the Lord's Supper are as follows:

The **Elements** of bread and wine are signs and seals of the body and blood of Christ.

The **Action of the Minister** is a symbol of God's action. The Minister's action is fourfold:

1. Taking the bread and wine into his own hands. This seals the action of God the Father by which he (from all eternity) separated and elected his Son to perform the duty of a Mediator between God and man. *"For on him God the Father has set his seal"* (John 6:27).
2. Blessing it. Here, by the recital of the promises and prayers given for that purpose, he separates the bread and wine from their common to a holy use. This seals that action of God by which he, in the fullness of time, sent Christ to perform the office of a Mediator, to which he was foreordained.
3. Breaking of the bread and pouring out of the wine. This seals the passion of Christ in which upon the cross he was truly bruised for our transgressions, both in soul and in body.
4. Distributing of the bread and wine into the hands of the communicants. This seals the action of God offering Christ to all (indeed, even to the hypocrites), but giving him actually to the faithful for the daily increase of their faith and repentance.

The **Action of the Receiver** is twofold:

1. Taking the bread and wine in his hand. This seals a spiritual action of the receiver, namely his apprehension of Christ by the

hand of faith (John 1:12).

2. Eating the bread and drinking the wine for the nourishment of his body. This seals his application of Christ by faith, so that the feeling of his true union and communion with Christ may daily be increased: *"The cup of blessing that we bless, is it not a participation in the blood of Christ? The bread that we break, is it not a participation in the body of Christ?"* (1 Cor. 10:16).

The (Roman Catholic) **Doctrine of Transubstantiation** teaches that the bread is turned into the very body of Christ, and the wine into his blood. This is an utter fable; the reasons why are these:

1. At the first institution of the Supper, which was before Christ's passion, the body of Christ was then eaten as though already crucified. How the crucified body of Christ should be eaten, he himself not yet being crucified, is impossible to imagine.
2. The bread after the consecration is distributed into parts, yet the whole body of Christ is received of every singular communicant.
3. The bread is the communion of Christ's body, therefore cannot be his body itself.
4. By this means the body of Christ would not only be made of the substance of the Virgin Mary, but also of the baker's bread.
5. Let the bread and wine be kept for a time and the bread will mould and the wine turn to vinegar, even after the consecration. By this we may conclude that the substance of bread and wine remained.
6. This opinion completely overthrows the sacramental union, namely the proper relation between the sign and the thing signed.

The same may be said of the **Lutherans' Consubstantiation**, whereby they teach that there is a coexistence by which the body of Christ is either *in*, *with*, or *about* the bread. Against this, these reasons may suffice:

1. The Supper is done in remembrance of Christ. But what need is there of that if the body of Christ were really present?

2. *"Whom heaven must receive until the time for restoring all the things about which God spoke by the mouth of his holy prophets long ago"* (Acts 3:21).
3. An essential property of a body is to be in one place, and this applies to the body of Christ also.
4. If Christ's body were physically eaten, then the wicked as well as the faithful would be partakers of the flesh of Christ. But to 'eat his flesh' is to believe in him and to have eternal life.
5. It is absurd to think that Christ, sitting among his Disciples, took his own body into his hands and give it, in its entirety, to each of his Disciples.

Those who would rightly prepare themselves to celebrate the Lord's Supper, must have:

1. A knowledge of God, of man's fall, and of the promised restoration into the covenant by Christ. *"For as often as you eat this bread and drink the cup, you proclaim the Lord's death until he comes .... discerning the body"* (1 Cor. 11:26, 29).
2. True faith in Christ. For every man receives as much as he believes he receives. *"For good news came to us just as to them, but the message they heard did not benefit them, because they were not united by faith with those who listened"* (Heb. 4:2).

   Furthermore, a true repentance of their sins. *"He who slaughters an ox is like one who kills a man; he who sacrifices a lamb, like one who breaks a dog's neck; he who presents a grain offering, like one who offers pig's blood; he who makes a memorial offering of frankincense, like one who blesses an idol. These have chosen their own ways, and their soul delights in their abominations"* (Isa. 66:3). *"I wash my hands in innocence and go around your altar, O LORD"* (Psalm 26:6).
3. Renewed faith and daily repentance for new sins committed upon infirmity. Every new sin requires a new act both of repentance and faith, and this renovation must be seen by our reconciliation of ourselves to our neighbours or injuries and wrongs. *"So if you are offering your gift at the altar and there remember that your brother has something against you, leave your gift there before the altar and go. First be reconciled*

to your brother, and then come and offer your gift" (Matt. 5:23-24). If you come furnished with these things, then do not abstain from the Lord's table because of your many infirmities.

If, being thus prepared, you feel that you have a corrupt and rebellious heart, know that you are well disposed to be at the Lord's table since you are touched with a lively sense of your crooked disposition. *"The Spirit of the Lord is upon me, because he has anointed me to proclaim good news to the poor. He has sent me to proclaim liberty to the captives and recovering of sight to the blind, to set at liberty those who are oppressed"* (Luke 4:18). *"He answered, 'I was sent only to the lost sheep of the house of Israel'"* (Matt. 15:24). The Lord's Supper is a medicine to the diseased and languishing soul. Therefore, men must seek to purify and heal their hearts in it, as much as to bring pure and sound hearts to it.

If you feel in yourself some great defect and lack of faith, pray earnestly to God that he would increase it. *"Immediately the father of the child cried out and said, 'I believe; help my unbelief!'"* (Mark 9:24). If you cannot do this yourself, ask for the aid of the faithful who may carry you by their faith, as the friends of the paralysed man carried him upon their shoulders and laid him before Christ (Mark 2:3).

If you come to the Lord's table ill prepared, you shall be judged guilty of the body and blood of Christ, just as a money counterfeiter is guilty of high treason. *"Whoever, therefore, eats the bread or drinks the cup of the Lord in an unworthy manner will be guilty concerning the body and blood of the Lord"* (1 Cor. 11:27).

Those who don't feel themselves to be penitent cannot come to the Lord's table without repentance, lest they eat and drink their own damnation. But neither can they defer repentance, by which they may come, lest they procure for themselves final destruction.

CHAPTER 35:

Degrees of Love

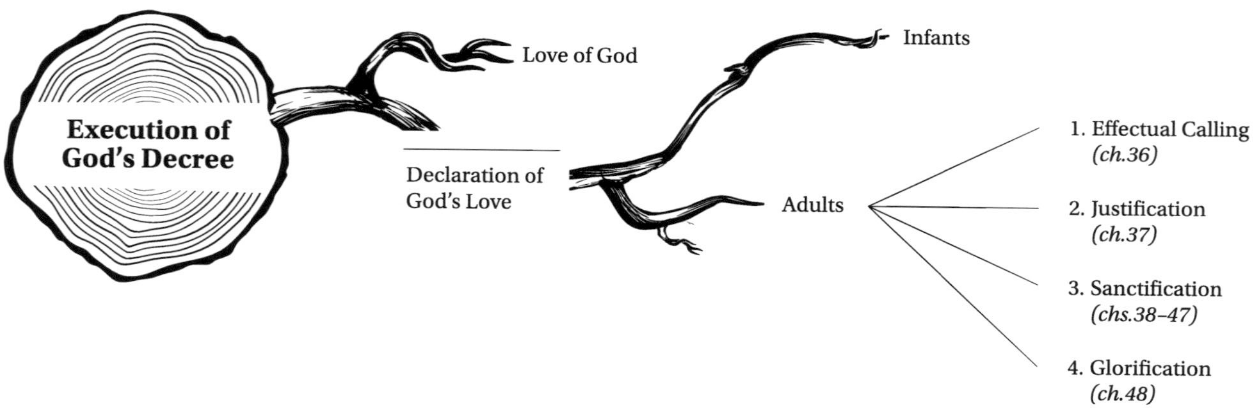

Chapter Thirty Five

THE DEGREES OF EXECUTING GOD'S DECREE OF ELECTION

We have hitherto declared the outward means by which God's decree is executed. Now follow the degrees of its execution.

There are two degrees of the **Execution of God's Decree**: the Love of God and the Declaration of his Love. *"To the praise of his glorious grace, with which he has blessed us in the Beloved .... making known to us the mystery of his will, according to his purpose, which he set forth in Christ"* (Eph. 1:6, 9).

God's Love is that whereby God freely loves all who he has chosen in Christ Jesus though they are, in themselves, altogether corrupt. *"We love because he first loved us"* (1 John 4:19). *"God shows his love for us in that while we were still sinners, Christ died for us .... For if while we were enemies we were reconciled to God by the death of his Son, much more, now that we are reconciled, shall we be saved by his life"* (Rom. 5:8, 10).

The **Declaration of God's Love** is twofold. The first is towards infants elected to salvation (***as follows***), the second towards men of riper years (***Chapter 36***).

The **Declaration of God's Love towards Infants** is of this manner:

Elect Infants who depart this life, either whilst still in the womb of their mother or after they are born, obtain eternal salvation by God's Spirit grafted them into Christ in a secret and indescribable manner. *"For in one Spirit we were all baptized into one body—Jews or Greeks, slaves or free—and all were made to drink of one Spirit"* (1 Cor. 12:13). *"And the angel answered her, "The Holy Spirit will come upon you, and the power of the Most High will overshadow you; therefore the child to be born will be called holy—the Son of God .... And when Elizabeth heard the greeting of Mary, the baby leaped in her womb. And Elizabeth was filled with the Holy Spirit .... And immediately his mouth was opened and his tongue loosed, and he spoke, blessing God .... And the child grew and became strong in spirit, and he was in the wilderness until the day of his public appearance to Israel"* (Luke 1:35, 41, 64, 80). *"Before I formed you in the womb I knew you, and before you were born I consecrated you"* (Jer. 1:5).

I call the manner of infants salvation secret and indescribable, because:

1. They lack actual faith to receive Christ. For actual faith necessarily presupposes a knowledge of God's free promise, which the believer applies to himself. But infants cannot possibly perform this in any way. And surely if infants have faith actually, they generally either lose it when they reach adulthood or at least show no signs of it, neither of which is possible if they had previously received actual faith. Rather, we see that in those of riper years, there is not so much as a shadow or spark of faith to be seen before they are called by the preaching of the gospel.
2. Infants are said to be regenerated only with regard to their internal inclinations, not in regard to any actions of the mind, will, or affections. Therefore, they lack those terrors of conscience which precede repentance in those who are of riper years of discretion. Again, they are not troubled with that conflict and combat between the flesh and the Spirit, with which the faithful of greater years are exercised (***chapters 40-43***).

CHAPTER 36:

Effectual Call

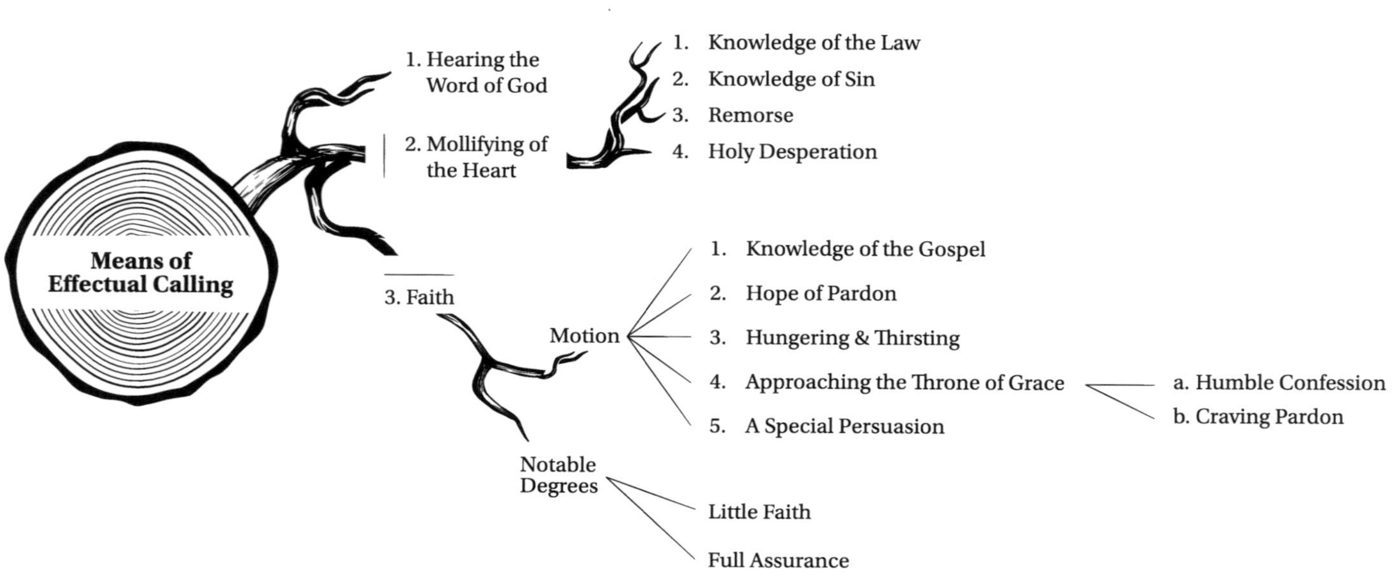

Chapter Thirty Six

THE FIRST DEGREE OF THE DECLARATION OF GOD'S LOVE: EFFECTUAL CALLING

The **Declaration of God's love in those of Years of Discretion** has four degrees (Rom. 8:30, 1 Cor. 1:30):

1. Effectual Calling (***as follows***),
2. Justification (***chapter 37***),
3. Sanctification (***chapters 38–47***), and
4. Glorification (***chapters 48–50***).

The **First Degree is Effectual Calling** whereby a sinner (being severed from the world) is welcomed into God's family. *"And he came and preached peace to you who were far off and peace to those who were near .... So then you are no longer strangers and aliens, but you are fellow citizens with the saints and members of the household of God"* (Eph. 2:17, 19).

Of this there are two parts:

1. Election, which is a separation of a sinner from the cursed estate of all mankind. *"If you were of the world, the world would love you as its own; but because you are not of the world, but I chose you out of the world, therefore the world hates you"* (John 15:19).
2. The reciprocal donation or free gift of God the Father, whereby he both gives the sinful man to be saved by Christ, and actually and most effectually gives Christ to that sinful man, so that he may boldly say: "Christ (both God and man) is mine, and I am his." We see a similar thing in marriage: the husband says: "this woman is my wife, whom her parents have given to me, so that

> (she being fully mine) I may both have her and govern her." Likewise, the woman may say: "this man is my husband, who has bestowed himself upon me and does cherish me as his wife." *"He who did not spare his own Son but gave him up for us all"* (Rom. 8:32). *"For to us a child is born, to us a son is given"* (Isa. 9:6). *"Since you have given him authority over all flesh, to give eternal life to all whom you have given him .... I have manifested your name to the people whom you gave me out of the world. Yours they were, and you gave them to me, and they have kept your word. Now they know that everything that you have given me is from you"* (John 17:2, 6–7). *"My Father, who has given them to me, is greater than all, and no one is able to snatch them out of the Father's hand"* (John 10:29).

Hence comes that admirable **Union**, which is the grafting in of those who are to be saved into Christ, and their growing up together with him. Thus, in a particular manner, Christ is made the head, and every repentant sinner a member of his mystical body. *"I do not ask for these only, but also for those who will believe in me through their word, that they may all be one, just as you, Father, are in me, and I in you, that they also may be in us, so that the world may believe that you have sent me"* (John 17:20). *"Because we are members of his body"* (Eph. 5:30). *"I am the true vine, and my Father is the vinedresser. Every branch in me that does not bear fruit he takes away, and every branch that does bear fruit he prunes, that it may bear more fruit"* (John 15:1–2). *"Built on the foundation of the apostles and prophets, Christ Jesus himself being the cornerstone, in whom the whole structure, being joined together, grows into a holy temple in the Lord. In him you also are being built together into a dwelling place for God by the Spirit"* (Eph. 2:20-22).

Although this is a very close and real union, we must not think of it, as mixing or soldering of one soul to another. Neither is it a mere agreement between souls. Rather, it is by the communion and operation of the infinite Spirit, who is of sufficient ability to join things together which are of themselves far distant from each other. We see the like in the soul of man, which joins the head with the foot (Eph. 2:22); *"by which he has granted to us his precious and very great promises, so that through them you may become partakers of the divine nature, having escaped from the corruption that is in the world because of sinful desire"* (2 Pet. 1:4).

"So if there is any encouragement in Christ, any comfort from love, any participation in the Spirit, any affection and sympathy, etc." (Phil. 2:1).

The Things United. In this union the whole person of every faithful man, is truly joined with the whole person of our Saviour Christ, God and man. (The union is not of our soul alone being united with Christ's soul, or our flesh with his flesh).

The **Manner of their Union** is as follows. A faithful man is, first of all, united to the human nature of Christ, then afterwards (by reason of Christ's humanity) to the Word itself, the divine nature. For salvation and life depend upon that fullness of the Godhead which is in Christ, yet it is not shared with us except in and by the flesh of Christ. *"So Jesus said to them, "Truly, truly, I say to you, unless you eat the flesh of the Son of Man and drink his blood, you have no life in you .... Whoever feeds on my flesh and drinks my blood abides in me, and I in him"* (John 6:53, 56).

The Bond of this Union. This union is made by the Spirit of God applying Christ to us, and we (on our part) receiving by faith Christ Jesus offered to us. This is why it is called a spiritual union.

Christ, as the head of the faithful, is to be considered a public man sustaining the person of all the elect. Hence is it that the faithful are said to be crucified with Christ, to die with him, to be buried (Rom. 6:4-6), to be enlivened (Eph. 2:5), and to be raised up and placed in heaven (Eph. 2:6, Col. 3:1). This is not only the hope of the faithful, but they are presently accepted by God to have done all these things in Christ, just as in Adam's first sin all his descendants afterwards were tainted by sin.

A member of Christ is **Distinguished** as such either before men or before God. Before men, the members of Christ are those who, outwardly professing the faith, are charitably regarded by the Church as true members. But such people may be reprobates, deceiving both themselves and the Church. In God's presence such persons are no more true members than are the noxious sicknesses in a man's body, or a wooden leg or another joint cunningly fastened to the body.

Before God, the members of Christ are those who are either decreed to be so, or actually are so already. Those decreed to be so are those who (being elect from all eternity) are either not yet born or not yet called. *"And I have other sheep that are not of this fold. I must bring them also"* (John 10:16).

Actual Members of Christ are either living or dying members.

Actual living members of Christ are everyone elected who, being grafted into Christ by faith and by the Spirit, do feel and show forth the power of Christ in them.

An actual dying or decayed member is everyone truly grafted into Christ, yet has no feeling of the power and efficacy of the enlivening Spirit in him. He is like a numb leg without sense. This is indeed a part of man's body, and yet receives no nourishment. Such are those faithful ones (who for a time) faint and are overcome by the heavy burden of temptations and their sins. Such also are excommunicated persons who are true members in regard of their grafting; however in regard to their external communion with the Church, and efficacy of the Spirit, they are not members until such a time as they are touched with repentance, and begin (as it were) to live again.

God executes this effectual calling by certain **Means**.

The first Means is the saving **Hearing of the word of God**, *"And when I passed by you and saw you wallowing in your blood, I said to you in your blood, 'Live!'"* (Ezek. 16:6). *"Come, everyone who thirsts, come to the waters; and he who has no money, come, buy and eat! Come, buy wine and milk without money and without price"* (Isa. 55:1). *"But to all who did receive him, who believed in his name, he gave the right to become children of God"* (John 1:12). This is when this word is outwardly preached to one who is both dead in his sins and does not so much as dream of his salvation. *"For I would not have known what it is to covet if the law had not said, 'You shall not covet'"* (Rom. 7:7). First the Law shows him his sin and its punishment which is eternal death. Afterwards the gospel shows them salvation by Christ Jesus to those who believe. *"But the anointing that you received from him abides in you, and you have no need that anyone should teach you. But as his anointing teaches you about everything, and is true, and is no lie—just as it has taught you, abide in him"* (1 John 2:27). Inwardly the eyes of the mind are enlightened, and the heart and ears are opened so that he may see, hear, and understand the preaching of the word of God. *"One who heard us was a woman named Lydia, from the city of Thyatira, a seller of purple goods, who was a worshipper of God. The Lord opened her heart to pay attention to what was said by Paul"* (Acts 16:14). *"In sacrifice and offering you have not delighted, but you have given me an open ear"* (Psalm 40:6). *"No one can come to me unless the*

Father who sent me draws him. And I will raise him up on the last day" (John 6:44). *"For the LORD has called you like a wife deserted and grieved in spirit, like a wife of youth when she is cast off, says your God"* (Isa. 54:6).

The second Means is the **Mollifying of the Heart**, which must be bruised and broken into pieces so that it may be fit to receive God's saving grace offered to it. *"And I will give them one heart, and a new spirit I will put within them. I will remove the heart of stone from their flesh and give them a heart of flesh"* (Ezek. 11:19).

There are four principle hammers for the bruising of this stony heart:

1. Knowledge of the law of God.
2. Knowledge of sin, both original and actual, and the punishment due to them.
3. Remorse, or pricking of the heart: namely a sense and feeling of the wrath of God for our sins.
4. Holy desperation of one's own power in the obtaining of eternal life. *"Now when they heard this they were cut to the heart, and said to Peter and the rest of the apostles, "Brothers, what shall we do?" And Peter said to them, "Repent and be baptized every one of you in the name of Jesus Christ for the forgiveness of your sins, and you will receive the gift of the Holy Spirit"* (Acts 2:37–38). *"But when he came to himself, he said, 'How many of my father's hired servants have more than enough bread, but I perish here with hunger! I will arise and go to my father, and I will say to him, 'Father, I have sinned against heaven and before you. I am no longer worthy to be called your son. Treat me as one of your hired servants,' etc."* (Luke 15:17–19). *"He answered, 'I was sent only to the lost sheep of the house of Israel'"* (Matt. 15:24).

The third Means is **Faith**, which is a miraculous and supernatural faculty of the heart, apprehending Christ Jesus, being applied by the operation of the Holy Spirit, and receiving him to itself (John 1:12); *"Jesus said to them, 'I am the bread of life; whoever comes to me shall not hunger, and whoever believes in me shall never thirst'"* (John 6:35). *"What shall we say, then? That Gentiles who did not pursue righteousness have attained it, that is, a righteousness that is by faith"* (Rom. 9:30).

Christ is received where a person particularly applies to himself Christ with his merits. This is done by an inward persuasion of the heart, which comes exclusively by effectual certification by the Holy Spirit concerning the mercy of God in Christ Jesus. *"Now we have received not the spirit of the world, but the Spirit who is from God, that we might understand the things freely given us by God"* (1 Cor. 2:12). *"And I will pour out on the house of David and the inhabitants of Jerusalem a spirit of grace and pleas for mercy, so that, when they look on me, on him whom they have pierced"* (Zech. 12:10). *"The Spirit himself bears witness with our spirit that we are children of God"* (Rom. 8:16). *"In him you also, when you heard the word of truth, the gospel of your salvation, and believed in him, were sealed with the promised Holy Spirit"* (Eph. 1:13). See also 2 Corinthians 1:22.

In the **Work of Faith** there are five motions of the heart, which are linked and united together, and which are worthy of the consideration of every Christian:

1. **Knowledge of the gospel** by the illumination of God's spirit. *"By his knowledge shall the righteous one, my servant, make many to be accounted righteous"* (Isa. 53:11). *"And this is eternal life, that they know you the only true God, and Jesus Christ whom you have sent"* (John 17:3).

    In those who are truly humbled, to this is joined a serious meditation on the promises of the gospel, stirred up by the distinct feeling of their own poverty.

    And after the foresaid knowledge comes a general faith (in all those who are enlightened) whereby they subscribe to the truth of the gospel. *"For good news came to us just as to them, but the message they heard did not benefit them, because they were not united by faith with those who listened"* (Heb. 4:2). *"Holding faith and a good conscience. By rejecting this, some have made shipwreck of their faith"* (1 Tim. 1:19). *"God our Saviour, who desires all people to be saved and to come to the knowledge of the truth"* (1 Tim. 2:4).

    When this knowledge is more full and complete, it is called the "full assurance of understanding" (πληροφορία). *"That their hearts may be encouraged, being knit together in love, to reach all the riches of full assurance of understanding and the knowledge of God's mystery, which is Christ"* (Col. 2:2). *"I know and am persuaded in the Lord Jesus that nothing is unclean in itself"* (Rom. 14:14). *"Because our gospel came to you not only in word, but also in power and in the*

Holy Spirit and with full conviction" (1 Thess. 1:5).

2. **Hope of pardon**, whereby a sinner believes that his sins are pardonable, though he does not yet feel this to be the case. *"I will arise and go to my father, and I will say to him, "'Father, I have sinned against heaven and before you. I am no longer worthy to be called your son. Treat me as one of your hired servants'"* (Luke 15:18).
3. **Hungering and Thirsting** after the grace offered to him in Christ Jesus, as a man hungers and thirsts after food and drink (John 6:35; 7:37). *"And he said to me, 'It is done! I am the Alpha and the Omega, the beginning and the end. To the thirsty I will give from the spring of the water of life without payment'"* (Rev. 21:6). *"Blessed are those who hunger and thirst for righteousness, for they shall be satisfied"* (Matt. 5:6).
4. **Approaching to the Throne of Grace**. Here a man flies from the terror of the Law, in order that he may take hold of Christ and find favour with God. *"Let us then with confidence draw near to the throne of grace, that we may receive mercy and find grace to help in time of need"* (Heb. 4:16).

   This approaching has two parts:

   a. A **Humble Confession** of our sins before God: confession of specific sins where they are known, and generally if unknown. This done, the Lord forthwith remits all our sins. *"I said, 'I will confess my transgressions to the LORD,' and you forgave the iniquity of my sin"* (Psalm 32:5). *"David said to Nathan, 'I have sinned against the LORD.' And Nathan said to David, 'The LORD also has put away your sin; you shall not die'"* (2 Sam. 12:13). See also Luke 15:19.

   b. **Craving Pardon** of some sins, with unspeakable sighs and with perseverance (Luke 15:21); *"Repent, therefore, of this wickedness of yours, and pray to the Lord that, if possible, the intent of your heart may be forgiven you"* (Acts 8:22). *"Likewise the Spirit helps us in our weakness. For we do not know what to pray for as we ought, but the Spirit himself intercedes for us with groanings too deep for words"* (Rom. 8:26). *"O Israel, return to the LORD your God, For you have stumbled because of your iniquity; Take words with you, And return to the LORD. Say to Him, 'Take away all iniquity; Receive us graciously'"* (Hos. 14:1–2 NKJV).

5. **A Special Persuasion** (arising from approaching Christ's throne) imprinted on the heart by the Holy Spirit. By this, every faithful man applies those promises made in the gospel particularly to himself. *"And behold, some people brought to him a paralytic, lying on a bed. And when Jesus saw their faith, he said to the paralytic, 'Take heart, my son; your sins are forgiven'"* (Matt. 9:2). *"O woman, great is your faith! Be it done for you as you desire"* (Matt. 15:28). *"It is no longer I who live, but Christ who lives in me. And the life I now live in the flesh I live by faith in the Son of God, who loved me and gave himself for me"* (Gal. 2:20).

   This persuasion is (and ought to be) in everyone even before he has any experience of God's mercies. *"And behold, a Canaanite woman from that region came out and was crying, 'Have mercy on me, O Lord, Son of David; my daughter is severely oppressed by a demon,' etc."* (Matt. 15:22. See also verses 23–27). *"Jesus said to him, 'Have you believed because you have seen me? Blessed are those who have not seen and yet have believed'"* (John 20:29). *"Now faith is the assurance of things hoped for, the conviction of things not seen"* (Heb. 11:1). In philosophy we first see that a thing is true by experience, and afterwards give our agreement to it. For example, in natural philosophy, I am persuaded that the water is hot because when I put my hand into it, I perceive it to be so by experience.

   But in the practice of faith it is the opposite. For first we must consent to the word of God, resisting all doubt and hesitancy, and afterwards our will, experience, and feeling of comfort will follow. *"Believe in the LORD your God, and you will be established; believe his prophets, and you will succeed"* (2 Chron. 20:20). They therefore do themselves harm, who are still in a doubt of their salvation because they do not (as yet) feel in themselves special motions of God's Spirit.

Thus much concerning the means which God uses in the begetting of faith. There are, beside this, **Two Notable Degrees of Faith**. One is the lowest degree; the other is the highest, or superlative degree.

The **Lowest Degree of Faith** is called *little* or *weak faith* (ὀλιγόπιστοι).[1]

1. For Perkins's fuller discussion of this lowest degree of faith, see his *A Grain of a Mustard Seed* (1597) in *The Works of William Perkins: Volume 8* (ed. J. Stephen Yuille; Grand Rapids: Reformation Heritage Books, 2019).

It is like a grain of mustard seed, or a smoking flax which can neither give out heat nor flame but only smoke. *"And they went and woke him, saying, 'Save us, Lord; we are perishing.' And he said to them, 'Why are you afraid, O you of little faith?'"* (Matt. 8:25–26). *"I say to you, if you have faith like a grain of mustard seed, you will say to this mountain, 'Move from here to there,' and it will move"* (Matt. 7:20). *"A faintly burning wick he will not quench"* (Isa. 42:3).

Faith is said to be weak and feeble when, of those five degrees mentioned above, either the first (knowledge) or the fifth (application of the promises) is very feeble, whilst the rest remain strong. "*One person believes he may eat anything, while the weak person eats only vegetables. Let not the one who eats despise the one who abstains, and let not the one who abstains pass judgement on the one who eats, for God has welcomed him"* (Rom. 14:2–3). Although the Apostles believed that Christ was the Son of the living God, they were ignorant of his death and resurrection (Matt. 16:16, John 6:69, Matt. 17:22); *"But they did not understand this saying, and it was concealed from them, so that they might not perceive it"* (Luke 9:45). *"They asked him, 'Lord, will you at this time restore the kingdom to Israel?'"* (Acts 1:6).

To better understand this kind of faith, we must observe these two rules:

1. The beginnings of faith is a serious desire to believe and an endeavour to obtain God's favour. *"Blessed are those who hunger and thirst for righteousness, for they shall be satisfied"* (Matt. 5:6). *"To the thirsty I will give from the spring of the water of life without payment"* (Rev. 21:6). *"He fulfils the desire of those who fear him; he also hears their cry and saves them"* (Psalm 145:19). For those who begin to believe and to be renewed, the mind will not lie idle. But being moved by the Holy Spirit, they will strive with doubt and distrust, and endeavour to bring their agreement to the sweet promises made in the gospel and firmly to apply the same to themselves; and amidst their sense of weakness, desire assistance from above. And thus faith is bestowed.

2. God does not despise the least spark of faith if it increases, even little by little, and such persons use the means of grace to increase it. *"The apostles said to the Lord, "Increase our faith!" And the Lord said, "If you had faith like a grain of mustard seed,*

you could say to this mulberry tree, 'Be uprooted and planted in the sea,' and it would obey you"' (Luke 17:5-6). Man must therefore stir up his faith by meditation on God's word, serious prayers, and by other spiritual exercises relating to faith.

The **Highest Degree of Faith** is a full assurance (πληροφορία), which is not only certain and true, but also *a full persuasion* of the heart. By this, a Christian (taking hold of Christ Jesus much more firmly) makes full and resolute account that God loves him, and that God will give Christ to him by name, along with all his graces pertaining to eternal life. *"No distrust made him waver concerning the promise of God, but he grew strong in his faith as he gave glory to God, fully convinced that God was able to do what he had promised"* (Rom. 4:20). *"For I am sure that neither death nor life, etc. .... will be able to separate us from the love of God in Christ Jesus our Lord"* (Rom. 8:38-39). *"Your servant has struck down both lions and bears, and this uncircumcised Philistine shall be like one of them, for he has defied the armies of the living God"* (1 Sam. 17:36). *"Surely goodness and mercy shall follow me all the days of my life"* (Psalm 23:6; cf. 23:1-4).

Man comes to this high degree after felt sense, observation, and long experience of God's favour and love.

Question: Is justifying faith commanded in the Law?

Answer: It is commanded in the law of faith, namely the gospel, but not in the law of works, that is, the moral law (Rom. 3:27).

The reasons are these:

a. The law does not command anything which it does not reveal. The law is so far from revealing justifying faith, that it never knew it.

b. Adam had (before his fall) fully written the moral law on his heart, yet he did not have justifying faith, which apprehends Christ.

Objection 1: Disbelief is condemned by the law.

Answer: Disbelief toward God is condemned in the law, but disbelief against the Messiah Christ Jesus is condemned by the gospel. For in the gospel disbelief in the Son as Mediator is shown to be a sin. This is not condemned by the law, but by the gospel, which commands us to hear the Son, and to believe in him (Matt. 17:5; 1 John 3:23). Thus it is plain that this sin (not to believe in Christ) is expressly made clear and condemned by the gospel. Whilst the knowledge of sin comes by the law, not everything which reproves or declares something a sin belongs to the Law of Works.

Objection 2: But ceremonies belong to the Decalogue.

Answer: Ceremonies relate to the Decalogue as examples, but in fact they are belong to the gospel.

Chapter Thirty Seven

THE SECOND DEGREE OF THE DECLARATION OF GOD'S LOVE: JUSTIFICATION

The **Second Degree is Justification** whereby those who believe are accounted just (or righteous) before God through the obedience of Christ Jesus. *"For our sake he made him to be sin who knew no sin, so that in him we might become the righteousness of God"* (2 Cor. 5:21. cf. 1 Cor. 1:30) *"For as by the one man's disobedience the many were made sinners, so by the one man's obedience* (that is Christ, 5:17) *the many will be made righteous"* (Rom. 5:19).

Question: Did Christ perform full obedience to the law for us men alone, or for himself also?

Answer:

1. Not for himself (as some would erroneously have him). For the flesh of Christ was in hypostatic union to the Word, and so was fully sanctified in itself, even from the first moment of conception, and was most worthy to be blessed with eternal life. Therefore, Christ merited nothing for himself by all that obedience which he performed after his conception.
2. For us (namely, the faithful) he fulfilled all the righteousness of the law. And hence is it that he is called: *"the end of the law for righteousness to everyone who believes"* (Rom. 10:4).

Here several things may be objected:

1. *Objection:* Christ, as he is man, is bound to obey the law for himself.

   Answer: He is not bound by nature (except of his own accord), for he was not a bare man, but God and man. And whilst Christ neither suffered nor fulfilled the law except in that flesh which he took upon him, yet (because of the hypostatic union) his passion and obedience has respect to the whole person, God and man. Therefore, obedience was not due on his part, and so was without merit to himself. Indeed, given that the flesh of Christ is united to the person of the Word, and so exalted in dignity and sanctity above all angels, it may seem to be exempted from this natural obligation of performing the law.

2. *Objection:* If Christ performed the law for us, we are no longer bound to observe it. We will not undergo eternal punishments for our sins since Christ bore them in his person upon the cross.

   Answer: If we keep the same relation to performing obedience to the law, then this consequence is very true. But it is not so, for Christ performed obedience to the law for us as the satisfaction of the law, whereas the faithful are bound to obedience, not as it is satisfactory, but as a certification of faith, a testimony of their gratitude towards God, or a means to edify their neighbours. Even as Christ suffered punishments for our sins, we also suffer punishments as trials or chastisements.

3. *Objection:* The law and justice of God do not demand both obedience and punishment.

   Answer: In man's perfect estate the justice of God required only obedience, but in his corrupted estate, God requires both obedience and punishment: punishment, as the law is violated; and obedience, that legal justice may be performed (Gal. 3:10). It is therefore plain that not only Christ's passion, but also his legal obedience, is our righteousness before God.

Justification has two parts: Remission of Sins and Imputation of Christ's Righteousness.

Remission of Sins is that part of justification whereby he who believes is freed from the guilt and punishment of sin by the merits of Christ's passion. *"And you, who once were alienated and hostile in mind, doing evil deeds, he has now reconciled in his body of flesh by his death, in order to present you holy and blameless and above reproach before him"* (Col. 1:21–22). *"He himself bore our sins in his body on the tree, that we might die to sin and live to righteousness. By his wounds you have been healed"* (1 Pet. 2:24).

Imputation of Righteousness is the other part of justification, whereby those who believe, having the guilt of their sins covered, are accounted just in the sight of God through Christ's righteousness (2 Cor. 5:21), *"Blessed is the one whose transgression is forgiven, whose sin is covered"* (Psalm 32:1). See also Romans 4 where the Apostle repeats imputation eleven times. *"I count everything as loss because of the surpassing worth of knowing Christ Jesus my Lord. For his sake I have suffered the loss of all things and count them as rubbish, in order that I may gain Christ and be found in him, not having a righteousness of my own that comes from the law, but that which comes through faith in Christ, the righteousness from God that depends on faith"* (Phil. 3:8–9).

The **Form of Justification** is a kind of transfer of the believer's sins to Christ and of Christ's righteousness to the believer by means of divine imputation. This is portrayed in the following diagram:

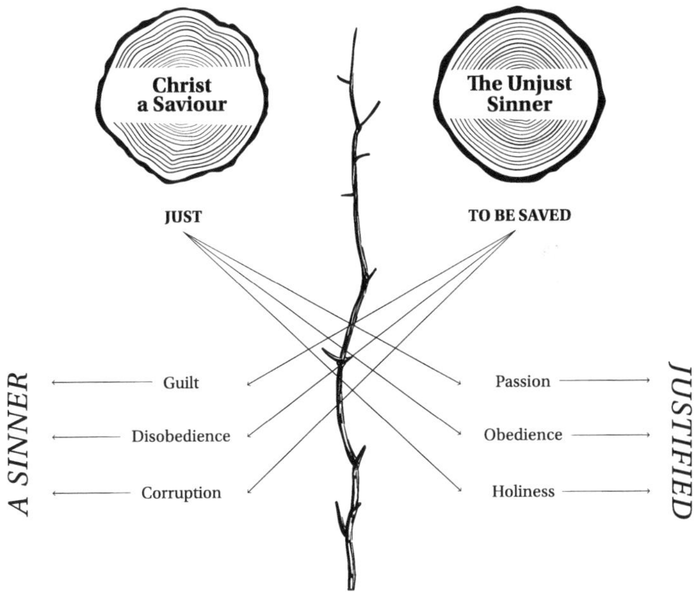

This **Obedience of Christ** is called both the Righteousness *of God,* and *of Christ.*

Of God.

1. Not because it is in God, but *of* God: for it takes all the power and merit it has from the deity of the Son. Hence Jeremiah says:

"Jehovah our righteousness" (Jer. 33:16).

2. God accepts it alone to save us. This alone makes us bold to approach God's throne of grace that we may have pardon for our sins and be received to eternal life. It is also called the Righteousness of Christ because, being outside of us, it is in the humanity of Christ.

   Objection 1: No man is made just by another man's justice.

   Answer: This justice is both another's and ours also. Another's, because it is in Christ; ours, because by our union with him, Christ with all his benefits is made ours.

   Objection 2: The ancient fathers never dreamed of this imputative justice. This teaching appears to be no more than fifty years old.[1]

   Answer: This is both false and impious. Augustine says: *"All who are justified by Christ are just, not in themselves, but in him"*.[2] Bernard says: *"Death in Christ his death is put to flight, and the justice of Christ is imputed to us."*[3] Also that: *"Where is there any rest* (he said) *but in the wounds of our Saviour? I will further sing, but what? My own justice? No, O Lord, I will remember your justice alone, for that is also my justice. For you were made of God unto me justice. But should I fear, whether that one justice would suffice two? No, it is not a short cloak that is not able to cover a couple. Your justice is justice for evermore, and will both cover thee and me, it is an exceedingly large and eternal justice, and in me it covers the multitude of my sins..."*.[4] Augustine says: *"We must understand this saying so. The doers of the law shall be justified," that we may know, that there are no doers of the law but those who are justified, so that they are not first doers of the law and then justified, but they are first justified and then doers of the law. So it is said they shall be justified, as if it should be said they shall be reputed just and accounted just."*[5]

---

1. This was a common Roman Catholic argument against Protestant theology in the sixteenth century. They argued that the doctrine of justification by faith alone through the imputation of Christ's sins to the believer was invented by the Protestant Reformers, and unprecedented in the history of the church.
2. Augustine, *Tractate on John*, 3.
3. Bernard of Clairvaux, *Book for the Knights of the Temple in Praise of the New Knighthood*, ch. 2.
4. Bernard of Clairvaux, *Sermons on the Canticles*, 62.
5. Augustine, *On the Spirit and the Letter*, chs. 9 & 26.

Justification has Adoption joined to it, whereby all who are predestined to be adopted are actually accounted the sons of God by Christ. *"He predestined us for adoption as sons through Jesus Christ, according to the purpose of his will"* (Eph. 1:5).

By means of **Adoption** God has bestowed many notable privileges upon his children.

1. They are the Lord's heirs apparent. *"And if children, then heirs—heirs of God and fellow heirs with Christ"* (Rom. 8:17).
2. They are fellow heirs with Christ, even kings (Rom. 8:17). *"And made us a kingdom, priests to his God and Father"* (Rev. 1:6).
3. All their afflictions, indeed their offences and even their deficiencies, are turned to trials or fatherly chastisements inflicted upon them for their good. *"And we know that for those who love God .... As it is written, "For your sake we are being killed all the day long; we are regarded as sheep to be slaughtered." No, in all these things we are more than conquerors through him who loved us"* (Rom. 8:28, 36–37). *"Then I will punish their transgression with the rod and their iniquity with stripes, but I will not remove from him my steadfast love or be false to my faithfulness"* (Psalm 89:32–33). *"A thorn was given me in the flesh, a messenger of Satan to harass me, to keep me from becoming conceited"* (2 Cor. 12:7). *"I will be to him a father, and he shall be to me a son. When he commits iniquity, I will discipline him with the rod of men, with the stripes of the sons of men"* (2 Sam. 7:14).
4. They have dominion over all creatures, yet such that in this life they only have the right to such dominion, but after this life shall actually enjoy it. Thus, it is apparent that the faithful alone make right use of the Lord's goods.
    a. Because their persons are acceptable to him in Christ, in whom also they have restitution made to them of all which they lost in Adam, that they may with a good conscience use them.
    b. They use them with thanksgiving to their ends appointed by God. *"Whether Paul or Apollos or Cephas or the world or life or death or the present or the future—all are yours, and you are Christ's, and Christ is God's"* (1 Cor. 3:22–23). *"You made him for a little while lower than the angels; you have*

crowned him with glory and honour, putting everything in subjection under his feet. Now in putting everything in subjection to him, he left nothing outside his control. At present, we do not yet see everything in subjection to him" (Heb. 2:7–8).

5. Lastly, they have the angels attending upon them for their good. *"Are they not all ministering spirits sent out to serve for the sake of those who are to inherit salvation?"* (Heb. 1:14). *"The angel of the LORD encamps around those who fear him, and delivers them"* (Psalm 34:7).

CHAPTER 38:

Sanctification

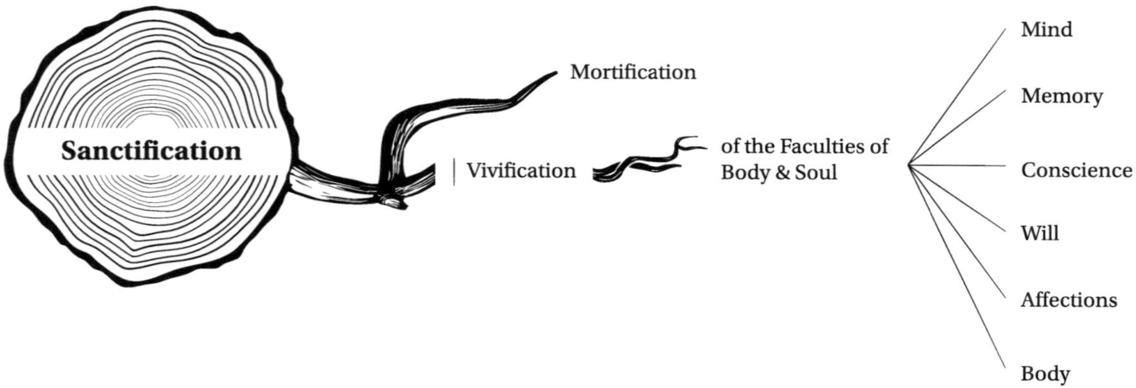

Chapter Thirty Eight

THE THIRD DEGREE OF THE DECLARATION OF GOD'S LOVE: SANCTIFICATION

The **Third Degree is Sanctification** whereby those who believe, being delivered from the tyranny of sin, are (little by little) renewed in holiness and righteousness. *"No one born of God makes a practice of sinning, for God's seed abides in him, and he cannot keep on sinning because he has been born of God"* (1 John 3:9). *"There is therefore now no condemnation for those who are in Christ Jesus"* (Rom. 8:1).

Sanctification has two parts: Mortification and Vivification.

Mortification of sin is the first part of sanctification, whereby the power of sin is subdued and crucified in the faithful. *"How can we who died to sin still live in it? Do you not know that all of us who have been baptized into Christ Jesus were baptized into his death? We were buried therefore with him by baptism into death, in order that, just as Christ was raised from the dead by the glory of the Father, we too might walk in newness of life"* (Rom. 6:2–4). See also Ecclesiastes 5:6–7, 11–13; *"And those who belong to Christ Jesus have crucified the flesh with its passions and desires"* (Gal. 5:24).

The means of this mortification is the death and burial of Christ, which first gave sin its mortal wound. From this proceeds such virtue as subdues sin, keeping it from breaking out as it would, and causing it to die in man as in a grave. *"We know that our old self was crucified with him in order that the body of sin might be brought to nothing"* (Rom. 6:6).

The power of Christ's death is a power which issued from his deity into his humanity when he died. By this he vanquished our sin in his humanity (both its guilt and punishment), since our sin was imputed to him as our substitute. Thus, he has the same power to abolish the corruption of sin in us, his members.

Vivification is the second part of sanctification, whereby our holiness begun is gradually enlarged. First, we receive the first fruits of the Spirit, then a continual increase of them. *"And to be renewed in the spirit of your minds, and to put on the new self, created after the likeness of God in true righteousness and holiness"* (Eph. 4:23–24). *"And you He made alive, who were dead in trespasses and sins"* (Eph. 2:1 NKJV). *"It is no longer I who live, but Christ who lives in me. And the life I now live in the flesh I live by faith in the Son of God, who loved me and gave himself for me"* (Gal. 2:20). *"But we ourselves, who have the firstfruits of the Spirit, groan inwardly as we wait eagerly for adoption as sons, the redemption of our bodies"* (Rom. 8:23). *"The first man Adam became a living being; the last Adam became a life-giving spirit"* (1 Cor. 15:45).

The **Cause** of both mortification and vivification is the Holy Spirit, who (by his divine power) conveys himself into believers' hearts, and creates holiness in them by applying the power of Christ's death and resurrection (Job 33:24–25); *"You, however, are not in the flesh but in the Spirit, if in fact the Spirit of God dwells in you. Anyone who does not have the Spirit of Christ does not belong to him .... If the Spirit of him who raised Jesus from the dead dwells in you, he who raised Christ Jesus from the dead will also give life to your mortal bodies through his Spirit who dwells in you"* (Rom. 8:9, 11).

The **Preservative** of vivification is derived from Christ's resurrection to those that are enlivened, which makes them to rise up to newness of life. *"That I may know him and the power of his resurrection"* (Phil. 3:10).

The power of Christ's resurrection is that whereby he first, in his own flesh and as conqueror over death and sin, began to live with God and to be exalted above every name. And then by this, sin being dead and buried, he causes in his members a goal and purpose to live according to the will of God.

Furthermore, this **Inherent Holiness** is to be distinguished into parts, according to the various faculties of the body and soul of man. *"Now may the God of peace himself sanctify you completely, and may your whole spirit and soul and body be kept blameless at the coming of our Lord Jesus Christ"* (1 Thess. 5:23).

1. The holiness or renewing of the **Mind**, which is the illumination thereof, to the knowledge of the will of God. *"We have not ceased to pray for you, asking that you may be filled with the knowledge of his will in all spiritual wisdom and understanding"* (Col. 1:9). *"For to one is given through the Spirit the utterance of wisdom, and to another the utterance of knowledge according to the same Spirit"* (1 Cor. 12:8).

   Illumination is either Spiritual Understanding or Spiritual Wisdom.

   a. **Spiritual Understanding** is an illumination of the mind, whereby it acknowledges the known truth of the word of God.

   b. **Spiritual Wisdom** is also an illumination of the mind, whereby this same truth is applied to the good ordering of particular things and actions, as persons, place, and time require.

      These two have these effects:

      i. To discern between good and evil. *"But solid food is for the mature, for those who have their powers of discernment trained by constant practice to distinguish good from evil"* (Heb. 5:14). *"that you may approve what is excellent"* (Phil. 1:10).

      ii. To discern of spirits. *"Beloved, do not believe every spirit, but test the spirits to see whether they are from God"* (1 John 4:1). *"Test everything; hold fast what is good"* (1 Thess. 5:21). *"Now these Jews were more noble than those in Thessalonica; they received the word with all eagerness, examining the Scriptures daily to see if these things were so"* (Acts 17:11).

      iii. To meditate upon the word and works of God. *"But his delight is in the law of the LORD, and on his law he meditates day and night"* (Psalm 1:2). *"I will meditate on your precepts and fix my eyes on your ways"* (Psalm 119:15; See also: Psalm 107).

      iv. To discern and acknowledge a man's own inward blindness. *"Teach me, O LORD, the way of your statutes; and I will keep it to the end .... Open my eyes, that I may behold wondrous things out of your law"* (Psalm 119:33, 18).

2. The sanctity of the **Memory** is an ability to keep a good thing when it is offered to the mind, and to remember it as need serves.[1] *"I have stored up your word in my heart, that I might not sin against you"* (Psalm 119:11. *"I bless the LORD who gives me counsel; in the night also my heart instructs me"* (Psalm 16:7). *"And his mother treasured up all these things in her heart"* (Luke 2:51).

3. The sanctity of **Conscience**, which is a grace of God whereby a man's conscience excuses him for all sins after they are forgiven him in Christ, as also of his upright walking in the whole course of his life.[2] *"Holding faith and a good conscience. By rejecting this, some have made shipwreck of their faith, etc."* (1 Tim. 1:19). *"For I am not aware of anything against myself, but I am not thereby acquitted"* (1 Cor. 4:4). *"Paul said, 'Brothers, I have lived my life before God in all good conscience up to this day'"* (Acts 23:1). *"So I always take pains to have a clear conscience toward both God and man"* (Acts 24:16). *"Vindicate me, O LORD, for I have walked in my integrity, and I have trusted in the LORD without wavering. Prove me, O LORD, and try me; test my heart and my mind. For your steadfast love is before my eyes, and I walk in your faithfulness"* (Psalm 26:1-3).

   Hence, there arises in all godly men the inward peace of God, and the outward alertness of disposition. *"And the peace of God, which surpasses all understanding, will guard your hearts and your minds in Christ Jesus"* (Phil. 4:7). *"The wicked flee when no one pursues, but the righteous are bold as a lion"* (Prov. 28:1).

4. Sanctity of **Will**, by which man begins to will what is good and to refuse the contrary. Therefore, in this state the will is partly freed, though also partly in bondage to sin. *"For it is God who works in*

---

1. Perkins' first published works defended his Ramist views of the art of memory against the esoteric views of Giordano Bruno (1548–1600) as advocated by his English disciple Alexander Dicson (1558–1603). See Perkins' *The Antidicson* (1584) and *A Handbook on Memory* (1584) in *The Works of William Perkins: Volume 6.* (ed. Joel R. Beeke & Greg A. Salazar; Grand Rapids: Reformation Heritage Books, 2018).
2. Perkins' fullest account of case-by-case, conscience-led decision making in the Christian life can be found in his *Whole Treatise of the Cases of Conscience* (1604) in *The Works of William Perkins: Volume 8* (ed. J. Stephen Yuille; Grand Rapids: Reformation Heritage Books, 2019).

you, both to will and to work for his good pleasure" (Phil. 2:13). *"For I know that nothing good dwells in me, that is, in my flesh. For I have the desire to do what is right, but not the ability to carry it out"* (Rom. 7:18 and verses 19–22).

5. Sanctity of **Affections** in the right moving of them (1 Thess. 5:23; Rom. 7:24). Those affections of most special note are:

    1. Hope, whereby men (with sighing) look for the accomplishment of their redemption. (Rom. 8:23).

       This hope, when it is strong and lively, also has the *full assurance* (πληροφορία) that faith has. *"And we desire each one of you to show the same earnestness to have the full assurance of hope until the end"* (Heb. 6:11). *"Blessed be the God and Father of our Lord Jesus Christ! According to his great mercy, he has caused us to be born again to a living hope through the resurrection of Jesus Christ from the dead"* (1 Pet. 1:3).

    2. Fear of offending God because of his mercy. *"And if you call on him as Father who judges impartially according to each one's deeds, conduct yourselves with fear throughout the time of your exile"* (1 Pet. 1:17). *"But with you there is forgiveness, that you may be feared"* (Psalm 130:4).

    3. A low regard of all worldly things with respect to Christ Jesus. *"But whatever gain I had, I counted as loss for the sake of Christ. Indeed, I count everything as loss because of the surpassing worth of knowing Christ Jesus my Lord. For his sake I have suffered the loss of all things and count them as rubbish, in order that I may gain Christ"* (Phil. 3:7–8).

    4. The love of God in Christ, which is as strong as death and a fire that cannot be quenched. *"For love is strong as death, jealousy is fierce as the grave. Its flashes are flashes of fire, the very flame of the LORD"* (Song 8:6).

    5. A fervent zeal for God's glory. *"For I could wish that I myself were accursed and cut off from Christ for the sake of my brothers, my kinsmen according to the flesh"* (Rom. 9:3).

    6. An anguish of mind for our own sins, and for those others also. *"My eyes shed streams of tears, because people do not keep your law"* (Psalm 119:136). *"And if he rescued righteous*

Lot, greatly distressed by the sensual conduct of the wicked (for as that righteous man lived among them day after day, he was tormenting his righteous soul over their lawless deeds that he saw and heard)" (2 Pet. 2:7–8).

7. Exceedingly great joy in the Holy Spirit. *"For the kingdom of God is not a matter of eating and drinking but of righteousness and peace and joy in the Holy Spirit"* (Rom. 14:17).

6. Sanctity of **Body** whereby it is a fitting instrument for the soul to accomplish that which is good. *"For just as you once presented your members as slaves to impurity and to lawlessness leading to more lawlessness, so now present your members as slaves to righteousness leading to sanctification"* (Rom. 6:19).

CHAPTER 39–44:

Repentance

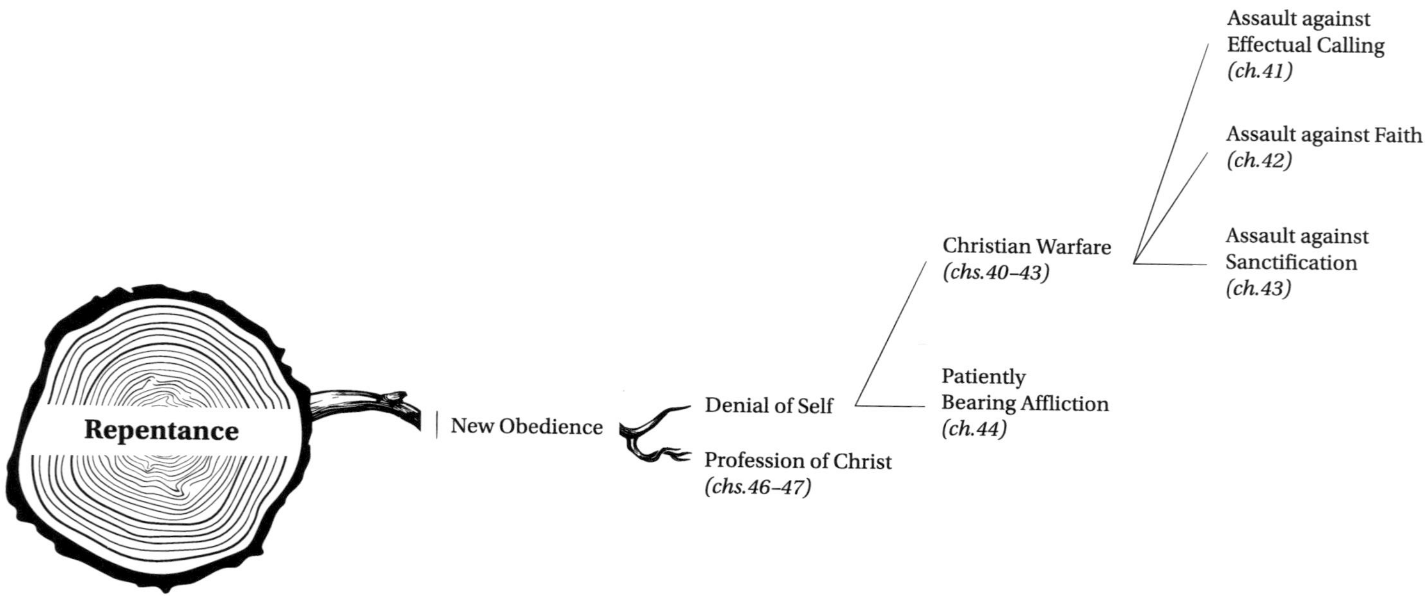

Chapter Thirty Nine

REPENTANCE AND ITS FRUITS

Repentance flows from sanctification, since no man can earnestly repent unless he (denying himself) first hates sin from his heart and embraces righteousness. No man can either will or perform this unless they are first regenerated and justified in the sight of God and endued with true faith. Therefore, although repentance is the first outward sign of conversion, yet in the order of nature it follows faith and sanctification.[1]

Hence also is it evident that this repentance is begotten by the preaching of the gospel. (Legal contrition offers some opportunity of preparation for true conversion).

Repentance is when a sinner turns to the Lord. *"I declared first to those in Damascus, then in Jerusalem and throughout all the region of Judea, and also to the Gentiles, that they should repent and turn to God, performing deeds in keeping with their repentance"* (Acts 26:20). *"And everyone who thus hopes in him purifies himself as he is pure"* (1 John 3:3).

This is performed when anyone (by the instinct of the Holy Spirit) does purpose, will, desire, and endeavour to relinquish his former sins and to become a new man. *"I incline my heart to perform your statutes forever, to the end"* (Psalm 119:112, 1 John 3:3); *"When he came and saw the grace of God, he was glad, and he exhorted them all to remain faithful to the Lord with steadfast purpose"* (Acts 11:23).

The fruit of Repentance is Christian Conduct,[2] namely a worthy and fruitful amendment of life. *"Bear fruit in keeping with repentance"* (Matt. 3:8).

1. That is, the order of experience differs from its proper causal order of the 'golden chain'.
2. Perkins' original term was 'Christian Conversation'.

Christian Conduct is a course of life in which we follow Christ's example, and by him perform New Obedience to God. *"Take my yoke upon you, and learn from me, for I am gentle and lowly in heart, and you will find rest for your souls"* (Matt. 11:29). *"Since therefore Christ suffered in the flesh, arm yourselves with the same way of thinking, for whoever has suffered in the flesh has ceased from sin"* (1 Pet. 4:1). *"For to this you have been called, because Christ also suffered for you, leaving you an example, so that you might follow in his steps"* (1 Pet. 2:21). *"For "Whoever desires to love life and see good days, let him keep his tongue from evil and his lips from speaking deceit; let him turn away from evil and do good; let him seek peace and pursue it"* (1 Pet. 3:10–11).

There are two parts of **New Obedience**: the Denial of Ourselves (***as follows***), and the Profession of Christ (***chapters 46–47***). *"If anyone would come after me, let him deny himself and take up his cross and follow me"* (Matt. 16:24).

The **Denial of Ourselves** consists partly in Christian Warfare (***chapters 40-43***) and partly in patiently bearing affliction (***chapter 44***).

Chapter Fourty

CHRISTIAN WARFARE

Christian Warfare concerns the right way of fighting the spiritual battle.

The parts thereof, are the Preparation to Battle, and the Combat itself.

In the **Preparation to Battle** we must use the complete armour of God. *"Therefore take up the whole armour of God, that you may be able to withstand in the evil day, and having done all, to stand firm"* (Eph. 6:13).

The parts are especially six:

1. Truth.
2. Justice.
3. Evangelical obedience.
4. Faith.
5. The word of God.
6. Continual and fervent prayer with watching.

> *Stand therefore, having fastened on the belt of truth, and having put on the breastplate of righteousness, and, as shoes for your feet, having put on the readiness given by the gospel of peace. In all circumstances take up the shield of faith, with which you can extinguish all the flaming darts of the evil one; and take the helmet of salvation, and the sword of the Spirit, which is the word of God, praying at all times in the Spirit, with all prayer and supplication. To that end keep alert with all perseverance, making supplication for all the saints."* (Eph. 6:14–18) *"Be sober-minded; be watchful. Your adversary the Devil prowls around like a roaring lion, seeking someone to devour."* (1 Pet. 5:8)

The **Combat** is a conflict between those who fight spiritually.

The combatants are the Tempter and the Christian soldier. *"For we do not wrestle against flesh and blood, but against the rulers, against the authorities, against the cosmic powers over this present darkness, against the spiritual forces of evil in the heavenly places"* (Eph. 6:12).

1. The **Tempter** is the prince (Satan) along with his helpers (his angels) which are spiritual wickedness in heavenly places. His helpers are the Flesh and the World.

   The conflict between them all is Temptation, whereby man is provoked to commit such wickedness as is hurtful to the salvation of his soul. *"Beloved, I urge you as sojourners and exiles to abstain from the passions of the flesh, which wage war against your soul"* (1 Pet. 2:11).

2. In the **Soldier** two things are to be considered: his Resisting and his Fall.

   1. **Resistance** is an action whereby the soldier withstands temptation through grace working inwardly within him. *"I write to you, fathers, because you know him who is from the beginning. I write to you, young men, because you are strong, and the word of God abides in you, and you have overcome the evil one"* (1 John 2:14). See also 1 Peter 5:8; Ephesians 6:16; *"You will tread on the lion and the adder; the young lion and the serpent you will trample underfoot"* (Psalm 91:13).

      To strengthen such resistance the following **Preservatives** are most necessary:

      i. When you are tempted to sin, do not only abstain from it but earnestly love and chase after the contrary (John 8:44).

      ii. Never yield or consent to Satan's words, whether he speaks the truth, accuses falsely, or flatters in order to deceive. *"You are of your father the Devil, and your will is to do your father's desires. He was a murderer from the beginning, and has nothing to do with the truth, because there is no truth in him. When he lies, he speaks out of his own character, for he is a liar and the father of lies"* (John 8:44). *"What have you to do with us, Jesus of Nazareth? Have you come to destroy us? I know who you are—the Holy One of God"* (Mark 1:24). *"She followed Paul and us, crying out, "These men are servants of the Most High God, who proclaim to you the way of salvation"* (Acts 16:17).[1]

iii. One temptation is to be expected after another, especially after our enemy has set his snares and is at rest, for the Devil never makes an end of his malice (1 Pet. 5:8).

2. The **Fall** is where the soldier faints through infirmity, being subdued by the power of the enemy. *"Brothers, if anyone is caught in any transgression, you who are spiritual should restore him in a spirit of gentleness. Keep watch on yourself, lest you too be tempted"* (Gal. 6:1).

   To this relates the **Spiritual Remedy**. A remedy is a thing which is able to restore him who is fallen to his former estate (Gal. 6:1).

   And here two things must always be thought on:

   i. Where there is a willing mind, everyone is accepted by God for that grace which he has, not for that which he has not *"For if the readiness is there, it is acceptable according to what a person has, not according to what he does not have"* (2 Cor. 8:12).

   ii. In all these things, the power of God is to be made perfect through their infirmity in all who would lead a godly life in Christ, *"But he said to me, "My grace is sufficient for you, for my power is made perfect in weakness." Therefore I will boast all the more gladly of my weaknesses, so that the power of Christ may rest upon me. For the sake of Christ, then, I am content with weaknesses, insults, hardships, persecutions, and calamities. For when I am weak, then I am strong."* (2 Cor. 12:9–10).

1. Augustine, Sermon 241.

Chapter Fourty One

THE FIRST ASSAULT: AGAINST EFFECTUAL CALLING

Assaults are threefold.

The First Assault concerns **Effectual Calling**.

The **Temptation** is the enterprise of the Devil to blindfold a man's mind and to harden his heart, lest the word of God should work in him unto salvation.

> *And as he sowed, some seeds fell along the path, and the birds came and devoured them. Other seeds fell on rocky ground, where they did not have much soil, and immediately they sprang up, since they had no depth of soil, but when the sun rose they were scorched. And since they had no root, they withered away. Other seeds fell among thorns, and the thorns grew up and choked them .... When anyone hears the word of the kingdom and does not understand it, the evil one comes and snatches away what has been sown in his heart. This is what was sown along the path.* (Matt. 13:4–7, 19)

A **Resistance** is created by the Spirit of God in those who are called. This causes men to lend their ears to hear, and grafts the word in their hearts, so that the immortal seed of regeneration may spring in them (Psalm 40:6; John 6:44; Acts 16:14); *"Therefore put away all filthiness and rampant wickedness and receive with meekness the implanted word, which is able to save your souls"* (James 1:21). *"Having purified your souls by your obedience to the truth for a sincere brotherly love, love one another earnestly from a pure heart"* (1 Pet. 1:22). *"No one born of God makes a practice of sinning, for God's seed abides in him, and he cannot keep on sinning because he has been born of God"* (1 John 3:9). A Resistance in those called is when by a sincere heart they join faith to the word which they have heard. *"As for that in the good soil, they are those who, hearing the word, hold it fast in an honest and good heart, and bear fruit with patience"* (Luke 8:15; cf. Heb. 4:2).

Here are certain **Preservatives** to be noted.

1. Meditation on the power and use of the word. *"Guard your steps when you go to the house of God. To draw near to listen is better than to offer the sacrifice of fools, for they do not know that they are doing evil. Be not rash with your mouth, nor let your heart be hasty to utter a word before God, for God is in heaven and you are on earth. Therefore let your words be few"* (Eccl. 5:1–2).
2. Diligent attention of the mind (Acts 16:14).
3. A hungering desire of the heart. *"On the last day of the feast, the great day, Jesus stood up and cried out, "If anyone thirsts, let him come to me and drink"* (John 7:37).
4. Integrity of life (Psalm 26:6).
5. The casting off of evil affections. *"But be doers of the word, and not hearers only, deceiving yourselves"* (James 1:22).
6. The inward consent and agreement of the heart with the word preached (Acts 2:37).
7. A storing up the word in the heart, lest we should sin. *"I have stored up your word in my heart, that I might not sin against you"* (Psalm 119:11).
8. A trembling at the presence of God in the Church. *"All these things my hand has made, and so all these things came to be, declares the LORD. But this is the one to whom I will look: he who is humble and contrite in spirit and trembles at my word"* (Isa. 66:2). *"So I sent for you at once, and you have been kind enough to come. Now therefore we are all here in the presence of God to hear all that you have been commanded by the Lord"* (Act 10:33).

The **Fall** is either a coldness in receiving the word, a neglect of it, or falling into error.

The **Remedy** for this is subjecting ourselves to the discipline and censure of the brethren and ministers (Gal 6:1). *"I know your works: you are neither cold nor hot"* (Rev. 3:15). *"Among whom are Hymenaeus and Alexander, whom I have handed over to Satan that they may learn not to blaspheme"* (1 Tim. 1:20).

Chapter Fourty Two

THE SECOND ASSAULT: AGAINST FAITH

The Second Assault concerns **Faith**.

This **Temptation** is an illusion which the Devil casts into the hearts of godly men. For example, when he says "you are not of the number of the elect", "you are not justified", "you have no faith", and "you must certainly be condemned for your sins". *"And the tempter came and said to him, 'If you are the Son of God, command these stones to become loaves of bread'"* (Matt. 4:3).

Helps which the Devil abuses for the strengthening of such illusions are these:

1. Adversity: dangers, loss, persecutions, jealousy, grievous offences, and so on. *"Behold, these are the wicked; always at ease, they increase in riches. All in vain have I kept my heart clean and washed my hands in innocence"* (Psalm 73:12–13). *"How many are my iniquities and my sins? Make me know my transgression and my sin. Why do you hide your face and count me as your enemy? Will you frighten a driven leaf and pursue dry chaff?"* (Job 13:23–25).
2. Remembrance of past sins. *"For you write bitter things against me and make me inherit the iniquities of my youth"* (Job 13:26).
3. A feeling that death is at hand.

The **Resistance** is made by a true faith, applying Christ with all his merits particularly to oneself in this way: "I assuredly believe that I shall not be condemned, but that I am elected and justified in Christ, and am of no doubt that all my sins are pardoned." *"Out of the anguish of his soul he shall see and be satisfied; by his knowledge shall the righteous one, my* *servant, make many to be accounted righteous, and he shall bear their iniquities"* (Isa. 53:11). *"For I am sure that neither death nor life, nor angels nor rulers, nor things present nor things to come, nor powers, nor height nor depth, nor anything else in all creation, will be able to separate us from the love of God in Christ Jesus our Lord"* (Rom. 8:38–39).

The **Preservative** in temptation is not to behold faith itself, but the object of faith, which is Christ. *"Not that I have already obtained this or am already perfect, but I press on to make it my own, because Christ Jesus has made me his own. Brothers, I do not consider that I have made it my own. But one thing I do: forgetting what lies behind and straining forward to what lies ahead, I press on toward the goal for the prize of the upward call of God in Christ Jesus"* (Phil. 3:12–14). *"And as Moses lifted up the serpent in the wilderness, so must the Son of Man be lifted up, etc."* (John 3:14).

The **Falling** is doubt and distrust of our election and of God's mercy. *"I said, "Let me remember my song in the night; let me meditate in my heart." Then my spirit made a diligent search: "Will the Lord spurn forever, and never again be favourable? Has his steadfast love forever ceased? Are his promises at an end for all time?"* (Psalm 77:6–8). So David of himself says: *"My God, my God, why have you forsaken me? Why are you so far from saving me, from the words of my groaning?"* (Psalm 22:1).

The **Remedy** is twofold:

1. The Operation of the Holy Spirit stirring up faith and increasing it. *"And I am sure of this, that he who began a good work in you will bring it to completion at the day of Jesus Christ"* (Phil. 1:6). *"The apostles said to the Lord, 'Increase our faith!'"* (Luke 17:5).
2. A Holy Meditation, which takes many forms:
    a. That it is the commandment of God that we should believe in Christ. *"And this is his commandment, that we believe in the name of his Son Jesus Christ and love one another, just as he has commanded us"* (1 John 3:23).
    b. That the evangelical promises are indefinite and exclude no man, unless any man excludes himself. *"Come, everyone who thirsts, come to the waters; and he who has no money,*

come, buy and eat! Come, buy wine and milk without money and without price" (Isa. 55:1). *"Come to me, all who labour and are heavy laden, and I will give you rest"* (Matt. 11:28). *"That whoever believes in him may have eternal life"* (John 3:15). Also the sacraments of Baptism and the Lord's Supper apply several indefinite promises to everyone, and therefore are very effective to cultivate full and particular assurance of the forgiveness of sins.

c. That doubt and despair are most grievous sins.

d. That contrary to hope, men must believe with Abraham. *"In hope he believed against hope, that he should become the father of many nations, as he had been told, 'So shall your offspring be'"* (Rom. 4:18).

e. That the mercy of God and the merit of Christ's obedience, being both God and man, are infinite. *"For the mountains may depart and the hills be removed, but my steadfast love shall not depart from you, and my covenant of peace shall not be removed, says the LORD, who has compassion on you"* (Isa. 54:10). *"For as high as the heavens are above the earth, so great is his steadfast love toward those who fear him"* (Psalm 103:11). *"My little children, I am writing these things to you so that you may not sin. But if anyone does sin, we have an advocate with the Father, Jesus Christ the righteous. He is the propitiation for our sins, and not for ours only but also for the sins of the whole world"* (1 John 2:1–2). *"O Israel, hope in the LORD! For with the LORD there is steadfast love, and with him is plentiful redemption"* (Psalm 130:7).

f. That God measures the obedience due to him by the affection and desire to obey, rather than by the act and performance of it. *"For those who live according to the flesh set their minds on the things of the flesh, but those who live according to the Spirit set their minds on the things of the Spirit .... For the mind that is set on the flesh is hostile to God, for it does not submit to God's law; indeed, it cannot"* (Rom. 8:5, 7). *"Now if I do what I do not want, it is no longer I who do it, but sin that dwells within me. So I find it to be a law that when I want to do right, evil lies close at hand. For I delight in the law of God, in my inner being"* (Rom. 7:20-22). *"They shall be mine, says the LORD of hosts, in the day when I make up my treasured possession, and I will spare them as a man spares his son who serves him"* (Mal. 3:17).

g. When one sin is forgiven, all the rest are remitted also. For remission given once, without any prescription of time, is given forever. *"For the gifts and the calling of God are irrevocable"* (Rom. 11:29). *"To him all the prophets bear witness that everyone who believes in him receives forgiveness of sins through his name"* (Acts 10:43).

h. That grace and faith are not taken away by falls of infirmity, but rather are declared and made clear by them. *"Now the law came in to increase the trespass, but where sin increased, grace abounded all the more"* (Rom. 5:20). *"So to keep me from becoming conceited because of the surpassing greatness of the revelations, a thorn was given me in the flesh, a messenger of Satan to harass me, to keep me from becoming conceited. Three times I pleaded with the Lord about this, that it should leave me. But he said to me, 'My grace is sufficient for you'"* (2 Cor. 12:7–9).

i. That all the works of God are by contrary means. *"For my power is made perfect in weakness"* (2 Cor. 12:9).

Chapter Fourty Three

THE THIRD ASSAULT: AGAINST SANCTIFICATION

The **Third Assault** concerns **Sanctification**.

The **Temptation** is a provoking to sin, according to the disposition of each particular man, and as occasion shall offer. *"Then Satan stood against Israel and incited David to number Israel"* (1 Chron. 21:1). *"During supper, when the Devil had already put it into the heart of Judas Iscariot, Simon's son, to betray him"* (John 13:2).

In this temptation, the Devil does strongly diminish and extenuate those sins, which men are about to commit, partly by pleading presumption on the mercy of God, and partly by covering or hiding the punishment which is due for the sin.

There are **Helps** to further the Devil in his temptation:

1. The **Flesh** which lusts against the Spirit (concupiscence), sometimes by begetting evil motions and affections, and sometimes by overwhelming and oppressing the good intents and motions. *"For the desires of the flesh are against the Spirit, and the desires of the Spirit are against the flesh, for these are opposed to each other, to keep you from doing the things you want to do .... Now the works of the flesh are evident: sexual immorality, impurity, sensuality, idolatry, sorcery, enmity, strife, jealousy, fits of anger, rivalries, dissensions, divisions, envy, drunkenness, orgies, and things like these. I warn you, as I warned you before, that those who do such things will not inherit the kingdom of God"* (Gal. 5:17, 19–21). *"But each person is tempted when he is lured and enticed by his own desire"* (James 1:14).

2. The **World**, which brings men to disobedience, through pleasure, profit, honour, and evil examples. *"Among whom we all once lived in the passions of our flesh, carrying out the desires of the body and the mind, and were by nature children of wrath, like the rest of mankind"* (Eph. 2:3). *"For all that is in the world—the desires of the flesh and the desires of the eyes and pride in possessions—is not from the Father but is from the world"* (1 John 2:16).

Resistance is made by the desires of the Spirit, which works good motions and affections in the faithful, and drives out evil ones. *"But the fruit of the Spirit is love, joy, peace, patience, kindness, goodness, faithfulness, gentleness, self-control; against such things there is no law. And those who belong to Christ Jesus have crucified the flesh with its passions and desires. If a little leaven leavens the whole lump we live by the Spirit, let us also walk by the Spirit. Let us not become conceited, provoking one another, envying one another"* (Gal. 5:22–26).

The **Preservatives** by which men are strengthened in resisting are these:

1. To account no sin light or small. *"A little leaven leavens the whole lump"* (Gal. 5:9). *"For the wages of sin is death, but the free gift of God is eternal life in Christ Jesus our Lord"* (Rom. 6:23).
2. To avoid all occasions of sin. To these rather agree the proverb used of the plague: "depart quickly, move far away, return slowly" (*citò, longè, tardè*). *"Abstain from every form of evil. Now may the God of peace himself sanctify you completely, and may your whole spirit and soul and body be kept blameless at the coming of our Lord Jesus Christ"* (1 Thess. 5:22–23). *"Save others by snatching them out of the fire; to others show mercy with fear, hating even the garment stained by the flesh"* (Jude 23).
3. To practice subduing lesser sins, that eventually you may also overcome the greater (Rom. 13:4).
4. To apply yourself to your appointed vocation, and to be always busily occupied in it.
5. To set against the rebellion of the flesh: the Law, God's judgements, the last judgement, the glorious presence of God, and so on. *"Blessed is the one who fears the LORD always, but*

whoever hardens his heart will fall into calamity" (Pro. 28:14). *"He is not greater in this house than I am, nor has he kept back anything from me except yourself, because you are his wife. How then can I do this great wickedness and sin against God?"* (Gen. 39:9).

Here certain **Remedies** take place:

1. Against unjust anger or private desire of revenge, meditate on:
    a. Injuries happen to us by the Lord's appointment for our good (2 Sam. 16:10).
    b. God, of his great goodness, forgives us for far more sins than it is possible for us to forgive in others.
    c. It is the duty of Christian love to forgive others.
    d. We must not desire to destroy those whom Christ has redeemed by his precious blood.
    e. We ourselves are in danger of the wrath of God, if we allow our wrath to burn against our brother. Forgive (Jesus said) and it shall be forgiven.
    f. We do not know the circumstances of the facts: what the mind and purpose was of the one against whom we are angry.
2. Bridles, or external remedies, are these:
    a. We should imitate the forgiveness of the Lord, who often tolerates the wicked for a very long season. *"Learn of me, for I am humble and meek"*. (Matt. 11:29)
    b. There must be pause and time of delay between our anger and its expression. Athenodorus counselled Augustus that he, being angry, should repeat all the letters of the alphabet before he spoke or did anything against another.
    c. To depart the place where those are with whom we are angry.
    d. To avoid contention, both in word and in deed. (Phil. 2:3)

3. Remedies against bad desires for riches and honour:

    a. God enlivens and revives those who fear him, even in famine. *"Behold, the eye of the LORD is on those who fear him, on those who hope in his steadfast love, that he may deliver their soul from death and keep them alive in famine"* (Psalm 33:18–19).

    b. Godliness is great gain, if the mind of man can be content with it (1 Tim. 6:6).

    c. We wait and look for the resurrection of the body and eternal life, therefore we should not place such anxious concern on this present mortal life.

    d. We are servants in our Father's house, therefore he will lovingly bestow upon us what is convenient for us.

    e. The ambitious mind is blind. It desires to be set aloft so as to have the greater downfall, and fears to be humbled lest he should not be exalted.

    f. When Adam sought to be the equal of God, he brought both himself and his descendants headlong to destruction.

    g. He is a very ambitious 'rob-God' who desires to take a commendation for himself which is appropriate only to the Lord.

4. Preservatives against the desires of the flesh:

    a. Whoever would be Christ's disciple must take up his cross every day (Luke 9:23).

    b. Those who live according to the Spirit savour such things as belong to the Spirit (Rom. 8:5).

    c. We ought to live as citizens of the kingdom of heaven (Phil. 3:20).

    d. We are the temple of God (1 Cor. 3:6). Our members are the members of Christ (1 Cor. 6:15). We have the Spirit of Christ dwelling within us, whom we should not grieve (Eph. 4:30). Concerning this, see further in the exposition of the seventh commandment (p. 189).

In this temptation, the **Fall** is when a man falls into some offence (Gal. 6:1). Here Satan aggravates the offence committed and accuses and terrifies the offender with the judgements of God. *"Then when Judas, his betrayer, saw that Jesus was condemned, he changed his mind and brought back the thirty pieces of silver to the chief priests and the elders, saying, "I have sinned by betraying innocent blood." They said, "What is that to us? See to it yourself." And throwing down the pieces of silver into the temple, he departed, and he went and hanged himself"* (Matt. 27:3–5).

The **Remedy** is a revived repentance, the beginning of which is sorrow toward God for the sin committed: the fruits hereof are especially seven. *"As it is, I rejoice, not because you were grieved, but because you were grieved into repenting. For you felt a godly grief, so that you suffered no loss through us. For godly grief produces a repentance that leads to salvation without regret, whereas worldly grief produces death. For see what earnestness this godly grief has produced in you, but also what eagerness to clear yourselves, what indignation, what fear, what longing, what zeal, what punishment! At every point you have proved yourselves innocent in the matter"* (2 Cor. 7:9–11).

1. A desire to do well.
2. A confession of the sin before God, requiring pardon for the offence. *"I acknowledged my sin to you, and I did not cover my iniquity; I said, 'I will confess my transgressions to the LORD,' and you forgave the iniquity of my sin"* (Psalm 32:5). *"David said to Nathan, 'I have sinned against the LORD.' And Nathan said to David, 'The LORD also has put away your sin; you shall not die'"* (2 Sam. 12:13).
3. Indignation against a man's self for his offence.
4. A fear, not so much for the punishment as for offending the Lord. *"If you, O LORD, should mark iniquities, O Lord, who could stand?"* (Psalm 130:3).
5. A desire to be fully renewed and to be delivered from sin.
6. A fervent zeal to love God, and to embrace and keep all his commandments.
7. Revenge, whereby the flesh may be tamed and subdued, lest at any time afterwards such offences be committed.

Chapter Fourty Four

THE PATIENT BEARING OF THE CROSS

The Patient Bearing of the Cross teaches how Christians should undergo the burden.

The **Cross** is a certain measure of affliction appointed by God to every one of the faithful. *"Then Jesus told his disciples, "'If anyone would come after me, let him deny himself and take up his cross and follow me'"* (Matt. 16:24). *"Now I rejoice in my sufferings for your sake, and in my flesh I am filling up what is lacking in Christ's afflictions for the sake of his body, that is, the church"* (Col. 1:24).

We ought to take up this cross willingly with both hands whenever it shall please God to lay it upon us. After we have taken it up, we must bear it with patience and perseverance. *"May you be strengthened with all power, according to his glorious might, for all endurance and patience with joy"* (Col. 1:11). *"By your patience possess your souls"* (Luke 21:19 NKJV).

The **Preservatives** of patience, are:

1. Strength from the Holy Spirit. *"I can do all things through him who strengthens me"* (Phil. 4:13). *"For it has been granted to you that for the sake of Christ you should not only believe in him but also suffer for his sake"* (Phil. 1:20).
2. A Holy Meditation, which is manifold:
    a. That the afflictions of the faithful do not come by chance, but by the counsel and providence of God. *"So Joseph said to his brothers, "Come near to me, please." And they came near. And he said, "I am your brother, Joseph, whom you sold into Egypt. And now do not be distressed or angry with yourselves because you sold me here, for God sent me before you to preserve life"* (Gen. 45:4–5). *"It is good for me that*

I was afflicted, that I might learn your statutes" (Psalm 119:71). Hence it is evident, that afflictions to the godly are inevitable. *"When they had preached the gospel to that city and had made many disciples, they returned to Lystra and to Iconium and to Antioch, strengthening the souls of the disciples, encouraging them to continue in the faith, and saying that through many tribulations we must enter the kingdom of God* (Acts 14:21-22)*." For the gate is narrow and the way is hard that leads to life, and those who find it are few"* (Matt. 7:14). *"In the world you will have tribulation"* (John 16:33).

b. That although afflictions are grievous, they are also good and profitable for they are helps whereby men (being humbled for their sins before God) obtain peace and holiness of life. *"Indeed, we felt that we had received the sentence of death. But that was to make us rely not on ourselves but on God who raises the dead"* (2 Cor. 1:9). *"O LORD, in distress they sought you; they poured out a whispered prayer when your discipline was upon them"* (Isa. 26:16). *"I will return again to my place, until they acknowledge their guilt and seek my face, and in their distress earnestly seek me"* (Hos. 5:15). *"When he killed them, they sought him; they repented and sought God earnestly"* (Psalm 78:34). *"I have heard Ephraim grieving, 'You have disciplined me, and I was disciplined, like an untrained calf; bring me back that I may be restored, for you are the LORD my God"* (Jer. 31:18). *"For the moment all discipline seems painful rather than pleasant, but later it yields the peaceful fruit of righteousness to those who have been trained by it"* (Heb. 12:11). *"His ways prosper at all times; your judgements are on high, out of his sight; as for all his foes, he puffs at them"* (Psalm 10:5). *"Every branch in me that does not bear fruit he takes away, and every branch that does bear fruit he prunes, that it may bear more fruit"* (John 15:2). *"In this you rejoice, though now for a little while, if necessary, you have been grieved by various trials"* (1 Pet. 1:6). *"Who comforts us in all our affliction, so that we may be able to comfort those who are in any affliction, with the comfort with which we ourselves are comforted by God"*

(2 Cor. 1:4). *"More than that, we rejoice in our sufferings, knowing that suffering produces endurance"* (Rom. 5:3). *"For it was fitting that he, ... should make the founder of their salvation perfect through suffering"* (Heb. 2:10). We permit surgeons to bind us laying diseased in our beds, to sear us with hot irons, even to lance and search our members with razors. Yet we usually send them away with friendly and kind speech, and often with a golden fee for thus handling us. Shall we then suffer so many things from a surgeon to cure a bodily disease, and not give God permission to cure the most festered diseases of our sick souls by afflictions?

By this also may we gather that the afflictions of the godly are signs of their adoption. *"For the Lord disciplines the one he loves, and chastises every son whom he receives. It is for discipline that you have to endure. God is treating you as sons. For what son is there whom his father does not discipline?"* (Heb. 12:6).

Moreover, to the godly they are the king's highway to heaven. *"Blessed is the man who remains steadfast under trial, for when he has stood the test he will receive the crown of life, which God has promised to those who love him"* (James 1:12). *"For this light momentary affliction is preparing for us an eternal weight of glory beyond all comparison"* (2 Cor. 4:17).

c. That God has promised favour, mitigation of punishment, his presence, and deliverance (Phil. 1:29); *"God is faithful, and he will not let you be tempted beyond your ability, but with the temptation he will also provide the way of escape"* (1 Cor. 10:13, see also 2 Sam. 7:14); *"Call upon me in the day of trouble; I will deliver you, and you shall glorify me"* (Psalm 50:15). *"Behold, he who keeps Israel will neither slumber nor sleep"* (Psalm 121:4). *"When you pass through the waters, I will be with you; and through the rivers, they shall not overwhelm you; when you walk through fire you shall not be burned, and the flame shall not consume you. For I am the LORD your God, the Holy One of Israel, your Savior. I give Egypt as your ransom, Cush and Seba in exchange for you"* (Isa. 43:2–3).

d. That Christ is a companion in all the troubles of the faithful. *"But rejoice insofar as you share Christ's sufferings"* (1 Pet. 4:13). *"Always carrying in the body the death of Jesus, so that the life of Jesus may also be manifested in our bodies"* (2 Cor. 4:10; cf. Col. 1:21).

e. That the angels are ready to defend those who fear God (Psalm 34:8); *"Do not be afraid, for those who are with us are more than those who are with them"* (2 Kings 6:16).

CHAPTER 45–47:

Profession of Christ

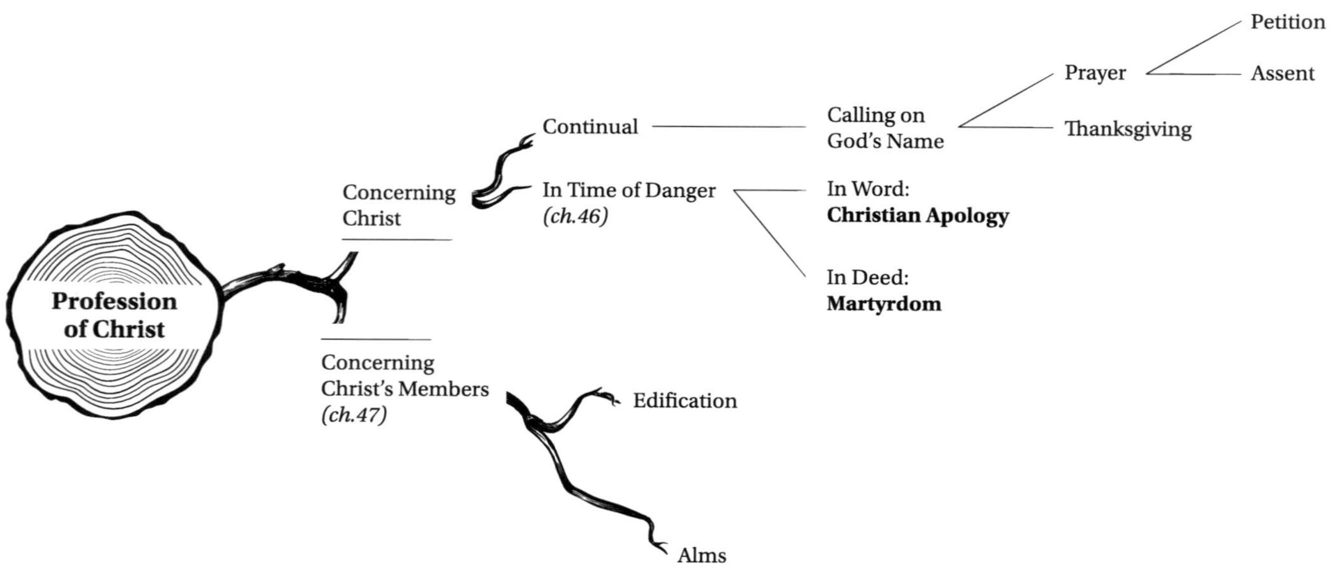

Chapter Fourty Five

PRAYER

Thus much concerning the denial of ourselves. Now follows the **Profession of Christ**, which concerns either Christ himself or his members (the faithful). *"Truly, I say to you, as you did it to one of the least of these my brothers, you did it to me"* (Matt. 25:40).

That profession which directly concerns Christ is either Continual (***as follows***) or only in the Time of Danger (***chapter 46***).

Continual Profession is the calling upon the Name of God, and ought ever to be performed by us in the name of Christ Jesus our mediator. *"To the church of God that is in Corinth, to those sanctified in Christ Jesus, called to be saints together with all those who in every place call upon the name of our Lord Jesus Christ, both their Lord and ours"* (1 Cor. 1:2). *"And here he has authority from the chief priests to bind all who call on your name"* (Acts 9:14). *"And whatever you do, in word or deed, do everything in the name of the Lord Jesus, giving thanks to God the Father through him"* (Col. 3:17).

The Calling upon God's Name is by Prayer or Thanksgiving. *"In everything by prayer and supplication with thanksgiving let your requests be made known to God"* (Phil. 4:6).

Prayer has two parts: Petition and Assent. *"Therefore I tell you, whatever you ask in prayer, believe that you have received it, and it will be yours"* (Mark 11:24).

1. **Petition** is the first part of prayer, whereby we (according to that rule of God's word) ask his help to obtain such things as we need. *"And this is the confidence that we have toward him, that if we ask anything according to his will he hears us"* (1 John 5:14).

   In every petition we must express two things:

   a. A sense of our needs.

b. A desire for the grace of God to supply those needs. *"She was deeply distressed and prayed to the LORD and wept bitterly"* (1 Sam. 1:10). *"I prayed to the LORD my God and made confession, saying, "O Lord, the great and awesome God, who keeps covenant and steadfast love with those who love him and keep his commandments, we have sinned and done wrong and acted wickedly and rebelled, turning aside from your commandments and rules, etc."* (Dan. 9:4, 5–20). *"Out of the depths I cry to you, O LORD!"* (Psalm 130:1). *"But Hannah answered, 'No, my lord, I am a woman troubled in spirit. I have drunk neither wine nor strong drink, but I have been pouring out my soul before the LORD,' etc."* (1 Sam. 1:15–16). *"I stretch out my hands to you; my soul thirsts for you like a parched land"* (Psalm 143:6).

2. **Assent** is the second part of prayer, whereby we believe and profess before God that he (in his due time) will grant the requests which we have made to his majesty. *"And this is the confidence that we have toward him, that if we ask anything according to his will he hears us. And if we know that he hears us in whatever we ask, we know that we have the requests that we have asked of him"* (1 John 5:14–15). *"And lead us not into temptation, but deliver us from evil"* (Matt. 6:13).

As for the faithful, however much they show infirmities in their prayers, they (no doubt) have a clear sense of God's favour, especially when they pray to the Lord zealously and often. *"Therefore, confess your sins to one another and pray for one another, that you may be healed. The prayer of a righteous person has great power as it is working"* (James 5:16). *"But the angel said to him, 'Do not be afraid, Zechariah, for your prayer has been heard'"* (Luke 1:13). *"But it displeased Jonah exceedingly, and he was angry. And he prayed to the LORD and said, 'O LORD, is not this what I said when I was yet in my country? That is why I made haste to flee to Tarshish; for I knew that you are a gracious God and merciful, slow to anger and abounding in steadfast love, and relenting from disaster'"* (Jonah 4:1–2), see also Romans. 8:26. *"O LORD, rebuke me not in your anger, nor discipline me in your wrath"* (Psalm 6:1–5). See also: Psalm 8:9; 16:7; 20:5; 35:9, 18, 28.

Thanksgiving is a calling upon God's name, whereby we praise God with joy and gladness of heart for benefits received or promised. *"My heart overflows with a pleasing theme; I address my verses to the king; my tongue is like the pen of a ready scribe"* (Psalm 45:1). *"Giving thanks always and for everything to God the Father in the name of our Lord Jesus Christ"* (Eph. 5:20). *"How precious is your steadfast love, O God! The children of mankind take refuge in the shadow of your wings. They feast on the abundance of your house, and you give them drink from the river of your delights"* (Psalm 36:7–8). See also: Col. 3:16.

Chapter Fourty Six

PROFESSION IN THE WORLD: APOLOGY AND MARTYRDOM

The Profession of Christ in Dangers is either in Word or in Deed.

Profession in Word is called Christian Apology or Confession of Christ. *"For with the heart one believes and is justified, and with the mouth one confesses and is saved"* (Rom. 10:10). *"I will tell of your name to my brothers; in the midst of the congregation I will praise you"* (Psalm 22:22).

Christian Apology is the profession of Christ in word, when we are ready (with fear and meekness) to confess the truth of the Christian religion as often as need requires and the glory of God is endangered. This includes before unbelievers, especially if they are not past all hope of repentance. *"But in your hearts honour Christ the Lord as holy, always being prepared to make a defence to anyone who asks you for a reason for the hope that is in you; yet do it with gentleness and respect, having a good conscience, so that, when you are slandered, those who revile your good behaviour in Christ may be put to shame"* (1 Pet. 3:15-16). See Acts 7, where Steven makes an Apology for himself. *"Do not give dogs what is holy, and do not throw your pearls before pigs, lest they trample them underfoot and turn to attack you"* (Matt. 7:6).

Profession in Deed is called Martyrdom. Martyrdom is a part of Christian profession, when a Christian man—for the doctrine of faith, for justice, and for the salvation of his brethren—undergoes the punishment of death imposed upon him by adversaries of Christ Jesus. *"For John had been saying to Herod, 'It is not lawful for you to have your brother's wife' .... And immediately the king sent an executioner with orders to bring*

John's head. He went and beheaded him in the prison" (Mark 6:18, 27). *"I will most gladly spend and be spent for your souls. If I love you more, am I to be loved less?"* (2 Cor. 12:15).

Nevertheless, it is lawful for Christians to flee persecution if they find themselves insufficiently resolved and strengthened by God's Spirit to stand. *"When they persecute you in one town, flee to the next, for truly, I say to you, you will not have gone through all the towns of Israel before the Son of Man comes"* (Matt. 10:23). *"Again they sought to arrest him, but he escaped from their hands"* (John 10:39). *"And when the brothers learned this, they brought him down to Caesarea and sent him off to Tarsus"* (Acts 9:30). *"Has it not been told my lord what I did when Jezebel killed the prophets of the LORD, how I hid a hundred men of the LORD's prophets by fifties in a cave and fed them with bread and water?"* (1 Kings 18:13). *"And now, behold, I am going to Jerusalem, constrained by the Spirit, not knowing what will happen to me there"* (Acts 20:22).

Chapter Fourty Seven

PROFESSION IN THE WORLD: EDIFICATION AND ALMS

Profession of Christ which concerns his members (namely, the saints and faithful ones) is either Edification or Alms.

Edification is every duty towards our brethren whereby they are furthered in their growth in Christ, or else are more surely united to him. *"So then let us pursue what makes for peace and for mutual upbuilding"* (Rom. 14:19).

The following relate to Edification:

1. To give a good example. *"Let your light shine before others, so that they may see your good works and give glory to your Father who is in heaven"* (Matt. 5:16). *"Keep your conduct among the Gentiles honourable, so that when they speak against you as evildoers, they may see your good deeds and glorify God on the day of visitation"* (1 Pet. 2:12).
2. To exhort. *"But exhort one another every day, as long as it is called "today," that none of you may be hardened by the deceitfulness of sin"* (Heb. 3:13). *"That is, that we may be mutually encouraged by each other's faith, both yours and mine"* (Rom. 1:12).
3. To comfort. *"And we urge you, brothers, admonish the idle, encourage the fainthearted, help the weak, be patient with them all"* (1 Thess. 5:14). *"Therefore, confess your sins to one another and pray for one another, that you may be healed .... let him know that whoever brings back a sinner from his*

wandering will save his soul from death and will cover a multitude of sins" (James 5:16, 20). *"Therefore encourage one another with these words"* (1 Thess. 4:18).

4. To admonish. *"I myself am satisfied about you, my brothers, that you yourselves are full of goodness, filled with all knowledge and able to instruct one another"* (Rom. 15:14). *"And we urge you, brothers, admonish the idle"* (1 Thess. 5:14).

   In admonition they shall conduct themselves in a holy manner, in the spirit of meekness, as though they were guilty of the infirmity themselves. They shall admonish all their brethren of such faults as they know, in accordance with God's word. *"Brothers, if anyone is caught in any transgression, you who are spiritual should restore him in a spirit of gentleness. Keep watch on yourself, lest you too be tempted"* (Gal. 6:1). *"You hypocrite, first take the log out of your own eye, and then you will see clearly to take the speck out of your brother's eye"* (Matt. 7:5). *"Preach the word; be ready in season and out of season; reprove, rebuke, and exhort, with complete patience and teaching"* (2 Tim. 4:2). *"If your brother sins against you, go and tell him his fault, between you and him alone. If he listens to you, you have gained your brother"* (Matt. 18:15). See also Romans. 15:14; 2 Timothy 4:2; *"You shall not hate your brother in your heart, but you shall reason frankly with your neighbour, lest you incur sin because of him"* (Lev. 19:17).

Alms. Financial relief among the godly is a duty, whereby the rich do out of their plenty supply the wants of the poor, both according to their ability, and sometimes beyond their ability. *"For they gave according to their means, as I can testify, and beyond their means, of their own accord"* (2 Cor. 8:3). *"And all who believed were together and had all things in common. And they were selling their possessions and belongings and distributing the proceeds to all, as any had need"* (Acts 2:44–45).

Chapter Fourty Eight

THE FOURTH DEGREE OF THE DECLARATION OF GOD'S LOVE: GLORIFICATION

The Fourth Degree of the Declaration of God's Love is Glorification (Rom. 8:30).

Glorification is the complete transformation of the saints into the image of the Son of God. *"Who will transform our lowly body to be like his glorious body, by the power that enables him even to subject all things to himself"* (Phil. 3:21). *"It is sown a natural body; it is raised a spiritual body. If there is a natural body, there is also a spiritual body. Thus it is written, "The first man Adam became a living being"; the last Adam became a life-giving spirit .... Just as we have borne the image of the man of dust, we shall also bear the image of the man of heaven"* (1 Cor. 15:44–45, 49). *"As for me, I shall behold your face in righteousness; when I awake, I shall be satisfied with your likeness"* (Psalm 17:15).

The beginning of glorification is in death, but it is not made complete before the last day of judgement.

The **Death of the Elect** is but a sleep in Christ, whereby body and soul are severed. The Body: that after corruption it may rise to greater glory. The Soul: that being fully sanctified it may immediately be transported into the kingdom of heaven after departure from the body. *"And if Christ has not been raised, ... then those also who have fallen asleep in Christ have perished"* (1 Cor. 15:17–18). *"And when he had said this, he (Stephen) fell asleep"* (Acts 7:60). *"You foolish person! What you sow does not come to life unless it dies"* (1 Cor. 15:36). *"But nothing unclean will ever enter it, nor anyone who does what is detestable or false, but only those who are written in the Lamb's book of life"* (Rev. 21:27). *"I myself serve the law of*

God with my mind, but with my flesh I serve the law of sin" (Rom. 7:25). *"And he said, 'Jesus, remember me when you come into your kingdom.' And he said to him, 'Truly, I say to you, today you will be with me in Paradise'"* (Luke 23:42–43). *"And I heard a voice from heaven saying, 'Write this: Blessed are the dead who die in the Lord from now on.' 'Blessed indeed,' says the Spirit, 'that they may rest from their labours, for their deeds follow them!'"* (Rev. 14:13).

Against the Fear of Death note these **Preservatives**:

1. Death, which frees the godly from the tyranny of Satan, sin, the world, the flesh, and eternal damnation indeed from infinite perils and loss. It places us both safe and happy under the shadow of Christ's wings.
2. By his death, Christ has sanctified both death and the grave to us.
3. Both in life and death, Christ is gain to the godly (Phil. 1:12).
4. The consolations which the Spirit of Christ suggests to the souls of the faithful overcome the sufferings of death by many degrees.
5. Desire of that most bright and glorious beholding of God, and of the presence of those saints who departed before us.
6. Instead of our bodies we shall be clothed with glory (2 Cor. 5:1).
7. The sting of death, namely sin, is then so taken away that the serpent can no more hurt us. *"O death, where is your victory? O death, where is your sting?"* (1 Cor. 15:55). *"And deliver all those who through fear of death were subject to lifelong slavery"* (Heb. 2:15).
8. We should not so much think of our death, as take an exact account of our life. For a man cannot die ill who has lived well, and he seldom dies well who has lived badly.
9. The angels stand at our elbows, so that as soon as a saint departs they may immediately transport his soul into heaven with all speed.

Once in heaven, souls remain there until the last day of judgement. There they partly magnify the name of God and partly wait, praying for the consummation of the kingdom of glory and for the bliss of body and soul being reunited in resurrection. *"And when he had taken the scroll, the four living creatures and the twenty-four elders fell down before the Lamb, each holding a harp, and golden bowls full of incense, which are the prayers of the saints. And they sang a new song, saying, "Worthy are you to take the scroll and to open its seals, for you were slain, and by your blood you ransomed people for God from every tribe and language and people and nation"* (Rev. 5:8–9). *"And I heard a voice from heaven like the roar of many waters and like the sound of loud thunder. The voice I heard was like the sound of harpists playing on their harps, and they were singing a new song before the throne and before the four living creatures and before the elders. No one could learn that song except the 144,000 who had been redeemed from the earth"* (Rev. 14:2–3).

Chapter Fourty Nine

THE STATE OF THE ELECT ON THE LAST DAY OF JUDGEMENT

The **Last day of Judgement** shall be of this manner:

1. Immediately before the coming of Christ the powers of heaven shall be shaken: the sun and moon shall be darkened and the stars will seem to fall from heaven. At this sight the Elect still living will rejoice, but every joint in the reprobate will shake. *"Immediately after the tribulation of those days the sun will be darkened, and the moon will not give its light, and the stars will fall from heaven, and the powers of the heavens will be shaken. Then will appear in heaven the sign of the Son of Man, and then all the tribes of the earth will mourn, and they will see the Son of Man coming on the clouds of heaven with power and great glory"* (Matt. 24:29–30). *"People fainting with fear and with foreboding of what is coming on the world. For the powers of the heavens will be shaken ... Now when these things begin to take place, straighten up and raise your heads, because your redemption is drawing near"* (Luke 21:26, 28). *"Henceforth there is laid up for me the crown of righteousness, which the Lord, the righteous judge, will award to me on that Day, and not only to me but also to all who have loved his appearing"* (2 Tim. 4:8).

2. Then all the heavens shall be set on fire and will suddenly pass away with a noise like chariot wheels. The earth, its elements, and everything on it will be dissolved with fire. *"Waiting for and hastening the coming of the day of God, because of which the heavens will be set on fire and dissolved, and the heavenly bodies will melt as they burn! But according to his promise we are waiting for new heavens and a new earth in which righteousness dwells"* (2 Pet. 3:12–13).

   At the same time, when all these things come to pass, the sound of the last trumpet shall be heard, sounded by the Archangel. And

Christ shall come suddenly in the clouds, with power, and glory, and a great train of Angels, *"And he will send out his angels with a loud trumpet call, and they will gather his elect from the four winds, from one end of heaven to the other"* (Matt. 24:31). *"For the Lord himself will descend from heaven with a cry of command, with the voice of an archangel, and with the sound of the trumpet of God. And the dead in Christ will rise first"* (1 Thess. 4:16). See also Matt. 24:30; *"Then we who are alive, who are left, will be caught up together with them in the clouds to meet the Lord in the air, and so we will always be with the Lord"* (1 Thess. 4:17).

3. At the sound of the trumpet, the elect who were dead shall arise with their bodies. Those very bodies which were turned to dust (one part rent from another) shall be restored by the omnipotent power of God, and their souls shall descend from heaven and be brought again into those bodies. As for those still living, they shall be changed in the twinkling of an eye rather than suffering death. At that time their bodies shall receive their full redemption, and all the bodies of the elect shall be made like the glorious body of Christ Jesus, and therefore shall be spiritual, immortal, glorious, and free from all infirmity. *"We shall not all sleep, but we shall all be changed, in a moment, in the twinkling of an eye, at the last trumpet .... It is sown in dishonour; it is raised in glory. It is sown in weakness; it is raised in power. It is sown a natural body; it is raised a spiritual body"* (1 Cor. 15:51–52, 43–44).

4. Last of all, when they are all convened before the tribunal seat of Christ, he will separate the elect from the reprobate and place them at his right hand. To these whose names are written in the book of life, he will he pronounce this sentence: *"Come, you who are blessed by my Father, inherit the kingdom prepared for you from the foundation of the world"* (Matt. 25:43). *"And he will place the sheep on his right, but the goats on the left"* Matt. 25:33. See also 1 Thessalonians. 4:17. *"And if anyone's name was not found written in the book of life, he was thrown into the lake of fire"* (Rev. 20:15).

Chapter Fifty

THE STATE OF THE ELECT AFTER JUDGEMENT

After the Last Judgement the elect shall immediately enjoy Blessedness in the kingdom of heaven.

Blessedness is that whereby God himself is 'all in all' in his Elect, *"When all things are subjected to him, then the Son himself will also be subjected to him who put all things in subjection under him, that God may be all in all"* (1 Cor. 15:28). And it is the reward of good works, not because works can merit, but by reason of God's favour, who thus accepts works, and that in respect of the merit of Christ's righteousness imputed to the Elect; *"For the wages of sin is death, but the free gift of God is eternal life in Christ Jesus our Lord"* (Rom. 6:23). See also 2 Timothy 4:8. *"Behold, I am coming soon, bringing my recompense with me, to repay everyone for what he has done"* (Rev. 22:12).

Blessedness has two parts: Eternal Life and Perfect Glory.

Eternal life is that fellowship with God whereby God himself is life to the elect, through Christ the lamb. For in the kingdom of heaven the elect shall not need food, drink, sleep, air, heat, cold, medicine, clothing, or the light of the sun and moon. In place of all these they shall have God's Spirit in them, by whom they shall be immediately made alive for ever. *"Jesus answered him, 'If anyone loves me, he will keep my word, and my Father will love him, and we will come to him and make our home with him'"* (John 14:23). *"Whoever confesses that Jesus is the Son of God, God abides in him, and he in God"* (1 John 4:15). *"And I heard a loud voice from the throne saying, "Behold, the dwelling place of God is with man. He will dwell with them, and they will be his people, and God himself will be with them as their God .... And the city has no need of sun or moon to shine on it, for the glory of God gives it light, and its lamp is the Lamb"* (Rev. 21:3,23). *"Through the middle of the street of the city; also, on either side of the river, the tree of life with its twelve kinds of fruit, yielding its fruit each month.*

The leaves of the tree were for the healing of the nations .... And night will be no more. They will need no light of lamp or sun, for the Lord God will be their light, and they will reign forever and ever" (Rev. 22:2, 5). See also 1 Corinthians 15:45. *"If the Spirit of him who raised Jesus from the dead dwells in you, he who raised Christ Jesus from the dead will also give life to your mortal bodies through his Spirit who dwells in you"* (Rom. 8:11).

Perfect Glory is that wonderful excellence of the elect whereby they shall be in a far better estate than any heart can wish. This glory is confessed in three points:

1. They shall behold the face of God, which is his glory and majesty. *"They will see his face, and his name will be on their foreheads"* (Rev. 22:4). *"As for me, I shall behold your face in righteousness; when I awake, I shall be satisfied with your likeness"* (Psalm 17:15).
2. They shall be most like Christ: just, holy, incorruptible, glorious, honourable, excellent, beautiful, strong, mighty, and nimble. *"Beloved, we are God's children now, and what we will be has not yet appeared; but we know that when he appears we shall be like him, because we shall see him as he is"* (1 John 3:2). *"Who will transform our lowly body to be like his glorious body, by the power that enables him even to subject all things to himself"* (Phil. 3:21).
3. They shall inherit the kingdom of heaven; the new heavens and new earth shall be their inheritance. *"To an inheritance that is imperishable, undefiled, and unfading, kept in heaven for you"* (1 Pet. 1:4). *"Then the King will say to those on his right, 'Come, you who are blessed by my Father, inherit the kingdom prepared for you from the foundation of the world"* (Matt. 25:34). *"And you have made them a kingdom and priests to our God, and they shall reign on the earth"* (Rev. 5:10). *"And you have made them a kingdom and priests to our God, and they shall reign on the earth"* (Rev. 21:7).

The **Fruit** that comes from both these parts of blessedness is of two sorts: Eternal Joy and the Perfect Service of God. *"You make known to me the path of life; in your presence there is fullness of joy; at your right hand are pleasures forevermore"* (Psalm 16:11). *"They feast on the abundance of your house, and you give them drink from the river of your delights. For* *with you is the fountain of life; in your light do we see light"* (Psalm 36:8–9).

The parts of **God's Service** are Praise and Thanksgiving. *"And I heard a loud voice from the throne saying, 'Behold, the dwelling place of God is with man. He will dwell with them, and they will be his people, and God himself will be with them as their God'"* (Rev. 21:3). *"Saying with a loud voice, 'Worthy is the Lamb who was slain, to receive power and wealth and wisdom and might and honour and glory and blessing!' etc."* (Rev. 5:12–13). *"And the twenty-four elders who sit on their thrones before God fell on their faces and worshiped God, saying, "We give thanks to you, Lord God Almighty, who is and who was, for you have taken your great power and begun to reign"* (Rev. 11:16–17).

The manner of performing this service is to worship God immediately by God himself. In heaven there shall neither be temple, ceremony, nor sacrament, but God will supply all these needs together with the lamb, that is Christ. *"And I saw no temple in the city, for its temple is the Lord God the Almighty and the Lamb"* (Rev. 21:22).

This service shall be daily and without ceasing. *"Therefore they are before the throne of God, and serve him day and night in his temple; and he who sits on the throne will shelter them with his presence"* (Rev. 7:15).

A Consequence (or the Last Conclusion)

Thus, God clearly sets forth his justice and mercy in saving the elect. His justice, in that he punished the sins of the elect in his Son; his mercy, in that he pardoned their sin by the merits of his Son. *"Having the eyes of your hearts enlightened, that you may know what is the hope to which he has called you, what are the riches of his glorious inheritance in the saints, and what is the immeasurable greatness of his power toward us who believe, according to the working of his great might that he worked in Christ"* (Eph. 1:18–20). *"(That you) may have strength to comprehend with all the saints what is the breadth and length and height and depth, and to know the love of Christ that surpasses knowledge, that you may be filled with all the fullness of God"* (Eph. 3:18–19).

All these things the Lord himself has thus decreed, and in his good time he will accomplish them to the glorious praise of his name. *"The LORD has made everything for its purpose, even the wicked for the day of trouble"* (Prov. 16:4).

CHAPTER 51:
Roman Predestination

A View of the Distribution of the Causes of Salvation & Damnation,
as the Church of Rome would have it.

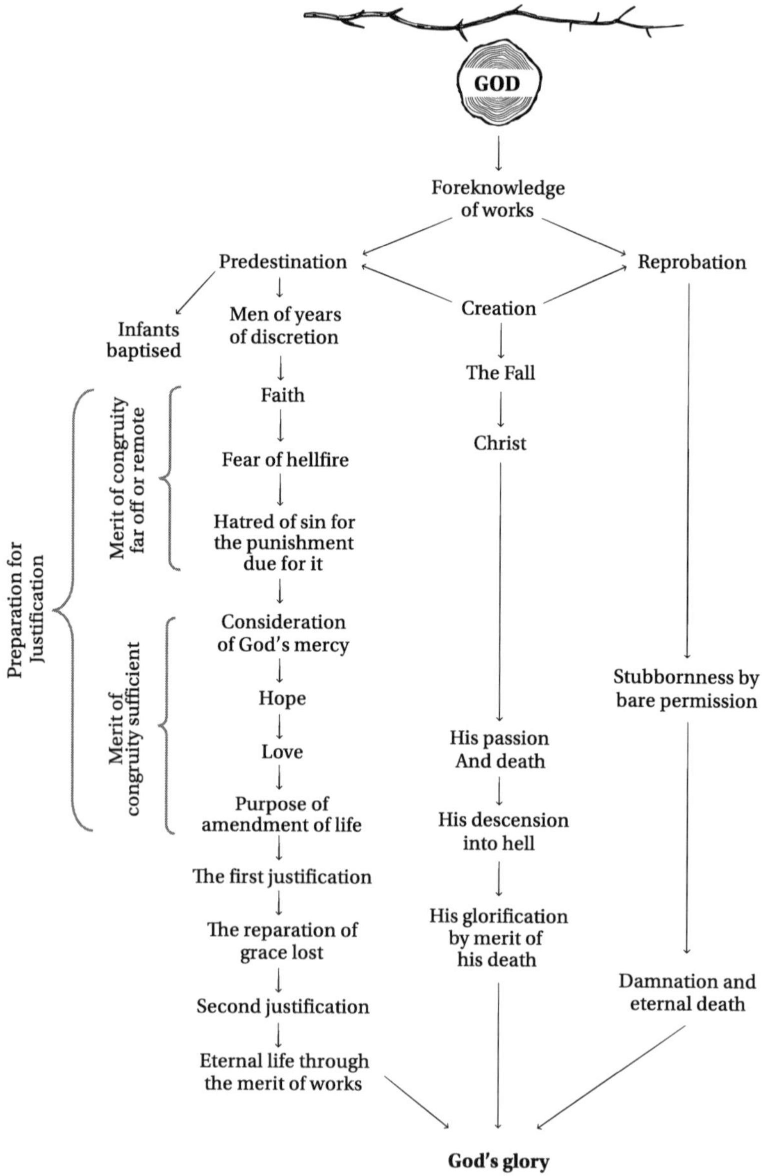

Chapter Fifty One

THE ORDER OF THE CAUSES OF SALVATION ACCORDING TO THE ROMAN CHURCH

According to the Roman Church, the Order of Causes of Salvation is as follows.[1]

There are two things required to obtain salvation: Predestination and its Execution.

Predestination is a foreordaining of the rational creature to grace in this life and glory in the life to come.

The first effects of Predestination (calling, election, and ordination to eternal life) are caused by God's will. However, the cause of its execution and the obtaining of eternal life are from man, because (according to the common opinion) God predestines according to his foresight of man's works. That is, God predestines or rejects a man because he foresees that he will use his grace well or badly. These seven conclusions draw this point out more clearly:

1. The Predestination and Reprobation of God do not constrain or enforce any necessity upon the will of man.
2. God has predestined all men, that is he has appointed and disposed all men to be able to obtain eternal salvation.
3. Man is neither saved nor condemned by necessity or chance,

1. For Perkins' fuller critique of Roman Catholic thought and practice, see his *A Reformed Catholic* (1597) and *The Problem of Forged Catholicism* (1604) in *The Works of William Perkins: Volume 7*. (ed. Shawn D. Wright; Grand Rapids: Reformation Heritage Books, 2018).

but voluntarily.

4. God has predestined some, and others he has rejected.
5. Those whom God has predestined by his absolute predestination cannot be lost and will infallibly die in grace. But those who are predestined according to present justice may be lost by some mortal sin which follows; they are not infallibly saved, but often such persons are condemned and lose their crown and glory. Hence arises their position that he who is justified may be a reprobate and perish eternally.[2] Therefore predestination is not certain since it may be lost.
6. God alone knows the certain and set number of those who are predestined.
7. There is one set number of those who are predestined, and this can neither be increased nor diminished.

The **Execution of Predestination** is either in Infants or in those of Years of Discretion.

The merit of Christ is applied to **Infants** by baptism whenever it is rightly administered. In baptism, whatever parts of original corruption may properly be accounted as sin are utterly taken away, and not merely decreased or not imputed. For there is nothing that God can hate in those who are renewed.[3]

Nevertheless, the baptised are urged to confess that concupiscence (the relics of sin) remains in them. However, man is able to wrestle with it and it has no power to harm those who will not yield to it.

The Execution of predestination in those who are of **Riper Years** has six degrees:

1. The first degree is **Calling**, whereby men are called to turn to God, not by their own merits but by God's enabling grace through Christ.
2. The second degree is a **Preparation for Righteousness**, whereby men apply themselves to justification through the

2. Augustine, *Confessions*, 2.4.20.
3. Council of Trent, sect 5, canon 5.

inherent power of free-will, after which the same power is stirred up by the Holy Spirit. For free-will is only somewhat diminished by sin, not extinguished. Therefore, as soon as the Holy Spirit touches and enlightens the heart, the heart works together with, and freely agrees with, the Spirit.

The beginning of this Preparation is Faith, which is a knowledge whereby men agree that those things revealed in the word of God concerning God and his will are true. This is the foundation of justification, wherein free-will is stirred up to affect the heart with the motions by which it is prepared for justification, as follows:

i. The act of faith apprehends the ugliness of sin and its wages.

ii. After this follows a fear of God's anger and of hellfire.

iii. Then men begin to dislike and detest sin. From this arises a certain disposition which, whilst imperfect, has a *merit of congruity* joined to it and so receives grace by God's generosity.[4]

iv. At length, faith returns to the contemplation of God's mercies, and believes that God is ready to forgive sins by the infusion of charity into those who are sufficiently prepared and disposed.

v. Out of this contemplation proceeds the act of hope, whereby faith begins to desire and to wait on God as the chief good.

vi. Out of this act of hope arises love, whereby God is loved above all things in the world.

vii. After this love follows a new dislike and detestation of sin, not so much from fear of punishment in hellfire, as from fear of offending God, who is simply loved more than all other things.

viii. After all these, follows a purpose of amendment of life. Here enters the immediate, sufficient, and last disposition before the infusion of grace.

4. In Roman Catholic theology, a *Merit of Congruity* is a merit which is insufficient to deserve grace (i.e. a 'half-merit'), but which receives grace nonetheless on account of God's generosity in Christ. See ***'The Ninth Error'*** below.

3. The third degree of predestination is **First Justification**, whereby unjust men are made just, not only through the remission of their sins but also by a sanctification of the inward man, by his voluntary reception of grace.

   The *efficient cause* of this justification is the mercy of God, and the meritorious passion of our Saviour Christ by which he purchased justification for men. The *instrumental cause* is Baptism. The *formal cause* is not that justice which was inherent in Christ, but that which he infuses into man, which is especially hope and charity.[5]

4. The fourth degree is the **Second Justification**, by which just men are made more just. The cause of this is faith joined with good works. It is possible for those who are renewed to keep the commandments, and therefore it is not true to say that a just man commits lesser sins (*venial sins*) even in his best actions, much less that he deserves eternal death for them.

5. The fifth degree is the **Reparation** of a sinner by the sacrament of Penance, which is a kind of second board to float on after a shipwreck. The reason that this reparation is necessary is because men lose the grace of justification by every mortal sin.

6. The sixth degree is the **Fruit of Justification**, namely the glory of eternal life, for which works done in grace actually attain merit of sufficient worthiness (that is, by *condign merit*).

Condign Merit is merit where reward is due, such that injustice will be committed if it is not given.[6] A condign merit is due by the rigour of justice.

---

5. These Aristotelian concepts were widely used by medieval and early modern theologians. Here, *efficient cause* fits naturally enough with the modern idea of 'cause': justification is caused by God's mercy by means of Jesus' death. The *instrumental cause* refers to the way that this is imparted to people, which (according to Roman Catholicism) is through baptism. Finally, *material cause* is what something is made out of, as a wall is made of bricks. According to Roman Catholicism, justification is not composed of the merits of Christ being imputed to God's people (as in Protestant theology), but of the transformation which God works within the believers, especially the production of hope and love in them.
6. That is, a *Condign Merit* (a full merit) is owed its reward, whereas a congruit merit (a half merit) is not owed a reward, but may receive it by God's generosity.

Two conditions are required to make a merit.

1. The reward should be due according to some compact or bargain. This condition is good works due to God, for in the Scriptures he has promised a reward to those who work well.
2. Besides this compact (by which the debtor is bound), there should be also some worthiness in the work itself: some proportion between the work and its reward.

The worthiness or dignity of the work depends:

1. On Christ. For Christ not only merited that his own actions would be meritorious but also those of his members.
2. On the Holy Spirit. For the Holy Spirit inspires, excites, and moves men to do good works.
3. On Habitual Grace (gracious dispositions toward obedience in the believer), which is a certain participation of the divine essence.

Thus much concerning the degrees of Executing Predestination. Now follows the **Applying of Predestination** particularly to the persons of men.

No man, so long as he lives in this mortal life, ought so much to presume on the secret mystery of God's predestination. Much less ought he to determine undoubtedly that he is in the number of the elect, whom God has ordained to eternal happiness. For no man (without special revelation) can know who God has chosen to be his heirs.

In Summary: By God's freely given, enabling grace (or *aid*), man may dispose himself to God's justifying grace, such that he may believe, fear, repent, love, and propound to himself newness of life, and so on.

Furthermore, if a sinner by his free-will yields his agreement to this divine motion, and consequently and accordingly rightly disposes himself, God forgives his sins and infuses justifying grace into him, by which he may do good works, and so by them merit eternal life.

Errors of the Papists in their Distribution of the causes of Salvation

Thus the doctrine of the Church of Rome is a very blasphemous doctrine, and should be considered no better than a gallows set up for the torture and massacre of the consciences of men. That this may more clearly appear to be the case, I here set down the most principle errors of Popish doctrine:

The First Error: *Predestination is only of the Elect, and the Reprobate are only foreknown.*

Rebuttal

'Predestination' is sometimes refers to its positive part alone, namely of the elect, as in Rom. 8:30, *"And those whom he predestined he also called, and those whom he called he also justified, and those whom he justified he also glorified".* So also, the Ephesians said to be predestined *"for adoption as sons (of God)"* (Eph. 1:5). Yet this word may generally be extended to the decree of God, including both predestination to eternal life and reprobation to eternal death. The reasons:

1. *"For truly in this city there were gathered together against your holy servant Jesus, ... to do whatever your hand and your plan had predestined (προώρισεν) to take place"* (Acts 4:27–28).
2. Augustine calls *Predestination* the disposition of future works,[7] and in his *City of God* he divides *"all mankind into two cities: whereof one is predestined to reign with God eternally, the other predestined to undergo eternal punishment with the Devil."*[8] In his *Enchiridion* he says, *"That God has justly predestined wicked men to punishment, and mercifully predestined the good to grace."*[9] Thomas Aquinas says: *"Regarding the name of predestination, it doesn't matter whether a man be said to be predestined to life eternal or not."*[10]

Furthermore, for a man to say that the Reprobates are foreknown

7. Augustine, *On the Gift of Perseverance*, ch. 17.
8. Augustine, *City of God*, 15.1.
9. Augustine, *Enchiridion*, ch. 100.
10. Thomas Aquinas, *Summa Theologica*, 1.23.4.

and not predestined is very injurious, since God's foreknowledge may not be severed from his will and eternal decree in anything which is to be. For all that shall be is foreknown of God, and all that shall come to pass is either by the will of God, or without his will. If with his will, then he both decreed and preordained the same; if without or against his will, then how is God then said to be omnipotent? And surely God wills evil itself, though not by his approving will but by his willing permission of it. Augustine has an excellent saying to this purpose. *"Although (he said) that those things which are evil in that they are evil cannot be good yet that there are not only good, but also evil things, it is very good: to the intent that after a marvellous and unspeakable manner, that thing may not be besides, or without his will, which also is done against his will, because it should not be done, unless he suffered it, neither does he suffer it against his will, but willingly."*[11]

The Second Error: *Predestination is changeable. For (according to the common opinion of the Papists) whosoever is predestined is conditionally predestined (on God's part as well as on man's). It follows that those predestined to salvation may be condemned, and he who is foreknown as damned may be saved.*

Rebuttal

The contrary is most true, namely that the decree of God concerning every man's eternal salvation or damnation is set down from all eternity and is unchangeable. The reasons:

1. Testimony of Scripture. *"For the gifts and the calling of God are irrevocable* (ἀμεταμέλητα)" (Rom. 11:29). *"For false christs and false prophets will arise and perform great signs and wonders, so as to lead astray, if possible, even the elect"* (Matt. 24:24). *"Who shall bring any charge against God's elect? It is God who justifies, Who is to condemn?"* (Rom. 8:33–34a). *"But God's firm foundation stands, bearing this seal: 'The Lord knows those who are his'"* (2 Tim. 2:19).
2. Election and reprobation are in God, not in men, and there can be nothing in God which is changeable. *"For I the LORD do not change"* (Mal. 3:6). *"My counsel shall stand, and I will accomplish*

11. Augustine, *Enchiridion*, 100.

all my purpose" (Isa. 46:10).

3. If this Popish conclusion should be granted, then it necessarily follows that the foreknowledge of God must be made void, his power weakened, and his will changed, each of which is impious even to dream of. For he which changes his counsel or will, changes it either because he sees that he might have taken better advice, or else in that he could not bring his former purpose about as he would have liked. Either of these are far from our Lord God.
4. If we resolve that the counsel of God is changeable in any way, then no man can be certain whether he is predestined to life or not. Thus, the ground of our full assurance of salvation is utterly shaken and overturned. Therefore, let us maintain this truth that both the election and reprobation of God stand unchangeable. The elect cannot become reprobates who are condemned, nor can reprobates become of the elect who are saved.

   Objection: The Popish sort object to this doctrine as follows. If you speak in a 'compound sense' (*in sensu composito*) it is very true that the predestined cannot be saved, nor can those foreknown perish. But if you speak in a 'divided sense' (*in sensu diviso*), this is it is not so. This distinction is plain by this example: white colour in a compound cannot be black, because blackness is contrary to whiteness. Similarly, one predestined to salvation may sin by his free will, and so be damned.

   > *Answer*. These are silly and fallacious arguments. Those who are predestined to the end, namely salvation, are necessarily predestined to the means of salvation also. They necessarily use such means and arrive at the end by them.

The Third Error: *All men are predestined, that is, disposed and ordained of God, and so may attain eternal life.*[12]

Rebuttal

This is clearly false. For:

1. Those who die as infants have no opportunity to use the means

12. Sebastian Cattaneo, *Enchiridion*, chapter of Predestination.

of salvation. They may have life eternal, yet they do not obtain it by the ordinary means.

2. Whatever the Lord actually does, he first determined to do. For he does nothing either unadvisedly or unwillingly, yet he actually forsakes a very great part of mankind, shut up under defiance and left to itself. *"In past generations he allowed all the nations to walk in their own ways"* (Acts 14:16). Hence also in Eph. 2:12 all the Gentiles are said to be *"without God in the world"* (ἄθεοι). Therefore God decreed to forsake some men in this life; he did not ordain all men to the obtaining of eternal life. Indeed, if God willed that all men should be saved then it would be impossible for any to perish. God's willing is his doing of it. If anyone ordained to salvation was to perish, then God will have failed in what he willed from all eternity, or else must have changed his will. These things cannot be said of God without blasphemy.
3. Paul says that there are certain men "who are perishing" (ἀπολλυμοι) (2 Thess. 2:10), who he distinguishes from the elect in verse 13. *"Has the potter no right..."* (Rom. 9:21-22). Where there is not only mention made of vessels of glory and mercy, but also of those made and fashioned (in God's eternal counsel) as vessels of wrath. God never disposed to obtain eternal life whom he made for wrath and destruction.

The Fourth Error: *The last effects of predestination are caused by man's free-will and works. For God predestined those whom he foresaw would receive grace offered in Christ and lead their life according to the law. This was not of works but of God's mercy, yet in such a way as had respect to works, or (as others say) to ordain them by their works foreseen. For example, God foresaw and foreknew from all eternity that Peter would be saved and Judas condemned, because from the same eternity he both foresaw and foreknew that Peter would accept the grace offered to him and afterwards rightly use it. He also foresaw that Judas would receive the grace offered yet use the same perversely.*

Rebuttal

Their doctrine of foreseen works is a man-made forgery:

1. Paul shows it to be plainly counterfeit when as he says that the Ephesians were chosen or elected *"in (Christ) before the foundation of the world"* (Eph. 1:4), and not because he foresaw that they would be holy, but so that they *"should be holy and blameless before him."* He goes on to say that they were *"created in Christ Jesus for good works, which God prepared beforehand, that we should walk in them"* (2:10). In these passages good works are effects of predestination, but the effect foreseen cannot be the cause of God's cause, cause goes before its effect, both in the order of nature and knowledge.
2. *"Not because of works done by us in righteousness, but according to his own mercy"* did God elect and save us (Titus 3:5).
3. In electing us God did not regard anything outside of himself, but elected us in himself (Eph. 1:4, 9). Therefore, he did not consider future works.
4. Even some Popish theologians confess that predestination puts nothing in the party predestined, for which God predestined them.[13]
5. Election is based on God's mercy alone (Rom. 9:16).
6. God saw no grace in man except what he himself must bestow upon him. Hence, the beginning of election proceeds from grace.
7. Since there is nothing above or greater than God, it is necessarily impious to assign any cause of his will outside or above his majesty. Therefore, we rightly deny that his foreknowledge of faith and works was the cause of his decree concerning man's salvation.

The Fifth Error: *By Baptism (rightly administered) both the guilt and corruption of original sin is so washed away, that it cannot afterwards properly be accounted as sin.*

13. Thomas Aquinas, *Summa Theologica*, 1.23.2.

Rebuttal

On the contrary, we do distinguish sin in this way. By the one act of baptism sin is taken away, both as guilt deserving of God's wrath and as punishment of corruption. However, the error and corruption of nature is not immediately taken away, but is extinguished gradually, little by little, just as our renovation by the Holy Spirit is begun and gradually increased in us. For these reasons:

1. Paul would not so greatly bewail his original sin, if it ceased any more to be sin after baptism. *"I see in my members another law waging war against the law of my mind and making me captive to the law of sin that dwells in my members. Wretched man that I am! Who will deliver me from this body of death?"* (Rom 7:23–24).
2. Original sin is called *"sinful beyond measure"* (Rom. 7:13), and *"sin which clings so closely"* (Heb. 12:1).
3. Concupiscence is the root of actual sin, and therefore it must properly be a sin even after baptism.
4. If concupiscence is not a sin, where does that fierce combat between the flesh and the Spirit come from?

The Sixth Error: *Baptism is absolutely necessary for salvation, especially for children.*

Rebuttal

We deny that baptism is absolutely necessity for salvation, for these reasons:

1. Sacraments do not confer grace, but rather confirm grace when God has conferred it. The children of faithful parents are born holy, not by natural generation, but by the grace of God. They are not first made holy by baptism, and those who reach the age of discretion before they are baptised cannot be baptised unless they believe. Now all who believe are both justified and reconciled to God, and therefore if they are (unwillingly) deprived of the sacraments, it remains impossible for them to perish.
2. God appointed circumcision to be precisely on the eighth day, not on the first or second. There is no doubt that many

infants died before their eight day and were thus prevented from receiving circumcision. To conclude that all these were condemned is absurd.

3. If circumcision was of such absolute necessity, why was it intermittent for the space of forty years in the desert? There can be no doubt that Moses and Aaron would never have omitted this sacrament so long if it had been absolutely necessary for salvation.
4. The doctrine of the absolute necessity of baptism was unknown to the ancient fathers. For the primitive Church tolerated very godly men deferring their baptism for many years, indeed often to the time of their death. Thus, Constantine the great was not baptised until a little before his death, and Valentinian was not baptised at all, yet Ambrose pronounces him to be in heaven. And Bernard argues that not every deprivation of baptism is damnable, but only the contempt or obvious negligence of it.[14]

The Seventh Error: *After the fall of Adam, man has free-will to do that which is good as well as that which is evil, although in different ways. That is, he has free-will to do evil simply and without any external aide, but can only will well the enabling grace of God. Every man has this grace, and our free-will can choose either to consent and work with the it, or not. Therefore, the power of free-will to do what is good and acceptable to God is only weakened before conversion, and thus man can prepare himself for justification.*

Rebuttal

Unregenerate man has free-will only to do evil; none to do good. The unconverted man cannot so much as desire to have faith and be converted. These are the reasons:

1. Man is not said to be weak or sick, but *"dead in sins"* (Eph. 2:1; Col. 1:13). Just as one who is physically dead cannot stir up himself to perform works of the living (even with the help of others), so the spiritually dead cannot move himself to live to God.

14. Bernard of Clairvaux, *Letters*, 77.

2. Man is the servant of Satan and bond-slave of sin (Eph. 2:2; Rom. 6:13). We know that a servant stands at the beck and pleasure of another, and cannot do otherwise.

3. Man cannot will what he cannot first know and believe. No man can know and believe the following things regarding the kingdom of God. *"The natural person does not accept the things of the Spirit of God"* (1 Cor. 2:14). *"Not that we are sufficient in ourselves to claim anything as coming from us"* (2 Cor. 3:5). Therefore, no man can, by himself, will those things that relate to God's kingdom.

4. Whatever is both a deadly enemy and repugnant to goodness does not desire what is good; and the human will is an enemy and directly repugnant to goodness. *"For the mind that is set on the flesh is hostile to God, for it does not submit to God's law; indeed, it cannot"* (Rom. 8:7).

Objection 1: *"But the word is very near you. It is in your mouth and in your heart, so that you can do it"* (Deut. 30:14).
Answer: It is easy to perform the law legally, but not evangelically. The latter is done when a man fulfils the law by a Mediator, and from him receives the Spirit of God, by whom he endeavours to perform new obedience.

Objection 2: God gives many precepts by which we are commanded to repent, believe, obey God, and so on. To obey these, we must have free-will.
Answer:

a. Such passages do not show us what we can do, but what we should do.

b. They are instruments of the Holy Spirit, by which he renews and converts those who shall be saved.

Objection 2a: In commanding these, God does not require the impossible.
Answer: He does not indeed to men in their innocence, but now to all those who fell in Adam he does, and that by their own failure, not God's.

Objection 3: *"Work out your own salvation with fear and trembling"* (Phil. 2:12).

Answer: Paul speaks of those who are already converted and have their will partly freed.

Objection 4: If the will is a mere passive patient of God's work, it is constrained to do good.

Answer: The will, both in and of itself, is a mere patient in her first conversion to God, but it is subsequently an agent as it is moved by the Spirit of God. For, being moved, it moves. It is not therefore compelled, since God makes a willing will out of a unwilling will.

The Eighth Error: *The Holy Spirit does not give grace to will, but only frees the will which was chained, and excites it so that the will (by her own power) disposes herself to justification.*

Rebuttal

This is false. To will things concerning the kingdom of God—such as faith, conversion, and new obedience—is the mere gift of God's Spirit. *"No one knows the Father except the Son and anyone to whom the Son chooses to reveal him"* (Matt. 11:27). *"To you it has been given to know the secrets of the kingdom of God"* (Luke 8:10). *"For it is God who works in you, both to will and to work for his good pleasure"* (Phil. 2:13). *"No one can say "Jesus is Lord" except in the Holy Spirit"* (1 Cor. 12:3). He who is to be *"created after the likeness of God in true righteousness and holiness"* (Eph. 4:24) cannot incline himself in any way to justification or new creation. For it is impossible that a thing not yet created should incline itself to its creation.

The Ninth Error: *That preparation to grace which is caused by the power of free-will may attain justification by the merit of congruity.*[15]

Rebuttal

These things smell of more than Satanic arrogance. For what man (except one not in his right mind) would believe that he, to whom so many millions of condemnations are due, could merit the least measure

15. On *Congruent Merit* see footnote 6 on page 334, above.

of grace? The prodigal son was not received into favour by reason of his deserving, but by favour. *"And the son said to him, 'Father, I have sinned against heaven and before you. I am no longer worthy to be called your son'"* (Luke 15:21).

The Tenth Error: *The faith which justifies is that by which a man generally believes the blessedness promised of God, and by which he also gives his agreement to other mysteries revealed of God concerning this blessedness.*

Rebuttal

Faith is not only a general knowledge and agreement to the history of the gospel but is also a certain power which apprehends and applies the promises of God in Christ, by which a man assuredly sets down that his sins are forgiven and that he is reconciled to God. The reasons are:

1. Assurance of God's favour toward oneself is of the nature of faith. *"In whom we have boldness and access with confidence through our faith in him"* (Eph. 3:12). *"No distrust made him waver concerning the promise of God, but he grew strong in his faith as he gave glory to God, fully convinced that God was able to do what he had promised"* (Rom. 4:20-21). *"Let us draw near with a true heart in full assurance of faith"* (Heb. 10:22).
2. Doubting regarding God's favour toward oneself is rebuked. *"O you of little faith, why did you doubt?"* (Matt. 14:31). *"Nor be worried"* (Luke 12:29b).
3. A man must assuredly believe that he will receive whatever he prays for from God (Mark 11:24). In their prayers the faithful make request for adoption, justification, and life eternal, and therefore they must certainly believe that they shall receive these benefits.
4. *"Therefore, since we have been justified by faith, we have peace with God"* (Rom. 5:1). But there can be no peace where there is not an assurance of God's favour towards oneself.
5. That which the Spirit of God testifies to us particularly must also be believed particularity. The Spirit of God gives a particular testimony of the adoption of the faithful (Rom. 8:16; Gal. 4:6).

Therefore, this is to be believed.

They say that no man has assurance of God's favour toward himself particularly except by special revelation (as it was with Abraham and Paul). But this is false, for the faith of these two is set down in Scripture as an example which we should all follow. For this reason, Abraham is called the *"father of the faithful"*, and Paul testifies the very same of himself: *"But I received mercy for this reason, that in me, as the foremost, Jesus Christ might display his perfect patience as an example to those who were to believe in him for eternal life"* (1 Tim. 1:16). Again, whereas they say that we have a moral assurance, but not the assurance of faith, this is a Popish device. For *"you have received the Spirit of adoption* (συμμαρτυρεῖ) *.... the Spirit himself bears witness with our spirit that we are children of God"* (Rom. 8:15–16). We see two witnesses of our adoption: our own spirit and the Spirit of God. Our spirit testifies morally of our adoption by sanctification and its fruits, and the Spirit of God also witnesses by the certainty of faith, declaring and applying the promises of God.

Objection 1: We are commanded to work out our salvation with fear and trembling.

Answer: This fear does not relate to God's mercy forgiving our sins, but in respect of us and our nature which is ever prone to slide away from God.

Objection 2: In respect of God's mercy, we must hope for salvation: but in respect of our unworthiness, we must doubt.

Answer:

a. We may not at all lawfully doubt God's mercy, because doubtfulness is not of the nature of faith, but rather a natural corruption.
b. If we consider our own unworthiness, there is no doubt that we must be out of all hope and despair of our salvation.

Objection 3: There are many sins unknown to us, and so it is uncertain whether they are pardoned.

Answer: He that certainly and truly knows that one sin is pardoned him, has all his sins remitted before God, whether they be known or unknown.

Objection 4: No man can dare swear or die in the defence of this proposition: *"I am the child of God"*, or in God's favour, and justified.

Answer: They which have a true faith, will (if they are lawfully called) not only testify to their adoption by an oath, but seal it also by their blood.

Objection 5: A man may have this faith which the Protestants talk of, and live in a mortal sin which they also intend to persevere in.

Answer: It is far otherwise, for true faith purifies the heart (Acts 15:9).

These sophisters further affirm that this faith (which to them is nothing but a knowledge and illumination of the mind concerning the truth of God's word) is the root and foundation of justification. If this is true, why should the Devil not be just? For he has both a knowledge of God's word and by believes it, yet he cannot be called one of the faithful.

Here they make an exception, saying that the Devil's faith is void of charity (love), which is the form of faith. But this is an invention of their own brain. For charity is the effect of faith (1 Tim. 1:5) and an effect cannot inform the cause.

The Eleventh Error: *Man's love of God goes before his justification and reconciliation with God in order and time.*

Rebuttal

On the contrary, unless we are first persuaded of God's love towards us, we never love him. *"We love (him) because he first loved us"* (1 John 4:19). Again, it is impossible that God's enemy should love him. He who is not as yet justified or reconciled to God is God's enemy (Rom. 5:9–10). Neither can any man be made God's friend before the act of justification.

The Twelfth Error: *Infused or inherent justice is the formal cause of justification, by which men are justified in the sight of God.*

Rebuttal

On the contrary, we hold that the material cause of man's justification is the obedience of Christ in suffering, and in fulfilling the law for us. The formal cause of justification is Imputation, which is an action of God the Father accepting the obedience of Christ for us, as if it were our own.[16] Reasons:

1. We are justified alone by whatever absolves us from all our sins and by which we obtain eternal life. We are absolved from all our sins thus accepted by God into eternal life by Christ's perfect obedience imputed to us, which we cannot do by inherent holiness. Therefore, we are justified by Christ's perfect obedience imputed to us, and this alone. This truth is reflected in the practices of calling on God's name and of repentance. For in temptation, and our conflicts with sin and Satan, faith does not reason thus: "Now I have charity and inherent grace, and for these God will accept of me". Rather, faith more rightly beholds the Son of God as he was made a sacrifice for us and sits at the right hand of his Father making intercession for us. To him, I say, faith flees and is assured that God will forgive us all our sins for the sake of his Son and will be reconciled to us. Indeed, he will account us just in his sight, not by any inherent quality in us, but rather by the merit of Jesus Christ (Rom. 5:19).
2. As Christ was made a sinner, so likewise those who believe are made just. But Christ was only made and accounted a sinner for us by imputation (2 Cor. 5:21). He became a guarantee for us: a sacrifice for our sins upon which all of our guilt and punishment was laid. Hence he is said to have become *"a curse"* (κατάρα) for us. Therefore, we are made just only by imputation.
3. The opposite of condemnation is remission of sins, and justification is the opposite of condemnation, *"It is God who justifies. Who is to condemn?"* (Rom. 8:33–34). Therefore justification is the remission of sins, which entirely depends upon this imputation of Christ's merits.
4. Although infused and inherent justice may have a due place, praise, and deserving, yet as it is a work of the Holy Spirit, it is not complete in this life. Due to the flesh to which it is united, it is both imperfect and infected with the dregs of sin (Isa. 64). Therefore, it cannot claim to absolve any from the sentence of condemnation before God's judgement seat.

---

16. On Aristotelian causal language, see footnote 5 on page 334, above.

Objection 1: This imputation is nothing else but a vain thought.

Answer:

a. Imputation is the foundation of its end goal.
b. As the imputation of our sins to Christ was indeed something, so the imputation of Christ's justice to us must not be thought a bare conceit.
c. The Church of Rome herself maintains imputed justice, namely when by ecclesiastical authority she applies the merits and satisfactions of certain persons to other members of that Church. From this it is apparent that even the Popes indulgences are imputed.

Objection 2: Imputed justice is not everlasting, but that justice which the Messiah brings is everlasting.

Answer: Although after this life there is no pardon of sins to be looked for, yet that which is given to us for salvation in this life shall continue in the life to come.

Objection 3: If justification is by imputation, a wicked man may be just before God.

Answer: Not at all, for he who is justified by imputation is also sanctified at that same instant.

The Thirteenth Error: *There is also a second justification which is obtained by works.*

Rebuttal

That Popish device of a second justification is a fantastic delusion. For:

1. The word of God acknowledges no more but one justification, and that is absolute and complete in itself. There is but one justice and one satisfaction of God being offended, therefore there cannot be a manifold justification.
2. If justification should be distinguished into several kinds or parts by reason of the increase of inherent justice, we might as well make a hundred kinds or parts of justification as make two.
3. That which follows after full justification before God by order of nature cannot be said to justify. But, by order of nature, good

works follow man's justification and his absolution from sins, for no work can please God unless the person who does it pleases him first. And no man can please God until they are reconciled to him and have peace with him by the merits of Christ.

4. Such works as are not agreeable to the rule of legal justice. Before the tribunal seat of God they cannot justify, but rather both in and of themselves are subject to God's eternal curse. For this is the sentence of the Law, *"Cursed be everyone who does not abide by all things written in the Book of the Law, and do them"* (Gal. 3:10). Now the works even of the regenerate are not squared according to the rule of legal justice. David was stricken with the consideration of this, and didn't dare to set even his best works before the judgement of God to plead pardon of his sins: *"Enter not into judgement with your servant, for no one living is righteous before you"* (Psalm 143:2). Similarly: *"If one (namely such a one as says he is just) wished to contend with him, one could not answer him once in a thousand times"* (Job 9:3). And: *"For we do not present our pleas before you because of our righteousness, but because of your great mercy"* (Dan. 9:18).

5. Justification by works overturns the foundation of our faith. *"If you accept circumcision, Christ will be of no advantage to you .... You are severed from Christ, you who would be justified by the law; you have fallen away from grace"* (Gal 5:2, 4). In this passage the Apostle does not speak of those who openly resist Christ and the gospel, but of those who mingle together the works of the Law with the merit of Christ as though some part of our salvation consisted in them.

Counter Claim: This passage only excludes such moral works of the flesh, which go before faith or the works of the law of Moses.

Answer: This is untrue. For it even speaks of regenerate Abraham, and of his works done when he was justified, in this way: *"And to the one who does not work but believes in him who justifies the ungodly, his faith is counted as righteousness"* (Rom. 4:5). Those works which God has prepared for the regenerate to walk in are moral works and works of grace, but these are excluded from justification and working man's salvation (Eph. 2:10). And Paul (being regenerate) says of himself, *"For I am not aware of anything against myself, but I am not thereby acquitted"* (1 Cor. 4:4).

6. The cause of the cause is the cause of the thing caused. Grace without works is the cause of man's predestination, which (in turn) is the cause of his justification. Therefore, grace without works must be the cause of justification.

Objection 1: *"If a person does them (God's statutes), he shall live by them"* (Lev. 18:5).

Answer: This saying is a legal sentence, and therefore does not show what men can do, but what they should do.

Objection 2: *"Blessed are those whose way is blameless, who walk in the law of the LORD!"* (Psalm 119:1).

Answer: Man is not here said to be blessed because he walks uprightly, but that he walks uprightly because he is justified before God by the merits of Christ.

Objection 3: *"Judge me, O LORD, according to my righteousness"* (Psalm 7:8). And the act of Phineas was imputed to him for righteousness (Numb. 25:11).

Answer: These passages are not about the righteousness of the person by which they are righteous before God, but of the righteousness of some particular cause or work. For whereas David was accused of this crime, in the words above mentioned, he testifies his innocence before God.

Objection 4: We are judged according to our works, therefore also by them justified.

Answer: The two are not alike because the last judgement is not the justifying of a man, but a declaration of that justification which he previously obtained. Therefore, the last judgement must be pronounced and taken from the effects and signs of justification, not from its causes.

Objection 5: *"Make friends for yourselves by means of unrighteous wealth, so that when it fails they may receive you into the eternal dwellings"* (Luke 16:9).

Answer: They do not do this as authors of salvation, but as its witnesses.

Objection 6: Redeem your sins by righteousness, and your iniquity by mercy to the poor (Dan. 4:27).

Answer: It is rather *"break off your sins"* than redeem in the original. Men break off their sins by ceasing from them, not by satisfying for them.

Objection 7: Evil works condemn, therefore good works justify.

Answer: This does not follow since good works are not perfectly good, whereas evil works are perfectly evil.

Objection 8: *"For in this hope we were saved"* (Rom. 8:24).

Answer: We must distinguish between justification and salvation. Salvation is the end, whereas justification is one degree toward that end. There is more required to the end than to one degree subordinate to it, therefore we are saved by hope and faith, but justified by faith alone.

Objection 9: Affliction causes eternal glory (2 Cor. 4:17).

Answer: Affliction does not effect glory, as by its own merit, but rather is the path to it.

Objection 10: Abraham was justified by works (James 2:21).

Answer: Not as a cause of justification, but as a proof of it.

Objection 11: He that is just may become more just.

Answer: This must be understood of justification before men, namely of sanctification or a holy life, and not of justification in the sight of God.

Objection 12: We are justified by faith, therefore by a work.

Answer: We are justified by faith, not as it is a virtue or a work, but as it is an instrument apprehending the justice of Christ, whereby we are justified. In this respect, faith is said to be imputed to us to righteousness.

Objection 13: The works of grace are dyed in the blood of Christ.

> *Answer*: They are indeed dyed in Christ's blood, but to the end they might better please God, not justify man. Moreover, they are so stained by sin that they need dying in the blood of Christ, therefore they cannot justify sinful man in any way. And the worker himself is also dyed in Christ's blood as well as his work, yet we cannot say that his own person therefore justifies him.

As I have now proved that this doctrine of the Papists is very erroneous, so I also assert that it is most ridiculous. For a man to say that inherent righteousness is by good works (namely the fruits of righteousness) is as if a man should say that the vine is made more fruitful by bearing grapes, or that the internal light of the sun is augmented by the external emission of the beams. Luther's saying is far more true: good works do not make a good man, but a good man does make works good.

The Fourteenth Error: *Grace is extinguished and utterly lost by any mortal sin.*

Rebuttal

1. The word of God plainly declares otherwise: *"All that the Father gives me will come to me, and whoever comes to me I will never cast out"* (John 6:37). *"And I tell you, you are Peter, and on this rock I will build my church, and the gates of hell shall not prevail against it"* (Matt. 16:18). *"They went out from us, but they were not of us; for if they had been of us, they would have continued with us"* (1 John 2:19). *"Therefore, since we have been justified by faith, we have peace with God"* (Rom. 5:1). Now how could this be true, if he who was before justified could in any way fall from grace and perish?
2. After grievously falling from God, the elect repent of their sins. We see this in the example of David, Peter, and so on. These show that they had not quite utterly fallen from grace and lost the Spirit of God.
3. If grace is ever utterly lost, then the grafting of that person into Christ is abolished, in which case those who repent require a second grafting into Christ. Then it would also follow that they

> require a new baptism, which is absurd to think.

But for all this, we do not deny that grace may be lost in part and for a time, to the end that the faithful may acknowledge and know their weakness and be humbled for it. But we utterly deny that there is any total or final falling from grace.

The Fifteenth Error: *It is possible to fulfil the Law in this life.*

Rebuttal

The Law is fulfilled evangelically by believing in Christ, but not legally by doing the works it commands. Reason: Those who are carnal cannot possibly fulfil the law of God, and even the most regenerate are partly carnal, so long as they live in this life. *"I am* (says Paul of himself) *of the flesh, sold under sin"* (Rom. 7:14). *"Who can say, 'I have made my heart pure; I am clean from my sin'?"* (Prov. 20:9). *"Surely there is not a righteous man on earth who does good and never sins"* (Eccl. 7:20). *"If you, O LORD, should mark iniquities, O Lord, who could stand?"* (Psalm 130:3). We are daily taught to pray to God, *"Forgive us our sins"* (Luke 11:4).

Counter Claim: Indeed, if the justice of the faithful is considered absolutely it is imperfect, but since God requires it out of our frailty, it is perfect.

> *Answer*: This is but the fancy of some doting Jesuit. For this sentence of the Law is simple, eternal, and immovable, *"Cursed be everyone who does not abide by all things written in the Book of the Law, and do them"* (Gal. 3:10). Neither may we imagine that God will not therefore exact the full accomplishing of the law, because we are frail. For we are creatures and debtors, and we know that the debt does not decrease because of a debtor's poverty.

Objection: The faithful are said to be perfect in this life.

> *Answer*: There is a twofold perfection. One is incomplete, namely an endeavour or care to obey God in the observation of all his precepts. The other is termed complete, and this is that justice which the law requires, a perfect and absolute justice like that which man performed to God in his innocence. In the first sense

the faithful are said to be perfect, not in this latter.

The Sixteenth Error: *Works done in grace merit eternal life (by condign merit).*[17]

Rebuttal

1. Eternal life is the free gift of God. *"For the wages of sin is death, but the free gift of God is eternal life in Christ Jesus our Lord"* (Rom. 6:23). Therefore, it is not obtained by the merit of works.
2. Condign Merit is an action belonging to such a nature as is both God and man, not to a bare creature. The angels themselves cannot merit anything at God's hands. Likewise, if he had stood in his first innocence, Adam could have deserved nothing from God since it is the bounden duty of the creature to obey his Creator. Condign Merit therefore only relates to Christ, God and man, in whom each nature performs that which belongs to it to the effecting of this merit. For the humanity contributes matter to the meritorious work by suffering and performing obedience, but the deity of Christ (to which the humanity is hypostatically united) confers full and sufficient worthiness to the work.[18] Hence the Father says of his Son, *"This is my beloved Son, with whom I am well pleased* (εὐδόκησα)*"* (Matt. 3:17).
3. In the second commandment God promises eternal life to the keepers of his commandments, yet he does not say that they shall obtain it by deserving it: *"but showing steadfast love to thousands of those who love me and keep my commandments"* (Deut. 5:10).
4. For a work to be meritorious, first there must be an equal proportion between it and legal justice. Second, merit also presupposes that God owes a debt towards man; that God ought to accept the person of man on the basis of duty, rather than by favour. But all our works, indeed our most holy work, cannot come near to legal righteousness. Since all the regenerate are partly carnal and partly spiritual, all their works are likewise imperfectly good. For look at what the causes are, and such must

17. On *Condign Merit* see footnote 6 on page 334, above.
18. On the hypostatic union, see ***chapters 16–17***.

the effects be. So then, good works presuppose a due debt in man, none in God.

5. The ancient fathers do not acknowledge this Condign Merit. Augustine: *"My merit is God's mercy"*[19] Bernard of Clairvaux: *"It is sufficient to know this, that merits are not sufficient"*, and *"Man's justice is God's goodness"*,[20] and *"That the satisfaction of one may be imputed to all, as the sins of all were born by one"*.[21] For the early theologians, merit was merely a good work acceptable to God: *"If it be grace, then is it not bestowed by reason of any merit, but upon free mercy. What merits of his own can be that is set at liberty brag of, who if he had his merits should have been condemned?"*[22] So the word "merit" signifies "to do well, to be acceptable, to please", as the old interpreter has for ευαρεσθαι signifying to please God, used this Latin word *promereri* ('to merit').

Objection 1: Works have reward attributed to them.

Answer: Reward is not so much attributed to the work as to the worker, and to him not for himself, but for Christ's merits apprehended by faith. Therefore our merit does not earn our reward, rather Christ's merit earns our reward.

Objection 2: *"God considers it just to repay with affliction those who afflict you"* (2 Thess. 1:6).

Answer: This is righteous, not because God ought to do so out of duty, but because he promised, and God keeping his word is a part of justice.

Objection 3: Christ has merited that works might merit.

Answer:

a. This ignores the intercession of Christ.

b. It is against the nature of a legal work, to merit (*ex condigno*) condignly, since both the law of nature and of creation bind man to perform legal works to God. Moreover, all our

19. Augustine, *Enchiridion*, ch. 22.
20. Bernard of Clairvaux, *Sermons on the Canticles*, 68, 61.
21. Bernard of Clairvaux, *Letters*, 190.
22. Augustine, *Letters*, 105 to Sixtus.

works are imperfect and mixed with sin.

c. This doctrine obscures and darkens the merit of Christ by withdrawing the obtaining of eternal life from his death and obedience, and attributing it to our works. For they say that Christ by his passion indeed merited justification for the sinner, but that once justified a sinner condignly merits eternal life for himself by his own merits.

Objection 4: The works of the regenerate are the works of the Holy Spirit, and therefore perfect and pure.

Answer:

a. The works of God are all perfect but come to perfection in their time and by degrees. Sanctification, which is a work of God, must remain incomplete in this life and is made perfect in the world to come.

b. The works of God are pure since they are of God alone, not of God and impure man together. But good works come immediately from the natural faculties of the soul, namely from the understanding and the will, where they are partly regenerated and some corrupt qualities of sin yet remain. Such works are not wholly derived from God's Spirit and hence it is that they are all stained with sin.

The Seventeenth Error: *Man does not know whether he is predestined or not, except by special revelation.*[23]

Rebuttal

The contrary to this is a plain truth. Reasons:

1. That which a man must certainly believe, that may he also certainly know without a special revelation: but every faithful man must believe that he is elected. It is God's commandment, that we should believe in Christ (1 John 3:23). Now to believe in Christ, is not only to believe that we are adopted, justified, and redeemed by him; but also that in him we were elected from

23. That is, somebody can only know that they are predestined if God directly and specifically reveals that to them.

eternity.

2. That which is sealed to us by the Spirit of God, of that we are very sure without special revelation: but our adoption (and so consequently our election) is sealed to us by the spirit of God. *"Now we have received not the spirit of the world, but the Spirit who is from God, that we might understand the things freely given us by God"* (1 Cor. 2:12). Therefore our election is certainly known to us, *"In him you also, when you heard the word of truth, the gospel of your salvation, and believed in him, were sealed with the promised Holy Spirit"* (Eph. 1:13).

Counter Claim: The Holy Spirit seals our adoption to us morally by works, and therefore the knowledge of our adoption is merely probable.

Answer:

a. It seals to us our adoption, by creating within us a special trust and confidence. For when as we hear God's promises and think upon them, then by the same promises the Holy Spirit moves our understandings and wills to embrace them, and in moving them, makes us both give our agreement to them and in them to rest ourselves. From this arises a special assurance that we are adopted, and in the favour of God.

b. *"But rejoice that your names are written in heaven"* (Luke 10:20). But no man can be glad for any good which he is in doubt of having received.

c. *"Be all the more diligent to make your calling and election sure (βεβαίαν ποιεῖσθαι)"* (2 Pet. 1:10): but this is not in respect of God, but ourselves.

Objection: No man of the Catholic faith must believe anything which God has not revealed either in the written or unwritten word (namely tradition). But there is no such either writing or tradition that a particular man, suppose Peter or Henry, is predestined of God. Therefore, no man must particularly believe that he is saved.

Answer: Whilst the proposition "I am elected" is not expressly set down in the Scriptures, yet is it comprehended in them as the species is in its genus (as the logicians speak), so that it may be gathered out of God's word by just consequence, if we reason thus:

> Those who truly believe are elected (John 6:35).
> I truly believe.
> Therefore, I am elected.

The first proposition is taken from the Scriptures, the second from the believer's conscience, and from them the conclusion is easily derived.

CHAPTER 52–53:

Reprobation

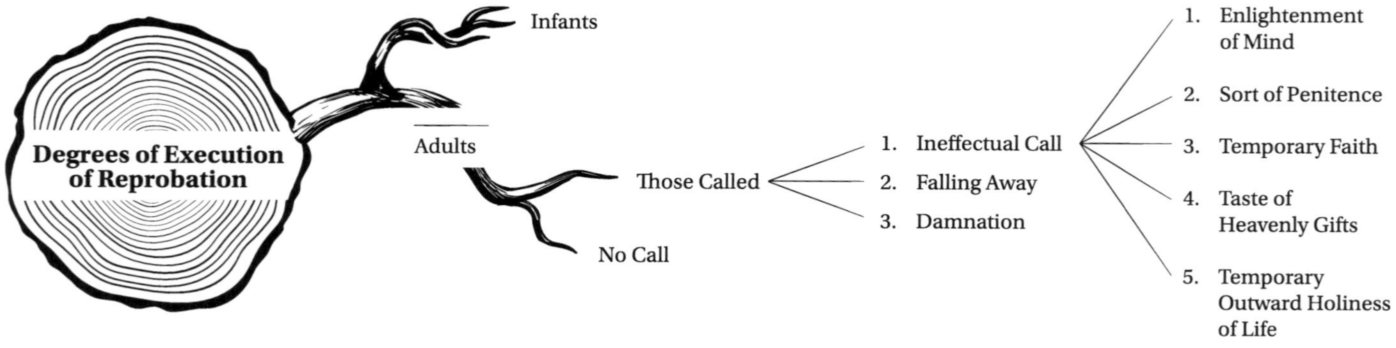

Chapter Fifty Two

THE DECREE OF REPROBATION

Thus much shall suffice for the Decree of Election. Now follows the Decree of Reprobation.

The **Decree of Reprobation** is that part of predestination, whereby God, (according to the most free and just purpose of his will) has determined to reject certain men to their eternal destruction and misery, to the praise of his justice. *"Has the potter no right over the clay, to make out of the same lump one vessel for honourable use and another for dishonourable use?"* (Rom. 9:21). *"They stumble because they disobey the word, as they were destined* (ἐτέθησαν) *to do"* (1 Pet. 2:8). *"For certain people have crept in unnoticed who long ago were designated* (προγεγραμμένοι) *for this condemnation"* (Jude 4). *"For God has not destined us for wrath, but to obtain salvation through our Lord Jesus Christ"* (1 Thess. 5:9). In the Scriptures Cain and Abel, Ishmael and Isaac, Esau and Jacob, are each presented to us as foreshadowing mankind partly elected and partly rejected.

We do not set down here any absolute decree of damnation, as though we should think that any were condemned by the mere will of God alone, without any inherent causes in those to be condemned. For there are certain subordinate means of execution joined to the decree of God itself. Therefore, though we can never separate God's decree from the means of its execution, yet we distinguish them. Thus, we may consider the purpose of God in two ways: by itself alone or not by itself but along with its subordinate middle causes. In this second respect Christ is said to be predestined, but in the former (namely, as the decree is considered by itself) he is not predestined, a predestinator together with God the Father.

Again, the decree of God is secret, since:

1. It only arises from the unsearchable good pleasure of God, adored by the angels themselves.
2. It is known only by its effects.

Chapter Fifty Three

THE EXECUTION OF THE DECREE OF REPROBATION

In the executing of this decree there is to be considered, the Foundation or beginning, and its Degrees or proceeding.

The Foundation of the Execution of the Decree of Reprobation is the fall of Adam, by which fall he was subject both to sin and damnation. *"For God has consigned all to disobedience, that he may have mercy on all"* (Rom. 11:32). In 1 Peter 2:8 we must note, that God has so decreed to condemn some, as that notwithstanding, all the fault and guilt of condemnation remains in the men only.

Further, God hates those whom he rejects unto condemnation. This hatred of God is that whereby he detests and abhors the reprobate for their sin when they are fallen into it. This hatred which God has to man comes by the fall of Adam, but is neither prior to God's decree, nor a cause of it. Rather it is only a consequence of, and follows from, God's decree.

Reprobates are either Infants or men of riper age.

In **Reprobate Infants** the execution of God's decree is this: as soon as they are born, for the guilt of original and natural sin, being left in God's secret judgement to themselves, they dying are rejected of God for ever. *"Yet death reigned from Adam to Moses, even over those whose sinning was not like the transgression of Adam, who was a type* (or, foreshadowing) *of the one who was to come"* (Rom. 5:14). *"Though they were not yet born and had done nothing either good or bad—in order that God's purpose of election might continue, not because of works but because of him who calls"* (Rom. 9:11).

Reprobates of Riper Age are of two sorts: those who are called (by an ineffectual calling), and those who are not called.

In the Reprobates who are called, the execution of the decree of Reprobation has three degrees: an acknowledgement of God's calling, a falling away again, and condemnation.

The acknowledgement of God's calling is that whereby Reprobates for a time, subject themselves to the calling of God produced by the preaching of the word. *"For many are called, but few are chosen"* (Matt. 22:14). And of this calling, there are five other degrees.

The first is an **Enlightening of their Minds**, whereby they are instructed by the Holy Spirit unto an understanding and knowledge of the word. *"For it is impossible, in the case of those who have once been enlightened, etc"* (Heb. 6:4). *"For if, after they have escaped the defilement of the world through the knowledge of our Lord and Saviour Jesus Christ, they are again entangled in them and overcome, the last state has become worse for them than the first"* (2 Pet. 2:20).

The second is **a Sort of Penitence** whereby the Reprobate:

1. Acknowledges his sin.
2. Is pricked with the feeling of God's wrath for sin.
3. Is grieved for the punishment of sin.
4. Confesses his sin.
5. Acknowledges God to be just in punishing sin.
6. Desires to be saved.
7. Promises repentance in his misery or affliction, in these words, *"I will sin no more". "Then when Judas, his betrayer, saw that Jesus was condemned, he changed his mind and brought back the thirty pieces of silver to the chief priests and the elders"* (Matt. 27:3). *"For you know that afterward, when he desired to inherit the blessing, he was rejected, for he found no chance to repent, though he sought it with tears"* (Heb. 12:17). *"And when Ahab heard those words, he tore his clothes and put sackcloth on his flesh and fasted and lay in sackcloth and went about dejectedly"* (1 Kings 21:27). *"Let me die the death of the upright, and let my end be like his!"* (Num. 23:10). *"In spite of all this, they still sinned; despite his wonders, they did not believe. So he made their days vanish like a breath, and their years in terror. When he killed*

them, they sought him; they repented and sought God earnestly. They remembered that God was their rock, the Most High God their redeemer" (Psalm 78:32-35).

The third degree is a **Temporary Faith** whereby the reprobate does confusedly believe the promises of God, made in Christ. I say confusedly because he believes that some shall be saved, but he does not believe that he himself particularly shall be saved, because he being content with a general faith, does never apply the promises of God to himself, neither does he so much as conceive any purpose, desire, or endeavour to apply the same, or any wrestling or striving against security or carelessness and distrust. *"You believe that God is one; you do well. Even the demons believe—and shudder!"* (James 2:19). *"As for what was sown on rocky ground, this is the one who hears the word and immediately receives it with joy, yet he has no root in himself, but endures for a while, and when tribulation or persecution arises on account of the word, immediately he falls away"* (Matt. 13:20-21). *"Now when he was in Jerusalem at the Passover Feast, many believed in his name when they saw the signs that he was doing. But Jesus on his part did not entrust himself to them, because he knew all people"* (John 2:23-24).

The fourth degree is a **Tasting of Heavenly Gifts**, such as of justification, of sanctification, and of the virtues of the world to come. This tasting is truly a sense in the hearts of reprobates whereby they perceive and feel the excellence of God's benefits, though they do not enjoy them. For it is one thing to taste the food at a banquet, and another thing to feed and to be nourished thereby. *"For it is impossible, in the case of those who have once been enlightened, who have tasted the heavenly gift, and have shared in the Holy Spirit"* (Heb. 6:4).

The fifth degree is, the **Outward Holiness of Life** for a time, under which, is comprehended a zeal in the profession of religion, a reverence and fear towards God's ministers, and amendment of life in many things. *"For Herod feared John, knowing that he was a righteous and holy man, and he kept him safe. When he heard him, he was greatly perplexed, and yet he heard him gladly"* (Mark 6:20). *"Even Simon himself believed, and after being baptized he continued with Philip. And seeing signs and great miracles performed, he was amazed"* (Acts 8:13). *"What shall I do with you, O Ephraim? What shall I do with you, O Judah? Your love is like a* *morning cloud, like the dew that goes early away"* (Hos. 6:4).

Thus much the five degrees of Ineffectual Calling.

The second degree of the Execution of God's decree of reprobation in men of ripe age who are called is a **Falling Away** again, which for the most part is effected in this way:

1. The reprobate is deceived by some sin.
2. His heart is hardened by the same sin.
3. His heart (being hardened) becomes wicked and perverse.
4. Then follows his incredulity and unbelief, whereby he refuses consent to God's word, when he has heard and known it.
5. An apostasy, or falling away from faith in Christ, immediately follows this unbelief. *"Take care, brothers, lest there be in any of you an evil, unbelieving heart, leading you to fall away from the living God. But exhort one another every day, as long as it is called 'today,' that none of you may be hardened by the deceitfulness of sin"* (Heb. 3:12–13). See also 1 Timothy 1:19.

This **Apostasy** is sometimes sin against the Holy Spirit. In the sin against the Holy Spirit, we have these several points to be considered:

1. The Name; it is called a sin against the Holy Spirit, not because it is done against the person, or Deity of the Holy Spirit (for in this respect he that sins against the Holy Spirit, sins in like sort against both the Father, and the Son) but it is so called because it is done contrary to the immediate action, namely, the illumination of the Holy Spirit. For albeit this be an action common to the whole Trinity, yet the Father and the Son do effect the same by the Holy Spirit.
2. The Efficient cause of it, which is a set and obstinate malice against God, and against his Christ. Therefore when a man does in the time of persecution, either for fear, or rashly deny Christ, he does not commit this sin against the Holy Spirit, as may appear by the example of Peter, who denied Christ (Matt. 26:73–75). Neither does he who persecutes Christ and his Church in ignorance fall into this sin. Paul persecuted the Church of Christ, and yet God had mercy on him, because he did it ignorantly

(1 Tim. 1:13). Many of the Jews crucified our Saviour Christ, who, afterwards, because they committed that grievous fact in ignorance, repenting at Peters sermon, they obtained remission of their sin (Acts 3:17, 37).

3. The Object, namely God himself, and the Mediator Christ Jesus. For the malice of this sin is directed against the very majesty of God himself, and against Christ. *"How much worse punishment, do you think, will be deserved by the one who has spurned the Son of God, and has profaned the blood of the covenant by which he was sanctified, and has outraged the Spirit of grace?"* (Heb. 10:29). Therefore this sin does directly relate to the first table of the moral law, and is not some particular slipping aside from the observation of those commandments which are contained in this first table, such as are some doubting concerning God, or of the truth of the Scriptures, or of Christ, etc. but it is a general defection and apostasy from God, and that totally.

4. The subject in which it is. This sin is found in none but those who have been enlightened by the Holy Spirit and have tasted of the good gift of God (Heb. 6:5–6). Neither is it in him a bare thought alone, but an external action, or rather such a blasphemy against God as proceeds from a malicious, and obstinate heart (Matt. 12:31).

5. The Elect cannot commit this sin. Therefore, they who feel in themselves a sure testimony of their election, need never to despair. Indeed, this sin is not in every reprobate, for many of them die before they have this illumination by God's Spirit.

6. This sin cannot be forgiven, not because it is greater than that Christ's merit can satisfy for it, but because after a man has once committed this sin, it is impossible for him to repent. For the gift of repentance proceeds from the Holy Spirit, and the Holy Spirit remains in us through Christ apprehended by faith: now no man does apprehend Christ, that does maliciously despise and contemn him.

7. It is very hard to know when a man commits this sin, because the root thereof, namely, set malice, lurks inwardly in the heart, and is not so easily discerned.

Out of all this which has been spoken, we may thus define this sin. The sin against the Holy Spirit is a voluntary, and obstinate denial of, and blasphemy against the Son of God, or that truth which was before acknowledged concerning him, and so consequently a universal defection from God and his true Church. We have an example of this sin partly in the Devil, who, though he knew that Jesus was that Christ, yet he never ceased both wittingly and willingly with all his power to oppugn the sacred majesty of God, together with the kingdom of Jesus Christ, and, as far forth as he could, utterly to supplant the same, partly in the Pharisees (Matt. 12:32; John 3:2).

After Apostasy follows **Pollution**, which is the very fullness of all iniquity, altogether contrary to sanctification. *"And they shall come back here in the fourth generation, for the iniquity of the Amorites is not yet complete"* (Gen. 15:16).

The third degree is **Damnation**, whereby the reprobates are delivered up to eternal punishment. The execution of damnation begins in death and is finished in the last judgement. *"The poor man died and was carried by the angels to Abraham's side. The rich man also died and was buried, and in Hades, being in torment, he lifted up his eyes and saw Abraham far off and Lazarus at his side"* (Luke 16:22).

The execution of the decree of reprobation in unbelievers who are not called, is this. First, they have by nature ignorance and vanity of mind. After that follows hardness of heart, whereby they become void of all sorrow for their sins. Then comes a reprobate sense, which is, when the natural light of reason and of the judgement of good and evil, is extinguished. Afterward, when the heart ceases to sorrow, then arises a committing of sin with greediness. Then comes pollution, which is the fullness of sin. Lastly, a just reward is given to all these, to wit, fearful condemnation. *"They are darkened in their understanding, alienated from the life of God because of the ignorance that is in them, due to their hardness of heart"* (Eph. 4:18). *"And since they did not see fit to acknowledge God, God gave them up to a debased mind to do what ought not to be done"* (Rom. 1:28).

CHAPTER 54:

Lutheran Predestination

A Framework of the Doctrine of Predestination
out of the writings of some recent Lutheran Theologians in Germany.

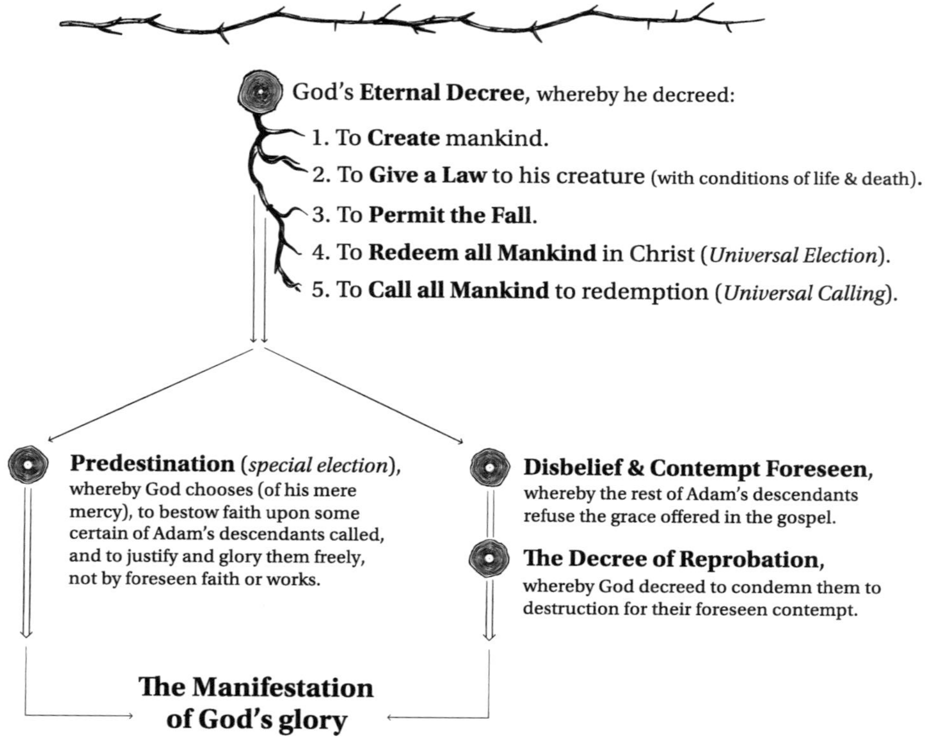

Chapter Fifty Four

THE NEWLY INVENTED LUTHERAN DOCTRINE OF PREDESTINATION

Certain new theologians of our age have constructed a new doctrine of predestination in which they turn the distribution of the causes of salvation and damnation upside down, fearing that they might otherwise make God both unjust and unmerciful. This appears by their description in this table.

Their doctrine has some foul errors and defects, which I will briefly highlight as follows.

The First Error: *Universal Election*

There is a certain universal or general election whereby God has decreed to redeem (by Christ) and to reconcile to himself all of fallen mankind in its entirety: every single person, both the Reprobate and the Elect.

Rebuttal

The very name 'election' fully disproves this. None can be said to be elected if God would have all men elected in Christ. For he who makes a choice cannot be said to choose all. Neither can he that accepts all be said to make choice only of some.

Objection. Election is nothing else but love. We know that God loves all his creatures, therefore he elects all his creatures.

Answer.

a. I deny that to elect is to love; rather it is to ordain and appoint to love (Rom. 9:13).

b. God does love all his creatures, yet not all equally, but each in their place.

Furthermore, this position flatly contradicts the clearest passages of holy Scripture. *"Who gave himself for us to redeem us from all lawlessness and to purify for himself a people for his own possession who are zealous for good works"* (Titus 2:14). *"I lay down my life for the sheep"* (John 10:15).

***Counter Claim*: "All men are the sheep of Christ".**

Answer: John adds, *"My sheep hear my voice, and I know them, and they follow me. I give them eternal life, and they will never perish"* (John 10:27-28). Christ is *"the head of the Church"* and the Saviour of his body (Eph. 5:23). *"Christ loved the church and gave himself up for her"* (Eph. 5:25). Redemption and remission of sins, is the inheritance of the Saints, and of those who are made heirs of the kingdom of Christ (Col. 1:13).

Again, look for whom Christ is an Advocate, and to them only is he a Redeemer: for redemption and intercession, which are parts of Christ's priesthood, the one is as general and large as the other, and are so surely united and fastened together, as that one cannot be without the other. But Christ is only an Advocate of the faithful. In that his solemn prayer in John 17, he first prays for his own, namely, his Disciples, elected not only to the Apostleship, but also to eternal life: and then (verse 20), he prays likewise for them that should believe in him by their word. Now against these, he opposes *the world*, for which he does not pray that it may attain eternal life. And, *"Who shall bring any charge against God's elect? .... who is at the right hand of God, who indeed is interceding for us"* (Rom. 8:33-34). Furthermore, the members of Christ's Church, are called the *"Redeemed of the Lord"* (Psalm 107:2). Therefore, this privilege is not given to all alike.

***Counter Claim*: "This universal reconciliation is not made with regard to man, but God himself, who both made it for all and offers it to all".**

Answer: If Christ became a reconciliation for all men's sins before God, and indeed satisfied for them all, it necessarily follows that all sins must be blotted out before God. For the actual blotting out of sins inseparably depends upon reconciliation for sins, and satisfaction necessarily infers the very real universal abolishing of the guilt and punishment of sin by God.

Objection 1: Christ took upon him man's nature, therefore he redeemed man's nature generally.

Answer:

a. This does not follow, unless we would say that Christ redeemed his own humanity, which cannot be possible.

b. Every woman partakes of the human nature of every man, yet every man isn't each woman's husband but hers alone with whom (by the covenant of matrimony) he is made one flesh. Likewise, by his incarnation (ἐν σαρκὼσει) Christ took man's nature upon himself. This nature is common to all Adams descendants, yet is he the husband of his Church alone, by the bond of the Spirit and of faith. And by this the Church has become flesh of his flesh and bone of his bone (Eph. 5:20), and therefore she alone may justly claim title to the death of Christ and all his merits.

Objection 2: Christ's redemption is as general as Adams fall was, thus it relates to all of Adams descendants.

Answer: Adam was a foreshadowing of Christ, and Christ the fulfilment corresponding to Adam. Adam was the root of all his successors, such that sin and death came from him. Again, Christ is also a root, but of the elect only. He cannot be said to be the root of every man since not all receive his righteousness and life (Rom. 12:17, 19).

Objection 2a: The benefit of Christ's death extended to all.

Answer: It extended to all that believe. For as Adam destroyed all those that were born of him, so Christ justifies and saves all who are born anew by him, and none other.

Objection 2b: If Adam's sin destroyed all and Christ's merit does not save all, then Adam's sin had more power to condemn than Christ's mercy has to save.

Answer: I grant that as Adams fall made all unjust, so the mercy of Christ and his redemption should actually justify all. However, we must not esteem the mercy of Christ by the number of men on whom it is bestowed, but rather measure it by its efficacy and dignity. For it was a far easier thing to destroy all by sin than to save but one by grace. Mere man could destroy all but could not save even one. None could do it, except such a one as was both God and man.

Objection 3: Many passages of Scripture there are which affirm this, that the benefit of Christ's death does appertain to all. *"For God has consigned all to disobedience, that he may have mercy on all"* (Rom. 11:32). *"(God) desires all people to be saved"* (1 Tim. 2:4). *"The Lord .... not wishing that any should perish"* (2 Pet. 3:9).

Answer:

a. You must understand "all that believe" in the same way as: *"all who labour and are heavy laden"* (Matt. 11:28), *"whoever believes"* (John 3:16), *"the Scripture imprisoned everything under sin, so that the promise by faith in Jesus Christ might be given to those who believe"* (Gal. 3:22), *"everyone who believes"* (Acts 10:43). And surely there are a multitude who believe out of the whole world.

b. We should understand "all" as meaning *of all sorts*, not every particular person. So, in Revelation 5:9, Christ is said to have redeemed some *"from every tribe and language and people and nation"*. And in Galatians 3:28, *"There is neither Jew nor Greek, there is neither slave nor free, there is no male and female, for you are all one in Christ Jesus"*. In Matthew 4:23 Christ is said to have healed *"every disease and every affliction"*, meaning every kind of disease and affliction. Augustine has a fitting rule for this purpose. "All" is often used for "many", as in Romans 5:18–19. *"It is thus said* (says Augustine) *God would have all to be saved. This does not mean that all men would have repented if only he had done miracles among them* (cf. Matthew 11:21), *but that by 'all men' we should understand all sorts of men howsoever distinguished, whether kings, private persons, and so on"*.[1] He states elsewhere: *"It is said he would have all to be saved, by which we must understand all those who are predestined to be saved, because amongst them there are*

1. Augustine, *Enchiridion*, ch. 103.

all sorts of men. As he said to the Pharisees: 'You tithe every herb'".[2]

c. These two truths—to be willing to save man and that man should come to the saving knowledge of the truth—are inseparably united together (1 Tim. 2:4). But we can see that the second does not apply to each and every individual person, therefore the first cannot either.

Objection 4: In many passages of Scripture Christ is said to redeem the world, as in 1 John 2:2, *"He is the propitiation for our sins, and not for ours only but also for the sins of the whole world"*.

Answer: This word 'world' signifies:

a. the frame of heaven and earth.

b. All men, both good and bad together.

c. The company of unbelievers, malignant haters of Christ.

d. The congregation of the elect dispersed over the face of the whole earth, who are to be gathered out of the same. We must understand such passages as are mentioned in this fourth sense. Abraham is called the *"heir of the world"* (Rom. 4:13), that is, of many nations (see also Gen. 17:4–5).

Objection 5: *"Have I any pleasure in the death of the wicked, declares the Lord God, and not rather that he should turn from his way and live?"* (Ezek. 18:23).

Answer: Augustine answers this question: *"You must distinguish between man as he is born man, and man as he is a sinner. For God is not delighted with the destruction of man as he is man, but as he of the sinner. Neither does he simply will the death of any as he is a sinner (or as it is the ruin and destruction of his creature) except that, by his detestation of sin and taking revenge upon it with eternal death, his glory is exceedingly advanced."*[3] God therefore wills the death of a sinner as it is a punishment; that is, as a means to declare and set forth his divine justice. Therefore, it is untrue to say that God would have none condemned. For where men are condemned it is either

2. Augustine, *On Rebuke and Grace*, ch. 14.
3. Augustine, *De Diversis Quaestionibus ad Simplicianum*, 1.2.

with God's will or without it. If without it, then the will of God suffers violence, and to affirm this is a great impiety. If with it, then God would appear to need to change his sentence already set down, but we must not presume to say this.

Objection 6: God is the Father of all (Mal. 2:10).

Answer: This passage refers to God's Church, outside of which all men stand in the corrupt estate of Adam, and are the children of wrath and of the Devil (Eph. 2:2; John 8:44).

Objection 7: If God elected some and rejected others, then he must be 'a respecter of persons' (προσωπολήπτης) and not impartial (cf. Acts 10:34).

Answer:

a. One is said to have 'respect of persons' when he is moved to do this or that by something inherent in the person. As for God, he elected some and rejected others out of his mere pleasure, and was not moved or urged by anything whatsoever outside of himself.

b. God is debtor to none. He may do with his creatures what seems good to him in his own eyes.

c. It is one thing for God to be a respecter of persons, and another to make choice of men. If we will not grant this, it follows that God must be deemed blameworthy for not making all his creatures to be most glorious angels.

Objection 8: If God decreed to reject certain men, then he hated his creature.

Answer: God decreed to reject his creature and workmanship not because he hated it, but because he appointed it to hatred. And it is one thing to hate, and another to appoint to hatred. Indeed, God does not actually hate anything, except due to sin. That saying of Augustine is fit for this purpose: *"When God makes the wicked, whom be does not justify, to be vessels of wrath, he doesn't do it to hate that which he made. For, in that he made them vessels, they have their use, namely that by the pains to which they were ordained, the vessels of honour might reap profit. Therefore, God does not hate them in that they are men or vessels; neither does he hate anything that he made in them by creation or ordination. For God hates nothing which he has made. But inasmuch as he made them vessels of destruction, he did it to instruct others. He utterly hates their impiety, which he never made. A judge hates theft in a man, but he does not hate his punishment to be sent to work in the mines. For the thief does the first, the judge the latter. So God, whereas he makes vessels of perdition of the company of them which perish, he does not therefore hate that which he does, that is the condemnation of those which perish in their due punishment for sin."*[4]

Objection 9: The reprobates are said in many passages of Scripture to be redeemed by Christ, as in 2 Peter 2:1.

Answer: First, we must not understand such passages to refer to all reprobates, but only those who are (for a time) in the Church. Second, they are said to be redeemed, justified, and sanctified, both in their own judgement and the Church's, inasmuch as they make an external profession of the faith. But this is a judgement of charity, not of certainty.

Objection 10: God might be thought cruel if he has ordained the greatest part of the world to destruction.

Answer: God could have decreed that all men should utterly have been rejected, and this would not have been even slightly cruel or unjust. Some reasons for this are:

a. He judged each and every one of those foul and wicked spirits which fell from him to eternal torments.

b. He decreed also (as is apparent by nature) that men should live by the slaughter of beasts, and yet God is not therefore cruel against them. Surely God is no more obligated to man than he is to the beasts.

Counter Claim: God appointed all to be saved with this condition: "if they believe".

Answer: This is absurd to affirm, for:

4. Augustine, *De Diversis Quaestionibus ad Simplicianum*.

a. By this means the decree of God would depend upon the will of man, whereas in reality God's decree limits and orders all inferior causes.
b. It takes away the certainty of God's decree since a conditional proposition doesn't assert anything.

Objection: If the merit of Christ does not extend as far as the fall of Adam, then the head of the serpent is not broken, nor Satan's kingdom abolished by Christ.

Answer: This bruising of the Serpents head is seen only in those who are at enmity with the serpent, namely in those who truly believe (Gen. 3:15; Rom. 16:20).

To conclude, it is not true that a universal and effectual redemption of every individual man is an effective remedy to comfort afflicted consciences. I appeal to the judgement of all men, whether there is any great comfort to an afflicted conscience in this manner of consolation:

> Christ died for all men:
> You are a man,
> Therefore Christ died for you.

The Second Error: *Passive Permission of the Fall*

God foreknew the fall of Adam but he did not foreordain it. And therefore, man's fall was without the active permission of God.

Rebuttal.

It is false. For the following reasons:

1. Absolutely nothing in nature comes to pass apart from the decree and will of God (Matt. 10:30). Therefore, those who affirm that God only foreknew this or that, either overturn the providence of God, or at least imagine that it is a very idle providence.
2. The fact that Herod and Pilate delivered over Christ against their own consciences to be crucified, may seem to be as heinous as was Adams fall, and yet they are said to have done *"whatever your hand and your plan had predestined to take place"* (Acts 4:28). Again, the

fall of Adam came by God's active permission in two ways:

a. Inasmuch as the fall was an action, for in God alone we live, move, and have our being.

b. Inasmuch as that his fall was a trial of his loyalty to God, whereby God would put both the power and will of his creature to the test.

The Third Error: *Foresight of Who would Reject the Gospel*

God only decreed the destruction and condemnation of those whom he foresaw would reject the gospel.

Rebuttal

We utterly deny that the foreseeing of the rejection of grace was the first and principle cause of the decree of reprobation. Our reasons are:

1. Paul derives the common condemnation of the Gentiles from the fact that they *"by their unrighteousness suppress the truth"* (Rom. 1:18). That is, they are condemned because they consciously extinguished the knowledge of God (which they had by the light of nature) by their wicked deeds and would not obey their consciences' condemnation of such acts.

2. If foreseen faith is not the cause of the decree of election, then neither can the lack of foreseen faith be the cause of the decree of reprobation. Rather, as faith follows election in order of causes, so must disbelief follow after reprobation. For these are of like reason or proportion of contrary.

3. Many infants depart this life, being both out of the true Church and before they have any use of reason. And again, there are many who live long yet are idiots and fools, or are born deaf, and cannot come to the true use of reason. In all these, it is not credible to suspect a contempt of the gospel which they could not learn.

4. Esau was hated by God for no other cause except that it pleased him (Rom. 9:13).

5. If this opinion were true, then would it follow that men should be condemned for nothing else but unbelief. Yet Christ does not say that the wrath of God came upon man for his unbelief, but that in

unbelief it "remains on him" (John 3:36). And why should we daily ask pardon for our sins if nothing but unbelief condemns us? Even if there were never any contempt of the gospel, the corruption of original sin would be sufficient to condemn men.

6. Also that admiration which Paul has—*"but who are you, O man, to answer back to God?"* (Rom. 9:20)—plainly shows that the cause of the decree of God in rejecting some is unsearchable. It does not at all depend upon foreseen defiance towards the grace of God offered in the gospel. For if it was otherwise, we might easily give a reason of God's decree. Augustine says it very well: *"Who created the reprobates but God? And why, but because it pleased him? But why did it please him? O man, who are you that disputes with God?"*.[5]

Some divines, perceiving that this is a hard sentence, set out to reduce its severity in this manner: *"The object of predestination is a reasonable creature, considered not simply or absolutely, but partly as it fell, partly as of itself it was subject to fall. And thereupon God preordaining men from everlasting, considered them not simply as he was to make them men, but as they were such men as might fall into sin, be redeemed by Christ, and after called to the light of the gospel. The efficient cause (or first motive) was not any foreknown cause of either this or that, but the mere will of God. For he disposes all things not of and by his foreknowledge, but rather according the same."* But these things are not altogether true, though they may seem to be subtle devices. Reasons:

1. When the potter chooses to make some vessel, he does not consider the clay and regard some inherent quality in it to make such vessel, but he makes it such and such a form, to this or that use, according to his free-will and pleasure alone.

2. *"Has the potter no right over the clay, to make out of the same lump one vessel for honourable use and another for dishonourable use?"* (Rom. 9:21). In this passage we may not understand the name 'lump' as referring to all mankind corrupted and fallen, and so to be redeemed in Christ, for then Paul would not have said that God made vessels of wrath, but rather that he forsook them after they were made.

3. It seems preposterous that God first foreknew mankind as created, fallen, and redeemed in Christ, and that afterwards he ordained

5. Augustine, *Letters*, 105.

them so foreknown to life or to death. For the end goal is the first thing in the intention of an agent. A skilful workman does not prepare means by which he may be helped to do a thing before he has the goal of his labour set down in his mind. We know that man's creation and his fall in Adam are but means to execute God's predestination, and therefore they are subordinate to it. The end of God's decree is the manifestation of his glory in saving some and condemning others. Therefore, we may not imagine that God first consulted the means by which he had determined to execute his decree, before he deliberated on the election and reprobation of man.

The Fourth Error: *Universal Calling*

God's calling to the knowledge of the gospel is universal: of all and every particular person without exception.

Rebuttal

This is a very unreasonable position. For the following reasons:

1. God does not call all: *"For many are called, but few are chosen"* (Matt. 22:14). He does not say that all are called, but *many*. When Christ first commissioned his disciples, he charged them not to proclaim his coming to the Gentiles (Matt. 10:5). To the Canaanite woman he says: *"It is not right to take the children's bread and throw it to the dogs"* (Matt. 15:26). *"To you it has been given to know the secrets of the kingdom of heaven, but to them it has not been given"* (Matt. 13:11). *"The mystery* (whether it is meant of Christ, or the calling of the Gentiles) *that was kept secret for long ages"* (Rom. 16:25).
2. There are many millions of men who have not even heard of Christ. *"In past generations he (God) allowed all the nations to walk in their own ways"* (Acts 14:16).
3. The greater part of the world has always been outside the covenant: *"You were at that time separated from Christ, alienated from the commonwealth of Israel and strangers to the covenants of promise, having no hope and without God in the world ..... So then you are no longer strangers and aliens, but you are fellow citizens with the saints and members of the household of God"* (Eph. 2:12, 19).

    a. ***Objection***: They are not simply said to be *alienated*, but *alienated from* (ἀπηλλοτριωμένοι) God. How can they be alienated from God unless they or their ancestors had been in the covenant?

Answer: The Gentiles are not said to be alienated from the covenant, but from the commonwealth of Israel, since God had at that time utterly severed and distinguished the Jews from all other nations by certain laws, rites, and ceremonies.

b. ***Objection***: This general calling is not to be understood simply of the ministry of the word, but of the will of God, delivered immediately after the fall in his unwritten word, but afterwards in his written word. All men ought to know this, though many do not know it (by their own evasion).

Answer: The Scriptures were committed to the custody of the Church of God, and not everyone was credited with them: *"the Jews were entrusted with the oracles of God"* (Rom. 3:2). *"The church of the living God, a pillar and buttress of the truth"* (1 Tim. 3:15). *"He declares his word to Jacob, his statutes and rules to Israel. He has not dealt thus with any other nation; they do not know his rules. Praise the LORD!"* (Psalm 147:19–20). *"In Judah God is known; his name is great in Israel"* (Psalm 76:1).

c. ***Objection***: The Covenant of Grace was made with Adam and Eve, and in them all mankind was received into both the Church and covenant, and also called to the knowledge of God.

Answer:

i. This reason lacks even common reason and sense, saying that God giving his promise in the days of Adam and Noah, in them called all mankind that should come after.

ii. Before his fall Adam indeed received grace both for himself and for others also, and in the fall he lost it both for himself and for all others. But after the fall he received the promise for himself alone, and not for the whole world. Otherwise the first Adam would not only have been a living creature, but a enlivening spirit, which is only true of the second Adam (1 Cor. 15:45).

The Conclusion

If we should grant this doctrine to be true, then by implication we must allow these theological absurdities:

1. That God would have each and every individual man to be saved, and yet he would have some ordained to perdition. Or else that in regard to God all men are elected and redeemed, but in regard to actual events, many perish.
2. The guilt of Adam's sin must not be imputed to any of his descendants since God, having mercy on all generally in Christ, took all mankind into the covenant of reconciliation. But if the guilt of Adam's fall is taken away, then punishment ceases to be a punishment and corruption itself is (little by little) abolished in all men.

Chapter Fifty Five

THE STATE OF THE REPROBATES AT DEATH

The Death of the Reprobate is a separation of the body and the soul. The body, for a time lays dead in the earth; and the soul experiences the torments of hell until the time of the last judgement. At that time the whole man shall be cast into the most terrible and fearful fire of hell: *"in which he went and proclaimed to the spirits in prison"* (1 Pet. 3:19, also Luke 8). *"For if God did not spare angels when they sinned, but cast them into hell and committed them to chains of gloomy darkness to be kept until the judgement, etc."* (2 Pet. 2:4).

When they die the reprobate become astonished and without sense, like a stone. Or else they are overwhelmed with a terrible horror of conscience, and despair of their salvation, as it were, with a gulf of the sea overturning them. *"In the morning, when the wine had gone out of Nabal, his wife told him these things, and his heart died within him, and he became as a stone. And about ten days later the LORD struck Nabal, and he died"* (1 Sam. 25:37–38). *"And throwing down the pieces of silver into the temple, he departed, and he went and hanged himself"* (Matt. 27:5).

Chapter Fifty Six

THE CONDEMNATION OF THE REPROBATES AT THE LAST JUDGEMENT

In the Last Judgement, at the sound of the trumpet, the living (being stricken with horror and fear) shall be changed in a moment. The dead shall rise again to condemnation. Both the living and the dead shall then have immortal bodies, but without glory. Those standing upon the earth at the left hand of Christ the Judge shall hear the sentence of condemnation: *"Then he will say to those on his left, 'Depart from me, you cursed, into the eternal fire prepared for the Devil and his angels'"* (Matt. 25:41). *"All who are in the tombs will hear his voice and come out, those who have done good to the resurrection of life, and those who have done evil to the resurrection of judgement"* (John 5:28–29). *"For the Lord himself will descend from heaven with a cry of command, with the voice of an archangel, and with the sound of the trumpet of God. And the dead in Christ will rise first. Then we who are alive, who are left, will be caught up together with them in the clouds to meet the Lord in the air, and so we will always be with the Lord"* (1 Thess. 4:16–17).

Chapter Fifty Seven

THE STATE OF THE REPROBATES IN HELL

After the sentence of condemnation is pronounced, then follows **Everlasting Death**, whereof this is the estate.

1. The Reprobates are separated from the presence and glory of God.
2. They are punished with eternal confusion and most bitter reproaches because all their secret wickedness and sins are revealed. *"They will suffer the punishment of eternal destruction, away from the presence of the Lord and from the glory of his might"* (2 Thess. 1:9). *"Blessed are the pure in heart, for they shall see God"* (Matt. 5:8*)*. *"And now, little children, abide in him, so that when he appears we may have confidence and not shrink from him in shame at his coming"* (1 John 2:28).
3. They have fellowship with the Devil and his angels (Matt. 25:41).
4. They are wholly in body and soul tormented with an incredible horror and exceeding great anguish through the sense and feeling of God's wrath poured out upon them for ever. *"And they shall go out and look on the dead bodies of the men who have rebelled against me. For their worm shall not die, their fire shall not be quenched, and they shall be an abhorrence to all flesh"* (Isa. 66:24).

Here is the punishment of those that are condemned, variously called hellfire, a worm, weeping and gnashing of teeth, utter darkness, and so on. *"But as for the cowardly, the faithless, the detestable, as for murderers, the sexually immoral, sorcerers, idolaters, and all liars, their portion will be in the lake that burns with fire and sulfur, which is the second death"* (Rev. 21:8). *"And throw them into the fiery furnace. In that place there will be weeping and gnashing of teeth"* (Matt. 13:42, see also Isa. 66:24).

A Corollary

And this is the full execution of God's decree of reprobation, by which appears the great justice of God in punishing sin. From this also comes God's glory which he sets forth to himself as the last and chief end in all these things. Therefore, let every Christian set forth the same end to himself. "*What shall we say then? Is there injustice on God's part? By no means! For he says to Moses, 'I will have mercy on whom I have mercy, and I will have compassion on whom I have compassion.' So then it depends not on human will or exertion, but on God, who has mercy. For the Scripture says to Pharaoh, 'For this very purpose I have raised you up, that I might show my power in you, and that my name might be proclaimed in all the earth'"* (Rom. 9:14–17). *"So, whether you eat or drink, or whatever you do, do all to the glory of God"* (1 Cor. 10:31).

Chapter Fifty Eight

THE APPLICATION OF PREDESTINATION

The right applying of Predestination to individuals is very necessary, and it has two parts. The first is the Judgement of Particular Predestination, and the second is the Use of it.

The **Judgement and Discerning of a Man's own Predestination** is to be performed by means of these rules which follow.

1. The elect alone, and all they that are elect, not only *may* be, but also (in God's good time) *are* sure of election in Christ to eternal life (1 Cor. 2:12; 2 Cor. 13:5).
2. They do not have this knowledge from the first causes of election, but rather from the last effects thereof. These are especially two: the testimony of God's Spirit, and the works of Sanctification (2 Pet. 1:10; Rom. 8:16).
3. If any are in doubt of this testimony, it will become clear to them whether it comes **from the Spirit of God** or their own carnal presumption by the following:

   First, by full persuasion which they shall have. For the Holy Spirit will not barely say it, but persuades the elect that they are the children of God in a manner which the flesh cannot do.

   Secondly, by the manner of persuasion. For the Holy Spirit does not draw reasons from the works or worthiness of a man but from God's favour and love. This kind of persuasion is far different from that which Satan uses.

   Thirdly, by the effects of that testimony. For if the persuasion arises from presumption, it is a dead persuasion. On the other hand, if it is most lively and stirring it comes from the Holy Spirit. For those who are persuaded that they are elected and adopted children of God will love God, will trust in him, and will call upon him with their whole heart.

4. If the testimony of God's Spirit is not so powerful in the elect, then they may judge their election by that other effect of the Holy Spirit—namely **Sanctification**—as we use to judge by heat that there is fire when we cannot see the flame itself.
5. Of all the effects of sanctification these are most notable:
    a. To feel our wants, and in bitterness of heart to bewail the offence to God in every sin.
    b. To strive against the flesh, that is, to resist and hate the ungodly motions thereof, and with grief to think them a burden and troublesome.
    c. To earnestly and vehemently desire the grace of God and merit of Christ to obtain eternal life.
    d. When it is obtained, to account it a most precious jewel (Phil. 3:8).
    e. To love the minister of God's word, in that he is a minister and a Christian. In that he is a Christian, to be ready to spend our blood with them if need be (Matt. 10:42; 1 John 3:16).
    f. To call upon God earnestly and with tears.
    g. To desire and love Christ's coming and the day of judgement so that an end may be made of the days of sin.
    h. To flee all occasions of sin and seriously to endeavour to come to newness of life.
    i. To persevere in these things to the last gasp of life. Luther has a good sentence for this purpose: *"He that will serve God must believe that which cannot be seen, hope for that which is deferred, and love God when he shows himself an enemy, and thus remain to the end."*

6. Now, if all the effects of the Spirit are very feeble in the godly, they must know that God tries them, not intending that they might be dismayed. For it is most sure that if they have faith, even but as much as a **Grain of Mustard Seed**, and be as weak as a young infant is, it

is sufficient to graft them into Christ. Therefore they must not doubt their election because they see their faith feeble and the effects of the Holy Spirit faint with them.[1]

7. Neither must he, that as yet has not felt in his heart any of these effects, presently conclude that he is a reprobate. Rather, let him use the word of God and the sacraments that he may have an inward sense of the power of Christ drawing him to Christ, and an assurance of his redemption by Christ's death and passion.

8. No man may conclude that himself or any other is a reprobate. For God often prefers those who seemed to be most estranged from his favour to be in his kingdom above others, who in man's judgement were the children of the kingdom. Hence Christ says: *"tax collectors and the prostitutes go into the kingdom of God before you"* (Matt. 21:31) and taught that many are called at the eleventh hour (Matt. 20:6), as appears by that notable example of the thief upon the cross.

The **Uses** which may be made of this doctrine of predestination are very many. First, for our instruction, we are taught these things:

1. That there is neither any justification by works, nor any works of ours that are meritorious. For election is by the free grace of God, and therefore so is justification. And for this reason, in the work of salvation, grace does wholly challenge all to itself. *"So too at the present time there is a remnant, chosen by grace"* (Rom. 11:5). *"Who saved us and called us to a holy calling, not because of our works but because of his own purpose and grace, which he gave us in Christ Jesus before the ages began"* (2 Tim. 1:9). *"For it has been granted to you that for the sake of Christ you should not only believe in him but also suffer for his sake"* (Phil. 1:29). *"And are justified by his grace as a gift"* (Rom. 3:24). *"he saved us, not because of works done by us in righteousness, but according to his own mercy"* (Titus 3:5). *"I will .... cause you to walk in my statutes"* (Ezek. 36:27). *"The free gift of God is eternal life in Christ Jesus our Lord"* (Rom. 6:23).

2. That Astrology (teaching what men will be by the casting of births) is ridiculous and impious. For it determines that such shall be very like in life and conduct whom God in his predestination has made unlike. Jacob and Esau, born of the same parents and almost in the

1. See further ***chapter 36***, above.

same moment of time (for Jacob held Esau by the heel as he was born, Gen. 25:26) were of most unlike dispositions and experienced very different events in their lives. We may see the same in all twins, and in others which are borne at the same time.

3. That God is most wise, omnipotent, just, and merciful. *"Oh, the depth of the riches and wisdom and knowledge of God! How unsearchable are his judgments and how inscrutable his ways!"* (Rom. 11:33). *"He predestined us for adoption as sons through Jesus Christ, according to the purpose of his will"* (Eph. 1:5).

Secondly, we are admonished as servants of Christ:

1. To fight against all doubting and loss of confidence of our salvation, for it neither depends upon works nor faith but upon God's decree which is unchanging (Matt. 24:24). *"Nevertheless, do not rejoice in this, that the spirits are subject to you, but rejoice that your names are written in heaven"* (Luke 10:20). *"Who shall bring any charge against God's elect? It is God who justifies. Who is to condemn?"* (Rom. 8:33, see also 2 Tim. 2:19). This teaches that the anchor of hope must be fixed in the truth, and in the stability of the unchanging good pleasure of God. So though our faith may be tossed so much as to be in danger of shipwreck, nevertheless it may never sink to the bottom. For even amidst danger it may take hold upon repentance, as on a board, and so recover itself.
2. To humble our souls under the mighty hand of God, for we are as clay in the hand of the potter. *"They were broken off because of their unbelief, but you stand fast through faith. So do not become proud, but fear"* (Rom. 11:20).
3. To give all glory to God. *"But we ought always to give thanks to God for you, brothers beloved by the Lord, because God chose you as the firstfruits to be saved, through sanctification by the Spirit and belief in the truth"* (2 Thess. 2:13).
4. To bear crosses patiently: *"For those whom he foreknew he also predestined to be conformed to the image of his Son"* (Rom. 8:29). This likeness to Christ is in bearing afflictions. *"That I may know him and the power of his resurrection, and may share his sufferings, becoming like him in his death"* (Phil. 3:10)
5. To do good works: *"For we are his workmanship, created in Christ*

Jesus for good works, which God prepared beforehand, that we should walk in them" (Eph. 2:10).

Thus much concerning Theology.

EDITORIAL POSTSCRIPT

A Golden Chain began as a slender Latin work (entitled *Armilla Aurea*) of 140 pages in 1590, after which it expanded to over 350 pages. It was first translated into English by Robert Hill in 1592. The text of this volume was transcribed by Mark Smith[1] from the 1597 edition which is also available on EEBO.[2] In this volume the original forward by Robert Hill has been removed, as has the appendix containing an excerpt of one of Theodore Beza's works.

The 1597 edition contains a few minor textual variations compared to the 1592 edition and to that published as part of Perkins' *Works.* Serious students of Perkins should also consult those authoritative seventeenth-century edition of his *Works* published by John Legatt (1626, 1631),[3] as well as the earliest Latin and English editions of *A Golden Chaine* which can be found on *Early English Books Online* (EEBO).

1. http://www.vor.org/rbdisk/pdf/a_golden_chaine_perkins.pdf
2. Perkins, William. *A Golden Chaine, or the Description of Theologie, containing the order of the causes of Salvation and Damnation, according to Gods word. A view whereof, is to be seene in the Table annexed. Written in Latine, and translated by R.H. Hereunto is adjoined the order which M. Theodore Beza used in comforting afflicted consciences. The Second Edition, much enlarged, with a Table at the end.* (Cambridge: John Legate, 1597). *Early English Books Online* (EEBO) can be found at: https://eebo.chadwyck.com
3. William Perkins, *The Workes of that Famous and Worthy Minister of Christ in the Uniuersitie of Cambridge, M. W. Perkins.* (2nd ed.; 3 vols; Cambridge: John Legatt, 1626, 1631).

ABOUT THE EDITORS

Mark Smith

By God's grace, Mark was brought up in a Christian home and came to Christ in his early teens. He attended Sydney University and completed a Bachelor of Science (Hons). While at University, Mark became a member of Stanmore Baptist Church, Sydney and came to understand the Doctrines of Grace. In the mid 1980s Mark made a computer program of the Second London Baptist Confession of Faith and subsequently has transcribed a number of works from the 16th and 17th Centuries. Mark is married to Carmel and God has blessed them with six children and 8 grandchildren. Mark has worked as a research scientist at Sydney University and for the last 20 years as a research administrator at Westmead Hospital, Sydney.

Matthew Payne

Matthew is a PhD student at the University of Sydney studying the life and thought of William Perkins. He has BD and MA (Theology) degrees from Moore Theological College, Sydney, and has previously served as a church pastor and as a high school teacher. Matthew is the author of several academic journal articles in biblical studies and historical theology, and has a particular passion for making deep theological content accessible to ordinary believers. Information about his ministry can be found at stretchtheology.com. He lives in Sydney with his three sons.

INDEX